Introduction to the Literature of Europe in the Fifteentth, Sixteenth, and Seventeenth Centuries
by Henry Hallam

Address:
HardPress
8345 NW 66TH ST #2561
MIAMI FL 33166-2626
USA
Email: info@hardpress.net

INTRODUCTION

TO THE

LITERATURE OF EUROPE,

IN THE

FIFTEENTH, SIXTEENTH, AND SEVENTEENTH CENTURIES.

BY HENRY HALLAM, LL.D., F.R.A.S.,

FOREIGN ASSOCIATE OF THE INSTITUTE OF FRANCE.

De modo autem hujusmodi historiæ conscribendæ, illud imprimis monemus, ut materia et copia ejus, non tantum ab historiis et criticis petatur, verum etiam per singulas annorum centurias, aut etiam minora intervalla, seriatim libri præcipui, qui eo temporis spatio conscripti sunt, in consilium adhibeantur; ut ex eorum non perlectione (id enim infinitum quiddam esset), sed degustatione, et observatione argumenti, styli, methodi, genius illius temporis literarius, veluti incantatione quadam, a mortuis evocetur.—BACON *de Augm. Scient.*

FIFTH EDITION.

IN FOUR VOLUMES.—VOL. IV.

LONDON:

JOHN MURRAY, ALBEMARLE STREET.

1855.

The right of Translation is reserved.

LONDON : PRINTED BY WILLIAM CLOWES AND SONS, STAMFORD STREET,
AND CHARING CROSS.

CONTENTS

OF

THE FOURTH VOLUME.

PART IV.

ON THE LITERATURE OF THE SECOND HALF OF THE SEVENTEENTH CENTURY.

CHAPTER I.

HISTORY OF ANCIENT LITERATURE IN EUROPE, FROM 1650 TO 1700.

CHAPTER II.

HISTORY OF THEOLOGICAL LITERATURE, FROM 1650 TO 1700.

a 2

CHAPTER III.

HISTORY OF SPECULATIVE PHILOSOPHY, FROM 1650 TO 1700.

CHAPTER IV.

HISTORY OF MORAL AND POLITICAL PHILOSOPHY AND OF JURISPRUDENCE, FROM 1650 TO 1700.

CHAPTER V.

HISTORY OF POETRY FROM 1650 TO 1700.

CHAPTER VI.

HISTORY OF DRAMATIC LITERATURE FROM 1650 TO 1700.

CHAPTER VII.

HISTORY OF POLITE LITERATURE IN PROSE, FROM 1650 TO 1700.

CHAPTER VIII.

HISTORY OF PHYSICAL AND OTHER LITERATURE, FROM 1650 TO 1700.

INTRODUCTION

TO THE

LITERATURE OF EUROPE

IN THE FIFTEENTH, SIXTEENTH, AND SEVENTEENTH CENTURIES.

PART IV.

ON THE LITERATURE OF THE SECOND HALF OF THE SEVENTEENTH CENTURY.

CHAPTER I.

HISTORY OF ANCIENT LITERATURE IN EUROPE, FROM 1650 TO 1700.

SECTION I.

Dutch Scholars — Jesuit and Jansenist Philologers — Delphin Editions — French Scholars — English Scholars — Bentley.

1. THE death of Salmasius about the beginning of this period left a chasm in critical literature which James Frederic Gronovius. no one was equal to fill. But the nearest to this giant of philology was James Frederic Gronovius, a native of Hamburg, but drawn, like several more of his countrymen, to the universities of Holland, the peculiarly learned state of Europe through the seventeenth century. The principal labours of Gronovius were those of correcting the text of Latin writers ; in Greek we find very little due to him.[a] His notes form an useful and considerable part of those which are collected in what are generally styled the Variorum editions, published, chiefly after 1660, by the Dutch book-

---

[a] Baillet, Critiques Grammairiens, n. 548. Blount. Biogr. Univ.

sellers. These contain selections from the older critics, some of them, especially those first edited, indifferently made and often mutilated; others with more attention to preserve entire the original notes. These, however, are for the most part only critical, as if explanatory observations were below the notice of an editor; though, as Le Clerc says, those of Manutius on Cicero's epistles cost him much more time than modern editors have given to their conjectures.[b] In general, the Variorum editions were not greatly prized, with the exception of those by the two Gronovii and Grævius.[c]

2. The place of the elder Gronovius, in the latter part of this present period, was filled by his son.

James Gronovius. James Gronovius, by indefatigable labour, and by a greater number of editions which bear his name, may be reckoned, if not a greater philologer, one not less celebrated than his father. He was at least a better Greek critic, and in this language, though far below those who were about to arise, and who did in fact eclipse him long before his death, Bentley and Burman, he kept a high place for several years.[d] *Grævius.* Grævius, another German, whom the Dutch universities had attracted and retained, contributed to the Variorum editions, chiefly those of Latin authors, an erudition not less copious than that of any contemporary scholar.

3. The philological character of Gerard Vossius himself, if we might believe some partial testimonies, *Isaac Vossius.* fell short of that of his son Isaac; whose observations on Pomponius Mela, and an edition of Catullus, did him extraordinary credit, and have placed him among the first philologers of this age. He was of a more lively genius, and perhaps hardly less erudition, than his father, but with a paradoxical judgment, and has certainly rendered much less service to letters.[e] Another son of a great father, Nicolas Heinsius, has by none been placed on a level with him; but his editions of Prudentius and Claudian are better than any that had preceded them.

4. Germany fell lower and lower in classical literature.

b Parrhasiana, i. 233.
c A list of the Variorum editions will be found in Baillet, Critiques Grammairiens, n. 604.
d Baillet, n. 548. Niceron, ii. 177.
e Niceron, vol. xiii.

A writer as late as 1714 complains, that only modern books of Latin were taught in the schools, Decline of German learning. and that the students in the universities despised all grammatical learning. The study " not of our own language, which we entirely neglect, but of French," he reckons among the causes of this decay in ancient learning; the French translations of the classics led many to imagine that the original could be dispensed with.[f] Ezekiel Spanheim, envoy Spanheim. from the court of Brandenburg to that of Louis XIV., was a distinguished exception; his edition of Julian, and his notes on several other writers, attest an extensive learning, which has still preserved his name in honour. As the century drew nigh to its close, Germany began to revive; a few men of real philological learning, especially Fabricius, appeared as heralds of those greater names which adorn her literary annals in the next age.

5. The Jesuits had long been conspicuously the classical scholars of France; in their colleges the Jesuit colleges in France. purest and most elegant Latinity was supposed to be found; they had early cultivated these graces of literature, while all polite writing was confined to the Latin language, and they still preserved them in its comparative disuse. " The Jesuits," Huet says, " write and speak Latin well, but their style is almost always too rhetorical. This is owing to their keeping regencies [an usual phrase for academical exercises] from their early youth, which causes them to speak incessantly in public, and become accustomed to a sustained and polished style, above the tone of common subjects."[g] Jouvancy, whose Latin orations were published in 1700, has had no equal, if we may trust a panegyrist, since Maffei and Muretus.[h]

6. The Jansenists appeared ready at one time to wrest this palm from their inveterate foes. Lancelot Port Royal writers. Lancelot. threw some additional lustre round Port Royal by the Latin and Greek grammars, which are more frequently called by the name of that famous cloister than by his own. Both were received with great approbation in the French schools, except, I suppose,

---

f Burckhardt, De Linguæ Latinæ hodie neglectæ Causis Oratio, p. 34.

g Huetiana, p. 71.
h Biogr. Univ.

where the Jesuits predominated, and their reputation lasted for many years. They were never so popular, though well known, in this country. " The public," says Baillet of the Greek grammar, which is rather the more eminent of the two, " bears witness that nothing of its kind has been more finished. The order is clear and concise. We find in it many remarks, both judicious and important for the full knowledge of the language. Though Lancelot has chiefly followed Caninius, Sylburgius, Sanctius, and Vossius, his arrangement is new, and he has selected what is most valuable in their works."[1] In fact, he professes to advance nothing of his own, being more indebted, he says, to Caninius than to any one else. The method of Clenardus he disapproves, and thinks that of Ramus intricate. He adopts the division into three declensions. But his notions of the proper meaning of the tenses are strangely confused and erroneous: several other mistakes of an obvious nature, as we should now say, will occur in his syntax; and upon the whole the Port Royal grammar does not give us a high idea of the critical knowledge of the seventeenth century, as to the more difficult language of antiquity.

7. The Latin, on the other hand, had been so minutely and laboriously studied, that little more than Latin grammars. Perizonius. gleanings after a great harvest could be obtained. The Aristarchus of Vossius, and his other grammatical works, though partly not published till this period, have been mentioned in the last volume. Perizonius, a professor at Franeker, and in many respects one of the most learned of this age, published a good edition of the Minerva of Sanctius in 1687. This celebrated grammar had become very scarce, as well as that of Scioppius, which contained nothing but remarks upon Sanctius. Perizonius combined the two with notes more ample than those of Scioppius, and more bold in differing from the Spanish grammarian.

8. If other editions of the classical authors have been Delphin editions. preferred by critics, none, at least of this period, have been more celebrated than those which Louis XIV., at the suggestion of the Duke de Montausier, caused to be prepared for the use of the Dauphin.

---

[1] Baillet, n. 714.

The object in view was to elucidate the Latin writers, both by a continual gloss in the margin, and by such notes as should bring a copious mass of ancient learning to bear on the explanation, not of the more difficult passages alone, but of all those in which an ordinary reader might require some aid.   The former of these is less useful and less satisfactorily executed than the latter ; as for the notes, it must be owned that, with much that is superfluous even to tolerable scholars, they bring together a great deal of very serviceable illustration.   The choice of authors as well as of editors was referred to Huet, who fixed the number of the former at forty.   The idea of an index, on a more extensive plan than in any earlier editions, was also due to Huet, who had designed to fuse those of each work into one more general, as a standing historical analysis of the Latin language.[k]   These editions are of very unequal merit, as might be expected from the number of persons employed ; a list of whom will be found in Baillet.[m]

9. Tanaquil Faber, thus better known than by his real name, Tanneguy le Fevre, a man learned, animated, not fearing the reproach of paradox, acquired a considerable name among French critics by several editions, as well as by other writings in philology.   But none of his literary productions were so celebrated as his daughter, Anne le Fevre, afterwards Madame Dacier.   The knowledge of Greek, though once not very uncommon in a woman, had become prodigious in the days of Louis XIV. ; and when this distinguished lady taught Homer and Sappho to speak French prose, she appeared a phœnix in the eyes of her countrymen. She was undoubtedly a person of very rare talents and estimable character ; her translations are numerous and reputed to be correct, though Niceron has observed that she did not raise Homer in the eyes of those who were not prejudiced in his favour.[n]   Her husband was a scholar of kindred mind and the same pursuits.   Their union was facetiously called the wedding of Latin and Greek. But each of this learned couple was skilled in both lan-

Le Fevre and the Daciers.

---

[k] Huetiana, p. 92.
[m] Critiques Grammairiens, n. 605.
[n] [It has been remarked that her edition of Callimachus, with critical notes, ought to have been mentioned, as the *chef-d'œuvre* of one whom Bentley calls " foeminarum doctissima."—1847.]

guages. Dacier was a great translator; his Horace is perhaps the best known of his versions; but the Poetics of Aristotle have done him most honour. The Daciers had to fight the battle of antiquity against a generation both ignorant and vain-glorious, yet keen-sighted in the detection of blemishes, and disposed to avenge the wrongs of their fathers, who had been trampled upon by pedants, with the help of a new pedantry, that of the court and the mode. With great learning they had a competent share of good sense, but not perhaps a sufficiently discerning taste, or liveliness enough of style, to maintain a cause that had so many prejudices of the world now enlisted against it.[o]

10. Henry Valois might have been mentioned before

Henry Valois. Complaints of decay of learning. for his edition of Ammianus Marcellinus, in 1636, which established his philological reputation. Many other works in the same line of criticism followed. He is among the great ornaments of learning in this period. Nor was France destitute of others that did her honour. Cotelier, it is said, deserved by his knowledge of Greek to be placed on a level with the great scholars of former times. Yet there seems to have been some decline, at least towards the close of the century, in that prodigious erudition which had distinguished the preceding period. "For we know no one," says Le Clerc, about 1699, "who equals in learning, in diligence, and in the quantity of his works, the Scaligers, the Lipsii, the Casaubons, the Salmasii, the Meursii, the Vossii, the Seldens, the Gronovii, and many more of former times."[p] Though perhaps in this reflection there was something of the customary bias against the present generation, we must own that the writings of scholars were less massive, and consequently gave less apparent evidence of industry, than formerly. But in classical philology, at least, a better day was about to arise, and the first omen of it came from a country not yet much known in that literature.

---

[o] Baillet. Niceron, vol. iii. Bibliothèque Universelle, x. 295, xxii. 176, xxiv. 241, 261. Biogr. Univ.

[p] Parrhasiana, vol. i. p. 225. Je viens d'apprendre, says Charles Patin in one of his letters, que M. Gronovius est mort à Leyden. Il restoit presque tout seul du nombre des savans d'Hollande. Il n'est plus dans ce pais-là des gens faits comme Jos. Scaliger, Baudius, Heinsius, Salmasius, et Grotius. (P. 582.)

11. It has been observed in a former passage, that while England was very far from wanting men English learning. Duport. of extensive erudition, she had not been at all eminent in ancient or classical literature. The proof which the absence of critical writings, or even of any respectable editions, furnishes, appears weighty; nor can it be repelled by sufficient testimony. In the middle of the century James Duport, Greek professor at Cambridge, deserves honour by standing almost alone. "He appears," says a late biographer, "to have been the main instrument by which literature was upheld in this university during the civil disturbances of the seventeenth century; and though little known at present, he enjoyed an almost transcendent reputation for a great length of time among his contemporaries as well as in the generation which immediately succeeded." [q] Duport, however, has little claim to this reputation, except by translations of the writings of Solomon, the book of Job, and the Psalms, into Greek hexameters; concerning which his biographer gently intimates that "his notions of versification were not formed in a severe or critical school;" and by what has certainly been more esteemed, his Homeri Gnomologia, which Le Clerc and Bishop Monk agree to praise, as very useful to the student of Homer. Duport gave also some lectures on Theophrastus about 1656, which were afterwards published in Needham's edition of that author. "In these," says Le Clerc, "he explains words with much exactness, and so as to show that he understood the analogy of the language." [r] "They are, upon the whole, calculated," says the Bishop of Gloucester, "to give no unfavourable opinion of the state of Greek learning in the university at that memorable crisis."

12. It cannot be fairly said that our universities declined in general learning under the usurpa- Greek not much studied. tion of Cromwell. They contained, on the contrary, more extraordinary men than in any earlier period, but not generally well affected to the predominant power. Greek however seems not much to have flourished, even immediately after the Restoration. Barrow, who was chosen Greek professor in 1660,

---

[q] Museum Criticum, vol. ii. p. 672 (by the Bishop of Gloucester and Bristol).
[r] Bibliothèque Choisie, xxv. 18.

complains that no one attended his lectures. "I sit like an Attic owl," he says, "driven out from the society of all other birds."* According indeed to the scheme of study retained from a more barbarous age, no knowledge of the Greek language appears to have been required from the students, as necessary for their degrees. And if we may believe a satirical writer of the time of Charles II., but one whose satire had great circulation and was not taxed with falsehood, the general state of education, both in the schools and universities, was as narrow, pedantic, and unprofitable as can be conceived.'

13. We were not, nevertheless, destitute of men dis-
Gataker's
Cinnus and
Antoninus.
tinguished for critical skill, even from the commencement of this period. The first was a very learned divine, Thomas Gataker, one whom a foreign writer has placed among the six Protestants most conspicuous, in his judgment, for depth of reading. His Cinnus, sive Adversaria Miscellanea, published in 1651, to which a longer work, entitled Adversaria Posthuma, is subjoined in later editions, may be introduced here; since, among a far greater number of Scriptural explanations, both of these miscellanies contain many relating to profane antiquity. He claims a higher place for his edition of Marcus Antoninus the next year. This is the earliest edition, if I am not mistaken, of any classical writer published in England with original annotations. Those of Gataker evince a very copious learning, and the edition is still, perhaps, reckoned the best that has been given of this author.

14. Thomas Stanley, author of the History of Ancient
Stanley's
Æschylus.
Philosophy, undertook a more difficult task, and gave in 1663 his celebrated edition of Æschylus. It was, as every one has admitted, by far supe-

---

* See a biographical memoir of Barrow prefixed to Hughes's edition of his works. This contains a sketch of studies pursued in the university of Cambridge from the twelfth to the seventeenth century, brief indeed, but such as I should have been glad to have seen before. P. 62. No alteration in the statutes, so far as they related to study, was made after the time of Henry VIII. or Edward VI.

[" The studies of the Cambridge schools about 1680 consisted of logic, ethics, natural philosophy, and mathematics; the latter branch of knowledge, which was destined subsequently to take the lead, and almost swallow up the rest, had then but recently become an object of much attention." Monk's Life of Bentley, p. 6.—1842.]

' Eachard's Grounds and Occasions of the Contempt of the Clergy. This little tract was published in 1670, and went through ten editions by 1696.

rior to any that had preceded it; nor can Stanley's real praise be effaced, though it may be diminished, by an unfortunate charge that has been brought against him, of having appropriated to himself the conjectures, most of them unpublished, of Casaubon, Dorat, and Scaliger, to the number of at least three hundred emendations of the text. It will hardly be reckoned a proof of our nationality, that a living English scholar was the first to detect and announce this plagiarism of a critic, in whom we had been accustomed to take pride, from these foreigners.[u] After these plumes have been withdrawn, Stanley's Æschylus will remain a great monument of critical learning.

15. Meric Casaubon by his notes on Persius, Antoninus, and Diogenes Laertius, Pearson by those on the last author, Gale on Iamblichus, Price on Apuleius, Hudson by his editions of Thucydides and Josephus, Potter by that of Lycophron, Baxter of Anacreon, attested the progress of classical learning in a soil so well fitted to give it nourishment. The same William Baxter published the first grammar, not quite elementary, which had appeared in England, entitled De Analogia, seu Arte Latinæ Linguæ Commentarius. It relates principally to etymology, and to the deduction of the different parts of the verb from a stem, which he conceives to be the imperative mood. Baxter was a man of some ability, but, in the style of critics, offensively contemptuous towards his brethren of the craft. *Other English philologers.*

16. We must hasten to the greatest of English critics in this, or possibly any other age, Richard Bentley. His first book was the epistle to Mill, subjoined to the latter's edition of the chronicle of John Malala, a Greek writer of the Lower Empire.[x] In a desultory and almost garrulous strain, Bentley pours forth an immense store of novel learning and of acute criticism, especially on his favourite subject, which *Bentley. His epistle to Mill.*

---

[u] Edinburgh Review, xix. 494. Museum Criticum, ii. 498 (both by the Bishop of London).

[x] [I am indebted to Mr. Dyce for reminding me that Mill only superintended the publication of Malala; the prolegomena having been written by Hody, the notes and Latin translation by Chilmead in the reign of Charles I. The notes, indeed, appear to have been written by John Gregory, whom Bishop Monk calls "a man of prodigious learning," not long before the Civil War. See a full account of this edition of Malala in l6ife of Bentley, i. 25.—1847.]

was destined to become his glory, the scattered relics of the ancient dramatists. The style of Bentley, always terse and lively, sometimes humorous and dryly sarcastic, whether he wrote in Latin or in English, could not but augment the admiration which his learning challenged. Grævius and Spanheim pronounced him the rising star of British literature, and a correspondence with the former began in 1692, which continued in unbroken friendship till his death.

17. But the rare qualities of Bentley were more abun-
Dissertation on Phalaris. dantly displayed, and before the eyes of a more numerous tribunal, in his famous dissertation on the epistles ascribed to Phalaris. This was provoked, in the first instance, by a few lines of eulogy on these epistles by Sir William Temple, who pretended to find in them indubitable marks of authenticity. Bentley, in a dissertation subjoined to Wotton's Reflections on Modern and Ancient Learning, gave tolerably conclusive proofs of the contrary. A young man of high family and respectable learning, Charles Boyle, had published an edition of the Epistles of Phalaris, with some reflection on Bentley for personal incivility; a charge which he seems to have satisfactorily disproved. Bentley animadverted on this in his dissertation. Boyle the next year, with the assistance of some leading men at Oxford, Aldrich, King, and Atterbury, published his Examination of Bentley's Dissertation on Phalaris; a book generally called, in familiar brevity, Boyle against Bentley.[y] The Cambridge giant of criticism replied in an answer which goes by the name of Bentley against Boyle. It was the first great literary war that had been waged in England; and like that of Troy, it has still the prerogative of being remembered, after the Epistles of Phalaris are almost as much buried as the walls of Troy itself. Both combatants were skilful in wielding the sword: the arms of Boyle, in Swift's language, were given him by all the gods; but his antagonist stood forward in no such figurative strength, master of a learning to which nothing parallel had been known in England, and that directed by an understanding prompt, discriminating,

---

[y] "The principal share in the undertaking fell to the lot of Atterbury; this was suspected at the time, and has since been placed beyond all doubt by the publication of a letter of his to Boyle."—Monk's Life of Bentley, p. 69.

not idly sceptical, but still farther removed from trust in authority, sagacious in perceiving corruptions of language, and ingenious, at the least, in removing them, with a style rapid, concise, amusing, and superior to Boyle in that which he had chiefly to boast, a sarcastic wit.[2]

18. It may now seem extraordinary to us, even without looking at the anachronisms or similar errors which Bentley has exposed, that any one should be deceived by the Epistles of Phalaris. The rhetorical commonplaces, the cold declamation of the sophist, the care to please the reader, the absence of that simplicity with which a man who has never known restraint in disguising his thoughts or choosing his words is sure to express himself, strike us in the pretended letters of this buskined tyrant, the Icon Basilice of the ancient world. But this was doubtless thought evidence of their authenticity by many who might say, as others have done, in a happy vein of metaphor, that they seemed " not written with a pen but with a sceptre." The argument from the use of the common dialect by a Sicilian tyrant, contemporary with Pythagoras, is of itself conclusive, and would leave no doubt in the present day.

19. " It may be remarked," says the Bishop of Gloucester, " that a scholar at that time possessed neither the aids nor the encouragements which are now presented to smooth the paths of literature. The grammars of the Latin and Greek languages were imperfectly and erroneously taught; and the critical scholar must have felt severely the absence of sufficient indexes, particularly of the voluminous scholiasts, grammarians, and later writers of Greece, in

Disadvantages of scholars in that age.

---

[2] " In point of classical learning the joint stock of the confederacy bore no proportion to that of Bentley; their acquaintance with several of the books upon which they comment appears' only to have begun upon that occasion, and sometimes they are indebted for their knowledge of them to their adversary; compared with his boundless erudition their learning was that of school-boys, and not always sufficient to preserve them from distressing mistakes. But profound literature was at that period confined to few, while wit and raillery found numerous and eager readers. It may be doubtful whether Busby himself, by whom every one of the confederated band had been educated, possessed knowledge which would have qualified him to enter the lists in such a controversy."—Monk's Bentley, p. 69. Warburton has justly said that Bentley by his wit foiled the Oxford men at their own weapons.

the examination of which no inconsiderable portion of a life might be consumed. Bentley, relying upon his own exertions and the resources of his own mind, pursued an original path of criticism, in which the intuitive quickness and subtilty of his genius qualified him to excel. In the faculty of memory, so important for such pursuits, he has himself candidly declared that he was not particularly gifted. Consequently he practised throughout life the precaution of noting in the margin of his books the suggestions and conjectures which rushed into his mind during their perusal. To this habit of laying up materials in store, we may partly attribute the surprising rapidity with which some of his most important works were completed. He was also at the trouble of constructing for his own use indexes of authors quoted by the principal scholiasts, by Eustathius and other ancient commentators, of a nature similar to those afterwards published by Fabricius in his Bibliotheca Græca ; which latter were the produce of the joint labour of various hands." *

SECT. II.—ON ANTIQUITIES.

Grævius and Gronovius — Fabretti — Numismatic Writers — Chronology.

20. THE two most industrious scholars of their time, Grævius and Gronovius, collected into one body such of the numerous treatises on Roman and Greek antiquities as they thought most worthy of preservation in an uniform and accessible work. These form the Thesaurus Antiquitatum Romanarum, by Grævius, in twelve volumes, the Thesaurus Antiquitatum Græcarum, by Gronovius, in thirteen volumes ; the former published in 1694, the first volumes of the latter in 1697. They comprehend many of the labours of the older antiquaries already commemorated from the middle of the sixteenth to that of the seventeenth century, and some also of a later date. Among these, in the collection of Grævius, are a treatise

Thesauri of Grævius and of Gronovius.

* Monk's Life of Bentley, p. 12.

of Albert Rubens, son of the great painter, on the dress of the Romans, particularly the laticlave, (Antwerp, 1665,) the enlarged edition of Octavius Ferrarius on the same subject, several treatises by Spanheim and Ursatus, and the Roma Antica of Nardini, published in 1666. Gronovius gave a place in his twelfth volume (1702) to the very recent work of a young Englishman, Potter's Antiquities, which the author, at the request of the veteran antiquary, had so much enlarged, that the Latin translation in Gronovius is nearly double in length the first edition of the English.[b] The warm eulogies of Gronovius attest the merit of this celebrated work. Potter was but twenty-three years of age; he had of course availed himself of the writings of Meursius, but he has also contributed to supersede them. It has been said that he is less exact in attending to the difference of times and places than our finer criticism requires.[c]

21. Bellori in a long list of antiquarian writings, Falconieri in several more, especially his Inscriptiones Athleticæ, maintained the honour of Italy in this province, so justly claimed as her own.[d] Fabretti. But no one has been accounted equal to Raphael Fabretti, by judges so competent as Maffei, Gravina, Fabroni, and Visconti.[e] His diligence in collecting inscriptions was only surpassed by his sagacity in explaining them; and his authority has been preferred to that of any other antiquary.[f] His time was spent in delving among ruins and vaults, to explore the subterranean treasures of Latium; no heat, nor cold, nor rain, nor badness of road, could deter him from these solitary peregrinations. Yet the glory of Fabretti must be partly shared with his horse. This wise and faithful animal, named Marco Polo, had acquired, it is said, the habit of standing still, and as it were *pointing*, when he came near an antiquity; his master candidly owning that several things which would have escaped him had been detected by the antiquarian quadruped.[g] Fabretti's principal works are three dissertations on the Roman

[b] The first edition of Potter's Antiquities was published in 1697 and 1698.
[c] Biogr. Univ.
[d] Salfi, vol. xi. p. 364.
[e] Fabretti's life has been written by two very favourable biographers, Fabroni, in Vitæ Italorum, vol. vi., and Visconti, in the Biographie Universelle.
[f] Fabroni, p. 187. Biogr. Univ.
[g] Fabroni, p. 192.

aqueducts, and one on the Trajan column. Little, says Fabroni, was known before about the Roman galleys or their naval affairs in general.[h] Fabretti was the first who reduced lapidary remains into classes, and arranged them so as to illustrate each other; a method, says one of his most distinguished successors, which has laid the foundations of the science.[i] A profusion of collateral learning is mingled with the main stream of all his investigations.

22. No one had ever come to the study of medals with such stores of erudition as Ezekiel Spanheim. The earlier writers on the subject, Vico, Erizzo, Angeloni, were not comparable to him, and had rather dwelt on the genuineness or rarity of coins than on their usefulness in illustrating history. Spanheim's Dissertations on the Use of Medals, the second improved edition of which appeared in 1671, first connected them with the most profound and critical research into antiquity.[k] Vaillant, travelling into the Levant, brought home great treasures of Greek coinage, especially those of the Seleucidæ, at once enriching the cabinets of the curious and establishing historical truth. Medallic evidence, in fact, may be reckoned among those checks upon the negligence of historians, that, having been retrieved by industrious antiquaries, have created a cautious and discerning spirit which has been exercised in later times upon facts, and which, beginning in scepticism, passes onward to a more rational, and therefore more secure, conviction of what can fairly be proved. Jobert, in 1692, consolidated the researches of Spanheim, Vaillant, and other numismatic writers, in his book entitled La Science des Médailles, a better system of the science than had been published.[m]

Numismatics. Spanheim —Vaillant.

23. It would of course not be difficult to fill these pages with brief notices of other books that fall within the extensive range of classical antiquity. But we have no space for more than a mere enumeration, which would give little satisfaction. Chronology has received some attention in former volumes. Our learned archbishop Usher might there have been named, since the first part of his Annals of the Old Tes-

Chronology. Usher.

h P. 201.   k Bibl. Choisie, vol. xxii.
i Biogr. Univ.   m Biogr. Univ.

tament, which goes down to the year of the world 3828, was published in 1650. The second part followed in 1654. This has been the chronology generally adopted by English historians, as well as by Bossuet, Calmet, and Rollin, so that for many years it might be called the orthodox scheme of Europe. No former annals of the world had been so exact in marking dates and collating sacred history with profane. It was therefore exceedingly convenient for those who, possessing no sufficient leisure or learning for these inquiries, might very reasonably confide in such authority.

24. Usher, like Scaliger and Petavius, had strictly conformed to the Hebrew chronology in all Scriptural dates. But it is well known that *Pezron.* the Septuagint version, and also the Samaritan Pentateuch, differ greatly from the Hebrew and from each other, so that the age of the world has nearly 2000 years more antiquity in the Greek than in the original text. Jerome had followed the latter in the Vulgate; and in the seventeenth century it was usual to maintain the incorrupt purity of the Hebrew manuscripts, so that when Pezron, in his Antiquité des Temps dévoilée, 1687, attempted to establish the Septuagint chronology, it excited a clamour in some of his church, as derogatory to the Vulgate translation. Martianay defended the received chronology, and the system of Pezron gained little favour in that age." It has since become more popular, chiefly, perhaps, on account of the greater latitude it gives to speculations on the origin of kingdoms and other events of the early world, which are certainly somewhat cramped in the common reckoning. But the Septuagint chronology is not free from its own difficulties, and the internal evidence seems rather against its having been the original. Where two must be wrong, it is possible that all three may be so; and the most judicious inquirers into ancient history have of late been coming to the opinion, that, with certain exceptions, there are no means of establishing an entire accuracy in dates before the Olympiads. While much of the more ancient history itself, even in leading and important events, is so precarious as must

---

" Biogr. Univ.: arts. Pezron and Martianay. Bibliothèque Univ., xxiv. 1C3.

be acknowledged, there can be little confidence in chronological schemes. They seem, however, to be very seducing, so that those who enter upon the subject as sceptics become believers in their own theory.

25. Among those who addressed their attention to *Marsham.* particular portions of chronology, Sir John Marsham ought to be mentioned. In his Canon Chronicus Ægyptiacus he attempted, as the learned were still more prone than they are now, to reconcile conflicting authorities without rejecting any. He is said to have first started the ingenious idea that the Egyptian dynasties, stretching to such immense antiquity, were not successive but collateral.[o] Marsham fell, like many others after him, into the unfortunate mistake of confounding Sesostris with Sesac. But in times when discoveries that Marsham could not have anticipated were yet at a distance, he is extolled by most of those who had laboured, by help of the Greek and Hebrew writers alone, to fix ancient history on a stable foundation, as the restorer of the Egyptian annals.

[o] Biograph. Britannica.

CHAPTER II.

HISTORY OF THEOLOGICAL LITERATURE FROM 1650 TO 1700.

SECT. I.

Papal Power limited by the Gallican Church — Dupin — Fleury — Protestant Contro-
versy — Bossuet — His Assaults on Protestantism — Jansenism — Progress of
Arminianism in England — Trinitarian Controversy — Defences of Christianity —
Pascal's Thoughts — Toleration — Boyle — Locke — French Sermons — And
English — Other Theological Works.

1. IT has been observed in the last volume, that while
little or no decline could be perceived in the Decline of
general church of Rome at the conclusion of papal in-
that period which we then had before us, yet fluence.
the papal authority itself had lost a part of that formidable character which, through the Jesuits, and especially Bellarmin, it had some years before assumed. This
was now still more decidedly manifest: the temporal
power over kings was not, certainly, renounced, for
Rome never retracts anything; nor was it perhaps
without Italian Jesuits to write in its behalf; but the
common consent of nations rejected it so strenuously,
that on no occasion has it been brought forward by any
accredited or eminent advocate. There was also a
growing disposition to control the court of Rome; the
treaty of Westphalia was concluded in utter disregard
of her protest. But such matters of history do not
belong to us, when they do not bear a close relation to
the warfare of the pen. Some events there were which
have had a remarkable influence on the theological literature of France, and indirectly of the rest of Europe.

2. Louis XIV., more arrogant, in his earlier life, than
bigoted, became involved in a contest with
Innocent XI., by a piece of his usual despotism Dispute of
Louis XIV.
and contempt of his subjects' rights. He ex- with Intended in 1673 the ancient prerogative, called nocent XI.

the regale, by which the king enjoyed the revenues of vacant bishoprics, to all the kingdom, though many sees had been legally exempt from it.   Two bishops appealed to the pope, who interfered in their favour more peremptorily than the times would permit.   Innocent, it is but just to say, was maintaining the fair rights of the church, rather than any claim of his own.   But the dispute took at length a different form.   France was rich in prelates of eminent worth, and among such, as is evident, the Cisalpine theories had never lain wholly dormant since the councils of Constance and Basle. Louis convened the famous assembly of the Gallican clergy in 1682.   Bossuet, who is said to have felt some apprehensions lest the spirit of resistance should become one of rebellion, was appointed to open this assembly; and his sermon on that occasion is among his most splendid works.   His posture was indeed magnificent: he stands forward not so much the minister of religion as her arbitrator; we see him poise in his hands earth and heaven, and draw that boundary line which neither was to transgress; he speaks the language of reverential love towards the mother-church, that of St. Peter, and the fairest of her daughters to which he belongs, conciliating their transient feud; yet in this majestic tone which he assumes, no arrogance betrays itself, no thought of himself as one endowed with transcendent influence; he speaks for his church, and yet we feel that he raises himself above those for whom he speaks.[p]

3. Bossuet was finally entrusted with drawing up the four articles, which the assembly, rather at the instigation perhaps of Colbert than of its own accord, promulgated as the Gallican creed on the limitations of papal authority.   These declare: 1. That kings are subject to no ecclesiastical power in temporals, nor can be deposed directly or indirectly by the chiefs of the church: 2. That the decrees of the council of Constance as to the papal authority are in full force and ought to be observed: 3. That this authority can only be exerted in conformity with the canons received in the Gallican church: 4. That though the pope has the principal share in determining controversies of faith,

Four articles of 1682.

---

[p] This sermon will be found in Œuvres de Bossuet, vol. ix.

and his decrees extend to all churches, they are not absolutely final, unless the consent of the catholic church be superadded.   It appears that some bishops would have willingly used stronger language, but Bossuet foresaw the risk of an absolute schism.   Even thus the Gallican church approached so nearly to it that, the pope refusing the usual bulls to bishops nominated by the king according to the concordat, between thirty and forty sees at last were left vacant.   No reconciliation was effected till 1693, in the pontificate of Innocent XII.   It is to be observed, whether the French writers slur this over or not, that the pope gained the honours of war ; the bishops who had sat in the assembly of 1682 writing separately letters which have the appearance of regretting, if not retracting, what they had done.   These were however worded with intentional equivocation ; and as the court of Rome yields to none in suspecting the subterfuges of words, it is plain that it contented itself with an exterior humiliation of its adversaries.   The old question of the regale was tacitly settled ; Louis enjoyed all that he had desired, and Rome might justly think herself not bound to fight for the privileges of those who had made her so bad a return.[q]

4. The doctrine of the four articles gained ground perhaps in the church of France through a Dupin on the ancient discipline. work of great boldness, and deriving authority from the learning and judgment of its author, Dupin.   In the height of the contest, while many were considering how far the Gallican church might dispense with the institution of bishops at Rome, that point in the established system which evidently secured the victory to their antagonist, in the year 1686, he published a treatise on the ancient discipline of the church. It is written in Latin, which he probably chose as less obnoxious than his own language.   It may be true, which I cannot affirm or deny, that each position in this work had been advanced before ; but the general tone seems undoubtedly more adverse to the papal supremacy than any book which could have come from a man of

[q] I have derived most of this account from Bausset's Life of Bossuet, vol. ii. Both the bishop and his biographer shuffle a good deal about the letter of the Gallican prelates in 1693.   But when the Roman legions had passed under the yoke at the Caudine Forks, they were ready to take up arms again.

reputed orthodoxy. It tends, notwithstanding a few necessary admissions, to represent almost all that can be called power or jurisdiction in the see of Rome as acquired, if not abusive, and would leave, in a practical sense, no real pope at all; mere primacy being a trifle, and even the right of interfering by admonition being of no great value, when there was no definite obligation to obey. The principle of Dupin is, that the church having reached her perfection in the fourth century, we should endeavour, as far as circumstances will admit, to restore the discipline of that age. But, even in the Gallican church, it has generally been held that he has urged his argument farther than is consistent with a necessary subordination to Rome.[r]

5. In the same year Dupin published the first volume of a more celebrated work, his Nouvelle Bibliothèque des Auteurs Ecclésiastiques, a complete history of theological literature, at least within the limits of the church, which, in a long series of volumes, he finally brought down to the close of the seventeenth century. It is unquestionably the most standard work of that kind extant, whatever deficiencies may have been found in its execution. The immense erudition requisite for such an undertaking must have rendered it inevitable to take some things at second hand, or to fall into some errors; and we may add other causes less necessary, the youth of the writer in the first volumes, and the rapidity with which they appeared. Integrity, love of truth, and moderation, distinguish this ecclesiastical history, perhaps beyond any other. Dupin is often near the frontier of orthodoxy, but he is careful, even in the eyes of jealous Catholics, not quite to overstep it. This work was soon translated into English, and furnished a large part of such knowledge on the subject as our own divines possessed. His free way of speaking, however, on the Roman supremacy and some other points, excited the animadversion of more rigid persons, and among others of Bossuet, who stood on his own vantage-ground, ready to strike on every side. The most impartial critics have been of Dupin's mind;

Marginal note: Dupin's Ecclesiastical Library.

---

[r] Bibliothèque Universelle, vi. 109. The book is very clear, concise, and learned, so that it is worth reading through by those who would understand such matters. I have not observed that it is much quoted by English writers.

but Bossuet, like all dogmatic champions of orthodoxy, never sought truth by an analytical process of investigation, assuming his own possession of it as an axiom in the controversy.[*]

6. Dupin was followed a few years afterwards by one not his superior in learning and candour (though deficient in neither), but in skill of narration and beauty of style, Claude Fleury. *Fleury's Ecclesiastical History.* The first volume of his Ecclesiastical History came forth in 1691; but a part only of the long series falls within this century. The learning of Fleury has been said to be frequently not original, and his prolixity to be too great for an elementary historian. The former is only blameable when he has concealed his immediate authorities; few works of great magnitude have been written wholly from the prime sources; with regard to his diffuseness, it is very convenient to those who want access to the original writers, or leisure to collate them. Fleury has been called by some credulous and uncritical; but he is esteemed faithful, moderate, and more respectful or cautious than Dupin. Yet many of his volumes are a continual protest against the vices and ambition of the mediæval popes, and his Ecclesiastical History must be reckoned among the causes of that estrangement, in spirit and affection, from the court of Rome, which leavens the theological literature of France in the eighteenth century.

7. The Dissertations of Fleury, interspersed with his History, were more generally read and more conspicuously excellent. Concise, but neither *His Dissertations.* dry nor superficial; luminous, yet appearing simple; philosophical without the affectation of profundity, seizing all that is most essential in their subject without the tediousness of detail or the pedantry of quotation; written, above all, with that clearness, that ease, that unaffected purity of taste, which belong to the French style of that best age, they present a contrast not only to the inferior writings on philosophical history with

---

[*] Bibliothèque Universelle, iii. 39, vii. 335, xxii. 120. Biogr. Universelle. Œuvres de Bossuet, vol. xxx. Dupin seems not to have held the superiority of bishops to priests jure divino, which provokes the prelate of Meaux. Ces grands critiques sont peu favorables aux supériorités ecclésiastiques, et n'aiment guère plus celles des évêques que celle du pape. P. 491.

which our age abounds, but, in some respects, even to
the best. It cannot be a crime that these dissertations
contain a good deal which, after more than a century's
labour in historical inquiry, has become more familiar
than it was.

8. The French Protestants, notwithstanding their dis-
armed condition, were not, I apprehend, much
oppressed under Richelieu and Mazarin. But
soon afterwards an eagerness to accelerate what
was taking place through natural causes, their return
into the church, brought on a series of harassing edicts,
which ended in the revocation of that of Nantes. During
this time they were assailed by less terrible weapons,
yet such as required no ordinary strength to resist, the
polemical writings of the three greatest men in the
church of France—Nicole, Arnauld, and Bossuet. The
two former were desirous to efface the reproaches of an
approximation to Calvinism, and of a disobedience to
the Catholic church, under which their Jansenist party
was labouring. Nicole began with a small treatise, entitled La Perpétuité de la Foi de l'Eglise Catholique,
touchant l'Eucharistie, in 1664. This aimed to prove
that the tenet of transubstantiation had been constant in
the church. Claude, the most able controvertist among
the French Protestants, replied in the next year. This
led to a much more considerable work by Nicole and
Arnauld conjointly, with the same title as the former ;
nor was Claude slow in combating his double-headed
adversary. Nicole is said to have written the greater
portion of this second treatise, though it commonly bears
the name of his more illustrious colleague.[t]

Protestant controversy in France.

9. Both Arnauld and Nicole were eclipsed by the
most distinguished and successful advocate of
the Catholic church, Bossuet. His Exposition
de la Foi Catholique was written in 1668, for
the use of two brothers of the Dangeau family ;
but having been communicated to Turenne, the most
eminent Protestant that remained in France, it contributed much to his conversion. It was published in
1671 ; and though enlarged from the first sketch, does
not exceed eighty pages in octavo. Nothing can be

Bossuet's exposition of Catholic faith.

t Biogr. Univ.

more precise, more clear, or more free from all circuity
and detail than this little book ; everything is put in
the most specious light ;' the authority of the ancient
church, recognised, at least nominally, by the majority
of Protestants, is alone kept in sight. Bossuet limits
himself to doctrines established by the council of Trent,
leaving out of the discussion not only all questionable
points, but, what is perhaps less fair, all rites and
usages, however general, or sanctioned by the regular
discipline of the church, except so far as formally
approved by that council. Hence he glides with a transient step over the invocation of saints and the worship
of images, but presses with his usual dexterity on the
inconsistencies and weak concessions of his antagonists.
The Calvinists, or some of them, had employed a jargon
of words about real presence, which he exposes with
admirable brevity and vigour." Nor does he gain less
advantage in favour of tradition and church authority
from the assumption of somewhat similar claims by the
same party. It has often been alleged that the Exposition of Bossuet was not well received by many on his
own side. And for this there seems to be some foundation, though the Protestant controvertists have made too
much of the facts. It was published at Rome in 1678,
and approved in the most formal manner by Innocent XI.
the next year. But it must have been perceived to separate the faith of the church, as it rested on dry propositions, from the same faith living and embodied in the
every-day worship of the people.ˣ

10. Bossuet was now the acknowledged champion of
the Roman church in France ; Claude was in His confer-
equal pre-eminence on the other side. These ence with
Claude,
great adversaries had a regular conference in
1678. Mademoiselle de Duras, a Protestant lady, like

ᵘ Bossuet observes, that most other
controversies are found to depend more
on words than substance, and the difference becomes less the more they are examined; but in that of the Eucharist the
contrary is the case, since the Calvinists
endeavour to accommodate their phraseology to the Catholics, while essentially
they differ. Vol. xviii. p. 135.
ˣ The writings of Bossuet against the

Protestants occupy nine volumes, xviii.-
xxvi., in the great edition of his works,
Versailles, 1816. The Exposition de la
Foi is in the eighteenth. Bausset, in his
Life of Bossuet, appears to have refuted
the exaggerations of many Protestants as
to the ill reception of this little book at
Rome. Yet there was a certain foundation for them. See Bibliothèque Universelle. vol. xi. p. 455.

most others of her rank at that time, was wavering about
religion, and in her presence the dispute was carried
on. It entirely turned on church authority. The arguments of Bossuet differ only from those which have often
been adduced by the spirit and conciseness with which
he presses them. We have his own account, which of
course gives himself the victory. It was almost as much
of course that the lady was converted; for it is seldom
that a woman can withstand the popular argument on
that side, when she has once gone far enough to admit
the possibility of its truth, by giving it a hearing. Yet
Bossuet deals in sophisms which, though always in the
mouths of those who call themselves orthodox, are contemptible to such as know facts as well as logic. " I
urged," he says, " in a few words, what presumption it
was to believe that we can better understand the word
of God than all the rest of the church, and that nothing
would thus prevent there being as many religions as
persons." [7] But there can be no presumption in supposing that we may understand anything better than
one who has never examined it at all; and if this rest
of the church, so magnificently brought forward, have
commonly acted on Bossuet's principle, and thought it
presumptuous to judge for themselves; if out of many
millions of persons a few only have deliberately reasoned
on religion, and the rest have been, like true zeros,
nothing in themselves, but much in sequence; if also,
as is most frequently the case, this presumptuousness is
not the assertion of a paradox or novelty, but the preference of one denomination of Christians, or of one
tenet maintained by respectable authority, to another,
we can only scorn the emptiness, as well as resent the
effrontery, of this commonplace that rings so often in
our ears. Certainly reason is so far from condemning a
deference to the judgment of the wise and good, that
nothing is more irrational than to neglect it; but when
this is claimed for those whom we need not believe to
have been wiser and better than ourselves, nay, sometimes whom without vain glory we may esteem less,
and that so as to set aside the real authority of the most
philosophical, unbiassed, and judicious of mankind, it is

[7] Œuvres de Bossuet, xxiii. 290.

not pride or presumption, but a sober use of our faculties
that rejects the jurisdiction.

11. Bossuet once more engaged in a similar discussion
about 1691. Among the German Lutherans Correspond-
there seems to have been for a long time a ence with
lurking notion that on some terms or other a and Leib-
reconciliation with the church of Rome could nitz.
be effected; and this was most countenanced in the
dominions of Brunswick, and above all in the University
of Helmstadt. Leibnitz himself, and Molanus, a Lutheran
divine, were the negotiators on that side with Bossuet.
Their treaty, for such it was apparently understood to
be, was conducted by writing; and when we read their
papers on both sides, nothing is more remarkable than
the tone of superiority which the Catholic plenipotentiary,
if such he could be deemed without powers from any
one but himself, has thought fit to assume. No concession is offered, no tenet explained away; the sacramental
cup to the laity, and a permission to the Lutheran clergy
already married to retain their wives after their reordi-
nation, is all that he holds forth; and in this, doubtless,
he had no authority from Rome. Bossuet could not
veil his haughty countenance, and his language is that
of asperity and contemptuousness instead of moderation.
He dictates terms of surrender as to a besieged city
when the breach is already practicable, and hardly
deigns to show his clemency by granting the smallest
favour to the garrison. It is curious to see the strained
constructions, the artifices of silence to which Molanus
has recourse, in order to make out some pretence for his
ignominious surrender. Leibnitz, with whom the correspondence broke off in 1693, and was renewed again
in 1699, seems not quite so yielding as the other; and
the last biographer of Bossuet suspects that the German
philosopher was insincere or tortuous in the negotiation.
If this were so, he must have entered upon it less of his
own accord than to satisfy the Princess Sophia, who,
like many of her family, had been a little wavering, till
our Act of Settlement became a true settlement to their
faith. This bias of the court of Hanover is intimated in
several passages. The success of this treaty of union,
or rather of subjection, was as little to be expected as it
was desirable; the old spirit of Lutheranism was much

worn out, but there must surely have been a determination to resist so unequal a compromise. Rome negotiated as a conqueror with these beaten Carthaginians; yet no one had beaten them but themselves.[*]

12. The warfare of the Roman church may be carried on either in a series of conflicts on the various doctrines wherein the reformers separated from her, or by one pitched battle on the main question of a conclusive authority somewhere in the church. Bossuet's temper, as well as his inferiority in original learning, led him in preference to the latter scheme of theological strategy. It was also manifestly that course of argument which was most likely to persuade the unlearned. He followed up the blow which he had already struck against Claude in his famous work on the Variations of Protestant Churches. Never did his genius find a subject more fit to display its characteristic impetuosity, its arrogance, or its cutting and merciless spirit of sarcasm. The weaknesses, the inconsistent evasions, the extravagancies of Luther, Zwingle, Calvin, and Beza, pass, one after another, before us, till these great reformers seem like victim prisoners to be hewn down by the indignant prophet. That Bossuet is candid in statement, or even faithful in quotation, I should much doubt; he gives the words of his adversaries in his own French, and the references are not made to any specified edition of their voluminous writings. The main point, as he contends it to be, that the Protestant churches (for he does not confine this to persons) fluctuated much in the sixteenth century, is sufficiently proved; but it remained to show that this was a reproach. Those who have taken a different view from Bossuet may perhaps think that a little more of this censure would have been well incurred; that they have varied too little rather than too much; and that it is far more difficult, even in controversy with the church of Rome, to withstand the inference which their long creeds and confessions, as well as the language too common with their theologians, have furnished to her more ancient and catholic claim of infallibility, than to vindicate those successive variations which are analogous to the neces-

His Variations of Protestant Churches.

---

[*] Œuvres de Bossuet, vols. xxv. and xxvi.

sary course of human reason on all other subjects. The essential fallacy of Romanism, that truth must ever exist visibly on earth, is implied in the whole strain of Bossuet's attack on the variances of Protestantism : it is evident that variance of opinion proves error somewhere ; but unless it can be shown that we have any certain method of excluding it, this should only lead us to be more indulgent towards the judgment of others, and less confident of our own. The notion of an intrinsic moral criminality in religious error is at the root of the whole argument; and till Protestants are well rid of this, there seems no secure mode of withstanding the effect which the vast weight of authority asserted by the Latin church, even where it has not the aid of the Eastern, must produce on timid and scrupulous minds.

13. In no period has the Anglican church stood up so powerfully in defence of the Protestant cause as in that before us. From the æra of the **Anglican writings against popery.** Restoration to the close of the century the war was unremitting and vigorous. And it is particularly to be remarked, that the principal champions of the church of England threw off that ambiguous syncretism which had displayed itself under the first Stuarts, and, comparatively at least with their immediate predecessors, avoided every admission which might facilitate a deceitful compromise. We can only mention a few of the writers who signalized themselves in this controversy.

14. Taylor's Dissuasive from Popery was published in 1664 ; and in this his latest work we find the **Taylor's Dissuasive.** same general strain of Protestant reasoning, the same rejection of all but Scriptural authority, the same free exposure of the inconsistencies and fallacies of tradition, the same tendency to excite a sceptical feeling as to all except the primary doctrines of religion, which had characterised the Liberty of Prophesying. These are mixed, indeed, in Taylor's manner, with a few passages (they are, I think, but few), which, singly taken, might seem to breathe not quite this spirit ; but the tide flows for the most part the same way, and it is evident that his mind had undergone no change. The learning, in all his writings, is profuse ; but Taylor never leaves me with the impression that he is exact and scrupulous

in its application.   In one part of this Dissuasive from
Popery, having been reproached with some inconsistency,
he has no scruple to avow that in a former work he had
employed weak arguments for a laudable purpose.[*]

15. Barrow, not so extensively learned as Taylor, who
Barrow.— had read rather too much, but inferior perhaps
Stillingfleet. even in that respect to hardly any one else, and
above him in closeness and strength of reasoning, maintained the combat against Rome in many of his sermons,
and especially in a long treatise on the papal supremacy.
Stillingfleet followed, a man deeply versed in ecclesiastical antiquity, of an argumentative mind, excellently
fitted for polemical dispute, but perhaps by those habits
of his life rendered too much of an advocate to satisfy an
impartial reader.   In the critical reign of James II. he
may be considered as the leader on the Protestant side;
but Wake, Tillotson, and several more, would deserve
mention in a fuller history of ecclesiastical literature.

16. The controversies always smouldering in the church
Jansenius. of Rome, and sometimes breaking into flame, to
which the Anti-Pelagian writings of Augustin
had originally given birth, have been slightly touched in
our former volumes.   It has been seen that the rigidly
predestinarian theories had been condemned by the court
of Rome in Baius, that the opposite doctrine of Molina
had narrowly escaped censure, that it was safest to abstain
from any language not verbally that of the church or of
Augustin, whom the church held incontrovertible.   But
now a more serious and celebrated controversy, that of
the Jansenists, pierced as it were to the heart of the
church.   It arose before the middle of the century.   Jansenius, bishop of Ypres, in his Augustinus, published
after his death in 1640, gave, as he professed, a faithful
statement of the tenets of that father.   " We do not inquire," he says, " what men ought to believe on the
powers of human nature, or on the grace and predestina-
tion of God, but what Augustin once preached with the
approbation of the church, and has consigned to writing
in many of his works."   This book is in three parts; the
first containing a history of the Pelagian controversy, the

---

[*] Taylor's Works, x. 304. This is
not surprising, as in his Ductor Dubitantium, xi. 484, he maintains the right
of using arguments and authorities in
controversy which we do not believe to
be valid.

second and third an exposition of the tenets of Augustin. Jansenius does not, however, confine himself so much to mere analysis, but that he attacks the Jesuits Lessius and Molina, and even reflects on the bull of Pius V. condemning Baius, which he cannot wholly approve.[b]

17. Richelieu, who is said to have retained some animosity against Jansenius on account of a book called Mars Gallicus, which he had written on the side of his sovereign the king of Spain, designed to obtain the condemnation of the Augustinus by the French clergy. The Jesuits, therefore, had gained ground so far that the doctrines of Augustin were out of fashion, though few besides themselves ventured to reject his nominal authority. It is certainly clear that Jansenius offended the greater part of the church. But he had some powerful advocates, and especially Antony Arnauld, the most renowned of a family long conspicuous for eloquence, for piety, and for opposition to the Jesuits. In 1649, after several years of obscure dispute, Cornet, syndic of the faculty of theology in the University of Paris, brought forward for censure seven propositions, five of which became afterwards so famous, without saying that they were found in the work of Jansenius. The faculty condemned them, though it had never been reckoned favourable to the Jesuits; a presumption that they were at least expressed in a manner repugnant to the prevalent doctrine. Yet Le Clerc declares his own opinion that there may be some ambiguity in the style of the first, but that the other four are decidedly conformable to the theology of Augustin.

Condemnation of his Augustinus in France.

18. The Jesuits now took the course of calling in the authority of Rome. They pressed Innocent X. to condemn the five propositions, which were maintained by some doctors in France. It is not the

and at Rome.

---

[b] A very copious history of Jansenism, taking it up from the Council of Trent, will be found in the fourteenth volume of the Bibliothèque. Universelle, p. 139-398, from which Mosheim has derived most of what we read in his Ecclesiastical History. And the History of Port Royal was written by Racine in so perspicuous and neat a style, that, though we may hardly think with Olivet that it places him as high in prose writing as his tragedies do in verse, it entitles him to rank in the list of those who have succeeded in both. Is it not probable that in some scenes of Athalie he had Port Royal before his eyes? The history and the tragedy were written about the same time. Racine, it is rather remarkable, had entered the field against Nicole in 1686, chiefly indeed to defend theatrical representations, but not without many sarcasms against Jansenism.

policy of that court to compromise so delicate a possession as infallibility by bringing it to the test of that personal judgment, which is of necessity the arbiter of each man's own obedience. The popes have, in fact, rarely taken a part, independently of councils, in these school debates. The bull of Pius V. (a man too zealous by character to regard prudence), in which he condemned many tenets of Baius, had not, nor could it, give satisfaction to those who saw with their own eyes that it swerved from the Augustinian theory. Innocent was, at first, unwilling to meddle with a subject which, as he owned to a friend, he did not understand. But after hearing some discussions, he grew more confident of his knowledge, which he ascribed, as in duty bound, to the inspiration of the Holy Ghost, and went so heartily along with the Anti-Jansenists that he refused to hear the deputies of the other party. On the 31st of May, 1653, he condemned the five propositions, four as erroneous, and the fifth in stronger language ; declaring, however, not in the bull, but orally, that he did not condemn the tenet of efficacious grace (which all the Dominicans held), nor the doctrine of St. Augustin, which was, and ever would be, that of the church.

19. The Jansenists were not bold enough to hint that they did not acknowledge the infallibility of the pope in an express and positive declaration. *The Jansenists take a distinction;* Even if they had done so, they had an evident recognition of this censure of the five propositions by their own church, and might dread its being so generally received as to give the sanction which no Catholic can withstand. They had recourse, unfortunately, to a subterfuge which put them in the wrong. They admitted that the propositions were false, but denied that they could be found in the book of Jansenius. Thus each party rested on the denial of a matter of fact, and each erroneously, according at least to the judgment of the most learned and impartial Protestants. The five propositions express the doctrine of Augustin himself; and if they do this, we can hardly doubt that they express that of Jansenius. In a short time this ground of evasion was taken from their party. An assembly of French prelates in the first place, and afterwards Alexander VII., successor of Innocent X., condemned the propositions as in Jansenius, and in the sense intended by Jansenius.

20. The Jansenists were now driven to the wall : the Sorbonne in 1655, in consequence of some pro-   and are per-
positions of Arnauld, expelled him from the   secuted.
theological faculty ; a formulary was drawn up to be
signed by the clergy, condemning the propositions of
Jansenius, which was finally established in 1661 ; and
those who refused, even nuns, underwent a harassing
persecution.   The most striking instance of this, which
still retains an historical character, was the dissolution of
the famous convent of Port-Royal, over which Angelica
Arnauld, sister of the great advocate of Jansenism, had
long presided with signal reputation.   This nunnery was
at Paris, having been removed in 1644 from an ancient
Cistertian convent of the same name about six leagues
distant, and called for distinction Port-Royal des Champs.
To this now unfrequented building some of the most
eminent men repaired for study, whose writings being
anonymously published have been usually known by the
name of their residence.   Arnauld, Pascal, Nicole, Lancelot, De Sacy, are among the Messieurs de Port-Royal,
an appellation so glorious in the seventeenth century.
The Jansenists now took a distinction, very reasonable,
as it seems, in its nature, between the authority which
asserts or denies a proposition, and that which does the
like as to a fact.   They refused to the pope, that is, in
this instance, to the church, the latter infallibility.   We
cannot prosecute this part of ecclesiastical history farther :
if writings of any literary importance had been produced
by the controversy, they would demand our attention ;
but this does not appear to have been the case.   The
controversy between Arnauld and Malebranche may perhaps be an exception.   The latter, carried forward by his
original genius, attempted to deal with the doctrines of
theology as with metaphysical problems, in his Traité de
la Nature et de la Grace.   Arnauld animadverted on this
in his Réflexions Philosophiques et Théologiques. · Malebranche replied in Lettres du Père Malebranche à un de
ses Amis.   This was published in 1686, and the controversy between such eminent masters of abstruse reasoning began to excite attention.   Malebranche seems to
have retired first from the field.   His antagonist had great
advantages in the dispute, according to received systems
of theology, with which he was much more conversant,
and perhaps on the whole in the philosophical part of the

question. This, however, cannot be reckoned entirely a Jansenistic controversy, though it involved those perilous difficulties which had raised that flame.[c]

21. The credit of Augustin was now as much shaken in the Protestant as in the Catholic regions of Europe. Episcopius had given to the Remonstrant party a reputation which no sect so inconsiderable in its separate character has ever possessed. The Dutch Arminians were at no time numerous; they took no hold of the people; they had few churches, and though not persecuted by the now lenient policy of Holland, were still under the ban of an orthodox clergy, as exclusive and bigoted as before. But their writings circulated over Europe, and made a silent impression on the adverse party. It became less usual to bring forward the Augustinian hypothesis in prominent or unequivocal language. Courcelles, born at Geneva, and the successor of Episcopius in the Remonstrant congregation at Amsterdam, with less genius than his predecessor, had perhaps a more extensive knowledge of ecclesiastical antiquity. His works were much in esteem with the theologians of that way of thinking; but they have not fallen in my way.

Progress of Arminianism.

Courcelles.

22. Limborch, great-nephew of Episcopius, seems more than any other Arminian divine to have inherited his mantle. His most important work is the Theologia Christiana, containing a system of divinity and morals, in seven books and more than 900 pages, published in 1686. It is the fullest delineation of the Arminian scheme; but as the Arminians were by their principle free inquirers, and not, like other churches, bondsmen of symbolical formularies, no one book can strictly be taken as their representative. The tenets of Limborch are, in the majority of disputable points, such as impartial men have generally found in the primitive or Ante-Nicene fathers; but in some he probably deviates from them, steering far away from all that the Protestants of the Swiss reform had abandoned as superstitious or unintelligible.

Limborch.

23. John Le Clerc, in the same relationship to Courcelles that Limborch was to Episcopius, and like him

---

[c] An account of this controversy will be found at length in the second volume of the Bibliothèque Universelle.

transplanted from Geneva to the more liberal air, at that time, of the United Provinces, claims a high place among the Dutch Arminians; for though he did not maintain their cause either in systematic or polemical writings, his commentary on the Old Testament, and still more his excellent and celebrated reviews, the Bibliothèques Universelle, Choisie, and Ancienne et Moderne, must be reckoned a perpetual combat on that side. These journals enjoyed an extraordinary influence over Europe, and deserved to enjoy it. Le Clerc is generally temperate, judicious, appeals to no passion, displays a very extensive, though not perhaps a very deep erudition, lies in wait for the weakness and temerity of those he reviews, thus sometimes gaining the advantage over more learned men than himself. He would have been a perfect master of that sort of criticism, then newly current in literature, if he could have repressed an irritability in matters personal to himself, and a degree of prejudice against the Romish writers, or perhaps those styled orthodox in general, which sometimes disturbs the phlegmatic steadiness with which a good reviewer, like a practised sportsman, brings down his game.[d]

d Bishop Monk observes that Le Clerc "seems to have been the first person who understood the power which may be exercised over literature by a reviewer." Life of Bentley, p. 209. This may be true, especially as he was nearly the first reviewer, and certainly better than his predecessors. But this remark is followed by a sarcastic animadversion upon Le Clerc's ignorance of Greek metres, and by the severe assertion, that "by an absolute system of terror he made himself a despot in the republic of letters."

[The former is certainly just: Le Clerc was not comparable to Bentley, or to many who have followed, in his critical knowledge of Greek metres; which, at the present day, would be held very cheap. He is, however, to be judged relatively to his predecessors; and, in the particular department of metrical rules, few had known much more than he did; as we may perceive by the Greek compositions of Casaubon and other eminent scholars. Le Clerc might have been more prudent in abstaining from interference with what he did not well understand; but this cannot warrant scornful language towards so general a scholar, and one who served literature so well. That he made himself a despot in the republic of letters by a system of terror is a charge not made out, as it seems to me, by the general character of Le Clerc's criticisms, which, where he has no personal quarrel, is temperate and moderate, neither traducing men nor imputing motives. I adhere to the character of his reviews given in the text; and having early in life become acquainted with them, and having been accustomed, by books then esteemed, to think highly of Le Clerc, I must be excused from following a change of fashion. This note has been modified on the complaint of the learned prelate quoted in it, whom I had not the slightest intention of offending, but who might take some expressions, with respect to periodical criticism, as personal to himself; which neither were so meant, nor, as far as I know, could apply to any reputed writings of his composition.—1847.]

24. The most remarkable progress made by the Armi-

nian theology was in England. This had begun under James and Charles; but it was then taken up in conjunction with that patristic learning which adopted the fourth and fifth centuries as the standard of orthodox faith. Perhaps the first very bold and unambiguous attack on the Calvinistic system which we shall mention came from this quarter. This was in an anonymous Latin pamphlet entitled Fur Prædestinatus, published in 1651, and generally ascribed to Sancroft, at that time a young man. It is a dialogue between a thief under sentence of death and his attendant minister, wherein the former insists upon his assurance of being predestinated to salvation. In this idea there is nothing but what is sufficiently obvious; but the dialogue is conducted with some spirit and vivacity. Every position in the thief's mouth is taken from eminent Calvinistic writers; and what is chiefly worth notice is that Sancroft, for the first time, has ventured to arraign the greatest heroes of the Reformation; not only Calvin, Beza, and Zanchius, but, who had been hitherto spared, Luther and Zwingle. It was in the nature of a manifesto from the Arminian party, that they would not defer in future to any modern authority.[*]

25. The loyal Anglican clergy, suffering persecution

at the hands of Calvinistic sectaries, might be naturally expected to cherish the opposite principles. These are manifest in the sermons of Barrow, rather perhaps by his silence than his tone, and more explicitly in those of South. But many exceptions might be found among leading men, such as Sanderson; while in an opposite quarter, among the younger generation who had conformed to the times, arose a more formidable spirit of Arminianism, which changed the face of the English church. This was displayed among those who, just about the epoch of the Restoration, were

[*] The Fur Prædestinatus is reprinted in D'Oyly's Life of Sancroft. It is much the best proof of ability that the worthy archbishop ever gave.

[The superiority of this little piece to anything else ascribed to Sancroft is easily explained. It was not his own; of which his biographers have been igno-rant. Leibnitz informs us that it is a translation from a Dutch tract, pub-lished at the beginning of the Arminian controversy. Bayle, he says, was not aware of this, and quotes it as written in English. Theodicea, sect. 167. San-croft, as appears by D'Oyly's Life of him, was in Holland from 1657 to 1659.—1853.]

denominated Latitude-men, or more commonly Latitudinarians, trained in the principles of Episcopius and
Chillingworth, strongly averse to every compromise
with popery, and thus distinguished from the high
church party ; learned rather in profane philosophy than
in the fathers, more full of Plato and Plotinus than
Jerome or Chrysostom, great maintainers of natural religion, and of the eternal laws of morality, not very
solicitous about systems of orthodoxy, and limiting very
considerably beyond the notions of former ages the fundamental tenets of Christianity. This is given as a
general character, but varying in the degree of its application to particular persons. Burnet enumerates as the
chief of this body of men, More, Cudworth, Whichcot,
Tillotson, Stillingfleet ; some, especially the last, more
tenacious of the authority of the fathers and of the church
than others, but all concurring in the adoption of an
Arminian theology.[f] This became so predominant before the Revolution, that few English divines of eminence
remained who so much as endeavoured to steer a middle
course, or to dissemble their renunciation of the doctrines which had been sanctioned at the synod of Dort
by the delegates of their church. " The Theological
Institutions of Episcopius," says a contemporary writer,
" were at that time (1685) generally in the hands of our
students of divinity in both universities, as the best
system of divinity that had appeared."[g] And he proceeds afterwards : " The Remonstrant writers, among
whom there were men of excellent learning and parts, had
now acquired a considerable reputation in our universities by the means of some great men among us." This
testimony seems irresistible ; and as one hundred years
before the Institutes of Calvin were read in the same
academical studies, we must own, unless Calvin and
Episcopius shall be maintained to have held the same
tenets, that Bossuet might have added a chapter to the
Variations of Protestant Churches.

26. The methods adopted in order to subvert the
Augustinian theology were sometimes direct, by explicit
controversy, or by an opposite train of Scriptural inter-

[f] Burnet's History of His Own Times,
i. 187. " Account of the new Sect called
Latitudinarians," in the collection of

tracts entitled The Phœnix, vol. ii. p. 499.
[g] Nelson's Life of Bull, in Bull's Works,
vol. viii. p. 257.

pretation in regular commentaries; more frequently per-
Bull's Harmonia Apostolica. haps indirect, by inculcating moral duties, and especially by magnifying the law of nature. Among the first class the Harmonia Apostolica of Bull seems to be reckoned the principal work of this period. It was published in 1669, and was fiercely encountered at first not merely by the Presbyterian party, but by many of the Church, the Lutheran tenets as to justification by faith being still deemed orthodox. Bull establishes as the groundwork of his harmony between the apostles Paul and James, on a subject where their language apparently clashes in terms, that we are to interpret St. Paul by St. James, and not St. James by St. Paul, because the latest authority, and that which may be presumed to have explained what was obscure in the former, ought to prevail [h]—a rule doubtless applicable in many cases, whatever it may be in this. It at least turned to his advantage; but it was not so easy for him to reconcile his opinions with those of the Reformers, or with the Anglican articles.

27. The Paraphrase and Annotations of Hammond on
Hammond— Locke— Wilkins. the New Testament give a different colour to the Epistles of St. Paul from that which they display in the hands of Beza and the other theologians of the sixteenth century. And the name of Hammond stood so high with the Anglican clergy, that he naturally turned the tide of interpretation his own way. The writings of Fowler, Wilkins, and Whichcot are chiefly intended to exhibit the moral lustre of Christianity, and to magnify the importance of virtuous life. Wilkins left an unfinished work on the Principles and Duties of Natural Religion. Twelve chapters only, about half the volume, were ready for the press at his death; the rest was compiled by Tillotson as well as the materials left by the author would allow; and the expressions employed lead us to believe that much was due to the editor. The latter's preface strongly presses the separate obligation of natural religion, upon which both the disciples of Hobbes, and many of the less learned sectaries, were at issue with him.

28. We do not find much of importance written on

h Nelson's Life of Bull.

the Trinitarian controversy before the middle of the
seventeenth century, except by the Socinians
themselves. But the case was now very different.
Though the Polish or rather German Unitarians did not
produce more distinguished men than before, they came
more forward in the field of dispute. Finally expelled
from Poland in 1660, they sought refuge in more learned
as well as more tolerant regions, and especially in the
genial soil of religious liberty, the United Provinces.
Even here they enjoyed no avowed toleration; but the
press, with a very slight concealment of place, under the
attractive words Eleutheropolis, Irenopolis, or Freystadt,
was ready to serve them with its natural impartiality.
They began to make a slight progress in England; the
writings of Biddle were such as even Cromwell, though
habitually tolerant, did not overlook; the author underwent an imprisonment both at that time and after the
Restoration. In general the Unitarian writers preserved
a disguise. Milton's treatise, not long since brought to
light, goes on the Arian hypothesis, which had probably
been countenanced by some others. It became common,
in the reign of Charles II., for the English divines to
attack the Anti-Trinitarians of each denomination.

29. An epoch is supposed to have been made in this
controversy by the famous work of Bull, Defensio Fidei Nicenæ. This was not primarily
directed against the heterodox party. In the
Dogmata Theologica of Petavius, published in 1644,
that learned Jesuit, laboriously compiling passages from
the fathers, had come to the conclusion, that most of
those before the Nicene council had seemed, by their
language, to run into nearly the same heresy as that
which the council had condemned, and this inference
appeared to rest on a long series of quotations. The
Arminian Courcelles, and even the English philosopher
Cudworth, the latter of whom was as little suspected of
an heterodox leaning as Petavius himself, had arrived
at the same result; so that a considerable triumph was
given to the Arians, in which the Socinians, perhaps at
that time more numerous, seem to have thought themselves entitled to partake. Bull had, therefore, to contend with authorities not to be despised by the learned.

30. The Defensio Fidei Nicenæ was published in

1685.   It did not want answerers in England ; but it obtained a great reputation, and an assembly of the French clergy, through the influence of Bossuet, returned thanks to the author.   It was indeed evident that Petavius, though he had certainly formed his opinion with perfect honesty, was preparing the way for an inference, that if the primitive fathers could be heterodox on a point of so great magnitude, we must look for infallibility not in them nor in the diffusive church, but in general councils presided over by the pope, or ultimately in the pope himself.   This, though not unsuitable to the notions of some Jesuits, was diametrically opposite to the principles of the Gallican church, which professed to repose on a perpetual and catholic tradition.

31. Notwithstanding the popularity of this defence of the Nicene faith, and the learning it displays, the author was far from ending the controversy, or from satisfying all his readers.   It was alleged that he does not meet the question with which he deals ; that the word ὁμοούσιος, being almost new at the time of the council, and being obscure and metaphysical in itself, required a precise definition to make the reader see his way before him, or at least one better than Bull has given, which the adversary might probably adopt without much scruple ; that the passages adduced from the fathers are often insufficient for his purpose ; that he confounds the eternal essence with the eternal personality or distinctness of the Logos, though well aware, of course, that many of the early writers employed different names (ἐνδιάθετος and προφορικὸς) for these ; and that he does not repel some of the passages which can hardly bear an orthodox interpretation.   It was urged, moreover, that his own hypothesis, taken altogether, is but a palliated Arianism ; that by insisting for more than one hundred pages on the subordination of the Son to the Father, he came close to what since has borne that name, though it might not be precisely what had been condemned at Nice, and could not be reconciled with the Athanasian creed, except by such an interpretation of the latter as is neither probable, nor has been reputed orthodox.

Not satisfactory to all.

32. Among the theological writers of the Roman Church, and in a less degree among Protestants, there has always been a class not inconsi-

Mystics.

derable for numbers or for influence, generally denominated mystics, or, when their language has been more
unmeasured, enthusiasts and fanatics. These may be
distinguished into two kinds, though it must readily be
understood that they may often run much into one another – the first believing that the soul, by immediate
communion with the Deity, receives a peculiar illumination and knowledge of truths not cognizable by the understanding; the second less solicitous about intellectual
than moral light, and aiming at such pure contemplation
of the attributes of God, and such an intimate perception of spiritual life, as may end in a sort of absorption
into the divine essence. But I should not probably have
alluded to any writings of this description, if the two most
conspicuous luminaries of the French church, Bossuet and Fenelon, had not clashed with each Fenelon.
other in that famous controversy of Quietism, to which
the enthusiastic writings of Madame Guyon gave birth.
The " Maximes des Saints " of Fenelon I have never
seen ; some editions of his entire works, as they affect
to be, do not include what the church has condemned ;
and the original book has probably become scarce.[i] Fenelon appears to have been treated by his friend, (shall we
call him ?) or rival, with remarkable harshness. Bossuet might have felt some jealousy at the rapid elevation
of the Archbishop of Cambray: but we need not have
recourse to this; the rigour of orthodoxy in a temper
like his will account for all. There could be little doubt
but that many saints honoured by the church had uttered
things quite as strong as any that Fenelon's work contained. Bossuet, however, succeeded in obtaining its
condemnation at Rome. Fenelon was of the second class
above mentioned among the mystics, and seems to have
been absolutely free from such pretences to illumination
as we find in Behmen or Barclay. The pure disinterested
love of God was the main spring of his religious theory.
The Divine Œconomy of Poiret, 1686, and the writings
of a German Quietist, Spener, do not require any particular mention.[k]

33. This later period of the seventeenth century was
marked by an increasing boldness in religious inquiry ;
we find more disregard of authority, more disposition to

i [It is reprinted in the edition of Fenelon's works, Versailles, 1820.—1847.]
k Bibl. Universelle, v. 412, xvi. 224.

question received tenets, a more suspicious criticism,
both as to the genuineness and the credibility
of ancient writings, a more ardent love of
truth, that is, of perceiving and understanding
what is true, instead of presuming that we
possess it without any understanding at all. Much of
this was associated, no doubt, with the other revolutions
in literary opinion ; with the philosophy of Bacon, Descartes, Gassendi, Hobbes, Bayle, and Locke, with the
spirit which a slightly learned, yet acute generation of
men rather conversant with the world than with libraries
(to whom the appeal in modern languages must be
made) was sure to breathe, with that incessant reference
to proof which the physical sciences taught mankind to
demand. Hence quotations are comparatively rare in
the theological writings of this age ; they are better reduced to their due office of testimony as to fact, sometimes of illustration or better statement of an argument,
but not so much alleged as argument or authority in
themselves. Even those who combated on the side of
established doctrines were compelled to argue more from
themselves, lest the public, their umpire, should reject,
with an opposite prejudice, what had enslaved the prejudices of their fathers.

34. It is well known that a disbelief in Christianity
became very frequent about this time. Several books more or less appear to indicate this
spirit, but the charge has often been made
with no sufficient reason. Of Hobbes enough has been
already said, and Spinosa's place as a metaphysician will
be in the next chapter. His Tractatus Theologico-Poli-
ticus, published anonymously at Amsterdam, with the
false date of Hamburg, in 1670, contains many observations on the Old Testament, which, though they do
not really affect its general authenticity and truth,
clashed with the commonly received opinion of its absolute inspiration. Some of these remarks were, if not
borrowed, at least repeated in a book of more celebrity,
Sentimens de quelques Théologiens d'Hollande sur l'Histoire Critique du Père Simon. This work is written by Le
Clerc, but it has been doubted whether he is the author
of those acute, but hardy, questions on the inspiration of
Scripture which it contains. They must however be

presumed to coincide for the most part with his own opinion ; but he has afterwards declared his dissent from the hypothesis contained .in these volumes, that Moses was not the author of the Pentateuch. The Archæologia Philosophica of Thomas Burnet is intended to dispute the literal history of the creation and fall. But few will pretend that either Le Clerc or Burnet were disbelievers in Revelation.

35. Among those who sustained the truth of Christianity by argument rather than authority, the first place both in order of time and of excellence is due to Pascal, though his Thoughts were not published till 1670, some years after his death, and, in the first edition, not without suppressions. They have been supposed to be fragments of a more systematic work that he had planned, or perhaps only reflections committed to paper, with no design of publication in their actual form. But, as is generally the case with works of genius, we do not easily persuade ourselves that they could have been improved by any such alteration as would have destroyed their type. They are at present bound together by a real coherence through the predominant character of the reasonings and sentiments, and give us everything that we could desire in a more regular treatise without the tedious verbosity which regularity is apt to produce. The style is not so polished as in the Provincial Letters, and the sentences are sometimes ill constructed and elliptical. Passages almost transcribed from Montaigne have been published by careless editors as Pascal's.

Thoughts of Pascal.

36. But the Thoughts of Pascal are to be ranked, as a monument of his genius, above the Provincial Letters, though some have asserted the contrary. They burn with an intense light; condensed in expression, sublime, energetic, rapid, they hurry away the reader till he is scarcely able or willing to distinguish the sophisms from the truth which they contain. For that many of them are incapable of bearing a calm scrutiny is very manifest to those who apply such a test. The notes of Voltaire, though always intended to detract, are sometimes unanswerable; but the splendour of Pascal's eloquence absolutely annihilates, in effect on the general reader, even this antagonist.

37. Pascal had probably not read very largely, which has given an ampler sweep to his genius. Except the Bible and the writings of Augustin, the book that seems most to have attracted him was the Essays of Montaigne. Yet no men could be more unlike in personal dispositions and in the cast of their intellect. But Pascal, though abhorring the religious and moral carelessness of Montaigne, found much that fell in with his own reflections in the contempt of human opinions, the perpetual humbling of human reason, which runs through the bold and original work of his predecessor. He quotes no book so frequently; and indeed, except Epictetus, and once or twice Descartes, he hardly quotes any other at all. Pascal was too acute a geometer, and too sincere a lover of truth, to countenance the sophisms of mere Pyrrhonism; but like many theological writers, in exalting faith he does not always give reason her value, and furnishes weapons which the sceptic might employ against himself. It has been said that he denies the validity of the proofs of natural religion. This seems to be in some measure an error, founded on mistaking the objections he puts in the mouths of unbelievers for his own. But it must, I think, be admitted that his arguments for the being of a God are too often à tutiori, that it is the safer side to take.

38. The Thoughts of Pascal on miracles abound in proofs of his acuteness and originality; an originality much more striking when we recollect that the subject had not been discussed as it has since, but with an intermixture of some sophistical and questionable positions. Several of them have a secret reference to the famous cure of his niece, Mademoiselle Perier, by the holy thorn. But he is embarrassed with the difficult question whether miraculous events are sure tests of the doctrine which they support, and is not wholly consistent in his reasoning, or satisfactory in his distinctions. I am unable to pronounce whether Pascal's other observations on the rational proofs of Christianity are as original as they are frequently ingenious and powerful.

39. But the leading principle of Pascal's theology, that from which he deduces the necessary truth of Revelation, is the fallen nature of mankind; dwelling less upon

Scriptural proofs, which he takes for granted, than on the evidence which he supposes man himself to supply. Nothing, however, can be more dissimilar than his beautiful visions to the vulgar Calvinism of the pulpit. It is not the sordid, grovelling, degraded Caliban of that school, but the ruined archangel, that he delights to paint. Man is so great, that his greatness is manifest even in his knowledge of his own misery. A tree does not know itself to be miserable. It is true that to know we are miserable is misery; but still it is greatness to know it. All his misery proves his greatness; it is the misery of a great lord, of a king, dispossessed of their own. Man is the feeblest branch of nature, but it is a branch that thinks. He requires not the universe to crush him. He may be killed by a vapour, by a drop of water. But if the whole universe should crush him, he would be nobler than that which causes his death, because he knows that he is dying, and the universe would not know its power over him. This is very evidently sophistical and declamatory; but it is the sophistry of a fine imagination. It would be easy, however, to find better passages. The dominant idea recurs in almost every page of Pascal. His melancholy genius plays in wild and rapid flashes, like lightning round the scathed oak, about the fallen greatness of man. He perceives every characteristic quality of his nature under these conditions. They are the solution of every problem, the clearing up of every inconsistency that perplexes us. "Man," he says very finely, " has a secret instinct that leads him to seek diversion and employment from without; which springs from the sense of his continual misery. And he has another secret instinct, remaining from the greatness of his original nature, which teaches him that happiness can only exist in repose. And from these two contrary instincts there arises in him an obscure propensity, concealed in his soul, which prompts him to seek repose through agitation, and even to fancy that the contentment he does not enjoy will be found, if by struggling yet a little longer he can open a door to rest." [m]

40. It can hardly be conceived that any one would think the worse of human nature or of himself by read-

***

[m] Œuvres de Pascal, vol. i. p. 121.

ing these magnificent lamentations of Pascal. He adorns and ennobles the degeneracy that he exaggerates. The ruined aqueduct, the broken column, the desolated city, suggest no ideas but of dignity and reverence. No one is ashamed of a misery which bears witness to his grandeur. If we should persuade a labourer that the blood of princes flows in his veins, we might spoil his contentment with the only lot he has drawn, but scarcely kill in him the seeds of pride.

41. Pascal, like many others who have dwelt on this alleged degeneracy of mankind, seems never to have disentangled his mind from the notion, that what we call human nature has not merely an arbitrary and grammatical, but an intrinsic objective reality. The common and convenient forms of language, the analogies of sensible things, which the imagination readily supplies, conspire to delude us into this fallacy. Yet though each man is born with certain powers and dispositions which constitute his own nature, and the resemblance of these in all his fellows produces a general idea, or a collective appellation, whichever we may prefer to say, called the nature of man, few would in this age explicitly contend for the existence of this as a substance capable of qualities, and those qualities variable, or subject to mutation. The corruption of human nature is therefore a phrase which may convey an intelligible meaning, if it is acknowledged to be merely analogical and inexact, but will mislead those who do not keep this in mind. Man's nature, as it now is, that which each man and all men possess, is the immediate workmanship of God, as much as at his creation; nor is any other hypothesis consistent with theism.

42. This notion of a real universal in human nature presents to us in an exaggerated light those anomalies from which writers of Pascal's school are apt to infer some vast change in our original constitution. Exaggerated, I say, for it cannot be denied that we frequently perceive a sort of incoherence, as it appears at least to our defective vision, in the same individual; and, like threads of various hues shot through one web, the love of vice and of virtue, the strength and weakness of the heart, are wonderfully blended in self-contradictory and self-destroying conjunction. But even if we should fail

altogether in solving the very first steps of this problem, there is no course for a reasonable being except to acknowledge the limitations of his own faculties; and it seems rather unwarrantable, on the credit of this humble confession, that we do not comprehend the depths of what has been withheld from us, to substitute something far more incomprehensible and revolting to our moral and rational capacities in its place. " What," says Pascal, " can be more contrary to the rules of our wretched justice, than to damn eternally an infant incapable of volition for an offence wherein he seems to have had no share, and which was committed six thousand years before he was born ? Certainly, nothing shocks us more rudely than this doctrine ; and yet, without this mystery, the most incomprehensible of all, we are incomprehensible to ourselves. Man is more inconceivable without this mystery, than the mystery is inconceivable to man."

43. It might be wandering from the proper subject of these volumes if we were to pause, even shortly, to inquire whether, while the creation of a world so full of evil must ever remain the most inscrutable of mysteries, we might not be led some way in tracing the connexion of moral and physical evil in mankind with his place in that creation ; and especially, whether the law of continuity, which it has not pleased his Maker to break with respect to his bodily structure, and which binds that, in the unity of one great type, to the lower forms of animal life by the common conditions of nourishment, reproduction, and self-defence, has not rendered necessary both the physical appetites and the propensities which terminate in self ; whether, again, the superior endowments of his intellectual nature, his susceptibility of moral emotion, and of those disinterested affections which, if not exclusively, he far more intensely possesses than any inferior being; above all, the gifts of conscience, and a capacity to know God, might not be expected, even beforehand, by their conflict with the animal passions, to produce some partial inconsistencies, some anomalies at least, which he could not himself explain, in so compound a being. Every link in the long chain of creation does not pass by easy transition into the next. There are necessary chasms, and, as it were,

leaps, from one creature to another, which, though not exceptions to the law of continuity, are accommodations of it to a new series of being. If man was made in the image of God, he was also made in the image of an ape. The framework of the body of him who has weighed the stars, and made the lightning his slave, approaches to that of a speechless brute who wanders in the forests of Sumatra. Thus standing on the frontier land between animal and angelic natures, what wonder that he should partake of both! But these are things which it is difficult to touch; nor would they have been here introduced, but in order to weaken the force of positions so confidently asserted by many, and so eloquently by Pascal.

44. Among the works immediately designed to confirm *Vindica-* the truth of Christianity, a certain reputation *tions of* was acquired, through the known erudition of *Christianity.* its author, by the Demonstratio Evangelica of Huet, Bishop of Avranches. This is paraded with definitions, axioms, and propositions, in order to challenge the name it assumes. But the axioms, upon which so much is to rest, are often questionable or equivocal; as, for instance: Omnis prophetia est verax, quæ prædixit res eventu deinde completas,—equivocal in the word *verax*. Huet also confirms his axioms by argument, which shows that they are not truly such. The whole book is full of learning; but he frequently loses sight of the points he would prove, and his quotations fall beside the mark. Yet he has furnished much to others, and possibly no earlier work on the same subject is so elaborate and comprehensive. The next place, if not a higher one, might be given to the treatise of Abbadie, a French refugee, published in 1684. His countrymen bestow on it the highest eulogies, but it was never so well known in England, and is now almost forgotten. The oral conferences of Limborch with Orobio, a Jew of considerable learning and ability, on the prophecies relating to the Messiah, were reduced into writing and published; they are still in some request. No book of this period, among many that were written, reached so high a reputation in England as Leslie's Short Method with the Deists, published in 1694; in which he has started an argument, pursued with more critical analysis

by others, on the peculiarly distinctive marks of credibility that pertain to the Scriptural miracles.   The authenticity of this little treatise has been idly questioned
on the Continent, for no better reason than that a translation of it has been published in a posthumous edition
(1732) of the works of Saint Real, who died in 1692.
But posthumous editions are never deemed of sufficient
authority to establish a literary title against possession ;
and Prosper Marchand informs us that several other
tracts, in this edition of Saint Real, are erroneously
ascribed to him.   The internal evidence that the Short
Method was written by a Protestant should be conclusive."

45. Every change in public opinion which this period
witnessed, confirmed the principles of religious   Progress of
toleration that had taken root in the earlier   tolerant
part of the century; the progress of a larger   principles.
and more catholic theology, the weakening of bigotry in
the minds of laymen, and the consequent disregard of
ecclesiastical clamour, not only in England and Holland,
but to a considerable extent in France ; we might even
add, the violent proceedings of the last government in
the revocation of the Edict of Nantes and the cruelties
which attended it.   Louis XIV., at a time when mankind were beginning to renounce the very theory of
persecution, renewed the ancient enormities of its practice, and thus unconsciously gave the aid of moral sympathy and indignation to the adverse argument.   The

---

[a] The Biographie Universelle, art.
Leslie, says, Cet ouvrage, qui passe pour
ce qu'il a fait de mieux, lui a été con-
testé.   Le Docteur Gleigh [sic] a fait de
grands efforts pour prouver qu'il ap-
partenait à Leslie, quoiqu'il fût publié
parmi les ouvrages de l'Abbé de Saint
Real, mort en 1692.   It is melancholy
to see this petty spirit of cavil against
an English writer in so respectable a
work as the Biographie Universelle.   No
grands efforts could be required from
Dr. Gleig or any one else to prove that
a book was written by Leslie, which
bore his name, which was addressed to
an English peer, and had gone through
many editions, when there is literally
no claimant on the other side; for a
posthumous edition, forty years after
the supposed author's death, without
attestation, is no literary evidence at all,
even where the book is published for the
first time, much less where it has a known
status as the production of a certain
author.   This is so manifest to any one
who has the slightest tincture of critical
judgment, that we need not urge the
palpable improbability of ascribing to
Saint Real, a Romish ecclesiastic, an
argument which turns peculiarly on the
distinction between the Scriptural miracles and those alleged upon inferior evidence.   I have lost, or never made, the
reference to Prosper Marchand; but the
passage will be found in his Dictionnaire
Historique, which contains a full article
on Saint Real.

Protestant refugees of France, scattered among their brethren, brought home to all minds the great question of free conscience ; not with the stupid and impudent limitation which even Protestants had sometimes employed, that truth indeed might not be restrained, but that error might ; a broader foundation was laid by the great advocates of toleration in this period, Bayle, Limborch, and Locke, as it had formerly been by Taylor and Episcopius.[o]

46. Bayle, in 1686, while yet the smart of his banishment was keenly felt, published his Philosophical Commentary on the text in Scripture, " Compel them to come in ;" a text which some of the advocates of persecution were accustomed to produce. He gives in the first part nine reasons against this literal meaning, among which none are philological. In the second part he replies to various objections. This work of Bayle does not seem to me as subtle and logical as he was wont to be, notwithstanding the formal syllogisms with which he commences each of his chapters. His argument against compulsory conversions, which the absurd interpretation of the text by his adversaries required, is indeed irresistible ; but this is far from sufficiently establishing the right of toleration itself. It appears not very difficult for a skilful sophist, and none was more so than Bayle himself, to have met some of his reasoning with a specious reply. The sceptical argument of Taylor, that we can rarely be sure of knowing the truth ourselves, and consequently of condemning in others what is error, he touches but slightly ; nor does he dwell on the political advantages which experience has shown a full toleration to possess. In the third part of the Philosophical Commentary, he refutes the apology of Augustin for persecution ; and a few years afterwards he published a supplement answering a book of Jurieu, which had appeared in the mean time.

Bayle's Philosophical Commentary.

[o] The Dutch clergy, and a French minister in Holland, Jurieu. of great polemical fame in his day, though now chiefly known by means of his adversaries, Bayle and Le Clerc, strenuously resisted both the theory of general toleration, and the moderate or liberal principles in religion which were connected with it. Le Clerc passed his life in fighting this battle, and many articles in the Bibliothèque Universelle relate to it.

47. Locke published anonymously his Letter on Toleration in 1689. The season was propitious ; a   Locke's
legal tolerance of public worship had first been   Letter on
granted to the dissenters after the Revolution,   Toleration.
limited indeed to such as held most of the doctrines of
the church, but preparing the nation for a more extensive
application of its spirit.   In the Liberty of Prophesying,
Taylor had chiefly in view to deduce the justice of
tolerating a diversity in religion, from the difficulty of
knowing the truth. He is not very consistent as to the
political question, and limits too narrowly the province
of tolerable opinions. Locke goes more expressly to the
right of the civil magistrate, not omitting, but dwelling
less forcibly on the chief arguments of his predecessor.
His own theory of government came to his aid.   The
clergy in general, and perhaps Taylor himself, had derived the magistrate's jurisdiction from paternal power.
And as they apparently assumed this power to extend
over adult children, it was natural to give those who
succeeded to it in political communities a large sway
over the moral and religious behaviour of subjects.
Locke, adopting the opposite theory of compact, defines
the commonwealth to be a society of men constituted
only for the procuring, preserving, and advancing their
own civil interests. He denies altogether that the care
of souls belongs to the civil magistrate, as it has never
been committed to him. " All the power of civil government relates only to men's civil interests, is confined to
the things of this world, and hath nothing to do with the
world to come." [p]

48. The admission of this principle would apparently
decide the controversy, so far as it rests on religious
grounds. But Locke has recourse to several other arguments independent of it. He proves, with no great

[p] [This principle, that the civil magistrate is not concerned with religion
as true, but only as useful, was strenuously maintained by Warburton, in his
Alliance of Church and State. It is
supported on Scriptural grounds by
Hoadly, in his famous sermon which
produced the Bangorian controversy, and
by Archbishop Whately, in a sermon on
the same text as Hoadly's, " My kingdom
is not of this world ;" but with more

closeness, though not less decision and
courage. I cannot, nevertheless, admit
the principle as a conclusion from their
premises, though very desirous to preserve it on other grounds. The late
respected Dr. Arnold was exceedingly
embarrassed by denying its truth, while
he was strenuous for toleration in the
amplest measure ; which leaves his writings on the subject unsatisfactory, and
weak against an adversary.—1847.]

difficulty, that the civil power cannot justly, or consistently with any true principle of religion, compel men to profess what they do not believe. This, however, is what very few would, at present, be inclined to maintain. The real question was as to the publicity of opinions deemed heterodox, and especially in social worship; and this is what those who held the magistrate to possess an authority patriarchal, universal, and arbitrary, and who were also rigidly tenacious of the necessity of an orthodox faith, as well as perfectly convinced that it was no other than their own, would hardly be persuaded to admit by any arguments that Locke has alleged. But the tendency of public opinion had begun to manifest itself against all these tenets of the high-church party, so that, in the eighteenth century, the principles of general tolerance became too popular to be disputed with any chance of attention. Locke was engaged in a controversy through his first Letter on Toleration, which produced a second and a third; but it does not appear to me that these, though longer than the first, have considerably modified its leading positions.[q] It is to be observed that he pleads for the universal toleration of all modes of worship not immoral in their nature, or involving doctrines inimical to good government; placing in the latter category some tenets of the church of Rome.

49. It is confessed by Goujet that, even in the middle of the seventeenth century, France could boast very little of pulpit eloquence. Frequent quotations from heathen writers, and from the schoolmen, with little solid morality and less good reasoning, make up the sermons of that age.[r] But the revolution in this style, as in all others, though perhaps gradual, was complete in the reign of Louis XIV. A slight sprinkling of passages from the fathers, and still more frequently from the Scriptures, but always short, and seeming to rise out of the preacher's heart, rather than to be sought

French sermons.

---

[q] Warburton has fancied that Locke's real sentiments are only discoverable in his first Letter on Toleration, and that in the two latter he "combats his intolerant adversary quite through the controversy with his own principles, well foreseeing that at such a time of prejudice arguments built on received opinions would have greatest weight, and make quickest impression on the body of the people whom it was his business to gain." Biogr. Britannica, art. Locke.

[r] Bibliothèque Française, vol. ii. p. 283.

for in his memory, replaced that intolerable parade of a theological commonplace book, which had been as customary in France as in England. The style was to be the perfection of French eloquence, the reasoning persuasive rather than dogmatic, the arrangement more methodical and distributive than at present, but without the excess we find in our old preachers. This is the general character of French sermons; but those who most adorned the pulpit had of course their individual distinctions. Without delaying to mention those who are now not greatly remembered, such as La Rue, Hubert, Mascaron, we must confine ourselves to three of high reputation, Bourdaloue, Bossuet, and Fléchier.

50. Bourdaloue, a Jesuit, but as little of a Jesuit in the worst acceptation of the word as the order Bourda-has produced, is remarkably simple, earnest, loue practical; he convinces rather than commands, and by convincing he persuades; for his discourses tend always to some duty, to something that is to be done or avoided. His sentences are short, interrogative, full of plain and solid reasoning, unambitious in expression, and wholly without that care in the choice of words and cadences which we detect in Bossuet and Fléchier. No one would call Bourdaloue a rhetorician, and though he continually introduces the fathers, he has not caught their vices of language.[*]

51. Bourdaloue is almost in the same relation to Bossuet as Patru to Le Maistre, though the two compared orators of the pulpit are far above those of the with Bos-bar. As the one is short, condensed, plain, suet. reasoning, and though never feeble, not often what is generally called eloquent, so the other is animated, figurative, rather diffuse and prodigal of ornament, addressing the imagination more than the judgment,

---

[*] The public did justice to Bourdaloue, as they generally do to a solid and impressive style of preaching. "Je crois," says Goujet, p. 300, "que tout le monde convient qu'aucun autre ne lui est supérieur. C'est le grand maître pour l'éloquence de la chaire; c'est le prince des prédicateurs. Le public n'a jamais été partagé sur son sujet; la ville et la cour l'ont également estimé et admiré. C'est qu'il avoit réuni en sa personne tous les grands caractères de la bonne éloquence; la simplicité du discours Chrétien avec la majesté et la grandeur, le sublime avec l'intelligible et le populaire, la force avec la douceur, la véhémence avec l'onction, la liberté avec la justesse, et la plus vive ardeur avec la plus pure lumière."

E 2

rich and copious in cadence, elevating the hearer to the pitch of his own sublimity. Bossuet is sometimes too declamatory; and Bourdaloue perhaps sometimes borders on dryness. Much in the sermons of the former is true poetry; but he has less of satisfactory and persuasive reasoning than the latter. His tone is also, as in all his writings, too domineering and dogmatical for those who demand something beyond the speaker's authority when they listen.

52. The sermons however of Bossuet, taken generally, are not reckoned in the highest class of his numerous writings; perhaps scarcely justice has been done to them. His genius, on the other hand, by universal confession, never shone higher than in the six which bear the name of Oraisons Funèbres. They belong in substance so much more naturally to the province of eloquence than of theology, that I should have reserved them for another place if the separation would not have seemed rather unexpected to the reader. Few works of genius perhaps in the French language are better known, or have been more prodigally extolled. In that style of eloquence which the ancients called demonstrative, or rather descriptive (ἐπιδεικτικὸς), the style of panegyric or commemoration, they are doubtless superior to those justly celebrated productions of Thucydides and Plato that have descended to us from Greece; nor has Bossuet been equalled by any later writer. Those on the Queen of England, on her daughter the Duchess of Orleans, and on the Prince of Condé, outshine the rest; and if a difference is to be made among these, we might perhaps, after some hesitation, confer the palm on the first. The range of topics is so various, the thoughts so just, the images so noble and poetical, the whole is in such perfect keeping, the tone of awful contemplation is so uniform, that if it has not any passages of such extraordinary beauty as occur in the other two, its general effect on the mind is more irresistible.[t]

Funeral discourses of Bossuet.

---

[t] An English preacher of conspicuous renown for eloquence was called upon, within no great length of time, to emulate the funeral discourse of Bossuet on the sudden death of Henrietta of Orleans. He had before him a subject incomparably more deep in interest, more fertile in great and touching associations—he had to describe, not the false sorrow of courtiers, not the shriek of sudden surprise that echoed by night in the halls of Versailles, not the apocryphal

53. In this style, much more of ornament, more of what speaks in the spirit, and even the very phrase, of poetry, to the imagination and the heart, is permitted by a rigorous criticism, than in forensic or in deliberative eloquence. The beauties that rise before the author's vision are not renounced ; the brilliant colours of his fancy are not subdued ; the periods assume a more rhythmical cadence, and emulate, like metre itself, the voluptuous harmony of musical intervals ; the whole composition is more evidently formed to delight ; but it will delight to little purpose, or even cease, in any strong sense of the word, to do so at all, unless it is ennobled by moral wisdom. In this Bossuet was pre-eminent ; his thoughts are never subtle or far-fetched ; they have a sort of breadth, a generality of application, which is peculiarly required in those who address a mixed assembly, and which many that aim at what is profound and original are apt to miss. It may be confessed, that these funeral discourses are not exempt from some defects, frequently inherent in panegyrical eloquence ; they are sometimes too rhetorical, and do not appear to show so little effort as some have fancied ; the amplifications are sometimes too unmeasured, the language sometimes borders too nearly on that of the stage ; above all, there is a tone of adulation not quite pleasing to a calm posterity.

54. Fléchier (the third name of the seventeenth century, for Massillon belongs only to the next), Fléchier. like Bossuet, has been more celebrated for his funeral sermons than for any others ; but in this line it is unfortunate for him to enter into unavoidable competition with one whom he cannot rival. The French critics extol Fléchier for the arrangement and harmony of his periods ; yet even in this, according to La Harpe, he is not essentially superior to Bossuet ; and to an English ear, accustomed to the long swell of our own writers and of the Ciceronian school in Latin, he will

penitence of one so tainted by the world's intercourse, but the manly grief of an entire nation in the withering of those visions of hope which wait upon the untried youth of royalty, in its sympathy with grandeur annihilated, with beauty and innocence precipitated into the tomb. Nor did he sink beneath his subject, except as compared with Bossuet. The sermon to which my allusion will be understood is esteemed by many the finest effort of this preacher ; but if read together with that of its prototype, it will be laid aside as almost feeble and unimpressive.

probably not give so much gratification. He does not want a moral dignity, or a certain elevation of thought, without which the funeral panegyric must be contemptible; but he has not the majestic tone of Bossuet; he does not, like him, raise the heroes and princes of the earth in order to abase them by paintings of mortality and weakness, or recall the hearer in every passage to something more awful than human power, and more magnificent than human grandeur. This religious solemnity, so characteristic in Bossuet, is hardly felt in the less emphatic sentences of Fléchier. Even where his exordium is almost worthy of comparison, as in the funeral discourse on Turenne, we find him degenerate into a trivial eulogy, and he flatters both more profusely and with less skill. His style is graceful, but not without affectation and false taste.[u] La Harpe has compared him to Isocrates among the orators of Greece, the place of Demosthenes being of course reserved for Bossuet.[x]

[u] [La Harpe justly ridicules an expression of Fléchier, in his funeral sermon on Madame de Montausier: Un ancien disait autrefois que les hommes étaient nés pour l'action et pour la conduite du monde, et que les *dames* n'étaient nées que pour le repos et pour la retraite.—1842.]

[x] The native critics ascribe a reform in the style of preaching to Paolo Segneri, whom Corniani does not hesitate to call, with the sanction, he says, of posterity, the father of Italian eloquence. It is to be remembered that in no country has the pulpit been so much degraded by empty declamation, and even by a stupid buffoonery. "The language of Segneri," the same writer observes, "is always full of dignity and harmony. He inlaid it with splendid and elegant expressions, and has thus obtained a place among the authors to whom authority has been given by the Della Crusca dictionary. His periods are flowing, natural, and intelligible, without the affectation of obsolete Tuscanisms, which pass for graces of the language with many." Tiraboschi, with much commendation of Segneri, admits that we find in him some vestiges of the false taste he endeavoured to reform. The very little that I have seen of the sermons of Segneri gives no impression of any merit that can be reckoned more than relative to the miserable tone of his predecessors. The following specimen is from one of his most admired sermons:—E Cristo non potrà ottenere da voi che gli rimettiate un torto, un affronto, un aggravio, una parolina? Che vorreste da Christo? Vorreste ch' egli vi si gettasse supplichevole a piedi a chiedervi questa grazia? Io son quasi per dire ch' egli il farebbe; perchè se non dubiti di prostrarsi a piedi di un traditore, qual' era Giuda, di lavarglieli, di asciugarglieli, di baciarglieli, non si vergognerebbe, cred' io, di farsi vedere ginocchioni a piè vostri. Ma vi fa bisogno di tanto per muovervi a compiacerlo? Ah Cavalieri, Cavalieri, io non vorrei questa volta farvi arrossire. Nel resto io so di certo, che se altrettanto fosse a voi domandato da quella donna che chiamate la vostra dama, da quella, di cui forsennati idolatrate il volto, indovinate le voglie, ambite le grazie, non vi farete pregar tanto a concederglielo. E poi vi fate pregar tanto da un Dio per voi crocefisso? O confusione! O vitupero! O vergogna!—Raccolta di Prose

55. The style of preaching in England was less orna- English
mental, and spoke less to the imagination and sermons—
affections, than these celebrated writers of the Barrow.
Gallican church; but in some of our chief divines
it had its own excellences.   The sermons of Barrow display a strength of mind, a comprehensiveness and fertility, which have rarely been equalled.   No better proof
can be given than his eight sermons on the government
of the tongue; copious and exhaustive without tautology
or superfluous declamation, they are, in moral preaching,
what the best parts of Aristotle are in ethical philosophy,
with more of development and a more extensive observation.   It would be said of these sermons, and indeed,
with a few exceptions, of all those of Barrow, that they
are not what is now called evangelical; they indicate
the ascendency of an Arminian party, dwelling far more
than is usual in the pulpit on moral and rational, or even
temporal inducements, and sometimes hardly abstaining
from what would give a little offence in later times.[y] His
quotations also from ancient philosophers, though not so
numerous as in Taylor, are equally uncongenial to our
ears.   In his style, notwithstanding its richness and
occasional vivacity, we may censure a redundancy and
excess of apposition: it is not sufficient to avoid strict
tautology; no second phrase (to lay down a general
rule not without exception) should be so like the first,
that the reader would naturally have understood it to
be comprised therein.   Barrow's language is more an-
tiquated and formal than that of his age; and he
abounds too much in uncommon words of Latin derivation, frequently such as appear to have no authority but
his own.

56. South's sermons begin, in order of date, before the

Italiane (in Classici Italiani), vol. ii. p.
345.
   This is certainly not the manner of
Bossuet, and more like that of a third-
rate Methodist among us.
   [y] Thus, in his sermon against evil
speaking (xvi.), Barrow treats it as fit
"for rustic boors or men of coarsest
education and employment, who having
their minds debased by being conversant
in meanest affairs, do vent their sorry

passions, and bicker about their petty
concernments in such strains, who also,
not being capable of a fair reputation, or
sensible of disgrace to themselves, do
little value the credit of others, or care
for aspersing it. But such language is
unworthy of those persons, and cannot
easily be drawn from them, who are
wont to exercise their thoughts about
nobler matters," &c.   No one would
venture this now from the pulpit.

Restoration, and come down to nearly the end of the
South. century. They were much celebrated at the
time, and retain a portion of their renown. This
is by no means surprising. South had great qualifica-
tions for that popularity which attends the pulpit, and
his manner was at that time original. Not diffuse, not
learned, not formal in argument like Barrow, with a
more natural structure of sentences, a more pointed,
though by no means a more fair and satisfactory turn of
reasoning, with a style clear and English, free from all
pedantry, but abounding with those colloquial novelties
of idiom, which, though now become vulgar and offen-
sive, the age of Charles II. affected, sparing no personal
or temporary sarcasm, but, if he seems for a moment to
tread on the verge of buffoonery, recovering himself
by some stroke of vigorous sense and language; such
was the witty Dr. South, whom the courtiers delighted
to hear. His sermons want all that is called unction,
and sometimes even earnestness, which is owing, in a
great measure, to a perpetual tone of gibing at rebels
and fanatics; but there is a masculine spirit about them,
which, combined with their peculiar characteristics,
would naturally fill the churches where he might be
heard. South appears to bend towards the Arminian
theology, without adopting so much of it as some of his
contemporaries.

57. The sermons of Tillotson were for half a century
Tillotson. more read than any in our language. They
are now bought almost as waste paper, and
hardly read at all. Such is the fickleness of religious
taste, as abundantly numerous instances would prove.
Tillotson is reckoned verbose and languid. He has not
the former defect in nearly so great a degree as some of
his eminent predecessors; but there is certainly little
vigour or vivacity in his style. Full of the Romish
controversy, he is perpetually recurring to that " world's
debate;" and he is not much less hostile to all the Calvinistic tenets. What is most remarkable in the theology of Tillotson is his strong assertion, in almost all
his sermons, of the principles of natural religion and
morality, not only as the basis of all revelation, without
a dependence on which it cannot be believed, but as

nearly coincident with Christianity in their extent; a length to which few at present would be ready to follow him. Tillotson is always of a tolerant and catholic spirit, enforcing right actions rather than orthodox opinions, and obnoxious, for that and other reasons, to all the bigots of his own age.

58. It has become necessary to draw towards a conclusion of this chapter; the materials are far Expository theology. from being exhausted. In expository, or, as some call it, exegetical theology, the English divines had already taken a conspicuous station. Andrès, no partial estimator of Protestant writers, extols them with marked praise.[z] Those who belonged to the earlier part of the century form a portion of a vast collection, the Critici Sacri, published by one Bee, a bookseller, in 1660. This was in nine folio volumes; and in 1669, Matthew Pool, a non-conforming minister, produced his Synopsis Criticorum in five volumes, being in great measure an abridgment and digest of the former. Bee complained of the infraction of his copyright, or rather his equitable interest; but such a dispute hardly pertains to our history.[a] The work of Pool was evidently a more original labour than the former. Hammond, Patrick, and other commentators, do honour to the Anglican church in the latter part of the century.

59. Pearson's Exposition of the Apostles' Creed, published in 1659, is a standard book in English Pearson on the Creed. divinity. It expands beyond the literal purport of the creed itself to most articles of orthodox belief, and is a valuable summary of arguments and authorities on that side. The closeness of Pearson, and his judicious selection of proofs, distinguish him from many, especially the earlier, theologians. Some might surmise that his undeviating adherence to what he calls the Church is hardly consistent with independence of thinking; but, considered as an advocate, he is one of much judgment and skill. Such men as Pearson and Stillingfleet would have been conspicuous at the bar, which we could not quite affirm of Jeremy Taylor.

[z] I soli Inglesi, che ampio spazio non dovrebbono occupare in questo capo dell' esegetica sacra, se l' istituto della nostr' opera ci permettesse tener dietro a tutti i più degni della nostra stima? Vol. xix. p. 253.   [a] Chalmers.

60. Simon, a regular priest of the congregation called
Simon's   The Oratory, which has been rich in eminent
Critical   men, owes much of his fame to his Critical
Histories. History of the Old Testament.   This work,
bold in many of its positions, as it then seemed to both
the Catholic and Protestant orthodox, after being nearly
strangled by Bossuet in France, appeared at Rotterdam
in 1685.   Bossuet attacked it with extreme vivacity,
but with a real inferiority to Simon both in learning
and candour.[b]   Le Clerc on his side carped more at the
Critical History than it seems to deserve.   Many paradoxes, as they then were called, in this famous work,
are now received as truth, or at least pass without
reproof.   Simon may possibly be too prone to novelty,
but a love of truth as well as great acuteness are visible
throughout.   His Critical History of the New Testament was published in 1689, and one or two more
works of a similar description before the close of the
century.

61. I have on a former occasion adverted, in a corresponding chapter, to publications on witchcraft and
similar superstitions.   Several might be mentioned at
this time; the belief in such tales was assailed by a
prevalent scepticism which called out their advocates.
Of these the most unworthy to have exhibited their
great talents in such a cause were our own philosophers
Henry More and Joseph Glanvil.   The Sadducismus
Triumphatus, or Treatise on Apparitions, by the latter,
has passed through several editions, while his Scepsis
Scientifica has hardly been seen, perhaps, by six living
persons.   A Dutch minister, by name Bekker, raised a
great clamour against himself by a downright denial of
all power to the devil, and consequently to his supposed
instruments, the ancient beldams of Holland and other
countries.   His Monde Enchanté, originally published
in Dutch, is in four volumes, written in a systematic manner, and with tedious prolixity.   There was no ground
for imputing infidelity to the author, except the usual
ground of calumniating every one who quits the beaten

b Défense de la Tradition des Saints   Imprimée à Trevoux, Id. vol. iv. p. 313.
Pères. Œuvres de Bossuet, vol. v., and   Bausset, Vie de Bossuet, iv. 276.
Instructions sur la Version du N. T.,

path in theology; but his explanations of Scripture in
the case of the demoniacs and the like are, as usual
with those who have taken the same line, rather forced.
The fourth volume, which contains several curious
stories of imagined possession, and some which resemble
what is now called magnetism, is the only part of Bekker's once celebrated book that can be read with any
pleasure. Bekker was a Cartesian, and his theory was
built too much on Cartesian assumptions of the impossibility of spirit *acting* on body.

CHAPTER III.

HISTORY OF SPECULATIVE PHILOSOPHY FROM 1650 TO 1700.

Aristotelians — Logicians — Cudworth — Sketch of the Philosophy of Gassendi — Cartesianism — Port-Royal Logic — Analysis of the Search for Truth of Malebranche, and of the Ethics of Spinosa — Glanvil — Locke's Essay on the Human Understanding.

1. THE Aristotelian and scholastic metaphysics, though shaken on every side, and especially by the rapid progress of the Cartesian theories, had not lost their hold over the theologians of the Roman church, or even the Protestant universities, at the beginning of this period, and hardly at its close. Brucker enumerates several writers of that class in Germany ;[a] and we find, as late as 1693, a formal injunction by the Sorbonne, that none who taught philosophy in the colleges under its jurisdiction should introduce any novelties, or swerve from the Aristotelian doctrine.[b] The Jesuits, rather unfortunately for their credit, distinguished themselves as strenuous advocates of the old philosophy, and thus lost the advantage they had obtained in philology as enemies of barbarous prejudice, and encouragers of a progressive spirit in their disciples. Rapin, one of their most accomplished men, after speaking with little respect of the Novum Organum, extols the disputations of the schools as the best method in

Aristotelian metaphysics. (marginal note)

---

[a] Vol. iv. See his long and laborious chapter on the Aristotelian philosophers of the sixteenth and seventeenth centuries ; no one else seems to have done more than copy Brucker.

[b] Cum relatum esset ad Societatem (Sorbonicam) nonnullos philosophiæ professores, ex iis etiam aliquando qui ad Societatem anhelant, novas quasdam doctrinas in philosophicis sectari, minusque Aristotelicæ doctrinæ studere, quam hactenus usurpatum fuerit in Acâdemiâ Parisiensi, censuit Societas injungendum esse illis, imo et iis qui docent philosophiam in collegiis suo regimini creditis, ne deinceps novitatibus studeant, aut ab Aristotelica doctrina deflectant. 31 Dec. 1693. Argentré, Collectio Judiciorum, ii. 150.

the education of young men, who, as he fancies, have too little experience to delight in physical science.[c]

2. It is a difficult and dangerous choice, in a new state of public opinion (and we have to make it at present), between that which may itself pass away, and that which must efface what has gone before. Those who clung to the ancient philosophy believed that Bacon and Descartes were the idols of a transitory fashion, and that the wisdom of long ages would regain its ascendency. They were deceived, and their own reputation has been swept off with the systems to which they adhered. Thomas White, an English Catholic priest, whose Latin appellation is Albius, endeavoured to maintain the Aristotelian metaphysics and the scholastic terminology in several works, and especially in an attack upon Glanvil's Vanity of Dogmatising. This book, entitled Sciri, I know only through Glanvil's reply in his second edition, by which White appears to be a mere Aristotelian. He was a friend of Sir Kenelm Digby, who was himself, though a man of considerable talents, incapable of disentangling his mind from the Peripatetic hypotheses. The power of words indeed is so great, the illusions of what is called realism, or of believing that general terms have an objective exterior being, are so natural, and especially so bound up both with our notions of essential, especially theological, truth, and with our popular language, that no man could in that age be much censured for not casting off his fetters, even when he had heard the call to liberty from some modern voices. We find that even after two centuries of a better method, many are always ready to fall back into a verbal process of theorising.

3. Logic was taught in the Aristotelian method, or rather in one which, with some change for the worse, had been gradually founded upon it.

Their decline. Thomas White.

Logic.

---

[c] Réflexions sur la Poëtique, p. 368. He admits, however, that to introduce more experiment and observation would be an improvement. Du reste il y a apparence que les loix, qui ne souffrent point d'innovation dans l'usage des choses universellement établies, n'autoriseront point d'autre méthode que celle qui est aujourd'hui en usage dans les universités; afin de ne pas donner trop de licence à la passion qu'on a naturellement pour les nouvelles opinions, dont le cours est d'une dangereuse conséquence dans un état bien réglé; vu particulièrement que la philosophie est un des organes dont se sert la religion pour s'expliquer dans ses décisions.

Burgersdicius, in this and in other sciences, seems to have been in repute; Smiglecius also is mentioned with praise.[d] These lived both in the former part of the century. But they were superseded, at least in England, by Wallis, whose Institutio Logicæ ad Communes Usus Accommodata was published in 1687. He claims as an improvement upon the received system, the classifying singular propositions among universals.[e] Ramus had made a third class of them, and in this he seems to have been generally followed. Aristotle, though it does not appear that he is explicit on the subject, does not rank them as particular. That Wallis is right will not be doubted by any one at present; but his originality we must not assert. The same had been perceived by the authors of the Port-Royal Logic; a work to which he has made no allusion.[f] Wallis claims also as his own the method of reducing hypothetical to categorical syllogisms, and proves it elaborately in a separate dissertation. A smaller treatise, still much used at Oxford, by Aldrich, Compendium Artis Logicæ, 1691, is clear and concise, but sems to contain nothing very important; and he alludes to the Art de Penser in a tone of insolence, which must rouse indignation in those who are acquainted with that excellent work. Aldrich's censures are, in many instances, mere cavil and misrepresentation; I do not know that they are right in any.[g]

---

[d] La Logique de Smiglecius, says Rapin, est un bel ouvrage. The same writer proceeds to observe that the Spaniards of the preceding century had corrupted logic by their subtilties. En se jetant dans des spéculations creuses qui n'avoient rien de réel, leurs philosophes trouvèrent l'art d'avoir de la raison malgré le bon sens, et de donner de la couleur, et même je ne sçais quoi de spécieuse, à ce qui étoit de plus déraisonnable. I'. 382. But this must have been rather the fault of their metaphysics than of what is strictly called logic.

[e] Atque hoc signanter notatum velim, quia novus forte hic videar, et præter aliorum loquendi formulam hæc dicere. Nam plerique logici propositionem quam vocant singularem, hoc est, de subjecto individuo sive singulari, pro particulari habent, non universali. Sed perperam hoc faciunt, et præter mentem Aristotelis, (qui, quantum memini, nunquam ejusmodi singularem, τὴν κατα μερος appellat aut pro tali habet), et præter rei naturam: Non enim hic agitur de particularitate subjecti (quod ατομον vocat Aristotelis, non κατα μερος) sed de partialitate prædicationis. . . . . 'Neque ego interim novator censendus sum qui hæc dixerim, sed illi potius novatores qui ab Aristotelica doctrina recesserint; eoque multa introduxerint incommoda de quibus suo loco dicetur. P. 125. He has afterwards a separate dissertation or thesis to prove this more at length. It seems that the Ramists held a third class of propositions, neither universal nor particular, to which they gave the name of propria, equivalent to singular.

[f] Art de Penser, part ii. chap. iii.

[g] One of Aldrich's charges against the author of the Art de Penser is, that he brings forward as a great discovery

Of the Art de Penser itself we shall have something to say in the course of this chapter.

4. Before we proceed to those whose philosophy may be reckoned original, or at least modern, a very few deserve mention who have endeavoured to maintain or restore that of antiquity. Stanley's History of Philosophy, in 1655, is in great measure confined to biography, and comprehends no name later than Carneades. Most is derived from Diogenes Laertius; but an analysis of the Platonic philosophy is given from Alcinous, and the author has compiled one of the Peripatetic system from Aristotle himself. The doctrine of the Stoics is also elaborately deduced from various sources. Stanley, on the whole, brought a good deal from an almost untrodden field; but he is merely an historian, and never a critic of philosophy.[h]

Stanley's History of Philosophy.

5. Gale's Court of the Gentiles, which appeared partly in 1669 and partly in later years, is incomparably a more learned work than that of Stanley. Its aim is to prove that all heathen philosophy, whether barbaric or Greek, was borrowed from the Scriptures, or at least from the Jews. The first part is entitled Of Philology, which traces the same leading principle by means of language; the second, Of Philosophy; the third treats of the Vanity of Philosophy, and the fourth of Reformed Philosophy, " wherein Plato's moral and metaphysic or prime philosophy is reduced to an usual form and method." Gale has been reckoned among Platonic philosophers, and indeed he professes to find a great resemblance between the philosophy of Plato and his own. But he is a determined Calvinist in all respects, and scruples not to say, " Whatever God wills is just, because he wills it;" and again, " God willeth nothing without himself because it is just, but it is therefore just because he willeth it. The reasons of

Gale's Court of Gentiles.

the equality of the angles of a chiliagon to 1996 right angles; and another is, that he gives as an example of a regular syllogism one that has obviously five terms; thus expecting the Oxford students for whom he wrote to believe that Antony Arnauld neither knew the first book of Euclid nor the mere rudiments of common logic.

h [In former editions, through an oversight altogether inexplicable by me at present, I had said that Stanley does not mention Epicurus, who occupies a considerable space in the History of Philosophy. I have searched my notes in vain for the source of this mistake, which was courteously pointed out to me; but I think it fitter to make this public acknowledgment than silently to withdraw the sentence.—1847.]

good and evil extrinsic to the divine essence are all
dependent on the divine will, either decernent or legislative."[1]   It is not likely that Plato would have acknowledged such a disciple.

6. A much more eminent and enlightened man than
Cudworth's Gale, Ralph Cudworth, by his Intellectual Sys-
Intellectual tem of the Universe, published in 1678, but
System.   written several years before, placed himself in
a middle point between the declining and rising schools
of philosophy; more independent of authority, and more
close, perhaps, in argument than the former, but more
prodigal of learning, more technical in language, and
less conversant with analytical and inductive processes
of reasoning than the latter.   Upon the whole, however,
he belongs to the school of antiquity, and probably his
wish was to be classed with it.   Cudworth was one of
those whom Hobbes had roused by the atheistic and
immoral theories of the Leviathan; nor did any antagonist perhaps of that philosopher bring a more vigorous
understanding to the combat.   This understanding was
not so much obstructed in its own exercise by a vast
erudition, as it is sometimes concealed by it from the
reader.   Cudworth has passed more for a recorder of
ancient philosophy, than for one who might stand in a
respectable class among philosophers; and his work,
though long, being unfinished, as well as full of digression, its object has not been fully apprehended.

7. This object was to establish the liberty of human
Its object.   actions against the fatalists.   Of these he lays
it down that there are three kinds: the first
atheistic; the second admitting a Deity, but one acting
necessarily and without moral perfections; the third
granting the moral attributes of God, but asserting all
human actions to be governed by necessary laws which
he has ordained.   The first book of the Intellectual System, which alone is extant, relates wholly to the proofs
of the existence of a Deity against the atheistic fatalists,
his moral nature being rarely or never touched; so that
the greater and more interesting part of the work, for
the sake of which the author projected it, is wholly wanting, unless we take for fragments of it some writings of
the author preserved in the British Museum.

[1] Part iv. p. 339.

8. The first chapter contains an account of the ancient corpuscular philosophy, which, till corrupted Sketch by Leucippus and Democritus, Cudworth takes of it. to have been not only theistic, but more consonant to theistic principles than any other. These two, however, brought in a fatalism grounded on their own atomic theory. In the second chapter he states very fully and fairly all their arguments, or rather all that have ever been adduced on the atheistic side. In the third he expatiates on the hylozoic atheism, as he calls it, of Strato, which accounts the universe to be animated in all its parts, but without a single controlling intelligence, and adverts to another hypothesis, which gives a vegetable but not sentient life to the world.

9. This leads Cudworth to his own famous theory of a plastic nature, a device to account for the ope- His plastic rations of physical laws without the continued nature. agency of the Deity. Of this plastic energy he speaks in rather a confused and indefinite manner, giving it in one place a sort of sentient life, or what he calls "a drowsy unawakened cogitation," and always treating it as an entity or real being. This language of Cudworth, and indeed the whole hypothesis of a plastic nature, was unable to stand the searching eye of Bayle, who, in an article of his dictionary, pointed out its unphilosophical and dangerous assumptions. Le Clerc endeavoured to support Cudworth against Bayle, but with little success.[a] It has had, however, some partisans, though rather among physiologists than metaphysicians. Grew adopted it to explain vegetation ; and the plastic nature differs only, as I conceive, from what Hunter and Abernethy have called life in organised bodies by its more extensive agency ; for if we are to believe that there is a vital power, not a mere name for the sequence of phænomena, which marshals the molecules of animal and vegetable substance, we can see no reason why a similar energy should not determine other molecules to assume geometrical figures in crystallization. The error or paradox consists in assigning a real unity of existence, and a real power of causation, to that which is unintelligent.

10. The fourth chapter of the Intellectual System, of vast length, and occupying half the entire work, launches

[a] Bibliothèque Choisie, vol. v.

into a sea of old philosophy, in order to show the unity
of a supreme God to have been a general belief of antiquity. " In this fourth chapter,"
he says, " we were necessitated by the matter
itself to run out into philology and antiquity, as also
in the other parts of the book we do often give an
account of the doctrine of the ancients; which, however some over-severe philosophers may look upon
fastidiously or undervalue and depreciate, yet as we
conceived it often necessary, so possibly may the variety
thereof not be ungrateful to others, and this mixture of
philology throughout the whole sweeten and allay the
severity of philosophy to them; the main thing which
the book pretends to, in the mean time, being the philosophy of religion. But for our part we neither call
philology, nor yet philosophy, our mistress, but serve
ourselves of either as occasion requireth."[o]

11. The whole fourth chapter may be reckoned one
great episode, and as it contains a store of useful knowledge on ancient philosophy, it has not only been more
read than the remaining part of the Intellectual System,
but has been the cause, in more than one respect, that
the work has been erroneously judged. Thus Cudworth
has been reckoned, by very respectable authorities, in
the Platonic school of philosophers, and even in that of
the later Platonists; for which I perceive little other
reason than that he has gone diffusely into a supposed
resemblance between the Platonic and Christian Trinity.
Whether we agree with him in this or no, the subject is
insulated, and belongs only to the history of theological
opinion; in Cudworth's own philosophy he appears to
be an eclectic, not the vassal of Plato, Plotinus, or
Aristotle, though deeply versed in them all.[p]

12. In the fifth and last chapter of the first and only
book of the Intellectual System, Cudworth, reverting

[o] Preface, p. 37.
[p] [" Cudworth," says a late very learned
and strong-minded writer, "should be
read with the notes of Mosheim; unless,
indeed, one be so acquainted with the
philosophy and religion of the ancients,
and so accustomed to reasoning, and to
estimating the power and the ambiguity
of language, as to be able to correct, for
himself his deceptive representations.
He deserves the highest praise for integrity as a writer; his learning was
superabundant, and his intellect vigorous
enough to wield it to his purpose. But
he transfers his own conceptions to the
heathen philosophers and religionists,"
&c. Norton on Genuineness of Gospels,
vol. ii. p. 215.—1847.]

to the various atheistical arguments which he had stated in the second chapter, answers them at great length, and though not without much erudition, perhaps more than was requisite, yet depending chiefly on his own stores of reasoning. And inasmuch as even a second-rate philosopher ranks higher in literary precedence than the most learned reporter of other men's doctrine, it may be unfortunate for Cudworth's reputation that he consumed so much time in the preceding chapter upon mere learning, even though that should be reckoned more useful than his own reasonings. These, however, are frequently valuable, and as I have intimated above, he is partially tinctured by the philosophy of his own generation, while he endeavours to tread in the ancient paths. Yet he seems not aware of the place which Bacon, Descartes, and Gassendi were to hold; and not only names them sometimes with censure, hardly with praise, but most inexcusably throws out several intimations that they had designedly served the cause of atheism. The disposition of the two former to slight the argument from final causes, though it might justly be animadverted upon, could not warrant this most uncandid and untrue aspersion. But justice was even-handed; Cudworth himself did not escape the slander of bigots; it was idly said by Dryden, that he had put the arguments against a Deity so well, that some thought he had not answered them; and if Warburton may be believed, the remaining part of the Intellectual System was never published, on account of the world's malignity in judging of the first.[q] Probably it was never written.

13. Cudworth is too credulous and uncritical about ancient writings, defending all as genuine, even where his own age had been sceptical. His terminology is stiff and pedantic, as is the case with all our older metaphysicians, abounding in words which the English language has not recognised. He is full of the ancients, but rarely quotes the schoolmen. Hobbes is the adversary with whom he most grapples; the materialism, the resolving all ideas into sensation, the low morality of that writer, were obnoxious to the animadversion of so

His arguments against atheism.

---

[q] Warburton's preface to Divine Legation, vol. ii.

F 2

strenuous an advocate of a more elevated philosophy. In some respects Cudworth has, as I conceive, much the advantage; in others, he will generally be thought by our metaphysicians to want precision and logical reasoning; and upon the whole we must rank him, in philosophical acumen, far below Hobbes, Malebranche, and Locke, but also far above any mere Aristotelians or retailers of Scotus and Aquinas.[r]

14. Henry More, though by no means less eminent

More.

than Cudworth in his own age, ought not to be placed on the same level. More fell not only into the mystical notions of the later Platonists, but even of the Cabalistic writers. His metaphysical philosophy was borrowed in great measure from them; and though he was in correspondence with Descartes, and enchanted with the new views that opened upon him, yet we find that he was reckoned much less of a Cartesian afterwards, and even wrote against parts of the theory.[*] The most peculiar tenet of More was the extension of spirit; acknowledging and even striving for the soul's immateriality, he still could not conceive it to be unextended. Yet it seems evident that if we give extension as well as figure, which is implied in finite extension, to the single self-conscious monad, qualities as heterogeneous to thinking as material impenetrability itself, we shall find it in vain to deny the possibility at least of the latter. Some indeed might question whether what we call matter is any real being at all, except as extension under peculiar conditions. But this conjecture need not here be pressed.

15. Gassendi himself, by the extensiveness of his eru-

Gassendi.

dition, may be said to have united the two schools of speculative philosophy, the historical and the experimental, though the character of his mind determined him far more towards the latter. He belongs in point of time rather to the earlier period of the century; but his Syntagma Philosophicum having been

---

[r] [The inferiority of Cudworth to Hobbes is not at present very manifest to me.—1847.]

[*] Baillet, Vie de Descartes, liv. vii. It must be observed that More never wholly agreed with Descartes. Thus they differed about the omnipresence of the Deity; Descartes thought that he was partout à raison de sa puissance, et qu'à raison de son essence il n'a absolument aucune relation au lieu. More, who may be called a lover of extension, maintained a strictly local presence. Œuvres de Descartes, vol. x. p. 239.

published in 1658, we have deferred the review of it for this volume. This posthumous work, in two volumes folio, and nearly 1600 pages closely printed in double columns, is divided into three parts, the Logic, the Physics, and the Ethics ; the second occupying more than five sixths of the whole. The Logic is introduced by two procemial books ; one containing a history of the science from Zeno of Elea, the parent of systematic logic, to Bacon and Descartes ;[t] the other, still more His Logic. valuable, on the criteria of truth ; shortly criticising also, in a chapter of this book, the several schemes of logic which he had merely described in the former. After stating very prolixly, as is usual with him, the arguments of the sceptics against the evidence of the senses, and those of the dogmatics, as he calls them, who refer the sole criterion of truth to the understanding, he propounds a sort of middle course. It is necessary, he observes, before we can infer truth, that there should be some sensible sign, $\alpha\iota\sigma\theta\eta\tau\grave{o}\nu \ \sigma\eta\mu\epsilon\tilde{\iota}o\nu$; for, since all the knowledge we possess is derived from the sense, the mind must first have some sensible image, by which it may be led to a knowledge of what is latent and not perceived by sense. Hence we may distinguish in ourselves a double criterion ; one by which we perceive the sign, namely, the senses ; another, by which we understand through reasoning the latent thing, namely, the intellect or rational faculty.[u] This he illustrates by the pores of the skin, which we do not perceive, but infer their existence by observing the permeation of moisture.

---

[t] Prætereundum porro non est ob eam, quâ est, celebritatem Organum, sive logica Francisci Baconis Verulamii. He extols Bacon highly, but gives an analysis of the Novum Organum without much criticism. De Logicæ Origine, c. x.

Logica Verulamii, Gassendi says in another place, tota ac per se ad physicam, atque adeo ad veritatem notitiamve rerum germanam habendam contendit. Præcipuè autem in eo est, ut bene imaginemur, quatenus vult esse imprimis exuenda omnia præjudicia, ac novas deinde notiones ideasve ex novis debitèque factis experimentis inducendas. Logica

Cartesii rectè quidem Verulamii imitatione ab eo exorditur, quod ad bene imaginandum prava præjudicia exuenda, recta vero induenda vult, &c. P. 90.

[u] P. 81. If this passage be well attended to, it will show how the philosophy of Gassendi has been misunderstood by those who confound it with the merely sensual school of metaphysicians. No one has more clearly, or more at length, distinguished the $\alpha\iota\sigma\theta\eta\tau\grave{o}\nu \ \sigma\eta\mu\epsilon\tilde{\iota}o\nu$, the sensible associated sign, from the unimaginable objects of pure intellect, as we shall soon see.

16. In the first part of the treatise itself on Logic, to
His theory which these two books are introductory, Gas-
of ideas, sendi lays down again his favourite principle,
that every idea in the mind is ultimately derived from
the senses. But while what the senses transmit are
only singular ideas, the mind has the faculty of making
general ideas out of a number of these singular ones when
they resemble each other.[x] In this part of his Logic he
expresses himself clearly and unequivocally a conceptualist.

17. The Physics were expanded with a prodigality of
learning upon every province of nature. Gassendi is
full of quotation, and his systematic method manifests
the comprehensiveness of his researches. In the third
book of the second part of the third section of the
Physics, he treats of the immateriality, and, in the fourteenth, of the immortality of the soul, and maintains the
affirmative of both propositions. This may not be what
those who judge of Gassendi merely from his objections
to the Meditations of Descartes have supposed. But a
clearer insight into his metaphysical theory will be
obtained from the ninth book of the same part of the
Physics, entitled De Intellectu, on the Human Understanding.

18. In this book, after much display of erudition on
and of the the tenets of philosophers, he determines the
nature of soul to be an incorporeal substance, created by
the soul. God, and infused into the body, so that it resides in it as an informing and not merely a present
nature, forma informans, et non simpliciter assistens.[y]
He next distinguishes intellection or understanding
from imagination or perception; which is worthy of
particular notice, because in his controversy with Descartes he had thrown out doubts as to any distinction
between them. We have in ourselves a kind of faculty
which enables us, by means of reasoning, to understand
that which by no endeavours we can imagine or represent to the mind.[z] Of this the size of the sun, or innu-

[x] P. 93.
[y] P. 440.
[z] Itaque est in nobis intellectûs species, qua ratiocinando eo provebimur,
ut aliquid intelligamus, quod imaginari,
vel cujus habere obversantem imaginem,

quantumcunque animi vires contenderi-
mus, non possimus. . . . After instancing
the size of the sun, possunt consimilia
sexcenta afferri. . . . Verum quidem istud
sufficiat, ut constet quidpiam nos intelligere quod imaginari non liceat, et intel-

merable other examples might be given; the mind having no idea suggested by the imagination of the sun's magnitude, but knowing it by a peculiar operation of reason. And hence we infer that the intellectual soul is immaterial, because it understands that which no material image presents to it, as we infer also that the imaginative faculty is material, because it employs the images supplied by sense. It is true that the intellect makes use of these sensible images as steps towards its reasoning upon things which cannot be imagined; but the proof of its immateriality is given by this, that it passes beyond all material images, and attains a true knowledge of that whereof it has no image.

19. Buhle observes that in what Gassendi has said on the power of the mind to understand what it cannot conceive, there is a forgetfulness of his principle, that nothing is in the understanding which has not been in the sense. But, unless we impute repeated contradictions to this philosopher, he must have meant that axiom in a less extended sense than it has been taken by some who have since employed it. By that which is "in the understanding," he could only intend definite images derived from sense, which must be present before the mind can exercise any faculty, or proceed to reason up to unimaginable things. The fallacy of the sensualist school, English and French, has been to conclude that we can have no knowledge of that which is not "in the understanding;" an inference true in the popular sense of words, but false in the metaphysical.

20. There is, moreover, Gassendi proceeds, a class of reflex operations, whereby the mind understands itself and its own faculties, and is conscious that it is exercising such acts. And this faculty is superior to any that a material sub-

Distinguishes ideas of reflection.

lectum ita esse distinctum a phantasia, ut cum phantasia habeat materiales species, sub quibus res imaginatur, non habeat tamen intellectus, sub quibus res intelligat: neque enim ullam, v. g. habet illius magnitudinis quam in sole intelligit; sed tantum vi propria, seu ratiocinando, eam esse in sole magnitudinem comprehendit, ac pari modo cætera. Nempe ex hoc efficitur, ut rem sine specie materiali intelligens, esse immaterialis debeat; si-

cuti phantasia ex eo materialis arguitur, quod materiali specie utatur. Ac utitur quidem etiam intellectus speciebus phantasia perceptis, tanquam gradibus, ut ratiocinando assequatur ea, quæ deinceps sine speciebus phantasmatisve intelligit; sed hoc ipsum est quod illius immaterialitatem arguit, quod ultra omnem speciem materialem se provehat, quidpiamque cujus nullam habeat phantasma revera agnoscat. —

stance possesses; for no body can act reflexly on itself, but must move from one place to another.* Our observation therefore of our own imaginings must be by a power superior to imagination itself; for imagination is employed on the image, not on the perception of the image, since there is no image of the act of perception.

21. The intellect also not only forms universal ideas, but perceives the nature of universality. And this seems peculiar to mankind; for brutes do not show anything more than a power of association by resemblance. In our own conception of an universal, it may be urged, there is always some admixture of singularity, as of a particular form, magnitude, or colour; yet we are able, Gassendi thinks, to strip the image successively of all these particular adjuncts.[b] He seems therefore, as has been remarked above, to have held the conceptualist theory in the strictest manner, admitting the reality of universal ideas even as images present to the mind.

22. Intellection being the proper operation of the soul, it is needless to inquire whether it does this by its own nature, or by a peculiar faculty called understanding, nor should we trouble ourselves about the Aristotelian distinction of the active and passive intellect.[c] We have only to distinguish this intellection from mere conception derived from the phantasy, which is necessarily associated with it. We cannot conceive God in this life, except under some image thus supplied; and it is the same with all other incorporeal things. Nor do we comprehend infinite quantities, but have a sort of confused image of indefinite extension. This is surely a right account of the matter; and if Stewart had paid any attention to these and several other passages, he could not have so much misconceived the philosophy of Gassendi.

Also intellect from imagination.

---

* Alterum est genus reflexarum actionum, quibus intellectus seipsum, suasque functiones intelligit, ac speciatim se intelligere animadvertit. Videlicet hoc munus est omni facultate corporea superius; quoniam quicquid corporeum est, ita certo loco, sive permanenter, sive succedenter alligatum est, ut non versus se, sed solum versus aliud diversum a se procedere possit.

b Et ne instes in nobis quoque, dum universale concipimus, admisceri semper aliquid singularitatis, ut certæ magnitudinis, certæ figuræ, certi coloris, &c. experimur tamen, nisi [sic] simul, saltem successivè spoliari à nobis naturam qualibet speciali magnitudine, qualibet speciali figurâ, quolibet speciali colore; atque ita de cæteris.

c P. 446.

23. The mind, as long as it dwells in the body, seems to have no intelligible species, except phantasms derived from sense. These he takes for impressions on the brain, driven to and fro by the animal spirits till they reach the *phantasia*, or imaginative faculty, and cause it to imagine sensible things. The soul, in Gassendi's theory, consists of an incorporeal part or intellect, and of a corporeal part, the phantasy or sensitive soul, which he conceives to be diffused throughout the body. The intellectual soul instantly perceives, by its union with the phantasy, the images impressed upon the latter, not by impulse of these sensible and material species, but by intuition of their images in the phantasy.[d] Thus, if I rightly apprehend his meaning, we are to distinguish; first, the species in the brain, derived from immediate sense or reminiscence; secondly, the image of these conceived by the phantasy; thirdly, the act of perception in the mind itself, by which it knows the phantasy to have imagined these species, and knows also the species themselves to have, or to have had, their external archetypes. This distinction of the *animus*, or reasonable, from the *anima*, or sensitive soul, he took, as he did a great part of his philosophy, from Epicurus.

24. The phantasy and intellect proceed together, so that they might appear at first to be the same faculty. Not only, however, are they different in their operation even as to objects which fall under the senses, and are represented to the mind, but the intellect has certain operations peculiar to itself. Such is the apprehension of things which cannot be perceived by sense, as the Deity, whom though we can only imagine as corporeal, we apprehend or understand to be otherwise.[e] He repeats a good deal of what he had before said on the dis-

---

d Eodem momento intellectus ob intimam sui, præsentiam cohærentiamque cum phantasia rem eandem contuetur. P. 450.

e Hoc est autem præter phantasiæ cancellos, intellectûsque ipsius proprium, potestque adeo talis apprehensio non jam imaginatio, sed intelligentia vel intellectio dici. Non quod intellectus non accipiat ansam ab ipsa phantasia ratiocinandi esse aliquid ultra id, quod specie imagineve repræsentatur, neque non simul comitantem talem speciem vel imaginationem habeat; sed quod apprehendat, intelligatve aliquid, ad quod apprehendendum sive percipiendum assurgere phantasia non possit, ut quæ omnino terminetur ad corporum speciem, seu imaginem, ex qua illius operatio imaginatio appellatur. Ibid.

tinctive province of the understanding, by which we reason on things incapable of being imagined; drawing several instances from the geometry of infinites, as in asymptotes, wherein, he says, something is always inferred by reasoning which we presume to be true, and yet cannot reach by any effort of the imagination.[f]

25. I have given a few extracts from Gassendi in order to confirm what has been said, his writings being little read in England, and his philosophy not having been always represented in the same manner. Degerando has claimed, on two occasions, the priority for Gassendi in that theory of the generation of ideas which has usually been ascribed to Locke.[g] But Stewart protests against this alleged similarity in the tenets of the French and English philosophers. "The remark," he says, "is certainly just, if restrained to Locke's doctrine as interpreted by the greater part of philosophers on the Continent; but it is very wide of the truth, if applied to it as now explained and modified by the most intelligent of his disciples in this country. The main scope, indeed, of Gassendi's argument against Descartes is to materialise that class of our ideas which the Lockists as well as the Cartesians

His philosophy misunderstood by Stewart.

---

[f] In quibus semper aliquid argumentando colligitur, quod et verum esse intelligimus et imaginando non assequimur tamen.

[Bernier well and clearly expressed the important distinction between αἰσθητά and νοήμενα, which separates the two schools of philosophy; and thus places Gassendi far apart from Hobbes. The passage, however, which I shall give in French, cannot be more decisive than the Latin sentence just quoted. Il ne faut pas confondre l'imagination, ou pour parler ainsi, l'intellection intuitive, ou directe, et qui se fait par l'application seule de l'entendement aux phantômes ou idées de la phantaisie, avec l'intellection pure que nous avons par le raisonnement, et que nous tirons par conséquence. D'où vient que ceux qui se persuadent qu'il n'y a aucune substance incorporelle, parce qu'ils ne conçoivent rien que dans une espèce ou image corporelle, se trompent en ce qu'ils ne reconnoissent pas qu'il y a une sorte d'intelligence qui n'est

pas imagination, à savoir celle par laquelle nous connoissons par raisonnement qu'il y a quelque chose outre ce qui tombe sous l'imagination. Abrégé du Système de Gassendi, vol. iii. p. 14. Gassendi plainly confines idea to phantasy or imagination, and so far differs from Locke.—1847.]

[g] Histoire comparée des Systèmes, 1804, vol. i. p. 301; and Biogr. Universelle, art. Gassendi. Yet in neither of these does M. Degerando advert expressly to the peculiar resemblance between the systems of Gassendi and Locke, in the account they give of ideas of reflection. He refers, however, to a more particular essay of his own on the Gassendian philosophy, which I have not seen. As to Locke's positive obligations to his predecessor, I should be perhaps inclined to doubt whether he, who was no great lover of large books, had read so unwieldy a work as the Syntagma Philosophicum; but the abridgment of Bernier would have sufficed.

consider as the exclusive objects of the power of *reflection*, and to show that these ideas are all ultimately resolvable into images or conceptions borrowed from things external. It is not therefore what is sound and valuable in this part of Locke's system, but the errors grafted on it in the comments of some of his followers, that can justly be said to have been borrowed from Gassendi. Nor has Gassendi the merit of originality even in these errors; for scarcely a remark on the subject occurs in his works, but what is copied from the accounts transmitted to us of the Epicurean metaphysics." [h]

26. It will probably appear to those who consider what I have quoted from Gassendi, that in his latest writings he did not differ so much from Locke, and lead the way so much to the school of the French metaphysicians of the eighteenth century, as Stewart has supposed. The resemblance to the Essay on the Human Understanding in several points, especially in the important distinction of what Locke has called ideas of reflection from those of sense, is too evident to be denied. I am at the same time unable to account in a satisfactory manner for the apparent discrepancy between the language of Gassendi in the Syntagma Philosophicum, and that which we find in his objections to the Meditations of Descartes. No great interval of time had intervened between the two works; for his correspondence with Descartes bears date in 1641, and it appears by that with Louis Count of Angoulême, in the succeeding year, that he was already employed on the first part of the Syntagma Philosophicum.[i] Whether he urged some of his objections against the Cartesian metaphysics with a regard to victory rather than truth, or, as would be the more candid and perhaps more reasonable hypothesis, he was induced by the acuteness of his great antagonist to review and reform his own opinions, I must leave to the philosophical reader.[k]

h Preliminary Dissertation to Encyclopædia.

i Gassendi Opera, vol. vi. p. 130. These letters are interesting to those who would study the philosophy of Gassendi.

k Baillet, in his Life of Descartes, would lead us to think that Gassendi was too much influenced by personal motives in writing against Descartes, who had mentioned the phænomena of parhelia, without alluding to a dissertation of Gassendi on the subject. The latter, it seems, owns in a letter to Rivet, that he should not have examined so closely the metaphysics of Descartes, if he had been treated by him with as much politeness as he had

27. Stewart had evidently little or no knowledge of
the Syntagma Philosophicum. But he had
seen an Abridgment of the Philosophy of Gassendi by Bernier, published at Lyons in 1678,
and finding in this the doctrine of Locke on ideas of
reflection, conceived that it did not faithfully represent
its own original. But this was hardly a very plausible
conjecture ; Bernier being a man of considerable ability,
an intimate friend of Gassendi, and his epitome being
so far from concise that it extends to eight small volumes. Having not indeed collated the two books, but
read them within a short interval of time, I can say that
Bernier has given a faithful account of the philosophy
of Gassendi, as it is contained in the Syntagma Philosophicum, for he takes notice of no other work; nor has
he here added anything of his own. But in 1682 he
published another little book, entitled Doutes de M.
Bernier sur quelques uns des principaux Chapitres de
son Abrégé de la Philosophie de Gassendi. One of
these doubts relates to the existence of space ; and in
another place he denies the reality of eternity or abstract duration. Bernier observes, as Descartes had
done, that it is vain and even dangerous to attempt a definition of evident things, such as motion, because we are
apt to mistake a definition of the word for one of the
thing ; and philosophers seem to conceive that motion
is a real being, when they talk of a billiard-ball commu-
nicating or losing it.[m]

28. The Cartesian philosophy, which its adversaries
had expected to expire with its founder, spread
more and more after his death, nor had it ever
depended on any personal favour or popularity
of Descartes, since he did not possess such except with
a few friends. The churches and schools of Holland
were full of Cartesians. The old scholastic philosophy
became ridiculous ; its distinctions, its maxims were

expected. Vie de Descartes, liv. vi. The
retort of Descartes, O caro! (see Vol. III.
of this work, p. 82) offended Gassendi,
and caused a coldness ; which, according
to Baillet, Sorbière aggravated, acting a
treacherous part in exasperating the mind
of Gassendi.

[m] Even Gassendi has defined duration

" an incorporeal flowing extension,"
which is a good instance of the success
that can attend such definitions of simple
ideas.

[Though this is not a proper definition
of duration, it is, perhaps, not ill expressed as an analogy.—1847.]

laughed at, as its adherents complain ; and probably a more fatal blow was given to the Aristotelian system by Descartes than even by Bacon.   The Cartesian theories were obnoxious to the rigid class of theologians; but two parties of considerable importance in Holland, the Arminians and the Coccejans, generally espoused the new philosophy.   Many speculations in theology were immediately connected with it, and it acted on the free and scrutinising spirit which began to sap the bulwarks of established orthodoxy.   The Cartesians were denounced in ecclesiastical synods, and were hardly admitted to any office in the church.   They were condemned by several universities, and especially by that of Leyden in 1678,[a] for the position that the truth of Scripture must be proved by reason.   Nor were they less exposed to persecution in France.[o]

29.   The Cartesian philosophy, in one sense, carried in itself the seeds of its own decline ; it was the Scylla of many dogs ; it taught men to think for themselves, and to think often better than Descartes had done.   A new eclectic philosophy, or rather the genuine spirit of free inquiry, made Cartesianism cease as a sect, though it left much that had been introduced by it.   We owe thanks to these Cartesians of the seventeenth century for their strenuous assertion of reason against prescrip-

[a] 'Leyden had condemned the whole Cartesian system as early as 1651, on the ground that it was an innovation on the Aristotelian philosophy so long received ; and ordained, ut in Academia intra Aristotelicæ philosophiæ limites, quæ hic hactenus recepta fuit, nos contineamus, utque in posterum nec philosophiæ, neque nominis Cartesiani in disputationibus, lectionibus aut publicis aliis exercitiis, nec pro nec contra mentio fiat. Utrecht, in 1644, had gone farther, and her decree is couched in terms which might have been used by any one who wished to ridicule university prejudice by a forgery. Rejicere novam istam philosophiam, primo quia veteri philosophiæ, quam Academiæ toto orbi terrarum hactenus optimo consilio docuere, adversatur, ejusque fundamenta subvertit; deinde quia juventutem a veteri et sana philosophia avertit, impeditque quo minus ad *culmen eruditionis provehatur;* eo quod istius

præsumptæ philosophiæ adminiculo *technologemata in auctorum libris professorumque lectionibus et disputationibus usitata, percipere nequit;* postremo quod ex eadem variæ falsæ et absurdæ opiniones partim consignantur, partim ab improvida juventute deduci possint pugnantes cum cæteris disciplinis et facultatibus, atque imprimis cum orthodoxa theologia ; censere igitur et statuere omnes philosophiam in hac Academia docentes imposterum a tall instituto et incepto abstinere debere, contentos *modica libertate dissentiendi* in singularibus nonnullis opinionibus ad aliarum celebrium Academiarum exemplum hic usitata, ita ut veteris et receptæ philosophiæ fundamenta non labefactent.   Tepel. Hist. Philos. Cartesianæ, p. 75.

[o] An account of the manner in which the Cartesians were harassed through the Jesuits is given by M. Cousin in the Journal des Savans, March, 1838.

tive authority : the latter part of this age was signalised
by the overthrow of a despotism which had fought every
inch in its retreat, and it was manifestly after a struggle,
on the Continent, with this new philosophy, that it was
ultimately vanquished.[p]

30. The Cartesian writers of France, the Low Countries, and Germany, were numerous and respectable. La Forge of Saumur first developed
the theory of occasional causes to explain the union of
soul and body, wherein he was followed by Geulinx,
Regis, Wittich, and Malebranche.[q] But this and other
innovations displeased the stricter Cartesians who did
not find them in their master. Clauberg in Germany,
Clerselier in France, Le Grand in the Low Countries,
should be mentioned among the leaders of the school.
But no one has left so comprehensive a statement and
defence of Cartesianism as Jean Silvain Regis, whose
Système de la Philosophie, in three quarto volumes,
appeared at Paris in 1690. It is divided into four parts,
on Logic, Metaphysics, Physics, and Ethics. In the
three latter Regis claims nothing as his own except
some explanations. " All that I have said being due to
M. Descartes, whose method and principles I have followed, even in explanations that are different from his
own." And in his Logic he professes to have gone little
beyond the author of the Art de Penser.[r] Notwithstanding this rare modesty, Regis is not a writer unworthy
of being consulted by the studious of philosophy, nor
deficient in clearer and fuller statements than will
always be found in Descartes. It might even be said
that he has many things which would be sought in vain
through his master's writings, though I am unable to
prove that they might not be traced in those of the

(margin notes: La Forge. Regis.)

[p] For the fate of the Cartesian philosophy in the life of its founder, see the
life of Descartes by Baillet, 2 vols. in
quarto, which he afterwards abridged in
12mo. After the death of Descartes, it
may be best traced by means of Brucker.
Buhle, as usual, is a mere copyist of his
predecessor. He has, however, given a
fuller account of Regis. A contemporary History of Cartesian Philosophy by
Tepel contains rather a neatly written
summary of the controversies it excited
both in the lifetime of Descartes and for
a few years afterwards.

[q] Tennemann (Manuel de la Philosophie, ii. 99) ascribes this theory to
Geulinx. See also Brucker, v. 704.
[r] It is remarkable that Regis says
nothing about figures and modes of syllogism : Nous ne dirons rien des figures
ni des syllogismes en général; car bien
que tout cela puisse servir de quelque
chose pour la spéculation de la logique,
il n'est au moins d'aucun usage pour la
pratique, laquelle est l'unique but que
nous nous sommes proposés dans ce
traité. P. 37.

intermediate Cartesians. Though our limits will not permit any further account of Regis, I will give a few passages in a note.*

31. Huet, Bishop of Avranches, a man of more general erudition than philosophical acuteness, yet not quite without this, arraigned the whole theory in his Censura

* Regis, in imitation of his master, and perhaps with more clearness, observes that our knowledge of our own existence is not derived from reasoning, mais par une connoissance simple et intérieure, qui précède toutes les connoissances acquises, et que j'appelle *conscience*. En effet, quand je dis que je connois ou que je crois connoître, ce *je* présuppose lui-même mon existence, étant impossible que je connoisse, ou seulement que je croie connoître, et que je ne sois pas quelque chose d'existant. P. 68. The Cartesian paradox, as it at first appears, that thinking is the essence of the soul, Regis has explained away. After coming to the conclusion, Je suis donc une pensée, he immediately corrects himself: Cependant je crains encore de me définir mal, quand je dis que je suis une pensée, qui a la propriété de douter et d'avoir de la certitude; car quelle apparence y a-t-il que ma nature, qui doit être une chose fixe et permanente, consiste dans la pensée, puisque je sais par expérience que mes pensées sont dans un flux continuel, et que je ne pense jamais à la même chose deux momens de suite; mais quand je considère la difficulté de plus près, je conçois aisément qu'elle vient de ce que le mot de *pensée* est équivoque, et que je m'en sers indifféremment pour signifier la pensée qui constitue ma nature, et pour désigner les différentes manières d'être de cette pensée; ce qui est une erreur extrême, car il y a cette différence entre la pensée qui constitue ma nature, et les pensées qui n'en sont que les manières d'être, que la première est une pensée fixe et permanente, et que les autres sont des pensées changeantes et passagères. C'est pourquoi, afin de donner une idée exacte de ma nature, je dirai que je suis une pensée qui existe en elle-même, et qui est le sujet de toutes mes manières de penser. Je dis que je suis une pensée pour marquer ce que la pensée qui constitue ma nature a de commun avec la pensée en général qui comprend sous soi toutes les manières particulières de penser: et j'ajoute, qui existe en elle-même,

et qui est le sujet de différentes manières de penser, pour désigner ce que cette pensée a de particulier qui la distingue de la pensée en général, vu qu'elle n'existe que dans l'entendement de celui qui la conçoit ainsi que toutes les autres natures universelles. P. 70.

Every mode supposes a substance wherein it exists. From this axiom Regis deduces the objective being of space, because we have the ideas of length, breadth, and depth, which cannot belong to ourselves, our souls having none of these properties; nor could the ideas be suggested by a superior being, if space did not exist, because they would be the representations of non-entity, which is impossible. But this transcendental proof is too subtle for the world.

It is an axiom of Regis that we only know things without us by means of ideas, and that things of which we have no ideas are in regard to us as if they did not exist at all. Another axiom is that all ideas, considered in respect to their representative property, depend on objects as their types, or *causes exemplaires*. And a third, that the "cause exemplaire" of ideas must contain all the properties which the ideas represent. These axioms, according to him, are the bases of all certainty in physical truth. From the second axiom he deduces the objectivity or "cause exemplaire" of his idea of a perfect being; and his proof seems at least more clearly put than by Descartes. Every idea implies an objective reality; for otherwise there would be an effect without a cause. Yet in this we have the sophisms and begging of questions of which we may see many instances in Spinosa.

In the second part of the first book of his metaphysics, Regis treats of the union of soul and body, and concludes that the motions of the body only act on the soul by a special will of God, who has determined to produce certain thoughts simultaneously with certain bodily motions. P. 124. God is the efficient first cause of all effects, his creatures are but se-

Philosophiæ Cartesianæ. He had been for many years,
Huet's Censure of Cartesianism. as he tells us, a favourer of Cartesianism, but
his retractation is very complete. It cannot be
denied that Huet strikes well at the vulnerable parts of the Cartesian metaphysics, and exposes their alternate scepticism and dogmatism with some justice. In other respects he displays an inferior knowledge of the human mind and of the principles of reasoning to Descartes. He repeats Gassendi's cavil that, Cogito, ergo sum, involves the truth of Quod cogitat, est. The Cartesians, Huet observes, assert the major, or universal, to be deduced from the minor; which, though true in things known by induction, is not so in propositions necessarily known, or as the schools say, à priori, as that the whole is greater than its part. It is not, however, probable that Descartes would have extended his reply to Gassendi's criticism so far as this; some have referred our knowledge of geometrical axioms to mere experience, but this seems not agreeable to the Cartesian theory.

32. The influence of the Cartesian philosophy was
Port-Royal Logic. displayed in a treatise of deserved reputation, L'Art de Penser, often called the Port-Royal Logic. It seems to have been the work of Antony Arnauld, with some assistance, perhaps, by Nicole. Arnauld was not an entire Cartesian; he had himself been engaged in controversy with Descartes; but his understanding was clear and calm, his love of truth sincere, and he could not avoid recognising the vast superiority of the new philosophy to that received in the schools. This logic, accordingly, is perhaps the first regular treatise on that science that contained a protestation, though in very moderate language, against the Aristotelian method. The author tells us that after some doubt he had resolved to insert a few things rather troublesome and of little value, such as the rules of conversion and the demonstration of the syllogistic figures, chiefly as exercises of the understanding, for which difficulties are not without utility. The method of syllo-

condarily efficient. But as they act immediately, we may ascribe all modal beings to the efficiency of second causes. And he prefers this expression to that of occasional causes, usual among the Cartesians, because he fancies the latter rather derogatory to the fixed will of God.

gism itself he deems little serviceable in the discovery
of truth; while many things dwelt upon in books of
logic, such as the ten categories, rather injure than
improve the reasoning faculties, because they accustom
men to satisfy themselves with words, and to mistake a
long catalogue of arbitrary definitions for real knowledge.
Of Aristotle he speaks in more honourable terms than
Bacon had done before, or than Malebranche did afterwards; acknowledging the extraordinary merit of some
of his writings, but pointing out with an independent
spirit his failings as a master in the art of reasoning.

33. The first part of L'Art de Penser is almost entirely
metaphysical, in the usual sense of that word.   It considers ideas in their nature and origin, in the chief differences of the objects they represent, in their simplicity
or composition, in their extent, as universal, particular,
or singular, and, lastly, in their distinctness or confusion.   The word idea, it is observed, is among those
which are so clear that we cannot explain them by
means of others, because none can be more clear and
simple than themselves.'   But here it may be doubtful
whether the sense in which the word is to be taken must
strike every one in the same way.   The clearness of a
word does not depend on its association with a distinct
conception in our own minds, but on the generality of
this same association in the minds of others.

34. No follower of Descartes has more unambiguously
than this author distinguished between imagination and
intellection, though he gives the name of idea to both.
Many suppose, he says, that they cannot conceive a
thing when they cannot imagine it.   But we cannot
imagine a figure of 1000 sides, though we can conceive
it and reason upon it.   We may indeed get a confused
image of a figure with many sides, but these are no more
1000 than they are 999.   Thus also we have ideas of
thinking, affirming, denying, and the like, though we
have no imagination of these operations.   By ideas
therefore we mean not images painted in the fancy, but
all that is in our minds when we say that we conceive
any thing, in whatever manner we may conceive it.
Hence it is easy to judge of the falsehood of some

' C. 1.

opinions held in this age. One philosopher has advanced that we have no idea of God; another that all reasoning is but an assemblage of words connected by an affirmation. He glances here at Gassendi and Hobbes.[u] Far from all our ideas coming from the senses, as the Aristotelians have said, and as Gassendi asserts in his Logic, we may say, on the contrary, that no idea in our minds is derived from the senses except occasionally (par occasion); that is, the movements of the brain, which is all that the organs of sense can affect, give occasion to the soul to form different ideas which it would not otherwise form, though these ideas have scarce ever any resemblance to what occurs in the organs of sense and in the brain, and though there are also very many ideas which, deriving nothing from any bodily image, cannot without absurdity be referred to the senses.[x] This is perhaps a clearer statement of an important truth than will be found in Malebranche or in Descartes himself.

35. In the second part Arnauld treats of words and propositions. Much of it may be reckoned more within the province of grammar than of logic. But as it is inconvenient to refer the student to works of a different class, especially if it should be the case that no good grammars, written with a regard to logical principles, were then to be found, this cannot justly be made an objection. In the latter chapters of this second part, he comes to much that is strictly logical, and taken from ordinary books on that science. The third part relates to syllogisms, and notwithstanding the author's low estimation of that method, in comparison with the general regard for it in the schools, he has not omitted the common explanations of mood and figure, ending with a concise but good account of the chief sophisms.

36. The fourth and last part is entitled, On Method, and contains the principles of connected reasoning, which he justly observes to be more important than the rules of

---

[u] The reflection on Gassendi is a mere cavil, as will appear by remarking what he has really said, and which we have quoted a few pages above. The Cartesians were resolute in using one sense of the word idea, while Gassendi used another. He had himself been to blame in this controversy with the father of the new philosophy, and the disciples (calling the author of L'Art de Penser such in a general sense) retaliated by equal captiousness.

[x] C. 1.

single syllogisms, wherein few make any mistake. The laws of demonstration given by Pascal are here laid down with some enlargement. Many observations not wholly bearing on merely logical proof are found in this part of the treatise.

37. The Port-Royal Logic, though not, perhaps, very much read in England, has always been reckoned among the best works in that science, and certainly had a great influence in rendering it more metaphysical, more ethical (for much is said by Arnauld on the moral discipline of the mind in order to fit it for the investigation of truth), more exempt from technical barbarisms and trifling definitions and divisions. It became more and more acknowledged that the rules of syllogism go a very little way in rendering the mind able to follow a course of inquiry without error, much less in assisting it to discover truth; and that even their vaunted prerogative of securing us from fallacy is nearly ineffectual in exercise. The substitution of the French language, in its highest polish, for the uncouth Latinity of the Aristotelians, was another advantage of which the Cartesian school legitimately availed themselves.

38. Malebranche, whose Recherche de la Vérité was published in 1674, was a warm and almost enthusiastic admirer of Descartes, but his mind was independent, searching, and fond of its own inventions; he acknowledged no master, and in some points dissents from the Cartesian school. His natural temperament was sincere and rigid; he judges the moral and intellectual failings of mankind with a severe scrutiny, and a contemptuousness not generally unjust in itself, but displaying too great confidence in his own superiority. This was enhanced by a religious mysticism, which enters, as an essential element, into his philosophy of the mind. The fame of Malebranche, and still more the popularity in modern times of his Search for Truth, has been affected by that peculiar hypothesis, so mystically expressed, the seeing all things in God, which has been more remembered than any other part of that treatise. "The union," he says, "of the soul to God is the only means by which we acquire a knowledge of truth. This union has indeed been rendered so obscure by original sin, that few can understand what it

G 2

means; to those who follow blindly the dictates of
sense and passion it appears imaginary. The same
cause has so fortified the connexion between the soul
and body that we look on them as one substance, of
which the latter is the principal part. And hence we
may all fear that we do not well discern the confused
sounds with which the senses fill the imagination from
that pure voice of truth which speaks to the soul. The
body speaks louder than God himself; and our pride
makes us presumptuous enough to judge without waiting
for those words of truth, without which we cannot
truly judge at all. And the present work," he adds,
" may give evidence of this; for it is not published
as being infallible. But let my readers judge of my
opinions according to the clear and distinct answers
they shall receive from the only Lord of all men, after
they shall have interrogated him by paying a serious
attention to the subject." This is a strong evidence of
the enthusiastic confidence in supernatural illumination
which belongs to Malebranche, and which we are almost
surprised to find united with so much cool and acute
reasoning as his writings contain.

39. The Recherche de la Vérité is in six books; the
first five on the errors springing from the

His style. senses, from the imagination, from the understanding, from the natural inclinations, and from the
passions. The sixth contains the method of avoiding
these, which however has been anticipated in great
measure throughout the preceding. Malebranche has
many repetitions, but little, I think, that can be called
digressive, though he takes a large range of illustration,
and dwells rather diffusely on topics of subordinate
importance. His style is admirable; clear, precise, elegant, sparing in metaphors, yet not wanting them in due
place, warm, and sometimes eloquent, a little redundant,
but never passionate or declamatory.

40. Error, according to Malebranche, is the source of
Sketch of   all human misery; man is miserable because
his theory.   he is a sinner, and he would not sin if he did
not consent to err. For the will alone judges and
reasons, the understanding only perceives things and
their relations—a deviation from common language, to
say the least, that seems quite unnecessary.[y] The will

ʸ L. 1. c. 2.

is active and free; not that we can avoid willing our own happiness; but it possesses a power of turning the understanding towards such objects as please us, and commanding it to examine every thing thoroughly, else we should be perpetually deceived, and without remedy, by the appearances of truth. And this liberty we should use on every occasion: it is to become slaves, against the will of God, when we acquiesce in false appearances; but it is in obedience to the voice of eternal truth which speaks within us, that we submit to those secret reproaches of reason, which accompany our refusal to yield to evidence. There are, therefore, two fundamental rules, one for science, the other for morals; never to give an entire consent to any propositions, except those which are so evidently true that we cannot refuse to admit them without an internal uneasiness and reproach of our reason; and, never fully to love anything which we can abstain from loving without remorse. We may feel a great inclination to consent absolutely to a probable opinion; yet on reflection, we shall find that we are not compelled to do so by any tacit self-reproach if we do not. And we ought to consent to such probable opinions for the time until we have more fully examined the question.

41. The sight is the noblest of our senses; and if they had been given us to discover truth, it is through vision that we should have done it. But it deceives us in all that it represents; in the size of bodies, their figures and motions, in light and colours. None of these are such as they appear, as he proves by many obvious instances. Thus we measure the velocity of motion by duration of time and extent of space; but of duration the mind can form no just estimate, and the eye cannot determine equality of spaces. The diameter of the moon is greater by measurement when she is high in the heavens; it appears greater to our eyes in the horizon.[a] On all sides we are beset with error through our senses. Not that the sensations themselves, properly speaking, deceive us. We are not deceived in supposing that we see an orb of light before the sun has risen above the horizon, but in supposing that what we see is the sun itself. Were we even delirious, we should see and feel

[a] L. i. c. 9. Malebranche was engaged afterwards in a controversy with Regis on this particular question of the horizontal moon.

what our senses present to us, though our judgment as
to its reality would be erroneous.   And this judgment
we may withhold by assenting to nothing without perfect certainty.

42. It would have been impossible for a man endowed
with such intrepidity and acuteness as Malebranche to
overlook the question, so naturally raised by this sceptical theory, as to the objective existence of an external
world.   There is no necessary connexion, he observes,
between the presence of an idea in the soul, and the
existence of the thing which it represents, as dreams
and delirium prove.   Yet we may be confident that
extension, figure, and movement do generally exist
without us when we perceive them.   These are not
imaginary; we are not deceived in believing their reality,
though it is very difficult to prove it.   But it is far otherwise with colours, smells, or sounds, for these do not
exist at all beyond the mind.   This he proceeds to show
at considerable length.[a]   In one of the illustrations subsequently written in order to obviate objections, and
subjoined to the Recherche de la Vérité, Malebranche
comes again to this problem of the reality of matter,
and concludes by subverting every argument in its
favour, except what he takes to be the assertion of Scripture.   Berkeley, who did not see this in the same light,
had scarcely a step to take in his own famous theory,
which we may consider as having been anticipated by
Malebranche, with the important exception that what
was only scepticism and denial of certainty in the one,
became a positive and dogmatic affirmation in the other.

43. In all our sensations, he proceeds to show, there
are four things distinct in themselves, but which, examined as they arise simultaneously, we are apt to confound; these are the action of the object, the effect upon
the organ of sense, the mere sensation, and the judgment
we form as to its cause.   We fall into errors as to all
these, confounding the sensation with the action of
bodies, as when we say there is heat in the fire or colour
in the rose, or confounding the motion of the nerves
with sensation, as when we refer heat to the hand; but
most of all, in drawing mistaken inferences as to the
nature of objects from our sensations.[b]   It may be here

[a] L. l. c. 10.   [b] C. 12.

remarked, that what Malebranche has properly called the judgment of the mind as to the cause of its sensations, is precisely what Reid denominates perception; a term less clear, and which seems to have led some of his school into important errors. The language of the Scottish philosopher appears to imply that he considered perception as a distinct and original faculty of the mind, rather than what it is, a complex operation of the judgment and memory, applying knowledge already acquired by experience. Neither he, nor his disciple Stewart, though aware of the mistakes that have arisen in this province of metaphysics by selecting our instances from the phænomena of vision instead of the other senses, have avoided the same source of error. The sense of sight has the prerogative of enabling us to pronounce instantly on the external cause of our sensation; and this perception is so intimately blended with the sensation itself, that it does not imply in our minds, whatever may be the case with young children, the least consciousness of a judgment. But we need only make our experiment upon sound or smell, and we shall at once acknowledge that there is no sort of necessary connexion between the sensation and our knowledge of its corresponding external object. We hear sounds continually, which we are incapable of referring to any particular body; nor does any one, I suppose, deny that it is by experience alone we learn to pronounce, with more or less of certainty according to its degree, on the causes from which these sensations proceed.[c]

[c] [The word "perception" has not, in this passage, been used in its most approved sense; but the language of philosophers is not uniform. Locke often confounds perception with sensation, so as to employ the words indifferently. But this is not the case when he writes with attention. "The ideas," he says, "we receive from sensation are often in grown people altered by the judgment without our taking notice of it;" instancing a globe, "of which the idea imprinted in our own mind is of a flat circle variously shadowed; but we, having been by use accustomed to perceive what kind of appearance convex bodies are wont to make in us, what alterations are made in the reflections of light by the difference of the sensible figures of bodies, the judgment presently, by an habitual custom, alters the appearances of things into their causes; so that, from that which truly is variety of shadow or colour, collecting the figure, it makes it pass for a mark of a figure, and frames to itself the *perception* of a convex figure and an uniform colour, when the idea we receive from thence is only a plane variously coloured." B. ii. ch. 9. M. Cousin, therefore, is hardly just in saying that "perception, according to Locke, does nothing but perceive the sensation—it is hardly more than an effect of the sensation." Cours de l'Hist. de la Philosophie, vol. ii. p. 136, edit. 1829. Doubtless perception is the *effect* of sensation; but

44. Sensation he defines to be "a modification of the soul in relation to something which passes in the body to which she is united." These sensations we know by experience; it is idle to go about defining or explaining them; this cannot be done by words. It is an error, according to Malebranche, to believe that all men have like sensations from the same objects. In this he goes farther than Pascal, who thinks it probable that they have; while Malebranche holds it indubitable, from the organs of men being constructed differently, that they do not receive similar impressions, instancing music, some smells and flavours, and many other things of the

Locke extends the word, in this passage at least, to much of which *mere* sensation has only furnished the materials, to the inferences derived from experience. Later metaphysicians limit more essentially the use of the word. La perception, says M. de Rémusat, dans sa plus grande complicité, n'est que la distinction mentale de l'objet de la sensation. Essais de Philosophie, vol. ii. p. 372. Kant, with his usual acuteness of discrimination, analyses the process. We have, first, the phænomenon, or appearance of the object, under which he comprehends the impression made on the organ of sense; secondly, the sensation itself; thirdly, the representation of the object by the mind; fourthly, the reference of this representation to the object. And there may be, but not necessarily, the conception or knowledge of what the object is. Id., vol. i. p. 270. Locke sometimes seems to use the word perception for the third of these; Reid very frequently for the fourth. In his first work, indeed, the Inquiry into the Human Mind, he expressly distinguishes perception from "that knowledge of the objects of sense, which is got by reasoning. There is no reasoning in perception. The belief which is implied in it is the effect of instinct." Chap. vi. § 20. But, in fact, he limits the strict province of perception to the primary qualities of matter, and to the idea of space. Both Locke and Reid, however, sometimes extend it to the conception or knowledge of the actual object. We have just quoted a passage from Locke. "In two of our senses," says Reid, "touch and taste, there must be an immediate application

of the object to the organ; in the other three the object is *perceived* at a distance, but still by means of a medium by which some impression is made upon the organ." Intellect. Powers, Essay II. ch. ii. But perception of the object, through the organs of sound, smell, and taste, must of necessity imply a knowledge of it derived from experience. Those senses, by themselves, give us no perception of external things. But the word has one meaning in modern philosophy, and another in popular usage, which philosophers sometimes inadvertently follow. In the first it is a mere reference of the sensation to some external object, more definite in sight, somewhat less so in touch, and not at all in the three other senses. In the other it is a reference of the sensation to a known object, and in all the senses; we *perceive* an oak-tree, the striking of the clock, the perfume of a violet. The more philosophical sense of the word perception limits greatly the extent of the faculty. "We perceive," says Sir W. Hamilton, on the passage last quoted from Reid, "nothing but what is in relation to the organ; and nothing is in relation to the organ that is not present to it. All the senses are, in fact, modifications of touch, as Democritus of old taught. We reach the distant reality, not by sense, not by perception, but by inference." Brown had said the same. This has been, in the case of sight, controverted by Dr. Whewell; but whether we see objects, strictly speaking, at a distance, or on the retina, it is evident that we do not know *what they are*, till we have been taught by experience.—1847.]

same kind. But it is obvious to reply that he has
argued from the exception to the rule; the great majority of mankind agreeing as to musical sounds (which
is the strongest case that can be put against his paradox),
and most other sensations. That the sensations of different men, subject to such exceptions, if not strictly
alike, are, so to say, in a constant ratio, seems as indisputable as any conclusion we can draw from their testimony.

45. The second book of Malebranche's treatise relates
to the imagination, and the errors connected with it.
"The imagination consists in the power of the mind to
form images of objects by producing a change in the
fibres of that part of the brain, which may be called
principal because it corresponds with all parts of the
body, and is the place where the soul, if we may so
speak, immediately resides." This he supposes to be
where all the filaments of the brain terminate : so difficult was it, especially in that age, for a philosopher who
had the clearest perception of the soul's immateriality to
free himself from the analogies of extended presence and
material impulse. The imagination, he says, comprehends two things; the action of the will and the obedience of the animal spirits which trace images on the
brain. The power of conception depends partly upon
the strength of those animal spirits, partly on the qualities of the brain itself. For just as the size, the depth,
and the clearness of the lines in an engraving depend
on the force with which the graver acts, and on the
obedience which the copper yields to it, so the depth
and clearness of the traces of the imagination depend on
the force of the animal spirits, and on the constitution
of the fibres of the brain; and it is the difference of
these which occasions almost the whole of that vast inequality which we find in the capacities of men.

46. This arbitrary, though rather specious hypothesis,
which in the present more advanced state of physiology
a philosopher might not in all points reject, but would
certainly not assume, is spread out by Malebranche
over a large part of his work, and especially the second
book. The delicacy of the fibres of the brain, he supposes, is one of the chief causes of our not giving sufficient application to difficult subjects. Women possess

this delicacy, and hence have more intelligence than men as to all sensible objects; but whatever is abstract is to them incomprehensible. The fibres are soft in children, and become stronger with age, the greatest perfection of the understanding being between thirty and fifty; but with prejudiced men, and especially when they are advanced in life, the hardness of the cerebral fibre confirms them in error. For we can understand nothing without attention, nor attend to it without having a strong image in the brain, nor can that image be formed without a suppleness and susceptibility of motion in the brain itself. It is therefore highly useful to get the habit of thinking on all subjects, and thus to give the brain a facility of motion analogous to that of the fingers in playing on a musical instrument. And this habit is best acquired by seeking truth in difficult things while we are young, because it is then that the fibres are most easily bent in all directions.[d]

47. This hypothesis, carried so far as it has been by Malebranche, goes very great lengths in asserting not merely a connexion between the cerebral motions and the operations of the mind, but something like a subordination of the latter to a plastic power in the animal spirits of the brain.. For if the differences in the intellectual powers of mankind, and also, as he afterwards maintains, in their moral emotions, are to be accounted for by mere bodily configuration as their regulating cause, little more than a naked individuality of consciousness seems to be left to the immaterial principle. No one, however, whether he were staggered by this difficulty or not; had a more decided conviction of the essential distinction between mind and matter than this disciple of Descartes. The soul, he says, does not become body, nor the body soul, by their union. Each substance remains as it is, the soul incapable of extension and motion, the body incapable of thought and desire. All the alliance between soul and body which is known to us consists in a natural and mutual correspondence of the thoughts of the former with the traces on the brain, and of its emotions with the traces of the animal spirits. As soon as the soul receives new ideas, new traces are imprinted on the brain; and as soon as

d L. ii. c. 1.

external objects imprint new traces, the soul receives new ideas. Not that it contemplates these traces, for it has no knowledge of them; nor that the traces contain the ideas, since they have no relation to them; nor that the soul receives her ideas from the traces, for it is inconceivable that the soul should receive anything from the body, and become more enlightened, as some philosophers (meaning Gassendi) express it, by turning itself towards the phantasms in the brain. Thus, also, when the soul wills that the arm should move, the arm moves, though she does not even know what else is necessary for its motion; and thus, when the animal spirits are put into movement, the soul is disturbed, though she does not even know that there are animal spirits in the body.

48. These remarks of Malebranche it is important to familiarise to our minds; and those who reflect upon them will neither fall into the gross materialism to which many physiologists appear prone, nor, on the other hand, out of fear of allowing too much to the bodily organs, reject any sufficient proof that may be adduced for the relation between the cerebral system and the intellectual processes. These opposite errors are by no means uncommon in the present age. But, without expressing an opinion on that peculiar hypothesis which is generally called phrenology, we might ask whether it is not quite as conceivable, that a certain state of portions of the brain may be the antecedent condition of memory or imagination, as that a certain state of nervous filaments may be, what we know it is, an invariable antecedent of sensation. In neither instance can there be any resemblance or proper representation of the organic motion transferred to the soul; nor ought we to employ, even in metaphor, the analogies of impulse or communication. But we have two phænomena, between which, by the constitution of our human nature, and probably by that of the very lowest animals, there is a perpetual harmony and concomitance; an ultimate fact, according to the present state of our faculties, which may in some senses be called mysterious, inasmuch as we can neither fully apprehend its final causes, nor all the conditions of its operation, but one which seems not to involve any appearance of con-

tradiction, and should therefore not lead us into the useless perplexity of seeking a solution that is almost evidently beyond our reach.

49. The association of ideas is far more extensively developed by Malebranche in this second book than by any of the old writers, not even, I think, with the exception of Hobbes; though he is too fond of mixing the psychological facts which experience furnishes with his precarious, however plausible, theory of cerebral traces. Many of his remarks are acute and valuable. Thus he observes that writers who make use of many new terms in science, under the notion of being more intelligible, are often not understood at all, whatever care they may take to define their words. We grant in theory their right to do this; but nature resists. The new words, having no ideas previously associated with them, fall out of the reader's mind, except in mathematics, where they can be rendered evident by diagrams. In all this part, Malebranche expatiates on the excessive deference shown to authority, which, because it is great in religion, we suppose equally conclusive in philosophy, and on the waste of time which mere reading of many books entails; experience, he says, having always shown that those who have studied most are the very persons who have led the world into the greatest errors. The whole of the chapters on this subject is worth perusal.

50. In another part of this second book, Malebranche has opened a new and fertile vein, which he is far from having exhausted, on what he calls the contagiousness of a powerful imagination. Minds of this character, he observes, rule those which are feebler in conception; they give them by degrees their own habit, they impress their own type; and as men of strong imagination are themselves for the most part very unreasonable, their brains being cut up, as it were, by deep traces, which leave no room for anything else, no source of human error is more dangerous than this contagiousness of their disorder. This he explains, in his favourite physiology, by a certain natural sympathy between the cerebral fibres of different men, which being wanting in any one with whom we converse, it is vain to expect

that he will enter into our views, and we must look for a more sympathetic tissue elsewhere.

51. The moral observations of Malebranche are worth more than these hypotheses with which they are mingled. Men of powerful imagination express themselves with force and vivacity, though not always in the most natural manner, and often with great animation of gesture; they deal with subjects that excite sensible images, and from all this they acquire a great power of persuasion. This is exercised especially over persons in subordinate relations; and thus children, servants, or courtiers adopt the opinions of their superiors. Even in religion nations have been found to take up the doctrines of their rulers, as has been seen in England. In certain authors, who influence our minds without any weight of argument, this despotism of a strong imagination is exercised, which he particularly illustrates by the examples of Tertullian, Seneca, and Montaigne. The contagious power of imagination is also manifest in the credulity of mankind as to apparitions and witchcraft; and he observes that where witches are burned, there is generally a great number of them, while, since some parliaments have ceased to punish for sorcery, the offence has diminished within their jurisdiction.

52. The application which these striking and original views will bear spreads far into the regions of moral philosophy in the largest sense of that word. It is needless to dwell upon, and idle to cavil at the physiological theories to which Malebranche has had recourse. False let them be, what is derived from the experience of human nature will always be true. No one general phænomenon in the intercommunity of mankind with each other is more worthy to be remembered, or more evident to an observing eye, than this contagiousness, as Malebranche phrases it, of a powerful imagination, especially when assisted by any circumstances that secure and augment its influence. The history of every popular delusion, and even the petty events of every day in private life, are witnesses to its power.

53. The third book is entitled. Of the Understanding or Pure Spirit (l'Esprit Pur). By the pure understanding he means the faculty of the soul to know the reality

of certain things without the aid of images in the brain.
And he warns the reader that the inquiry will be found
dry and obscure.   The essence of the soul, he says,
following his Cartesian theory,. consists in thought, as
that of matter does in extension; will, imagination,
memory, and the like, are modifications of thought or
forms of the soul, as water, wood, or fire are modifications of matter.   This sort of expression has been
adopted by our metaphysicians of the Scots school in
preference to the ideas of reflection, as these operations
are called by Locke. But by the word thought (pensée),
Malebranche, like Regis, does not mean these modifications, but the soul or thinking principle absolutely,
capable of all these modifications, as extension is neither
round nor square, though capable of either form.   The
power of volition, and, by parity of reasoning we may
add, of thinking, is inseparable from the soul, but not
the acts of volition or thinking themselves; as a body
is always moveable, though it be not always in motion.

54. In this book it does not seem that Malebranche
has been very successful in distinguishing the ideas of
pure intellect from those which the senses or imagination present to us; nor do we clearly see what he means
by the former, except those of existence and a few more.
But he now hastens to his peculiar hypothesis as to the
mode of perception. By ideas he understands the immediate object of the soul, which all the world, he supposes, will agree not to be the same with the external
objects of sense. Ideas are real existences; for they
have properties, and represent very different things;
but nothing can have no property.* How then do they
enter into the mind, or become present to it? Is it, as
the Aristotelians hold, by means of species transmitted
from the external objects? Or are they produced in-
stantaneously by some faculty of the soul?. Or have

---

* [Cudworth uses the same argument
for the reality of ideas. "It is a ridiculous conceit of a modern atheistic
writer that universals are nothing else
but names, attributed to many singular
bodies, because whatever is is singular.
For though whatever exists without the
mind be singular, yet it is plain that
there are conceptions in our minds objectively universal. Which universal objects
of our mind, though they exist not as such
anywhere without it, yet are they not
therefore nothing, but have an intelligible
entity, for this very reason, because they
are conceivable; for since non-entity is
not conceivable, whatever is conceivable
as an object of the mind is therefore
something." Intellectual System, p. 731.
—1842.]

they been created and posited as it were in the soul, when it began to exist? Or does God produce them in us whenever we think or perceive? Or does the soul contain in herself in some transcendental manner whatever is in the sensible world? These hypotheses of elder philosophers, some of which are not quite intelligibly distinct from each other, Malebranche having successfully refuted, comes to what he considers the only possible alternative; namely, that the soul is united to an all-perfect Being, in whom all that belongs to his creatures is contained. Besides the exclusion of every other supposition which he conceives himself to have given, he subjoins several direct arguments in favour of his own theory, but in general so obscure and full of arbitrary assumption that they cannot be stated in this brief sketch.[f]

55. The mysticism of this eminent man displays itself throughout this part of his treatise, but rarely leading him into that figurative and unmeaning language from which the inferior class of enthusiasts are never free. His philosophy, which has hitherto appeared so sceptical, assumes now the character of intense irresistible conviction. The scepticism of Malebranche is merely ancillary to his mysticism. His philosophy, if we may use so quaint a description of it, is subjectivity leading objectivity in chains. He seems to triumph in his restoration of the inner man to his pristine greatness, by subduing those false traitors and rebels, the nerves and brain, to whom, since the great lapse of Adam, his posterity had been in thrall. It has been justly remarked by Brown, that in the writings of Malebranche, as in all theological metaphysicians of the Catholic church, we perceive the commanding influence of Augustin.[g] From him, rather than, in the first instance,

[f] L. iii. c. 6.

[g] Philosophy of the Human Mind, Lecture xxx. Brown's own position, that "the idea is the mind," seems to me as paradoxical, in expression at least, as anything in Malebranche.

[Brown meant to guard against the notion of Berkeley and Malebranche, that ideas are any how separable from the mind, or capable of being considered as real beings. But he did not sufficiently distinguish between the percipient and the perception, or what M. de Rémusat has called, le moi observé par le moi. As for the word modification, which we owe to Malebranche, though it does not well express his own theory of independent ideas, I cannot help agreeing with Locke: "What service does that word do us in one case or the other, when it is only a new word brought in without any new conception at all? For my mind,

from Plato or Plotinus, it may be suspected that Male-branche, who was not very learned in ancient philo-sophy, derived the manifest tinge of Platonism, that, mingling with his warm admiration of Descartes, has rendered him a link between two famous systems, not very harmonious in their spirit and turn of reasoning. But his genius, more clear, or at least disciplined in a more accurate logic, than that of Augustin, taught him to dissent from that father by denying objective reality to eternal truths, such as that two and two are equal to four; descending thus one step from unintelligible mys-ticism.

56. " Let us repose," he concludes, " in this tenet, that God is the intelligible world, or the place of spirits, like as the material world is the place of bodies; that it is from his power they receive all their modifications; that it is in his wisdom they find all their ideas; and that it is by his love they feel all their well-regulated emotions. And since his power and his wisdom and his love are but himself, let us believe with St. Paul, that he is not far from each of us, and that in him we live, and move, and have our being." But sometimes Male-branche does not content himself with these fine effu-sions of piety. His theism, as has often been the case with mystical writers, expands till it becomes as it were dark with excessive light, and almost vanishes in its own effulgence. He has passages that approach very closely to the pantheism of Jordano Bruno and Spinosa; one especially, wherein he vindicates the Cartesian argu-ment for a being of necessary existence in a strain which perhaps renders that argument less incomprehen-sible, but certainly cannot be said, in any legitimate sense, to establish the existence of a Deity.[h]

57. It is from the effect which the invention of so original and striking an hypothesis, and one that raises such magnificent conceptions of the union between the

---

when it sees a colour or figure, is altered. I know, from the not having such or such a perception to the having it; but when, to explain this, I am told that either of these perceptions is a modification of the mind, what do I conceive more than that, from not having such a perception, my mind is come to have such a perception? Which is what I as well knew before the word 'modification' was made use of, which by its use has made me conceive nothing more than what I conceived before." Examination of Malebranche's theory, in, Locke's works, vol. iii. p. 427, ed. 1719.—1847.]

h L. iii. c. 8.

Deity and the human soul, would produce on a man of an elevated and contemplative genius, that we must account for Malebranche's forgetfulness of much that he has judiciously said in part of his treatise, on the limitation of our faculties and the imperfect knowledge we can attain as to our intellectual nature. For, if we should admit that ideas are substances, and not accidents of the thinking spirit, it would still be doubtful whether he has wholly enumerated, or conclusively refuted, the possible hypotheses as to their existence in the mind. And his more direct reasonings labour under the same difficulty from the manifest incapacity of our understandings to do more than form conjectures and dim notions of what we can so imperfectly bring before them.

58. The fourth and fifth books of the Recherche de la Vérité treat of the natural inclinations and passions, and of the errors which spring from those sources. These books are various and discursive, and very characteristic of the author's mind; abounding with a mystical theology, which extends to an absolute negation of secondary causes, as well as with poignant satire on the follies of mankind. In every part of his treatise, but especially in these books, Malebranche pursues with unsparing ridicule two classes, the men of learning, and the men of the world. With Aristotle and the whole school of his disciples he has an inveterate quarrel, and omits no occasion of holding them forth to contempt. This seems to have been in a great measure warranted by their dogmatism, their bigotry, their pertinacious resistance to modern science, especially to the Cartesian philosophy, which Malebranche in general followed. "Let them," he exclaims, "prove, if they can, that Aristotle, or any of themselves, has deduced one truth in physical philosophy from any principle peculiar to himself, and we will promise never to speak of him but in eulogy."[1] But, until this gauntlet should be taken up, he thought himself at liberty to use very different language. "The works of the Stagirite," he observes, "are so obscure and full of indefinite words, that we have a colour for ascribing to him the most opposite opinions. In fact, we make him say what we please, because he says very

[1] L. iv. c. 3.

little, though with much parade; just as children fancy
bells to say anything, because they make a great noise,
and in reality say nothing at all."

59. But such philosophers are not the only class of
the learned he depreciates. Those who pass their time
in gazing through telescopes, and distribute provinces
in the moon to their friends, those who pore over
worthless books, such as the Rabbinical and other Oriental writers, or compose folio volumes on the animals
mentioned in Scripture, while they can hardly tell what
are found in their own province, those who accumulate
quotations to inform us not of truth, but of what other
men have taken for truth, are exposed to his sharp, but
doubtless exaggerated and unreasonable ridicule. Malebranche, like many men of genius, was much too intolerant of what might give pleasure to other men, and
too narrow in his measure of utility. He seems to think
little valuable in human learning but metaphysics and
algebra.[k] From the learned he passes to the great, and
after enumerating the circumstances which obstruct
their perception of truth, comes to the blunt conclusion
that men "much raised above the rest by rank, dignity,
or wealth, or whose minds are occupied in gaining these
advantages, are remarkably subject to error, and hardly
capable of discerning any truths which lie a little out of
the common way."[m]

60. The sixth and last book announces a method of
directing our pursuit of truth, by which we may avoid
the many errors to which our understandings are liable.
It promises to give them all the perfection of which our
nature is capable, by prescribing the rules we should

[k] It is rather amusing to find that,
while lamenting the want of a review of
books, he predicts that we shall never
see one, on account of the prejudice of
mankind in favour of authors. The pro-
phecy was falsified almost at the time.
On regarde ordinairement les auteurs
comme des hommes rares et extraor-
dinaires, et [beaucoup élevés au-dessus
des autres; on les révère donc au lieu
de les mépriser et de les punir. Ainsi
il n'y a guères d'apparence que les
hommes érigent jamais un tribunal pour
examiner et pour condamner tous les
livres, qui ne font que corrompre la
raison. c. 8.

La plupart de livres de certains savans
ne sont fabriqués qu'à coups de diction-
naires, et ils n'ont guères lû que les
tables des livres qu'ils citent, ou quelques
lieux communs, ramassés de différens
auteurs. On n'oseroit entrer d'avan-
tage dans le détail de ces choses, ni en
donner des exemples, de peur de choquer
des personnes aussi fières et aussi bi-
lieuses que sont ces faux savans; car on
ne prend pas plaisir à se faire injurier en
Grec et en Arabe.   [m] C. 9.

invariably observe.   But it must, I think, be confessed
that there is less originality in this method than we
might expect.   We find, however, many · acute and
useful, if not always novel, observations on the conduct
of the understanding, and it may be reckoned among
the books which would supply materials for what is still
wanting to philosophical literature, an ample and useful
logic.   We are so frequently inattentive, he observes,
especially to the pure ideas of the understanding, that
all resources should be employed to fix our thoughts.
And for this purpose we may make use of the passions,
the senses, or the imagination, but the second with less
danger than the first, and the third than the second.
Geometrical figures he ranges under the aids supplied to
the imagination rather than to the senses.   He dwells
much at length on the utility of geometry in fixing our
attention, and of algebra in compressing and arranging
our thoughts.   All sciences, he well remarks (and I do
not know that it had been said before), which treat of
things distinguishable by more or less in quantity, and
which consequently may be represented by extension,
are capable of illustration by diagrams.   But these, he
conceives, are inapplicable to moral truths, though sure
consequences may be derived from them.   Algebra,
however, is far more useful in improving the understanding than geometry, and is in fact, with its sister
arithmetic, the best means that we possess."   But as men
like better to exercise the imagination than the pure

" L. vi. c. 4.   All conceptions of abstract ideas, he justly remarks in another
place, are accompanied with some imagination, though we are often not aware
of it, because these ideas have no natural
images or traces associated with them,
but such only as the will of man or
chance has given.   Thus, in analysis,
however general the ideas, we use letters
and signs always associated with the
ideas of the things, though they are not
really related, and for this reason do not
give us false and confused notions.
Hence, he thinks, the ideas of things
which can only be perceived by the understanding may become associated with
the traces on the brain, l. v., c. 2.   This
is evidently as applicable to language as
it is to algebra.

Cudworth has a somewhat similar remark in his Immutable Morality, that
the cogitations we have of corporeal
things are usually, in his technical style,
both noematical and phantasmatical together, the one being as it were the soul,
and the other the body of them.   "Whenever we think of a phantasmatical universal or universalised phantasm, or a thing
which we have no clear intellection of
(as, for example, of the nature of a rose
in general), there is a complication of
something noematical and something
phantasmatical together; for phantasms
themselves as well as sensations are always individual things."   p. 143.—[See
also the quotation from Gassendi, supra,
§ 16.—1842.]

H 2

intellect, geometry is the more favourite study of the two.

61. Malebranche may, perhaps, be thought to have occupied too much of our attention at the expense of more popular writers. But for this very reason, that the Recherche de la Vérité is not at present much read, I have dwelt long on a treatise of so great celebrity in its own age, and which, even more perhaps than the metaphysical writings of Descartes, has influenced that department of philosophy. Malebranche never loses sight of the great principle of the soul's immateriality, even in his long and rather hypothetical disquisitions on the instrumentality of the brain in acts of thought; and his language is far less objectionable on this subject than that of succeeding philosophers. He is always consistent and clear in distinguishing the soul itself from its modifications and properties. He knew well and had deeply considered the application of mathematical and physical science to the philosophy of the human mind. He is very copious and diligent in illustration, and very clear in definition. His principal errors, and the sources of them in his peculiar temperament, have appeared in the course of these pages. And to these we may add his maintaining some Cartesian paradoxes, such as the system of vortices, and the want of sensation in brutes. The latter he deduced from the immateriality of a thinking principle, supposing it incredible, though he owns it had been the tenet of Augustin, that there could be an immaterial spirit in the lower animals, and also from the incompatibility of any unmerited suffering with the justice of God.° Nor was Malebranche exempt from some prejudices of scholastic theology; and though he generally took care to avoid its technical language, is content to repel the objection to his denial of all secondary causation from its making God the sole author of sin, by saying that sin, being a privation of righteousness, is negative, and consequently requires no cause.

62. Malebranche bears a striking resemblance to his great contemporary Pascal, though they were not, I

Character of Malebranche.

° This he had borrowed from a maxim of Augustin : sub justo Deo quisquam nisi mereatur, miser esse non potest ; whence, it seems, that father had inferred the imputation of original sin to infants; a happy mode of escaping the difficulty.

believe, in any personal relation to each other, nor could
either have availed himself of the other's Compared
writings. Both of ardent minds, endowed with with Pascal.
strong imagination and lively wit, sarcastic, severe,
fearless, disdainful of popular opinion and accredited
reputations; both imbued with the notion of a vast
difference between the original and actual state of man,
and thus solving many phænomena of his being; both,
in different modes and degrees, sceptical, and rigorous
in the exaction of proof; both undervaluing all human
knowledge beyond the regions of mathematics; both of
rigid strictness in morals, and a fervid enthusiastic
piety. But in Malebranche there is a less overpowering
sense of religion; his eye roams unblenched in the
light, before which that of Pascal had been veiled in
awe; he is sustained by a less timid desire of truth, by
greater confidence in the inspirations that are breathed
into his mind; he is more quick in adopting a novel
opinion, but less apt to embrace a sophism in defence of
an old one; he has less energy, but more copiousness
and variety.

63. Arnauld, who, though at first in personal friendship with Malebranche, held no friendship in a Arnauld on
balance with his steady love of truth, combated true and
the chief points of the other's theory in a trea- false ideas.
tise on True and False Ideas. This work I have never
had the good fortune to see; it appears to assail a
leading principle of Malebranche, the separate existence
of ideas, as objects in the mind, independent and distinguishable from the sensation itself. Arnauld maintained, as Reid and others have since done, that we do
not perceive or feel ideas, but real objects, and thus led
the way to a school which has been called that of Scot-
land, and has had a great popularity among our later
metaphysicians. It would require a critical examination of his work, which I have not been able to make,
to determine precisely what were the opinions of this
philosopher.[P]

64. The peculiar hypothesis of Malebranche, that we

[P] Brucker; Buhle; Reid's Intellectual
Powers. [But see what Sir W. Hamilton has said in Edinb. Rev., vol. lii., and
in his edition of Reid, p. 296 et alibi.
Though Arnauld denied the *separate* existence of ideas, as held by Malebranche,
he admitted them as modifications of the
mind, and supposed, like Descartes and
most others, that perception of external
objects is representation, and not intuition.—1847.]

see all things in God, was examined by Locke in a short piece, contained in the collection of his works. It will readily be conceived that two philosophers, one eminently mystical, and endeavouring upon this highly transcendental theme to grasp in his mind and express in his language something beyond the faculties of man, the other as characteristically averse to mystery, and slow to admit anything without proof, would have hardly any common ground even to fight upon. Locke, therefore, does little else than complain that he cannot understand what Malebranche has advanced; and most of his readers will probably find themselves in the same position.

Norris.

65. He had, however, an English supporter of some celebrity in his own age, Norris; a disciple, and one of the latest we have had, of the Platonic school of Henry More. The principal metaphysical treatise of Norris, his Essay on the Ideal World, was published in two parts, 1701 and 1702. It does not therefore come within our limits. Norris is more thoroughly Platonic than Malebranche, to whom, however, he pays great deference, and adopts his fundamental hypothesis of seeing all things in God. He is a writer of fine genius and a noble elevation of moral sentiments, such as predisposes men for the Platonic schemes of theosophy. He looked up to Augustin with as much veneration as to Plato, and respected, more perhaps than Malebranche, certainly more than the generality of English writers, the theological metaphysicians of the schools. With these he mingled some visions of a later mysticism. But his reasonings will seldom bear a close scrutiny.

Pascal.

66. In the Thoughts of Pascal we find many striking remarks on the logic of that science with which he was peculiarly conversant, and upon the general foundations of certainty. He had reflected deeply upon the sceptical objections to all human reasoning, and, though sometimes out of a desire to elevate religious faith at its expense, he seems to consider them unanswerable, he was too clear-headed to believe them just. "Reason," he says, "confounds the dogmatists, and nature the sceptics."[q] "We have an incapacity of

[q] Œuvres de Pascal, vol. i. p. 205.

demonstration, which the one cannot overcome: we have a conception of truth which the others cannot disturb."[r] He throws out a notion of a more complete method of reasoning than that of geometry, wherein everything shall be demonstrated, which however he holds to be unattainable;[s] and perhaps on this account he might think the cavils of pyrrhonism invincible by pure reason. But as he afterwards admits that we may have a full certainty of propositions that cannot be demonstrated, such as the infinity of number and space, and that such incapability of direct proof is rather a perfection than a defect, this notion of a greater completeness in evidence seems neither clear nor consistent.[t]

67. Geometry, Pascal observes, is almost the only subject as to which we find truths wherein all men agree. And one cause of this is that geometers alone regard the true laws of demonstration. These, as enumerated by him, are eight in number. 1. To define nothing which cannot be expressed in clearer terms than those in which it is already expressed: 2. To leave no obscure or equivocal terms undefined: 3. To employ in the definition no terms not already known: 4. To omit nothing in the principles from which we argue unless we are sure it is granted: 5. To lay down no axiom which is not perfectly evident: 6. To demonstrate nothing which is as clear already as we can make it: 7. To prove everything in the least doubtful, by means of self-evident axioms, or of propositions already demonstrated: 8. To substitute mentally the definition instead of the thing defined. Of these rules, he says, the first, fourth, and sixth are not absolutely necessary in order to avoid error, but the other five are indispensable. Yet, though they may be found in books of logic, none but the geometers have paid any regard to them. The authors of these books seem not to have entered into the spirit of their own precepts. All other rules than those he has given are useless or mischievous; they contain, he says, the whole art of demonstration.[u]

---

[r] P. 208.
[s] Pensées de Pascal, part I. art. 2.
[t] Comme la cause qui les rend incapables de démonstration n'est pas leur obscurité, mais au contraire leur extrême évidence, ce manque de preuve n'est pas un défaut, mais plutôt une perfection.
[u] Œuvres de Pascal, i. 66.

68. The reverence of Pascal, like that of Malebranche, for what is established in religion does not extend to philosophy. We do not find in them, as we may sometimes perceive in the present day, all sorts of prejudices against the liberties of the human mind clustering together like a herd of bats, by an instinctive association. He has the same idea as Bacon, that the ancients were properly the children among mankind. Not only each man, he says, advances daily in science, but all men collectively make a constant progress, so that all generations of mankind during so many ages may be considered as one man, always subsisting and always learning ; and the old age of this universal man is not to be sought in the period next to his birth, but in that which is most removed from it. Those we call ancients were truly novices in all things; and we who have added to all they knew the experience of so many succeeding ages, have a better claim to that antiquity which we revere in them. In this, with much ingenuity and much truth, there is a certain mixture of fallacy, which I shall not wait to point out.

69. The genius of Pascal was admirably fitted for acute observation on the constitution of human nature, if he had not seen everything through a refracting medium of religious prejudice. When this does not interfere to bias his judgment he abounds with fine remarks, though always a little tending towards severity. One of the most useful and original is the following : " When we would show any one that he is mistaken, our best course is to observe on what side he considers the subject, for his view of it is generally right on this side, and admit to him that he is right so far. He will be satisfied with this acknowledgment that he was not wrong in his judgment, but only inadvertent in not looking at the whole of the case. For we are less ashamed of not having seen the whole, than of being deceived in what we do see ; and this may perhaps arise from an impossibility of the understanding's being deceived in what it does see, just as the perceptions of the senses, as such, must be always true." [x]

---

[x] Œuvres de Pascal, p. 149. Though Pascal here says that the perceptions of the senses are always true, we find the contrary asserted in other passages ; he is not uniformly consistent with himself.

70. The Cartesian philosophy has been supposed to have produced a metaphysician very divergent in most of his theory from that school, Benedict Spinosa. No treatise is written in a more rigidly geometrical method than his Ethics. It rests on definitions and axioms, from which the propositions are derived in close, brief, and usually perspicuous demonstrations. The few explanations he has thought necessary are contained in scholia. Thus a fabric is erected, astonishing and bewildering in its entire effect, yet so regularly constructed, that the reader must pause and return on his steps to discover an error in the workmanship, while he cannot also but acknowledge the good faith and intimate persuasion of having attained the truth, which the acute and deep-reflecting author every where displays. *Spinosa's Ethics.*

71. Spinosa was born in 1632; we find by his correspondence with Oldenburg in 1661, that he had already developed his entire scheme, and in that with De Vries in 1663, the propositions of the Ethics are alluded to numerically, as we now read them.[y] It was therefore the fruit of early meditation, as its fearlessness, its general disregard of the slow process of observation, its unhesitating dogmatism, might lead us to expect. In what degree he had availed himself of prior writers is not evident; with Descartes and Lord Bacon he was familiar, and from the former he had derived some leading tenets; but he observes both in him and Bacon what he calls mistakes as to the first cause and origin of things, their ignorance of the real nature of the human mind, and of the true sources of error.[z] The pantheistic theory of Jordano Bruno is not very remote from that of Spinosa; but the rhapsodies of the Italian, who seldom aims at proof, can hardly have supplied much to the subtle mind of the Jew of Amsterdam. Buhle has given us an exposition of the Spinosistic theory.[a] But several propositions in this I do not find in the author, and Buhle has at least, without any necessity, entirely deviated from the arrangement he *Its general originality.*

[y] Spinosæ Opera Posthuma, p. 398, 460.

[z] Cartes et Bacon tam longè a cognitione primæ causæ et originis omnium rerum aberrarunt. . . . Veram naturam humanæ mentis non cognoverunt . . . . veram causam erroris nunquam operati sunt.

[a] Hist. de la Philosophie, vol. iii. p. 440.

found in the Ethics. This seems as unreasonable in a work so rigorously systematic, as it would be in the elements of Euclid; and I believe the following pages will prove more faithful to the text. But it is no easy task to translate and abridge a writer of such extraordinary conciseness as well as subtlety; nor is it probable that my attempt will be intelligible to those who have not habituated themselves to metaphysical inquiry.

72. The first book or part of the Ethics is entitled View of his Concerning God, and contains the entire theory metaphysi- of Spinosa. It may even be said that this is cal theory. found in a few of the first propositions; which being granted, the rest could not easily be denied; presenting, as they do, little more than new aspects of the former, or evident deductions from them. Upon eight definitions and seven axioms reposes this philosophical superstructure. A substance, by the third definition, is that, the conception of which does not require the conception of anything else as antecedent to it.[b] The attribute of a substance is whatever the mind perceives to constitute its essence.[c] The mode of a substance is its accident or affection, by means of which it is conceived.[d] In the sixth definition he says, I understand by the name of God a being absolutely infinite; that is, a substance consisting of infinite attributes, each of which expresses an eternal and infinite essence. Whatever expresses an essence, and involves no contradiction, may be predicated of an absolutely infinite being.[e] The most important of the axioms are the following: From a given determinate cause the effect necessarily follows; but if there be no determinate cause, no effect can follow.——The knowledge of an effect depends upon the

---

[b] Per substantiam intelligo id quod in se est, et per se concipitur; hoc est, id cujus conceptus non indiget conceptu alterius rei, a quo formari debeat. The last words are omitted by Spinosa in a letter to De Vries (p. 463), where he repeats this definition.

[c] Per attributum intelligo id quod intellectus de substantiâ percipit, tanquam ejusdem essentiam constituens.

[d] Per modum intelligo substantiæ affectiones, sive id, quod in alio est, per quod etiam concipitur.

[e] Per Deum intelligo Ens absolutè infinitum, hoc est, substantiam constantem infinitis attributis, quorum unumquodque æternam et infinitam essentiam exprimit. Dico absolutè infinitum, non autem in suo genere; quicquid enim in suo genere tantum infinitum est, infinita de eo attributa negare possumus; quod autem absolutè infinitum est, ad ejus essentiam pertinet, quicquid essentiam exprimit et negationem nullam involvit.

knowledge of the cause, and includes it.—Things that have nothing in common with each other cannot be understood by means of each other; that is, the conception of one does not include that of the other.—A true idea must agree with its object.[f]

73. Spinosa proceeds to his demonstrations upon the basis of these assumptions alone.   Two substances, having different attributes, have nothing in common with each other; and hence one cannot be the cause of the other, since one may be conceived without involving the conception of the other; but an effect cannot be conceived without involving the knowledge of the cause.[g]   It seems to be in this fourth axiom, and in the proposition grounded upon it, that the fundamental fallacy lurks. The relation between a cause and effect is surely something different from our perfect comprehension of it, or indeed from our having any knowledge of it at all; much less can the contrary assertion be deemed axiomatic.   But if we should concede this postulate, it might perhaps be very difficult to resist the subsequent proofs, so ingeniously and with such geometrical rigour are they arranged.

74. Two or more things cannot be distinguished, except by the diversity of their attributes, or by that of their modes.   For there is nothing out of ourselves except substances and their modes.   But there cannot be two substances of the same attribute, since there would be no means of distinguishing them except their modes or affections; and every substance, being prior in order of time to its modes, may be considered independently of them; hence two such substances could not be distinguished at all.   One substance therefore cannot be the cause of another; for they cannot have the same attribute, that is, anything in common with one another.[h]   Every substance therefore is self-caused; that is, its essence implies its existence.[i]   It is also necessarily infinite, for it would otherwise be terminated by some other of the same nature and necessarily existing; ●but two substances cannot have the same attribute, and therefore cannot both possess necessary existence.[k]   The more reality or existence any being

---

f Axiomata, iii. iv. v. and vi.   h Prop. vi.   i Prop. vii.
g Prop. ii. and iii.   k Prop. viii.

possesses, the more attributes are to be ascribed to it.
This, he says, appears by the definition of an attribute.[m]
The proof however is surely not manifest, nor do we
clearly apprehend what he meant by degrees of reality
or existence.   But of this theorem he was very proud.
I look upon the demonstration, he says in a letter, as
capital (palmariam), that the more attributes we ascribe
to any being, the more we are compelled to acknowledge
its existence; that is, the more we conceive it as true
and not a mere chimera.[n]   And from this he derived the
real existence of God, though the former proof seems
collateral to it.   God, or a substance consisting of infinite attributes, each expressing an eternal and infinite
power, necessarily exists.[o]   For such an essence involves
existence.   And, besides this, if anything does not exist,
a cause must be given for its non-existence, since this
requires one as much as existence itself.[p]   The cause
may be either in the nature of the thing, as, e. gr. a
square circle cannot exist by the circle's nature, or in
something extrinsic.   But neither of these can prevent
the existence of God.   The later propositions in Spinosa
are chiefly obvious corollaries from the definitions and
a few of the first propositions which contain the whole
theory, which he proceeds to expand.

75. There can be no substance but God.   Whatever
is, is in God, and nothing can be conceived without
God.[q]   For he is the sole substance, and modes cannot
be conceived without a substance; but besides substance
and mode nothing exists.   God is not corporeal, but
body is a mode of God, and therefore uncreated.   God
is the permanent, but not the transient cause of all
things.[r]   He is the efficient cause of their essence, as
well as their existence, since otherwise their essence
might be conceived without God, which has been shown
to be absurd.   Thus particular things are but the affections of God's attributes, or modes in which they are
determinately expressed.[s]

[m] Prop. ix.
[n] P. 463.   This is in the letter to De
Vries, above quoted.
[o] Prop. xi.
[p] If twenty men exist, neither more
nor less, an extrinsic reason must be
given for this precise number, since the
definition of a man does not involve it.
Prop. viii.   Schol. ii.
[q] Prop. xiv.
[r] Deus est omnium rerum causa im-
manens, sed non transiens.   Prop. xviii.
[s] Prop. xxv. and Coroll.

76. This pantheistic scheme is the fruitful mother of many paradoxes, upon which Spinosa proceeds to dwell. There is no contingency, but everything is determined by the necessity of the divine nature, both as to its existence and operation; nor could anything be produced by God otherwise than as it is.[t] His power is the same as his essence; for he is the necessary cause both of himself and of all things, and it is as impossible for us to conceive him not to act as not to exist.[u] God, considered in the attributes of his infinite substance, is the same as nature, that is, *natura naturans;* but nature, in another sense, or *natura naturata*, expresses but the modes under which the divine attributes appear.[x] And intelligence, considered in act, even though infinite, should be referred to *natura naturata;* for intelligence, in this sense, is but a mode of thinking, which can only be conceived by means of our conception of thinking in the abstract, that is, by an attribute of God.[y] The faculty of thinking, as distinguished from the act, as also those of desiring, loving, and the rest, Spinosa explicitly denies to exist at all.

77. In an appendix to the first chapter, De Deo, Spinosa controverts what he calls the prejudice about final causes. Men are born ignorant of causes, but merely conscious of their own appetites, by which they desire their own good. Hence they only care for the final cause of their own actions or those of others, and inquire no farther when they are satisfied about these. And finding many things in themselves and in nature, serving as means to a certain good, which things they know not to be provided by themselves, they have believed that some one has provided them, arguing from the analogy of the means which they in other instances themselves employ. Hence they have imagined gods, and these gods they suppose to consult the good of men in order to be worshipped by them, and have devised every mode of superstitious devotion to ensure the favour of these divinities. And finding in the midst of so many beneficial things in nature not a few of an opposite effect, they have ascribed them to the anger of the gods on

---

[t] Prop. xxix.-xxxiii.
[u] Prop. xxxix., and part ii. prop. iii. Schol.

[x] Schol. in prop. xxix.
[y] Prop. xxxi. The atheism of Spinosa is manifest from this single proposition.

account of the neglect of men to worship them; nor
has experience of calamities falling alike on the pious
and impious cured them of this belief, choosing rather
to acknowledge their ignorance of the reason why good
and evil are thus distributed, than to give up their
theory. Spinosa thinks the hypothesis of final causes
refuted by his proposition that all things happen by
eternal necessity. Moreover, if God were to act for an
end, he must desire something which he wants; for it
is acknowledged by theologians that he acts for his own
sake, and not for the sake of things created.

78. Men having satisfied themselves that all things
were created for them, have invented names to distinguish that as good which tends to their benefit; and believing themselves free, have gotten the notions of right
and wrong, praise and dispraise. And when they can
easily apprehend and recollect the relations of things,
they call them well ordered, if not, ill ordered; and then
say that God created all things in order, as if order were
any thing except in regard to our imagination of it; and
thus they ascribe imagination to God himself, unless they
mean that he created things for the sake of our imagining
them.

79. It has been sometimes doubted whether the Spinosistic philosophy excludes altogether an infinite intelligence. That it rejects a moral providence or creative
mind is manifest in every proposition. His Deity could
at most be but a cold passive intelligence, lost to our
understandings and feelings in its metaphysical infinity.
It was not, however, in fact so much as this. It is true
that in a few passages we find what seems at first a dim
recognition of the fundamental principle of theism. In
one of his letters to Oldenburg, he asserts an infinite
power of thinking, which, considered in its infinity, embraces all nature as its object, and of which the thoughts
proceed according to the order of nature, being its correlative ideas.* But afterwards he rejected the term,

---

* Statuo dari in naturâ potentiam
infinitam cogitandi quæ quatenus infinita in se continet totam naturam ob-
jectivè, et cujus cogitationes procedunt
eodem modo ac natura, ejus nimirum
edictum. p. 441. In another place he
says, perhaps at some expense of his

usual candour, Agnosco interim, id quod
summam mihi præbet satisfactionem et
mentis tranquillitatem, cuncta potentia
Entis summè perfecti et ejus immutabili
ita fieri decreto. p. 498. What follows
is in the same strain. But Spinosa had
wrought himself up, like Bruno, to a

power of thinking, altogether. The first proposition of the second part of the Ethics, or that entitled On the Mind, runs thus : Thought is an attribute of God, or, God is a thinking being. Yet this, when we look at the demonstration, vanishes in an abstraction destructive of personality.* And in fact we cannot reflect at all on the propositions already laid down by Spinosa, without perceiving that they annihilate every possible hypothesis in which the being of a God can be intelligibly stated.'

80. The second book of the Ethics begins, like the first, with definitions and axioms. Body he defines to be a certain and determinate mode expressing the essence of God, considered as extended. The essence of anything he defines to be that, according to the affirmation or negation of which the thing exists or otherwise. An idea is a conception which the mind forms as a thinking being. And he would rather say conception than perception, because the latter seems to imply the presence of an object. In the third axiom he says, Modes of thinking, such as love, desire, or whatever name we may give to the affections of the mind, cannot exist without an idea of their object, but an idea may exist with no other mode of thinking.[b] And in the fifth : We perceive no singular things besides bodies and modes of thinking ; thus distinguishing, like Locke, between ideas of sensation and of reflection.

81. Extension, by the second proposition, is an attribute of God as well as thought. As it follows from the infinite extension of God, that all bodies are portions of his substance, inasmuch as they cannot be conceived without it, so all particular acts of intelligence are portions of God's infinite intelligence, and thus all things are in him. Man is not a substance, but something which is in God, and cannot be conceived without him ; that is,

mystical personification of his infinite unity.

* Singulares cogitationes, sive hæc et illa cogitatio, modi sunt, qui Dei naturam certo et determinato modo exprimunt. Competit ergo Dei attributum, cujus conceptum singulares omnes cogitationes involvunt, per quod etiam concipiuntur. Est igitur cogitatio unum ex infinitis Dei attributis quod Dei æternam et infinitam essentiam exprimit, sive Deus est res cogitans.

b Modi cogitandi, ut amor, cupiditas, vel quocunque nomine affectus animi insigniuntur, non dantur nisi in eodem individuo detur idea rei amatæ, desideratæ, &c. At idea dari potest, quamvis nullus alius detur cogitandi modus.

an affection or mode of the divine substance expressing its nature in a determinate manner.[c] The human mind is not a substance, but an idea constitutes its actual being, and it must be the idea of an existing thing.[d] In this he plainly loses sight of the percipient in the perception; but it was the inevitable result of the fundamental sophisms of Spinosa to annihilate personal consciousness. The human mind, he afterwards asserts, is part of the infinite intellect of God; and when we say, the mind perceives this or that, it is only that God, not as infinite, but so far as he constitutes the essence of the human mind, has such or such ideas.[e]

82. The object of the human mind is body actually existing.[f] He proceeds to explain the connexion of the human body with the mind, and the association of ideas. But in all this, advancing always synthetically and by demonstration, he becomes frequently obscure if not sophistical. The idea of the human mind is in God, and is united to the mind itself in the same manner as the latter is to the body.[g] The obscurity and subtilty of this proposition are not relieved by the demonstration; but in some of these passages we may observe a singular approximation to the theory of Malebranche. Both, though with very different tenets on the highest subjects, had been trained in the same school; and if Spinosa had brought himself to acknowledge the personal distinctness of the Supreme Being from his intelligent creation, he might have passed for one of those mystical theosophists who were not averse to an objective pantheism.

83. The mind does not know itself, except so far as it receives ideas of the affections of the body.[h] But these ideas of sensation do not give an adequate knowledge of an external body, nor of the human body itself.[i] The mind therefore has but an inadequate and confused know-

---

[c] Prop. x.

[d] Quod actuale mentis humanæ esse constituit, nihil aliud est quam idea rei alicujus singularis actu existentis. This is an anticipation of what we find in Hume's Treatise on Human Nature, the negation of a substance, or Ego, to which paradox no one can come except a professed metaphysician.

[e] Prop. xl., coroll.

[f] Prop. xiii.

[g] Mentis humanæ datur etiam in Deo idea, sive cognitio, quæ in Deo eodem modo sequitur, et ad Deum eodem modo refertur, ac idea sive cognitio corporis humani. Prop. xx. Hæc mentis idea eodem modo unita est menti, ac ipsa mens unita est corpori.

[h] Prop. xxiii.

[i] Prop. xxv.

ledge of anything, so long as it judges only by fortuitous perceptions; but may attain one clear and distinct by internal reflection and comparison.[k] No positive idea can be called false; for there can be no such idea without God, and all ideas in God are true, that is, correspond with their object.[m] Falsity, therefore, consists in that privation of truth which arises from inadequate ideas. An adequate idea he has defined to be one which contains no incompatibility, without regard to the reality of its supposed correlative object.

84. All bodies agree in some things, or have something in common: of these all men have adequate ideas;[n] and this is the origin of what are called common notions, which all men possess; as extension, duration, number. But to explain the nature of universals, Spinosa observes, that the human body can only form at the same time a certain number of distinct images; if this number be exceeded, they become confused; and as the mind perceives distinctly just so many images as can be formed in the body, when these are confused the mind will also perceive them confusedly, and will comprehend them under one attribute, as Man, Horse, Dog; the mind perceiving a number of such images, but not their differences of stature, colours, and the like. And these notions will not be alike in all minds, varying according to the frequency with which the parts of the complex image have occurred. Thus those who have contemplated most frequently the erect figure of man will think of him as a perpendicular animal, others as two-legged, others as unfeathered, others as rational. Hence so many disputes among philosophers who have tried to explain natural things by mere images.[o]

85. Thus we form universal ideas; first by singulars, represented by the senses confusedly, imperfectly, and disorderly; secondly, by signs, that is, by associating the remembrance of things with words; both of which he calls imagination, or primi generis cognitio; thirdly, by what he calls reason, or secundi generis cognitio; and fourthly, by intuitive knowledge, or tertii generis cognitio.[p] Knowledge of the first kind, or imagination, is the only source of error; the second and third being

k Schol., prop. xxix.　　　　　　　　n Prop. viii.　　o Schol., prop. xl.
m Prop. xxxii., xxxiii., xxxv.　　　　p Schol. ii., prop. xl.
VOL. IV.　　　　　　　　　　　　　　　　　　　　　I

necessarily true.[q]　These alone enable us to distinguish truth from falsehood.　Reason contemplates things not as contingent but necessary; and whoever has a true idea, knows certainly that his idea is true.　Every idea of a singular existing thing involves the eternal and infinite being of God.　For nothing can be conceived without God, and the ideas of all things, having God for their cause, considered under the attribute of which they are modes, must involve the conception of the attribute, that is, the being of God.[r]

86. It is highly necessary to distinguish images, ideas, and words, which many confound.　Those who think ideas consist in images which they perceive, fancy that ideas of which we can form no image are but arbitrary figments.　They look at ideas as pictures on a tablet, and hence do not understand that an idea, as such, involves an affirmation or negation.　And those who confound words with ideas, fancy they can will something contrary to what they perceive, because they can affirm or deny it in words.　But these prejudices will be laid aside by him who reflects that thought does not involve the conception of extension; and therefore that an idea, being a mode of thought, neither consists in images nor in words, the essence of which consists in corporeal motions, not involving the conception of thought.[s]

87. The human mind has an adequate knowledge of the eternal and infinite being of God.　But men cannot imagine God as they can bodies, and hence have not that clear perception of his being which they have of that of bodies, and have also perplexed themselves by associating the word God with sensible images, which it is hard to avoid.　This is the chief source of all error, that men do not apply names to things rightly.　For they do not err in their own minds, but in this application: as men who cast up wrong see different numbers in their minds from those in the true result.[t]

88. The mind has no free will, but is determined by a cause, which itself is determined by some other, and so

[q] Prop. xll., xlii. et sequent.
[r] Prop. xlv.
[s] Schol. prop. xlix.
[t] Prop. xlvii. Atque hinc pleræque oriuntur controversiæ, nempe, quia homines mentem suam non recte explicant, vel quia alterius mentem male interpretantur.

for ever.   For the mind is but a mode of thinking, and therefore cannot be the free cause of its own actions. Nor has it any absolute faculty of loving, desiring, understanding; these being only metaphysical abstractions.[u] Will and understanding are one and the same thing; and volitions are only affirmations or negations, each of which belongs to the essence of the idea affirmed or denied.[x] In this there seems to be not only an extraordinary deviation from common language, but an absence of any meaning which, to my apprehension at least, is capable of being given to his words.   Yet we have seen something of the same kind said by Malebranche; and it will also be found in a recently published work of Cudworth,[y] a writer certainly uninfluenced by either of these, so that it may be suspected of having some older authority.

89. In the third part of this treatise, Spinosa comes to the consideration of the passions.   Most who have written on moral subjects, he says, have rather treated man as something out of nature, or as a kind of imperium in imperio, than as part of the general order.   They have conceived him to enjoy a power of disturbing that order by his own determination, and ascribed his weakness and inconstancy not to the necessary laws of the system, but to some strange defect in himself, which they cease not to lament, deride, or execrate.   But the acts of mankind, and the passions from which they proceed, are in reality but links in the series, and proceed in harmony with the common laws of universal nature.

Spinosa's theory of action and passion.

90. We are said to act when anything takes place within us, or without us, for which we are an adequate cause; that is, when it may be explained by means of our own nature alone.   We are said to be acted upon, when anything takes place within us which cannot wholly be explained by our own nature.   The affections of the body which increase or diminish its power of action, and the ideas of those affections, he denominates passions (affectus).   Neither the body can determine the mind to thinking, nor can the mind determine the body

[u] Prop. xlviii.
[x] Prop. xlix.
[y] See Cudworth's Treatise on Free-will (1838), p. 20, where the will and understanding are purposely, and, I think, very erroneously confounded.

to motion or rest.   For all that takes place in body must be caused by God, considered under his attribute of extension, and all that takes place in mind must be caused by God under his attribute of thinking.   The mind and body are but one thing, considered under different attributes; the order of action and passion in the body being the same in nature with that of action and passion in the mind.   But men, though ignorant how far the natural powers of the body reach, ascribe its operations to the determination of the mind, veiling their ignorance in specious words.   For if they allege that the body cannot act without the mind, it may be answered that the mind cannot think till it is impelled by the body, nor are the volitions of the mind anything else than its appetites, which are modified by the body.

91. All things endeavour to continue in their actual being; this endeavour being nothing else than their essence, which causes them to be, until some exterior cause destroys their being.   The mind is conscious of its own endeavour to continue as it is, which is, in other words, the appetite that seeks self-preservation; what the mind is thus conscious of seeking it judges to be good, and not inversely.   Many things increase or diminish the power of action in the body; and all such things have a corresponding effect on the power of thinking in the mind.   Thus it undergoes many changes, and passes through different stages of more or less perfect power of thinking.   Joy is the name of a passion, in which the mind passes to a greater perfection or power of thinking; grief, one in which it passes to a less.   Spinosa, in the rest of this book, deduces all the passions from these two and from desire; but as the development of his theory is rather long, and we have already seen that its basis is not quite intelligible, it will be unnecessary to dwell longer upon the subject.   His analysis of the passions may be compared with that of Hobbes.

92. Such is the metaphysical theory of Spinosa, in as
Character of concise a form as I have found myself able to
Spinosism. derive it from his Ethics.   It is a remarkable proof, and his moral system will furnish another, how an undeviating adherence to strict reasoning may lead a man of great acuteness and sincerity from the paths of truth.   Spinosa was truly what Voltaire has with rather

less justice called Clarke, a reasoning machine. A few leading theorems, too hastily taken up as axiomatic, were sufficient to make him sacrifice, with no compromise or hesitation, not only every principle of religion and moral right, but the clear intuitive notions of common sense. If there are two axioms more indisputable than any others, they are, that ourselves exist, and that our existence, simply considered, is independent of any other being. Yet both these are lost in the pantheism of Spinosa, as they had always been in that delusive reverie of the imagination. In asserting that the being of the human mind consists in the idea of an existing thing presented to it, this subtle metaphysician fell into the error of the school which he most disdained, as deriving all knowledge from perception, that of the Aristotelians. And, extending this confusion of consciousness with perception to the infinite substance, or substratum of particular ideas, he was led to deny it the self, or conscious personality, without which the name of Deity can only be given in a sense deceptive of the careless reader, and inconsistent with the use of language. It was an equally legitimate consequence of his original sophism to deny all moral agency, in the sense usually received, to the human mind, and even, as we-have seen, to confound action and passion themselves, in all but name, as mere phænomena in the eternal sequence of things.

93. It was one great error of Spinosa to entertain too arrogant a notion of the human faculties, in which, by dint of his own subtle demonstrations, he pretended to show a capacity of adequately comprehending the nature of what he denominated God. And this was accompanied by a rigid dogmatism, no one proposition being stated with hesitation, by a disregard of experience, at least as the basis of reasoning, and by an uniform preference of the synthetic method. Most of those, he says, who have turned their minds to those subjects have fallen into error, because they have not begun with the contemplation of the divine nature, which both in itself and in order of knowledge is first, but with sensible things, which ought to have been last. Hence he seems to have reckoned Bacon, and even Descartes, mistaken in their methods.

94. All pantheism must have originated in overstrain-

ing the infinity of the divine attributes till the moral part of religion was annihilated in its metaphysics. It was the corruption, or rather, if we may venture the phrase, the suicide of theism ; nor could this theory have arisen, except where we know it did arise, among those who had elevated their conceptions above the vulgar polytheism that surrounded them to a sense of the unity of the Divine nature.

95. Spinosa does not essentially differ from the pantheists of old. He conceived, as they had done, that the infinity of God required the exclusion of all other substance ; that he was infinite *ab omni parte*, and not only in certain senses. And probably the loose and hyperbolical tenets of the schoolmen, derived from ancient philosophy, ascribing, as a matter of course, a metaphysical infinity to all the divine attributes, might appear to sanction those primary positions, from which Spinosa, unfettered by religion, even in outward profession, went on " sounding his dim and perilous track " to the paradoxes that have thrown discredit on his name. He had certainly built much on the notion that the essence or definition of the Deity involved his actuality or existence, to which Descartes had given vogue.

96. Notwithstanding the leading errors of this philosopher, his clear and acute understanding perceived many things which baffle ordinary minds. Thus he well saw and well stated the immateriality of thought. Oldenburg, in one of his letters, had demurred to this, and reminded Spinosa that it was still controverted whether thought might not be a bodily motion. " Be it so," replied the other, " though I am far from admitting it ; but at least you must allow that extension, so far as extension, is not the same as thought." [x] It is from inattention to this simple truth that all materialism, as it has been called, has sprung. Its advocates confound the union between thinking and extension or matter (be it, if they will, an indissoluble one) with the identity of the two, which is absurd and inconceivable. " Body," says Spinosa, in one of his definitions, " is not terminated by thinking, nor

---

[x] At als, forte cogitatio est actus corporeus. Sit, quamvis nullus concedam ; sed hoc unum non negabis, extensionem quoad extensionem, non esse cogitationem. Epist. iv.

thinking by body." *   This, also, does not ill express the
fundamental difference of matter and mind; there is an
incommensurability about them, which prevents one from
bounding the other, because they can never be placed in
juxtaposition.

97. England, about the era of the Restoration, began
to make a struggle against the metaphysical   Glanvil's
creed of the Aristotelians, as well as against   Scepsis
their natural philosophy.   A remarkable work,   Scientifica.
but one so scarce as to be hardly known at all, except by
name, was published by Glanvil in 1661, with the title,
The Vanity of Dogmatizing.   A second edition, in 1665,
considerably altered, is entitled Scepsis Scientifica.[b]
This edition has a dedication to the Royal Society, which
comes in place of a fanciful preface, wherein he had ex-
patiated on the bodily and mental perfections of his pro-
toplast, the father of mankind.[c]   But in proportion to
the extravagant language he employs to extol Adam
before his lapse is the depreciation of his unfortunate
posterity, not, as common among theologians, with
respect to their moral nature, but to their reasoning
faculties.   The scheme of Glanvil's book is to display
the ignorance of man, and especially to censure the
Peripatetic philosophy of the schools.   It is, he says,
captious and verbal, and yet does not adhere itself to any
constant sense of words, but huddles together insignificant terms and unintelligible definitions; it deals with
controversies, and seeks for no new discovery or physical
truth.   Nothing, he says, can be demonstrated but when
the contrary is impossible, and of this there are not many

* Corpus dicitur finitum, quia aliud
semper majus concipimus.   Sic cogitatio
alia cogitatione terminatur.   At corpus
non terminatur cogitatione, nec cogitatio
corpore.

b This book, I believe, especially in
the second edition, is exceedingly scarce.
The editors, however, of the Biographia
Britannica, art. Glanvil, had seen it, and
also Dugald Stewart.   The first edition,
or Vanity of Dogmatizing, is in the Bod-
leian Catalogue, and both are in the
British Museum.

c Thus, among other extravagances
worthy of the Talmud, he says, "Adam
needed no spectacles.   The acuteness of
his natural optics (if conjecture may

have credit) showed him much of the
celestial magnificence and bravery without a Galileo's tube; and it is most probable that his naked eyes could reach
near as much of this upper world as we
with all the advantages of art.   It may
be it was as absurd even in the judgment of his senses, that the sun and stars
should be so very much less than this
globe, as the contrary seems in ours: and
it is not unlikely that he had as clear
a perception of the earth's motion as we
have of its quiescence."   p. 5, edit. 1661.
In the second edition, he still adheres to
the hypothesis of intellectual degeneracy,
but states it with less of rhapsody.

instances.   He launches into a strain of what may be
called scepticism ; but answered his purpose in combating the dogmatic spirit still unconquered in our academical schools.   Glanvil had studied the new philosophy, and speaks with ardent eulogy of " that miracle of
men, the illustrious Descartes."   Many, if not most, of his
own speculations are tinged with a Cartesian colouring.
He was, however, far more sceptical than Descartes, or
even than Malebranche. Some passages from so rare and so
acute a work may deserve to be chosen, both for their
own sakes and in order to display the revolution which
was at work in speculative philosophy.

98. " In the unions which we understand the extremes
are reconciled by interceding participations of natures
which have somewhat of either.   But body and spirit
stand at such a distance in their essential compositions
that to suppose an uniter of a middle construction that
should partake of some of the qualities of both is un-
warranted by any of our faculties, yea, most absonous to
our reasons ; since there is not any the least affinity be-
twixt length, breadth, and thickness, and apprehension,
judgment, and discourse ; the former of which are the
most immediate results, if not essentials of matter, the
latter of spirit." [d]

99. " How is it, and by what art does it (the soul)
read that such an image or stroke in matter (whether
that of her vehicle or of the brain, the case is the same)
signifies such an object ?   Did we learn an alphabet in
our embryo state ?   And how comes it to pass that we
are not aware of any such congenite apprehensions ? We
know what we know ; but do we know any more ? That
by diversity of motions we should spell out figures, distances, magnitudes, colours, things not resembled by
them, we must attribute to some secret deduction.   But
what this deduction should be, or by what medium this
knowledge is advanced, is as dark as ignorance.   One
that hath not the knowledge of letters may see the
figures, but comprehends not the meaning included in
them : an infant may hear the sounds and see the motion
of the lips, but hath no conception conveyed by them,
not knowing what they are intended to signify.   So our

---

[d] Scepsis Scientifica, p. 16.   We have just seen something similar in Spinosa.

souls, though they might have perceived the motions and images themselves by simple sense, yet without some implicit inference it seems inconceivable how by that means they should apprehend their antitypes. The striking of divers filaments of the brain cannot well be supposed to represent distances, except some kind of inference be allotted us in our faculties; the concession of which will only stead us as a refuge for ignorance, when we shall meet what we would seem to shun." [e] Glanvil, in this forcible statement of the heterogeneity of sensations with the objects that suggest them, has but trod in the steps of the whole Cartesian school, but he did not mix this up with those crude notions that halt half-way between immaterialism and its opposite; and afterwards well exposes the theories of accounting for the memory by means of images in the brain, which, in various ways, Aristotle, Descartes, Digby, Gassendi, and Hobbes had propounded, and which we have seen so favourite a speculation of Malebranche.

100. It would be easy to quote many paragraphs of uncommon vivacity and acuteness from this forgotten treatise. The style is eminently spirited and eloquent; a little too figurative, like that of Locke, but less blameably, because Glanvil is rather destroying than building up. Every bold and original thought of others finds a willing reception in Glanvil's mind; and his confident impetuous style gives them an air of novelty which makes them pass for his own. He stands forward as a mutineer against authority, against educational prejudice, against reverence for antiquity. [f] No one thinks more intrepidly for himself; and it is probable that, even in what seems mere superstition, he had been rather

---

[e] P. 22, 23.

[f] " Now if we inquire the reason why the mathematics and mechanic arts have so much got the start in growth of other sciences, we shall find it probably resolved into this as one considerable cause, that their progress hath not been retarded by that reverential awe of former discoveries, which hath been so great a hindrance to theoretical improvements. For, as the noble Lord Verulam hath noted, we have a mistaken apprehension of antiquity, calling that so which in truth is the world's non-age. Antiquitas seculi est juventus mundi. 'Twas this vain idolizing of authors which gave birth to that silly vanity of impertinent citations, and inducing authority in things neither requiring nor deserving it.—Methinks it is a pitiful piece of knowledge that can be learned from an index, and a poor ambition to be rich in the inventory of another's treasure. To boast a memory, the most that these pedants can aim at, is but a humble ostentation." p. 104.

misled by some paradoxical hypothesis of his own ardent genius than by slavishly treading in the steps of others.[s]

101. Glanvil sometimes quotes Lord Bacon, but he seems to have had the ambition of contending with the Novum Organum in some of his brilliant passages, and has really developed the doctrine of *idols* with uncommon penetration, as well as force of language. " Our initial age is like the melted wax to the prepared seal, capable of any impression from the documents of our teachers. The half-moon or cross are indifferent to its reception; and we may with equal facility write on this *rasa tabula* Turk or Christian. To determine this indifferency, our first task is to learn the creed of our country, and our next to maintain it. We seldom examine our receptions more than children do their catechisms, but by a careless greediness swallow all at a venture. For implicit faith is a virtue where orthodoxy is the object. Some will not be at the trouble of a trial, others are scared from attempting it. If we do, 'tis not by a sunbeam or ray of light, but by a flame that is kindled by our affections, and fed by the fuel of our anticipations. And thus, like the hermit, we think the sun shines nowhere but in our cell, and all the world to be darkness but ourselves. We judge truth to be circumscribed by the confines of our belief and the doctrines we were brought up in."[h] Few books, I think, are more deserving of being reprinted than the Scepsis Scientifica of Glanvil.

102. Another bold and able attack was made on the His Plus   ancient philosophy by Glanvil in his " Plus Ultra.   Ultra, or the Progress and Advancement of Knowledge since the Days of Aristotle. 1668." His tone is peremptory and imposing, animated and intrepid, such as befits a warrior in literature. Yet he was rather acute by nature than deeply versed in learning, and talks of Vieta and Descartes's algebra so as to show he had little knowledge of the science, or of what they had done

[s] " That the fancy of one man should bind the thoughts of another, and determine them to their particular objects, will be thought impossible; which yet, if we look deeply into the matter, wants not its probability." p. 146. He dwells more on this, but the passage is too long to extract. It is remarkable that he sup-poses a subtle ether (like that of the modern Mesmerists) to be the medium of communication in such cases; and had also a notion of explaining these sympathies by help of the anima mundi, or mundane spirit.

[h] P. 95.

for it.[i] His animosity against Aristotle is unreasonable;
and he was plainly an incompetent judge of that philosopher's general deserts. Of Bacon and Boyle he speaks
with just eulogy. Nothing can be more free and bold
than Glanvil's assertion of the privilege of judging for
himself in religion;[k] and he had doubtless a perfect
right to believe in witchcraft.

103. George Dalgarno, a native of Aberdeen, conceived and, as it seemed to him, carried into
effect, the idea of an universal language and Dalgarno.
character. His Ars Signorum, vulgo Character Universalis et Lingua Philosophica, Lond. 1661, is dedicated
to Charles II., in this philosophical character, which
must have been as great a mystery to the sovereign as
to his subjects. This dedication is followed by a royal
proclamation in good English, inviting all to study this
useful art, which had been recommended by divers
learned men, Wilkins, Wallis, Ward, and others, "judging it to be of singular use for facilitating the matter of
communication and intercourse between people of different languages." The scheme of Dalgarno is funda-
mentally bad, in that he assumes himself, or the authors
he follows, to have given a complete distribution of all
things and ideas; after which his language is only an
artificial scheme of symbols. It is evident that until
objects are truly classified, a representative method of
signs can only rivet and perpetuate error. We have but
to look at his tabular synopsis to see that his ignorance
of physics, in the largest sense of the word, renders his
scheme deficient; and he has also committed the error
of adopting the combinations of the ordinary alphabet,
with a little help from the Greek, which, even with his
slender knowledge of species, soon leave him incapable
of expressing them. But Dalgarno has several acute
remarks; and it deserves especially to be observed that
he anticipated the famous discovery of the Dutch philologers, namely, that all other parts of speech may be
reduced to the noun, dexterously, if not successfully,
resolving the verb-substantive into an affirmative
particle.[m]

i Plus Ultra, p. 24 and 33.
k P. 142.
m Tandem mihi affulsit clarior lux;
accuratius enim examinando omnium no-
tionum analysin logicam, percepi nullam
esse particulam quae non derivetur a

104. Wilkins, bishop of Chester, one of the most ingenious men of his age, published in 1668 his
Essay towards a Philosophical Language, which
has this advantage over that of Dalgarno, that it abandons
the alphabet, and consequently admits of a greater variety
of characters. It is not a new language, but a more
analytical scheme of characters for English. Dalgarno
seems to have known something of it, though he was
the first to publish, and glances at "a more difficult
way of writing English." Wilkins also intimates that
Dalgarno's compendious method would not succeed. His
own has the same fault of a premature classification of
things; and it is very fortunate that neither of these
ingenious but presumptuous attempts to fasten down the
progressive powers of the human mind by the cramps
of association had the least success.[a]

105. But from these partial and now very obscure
endeavours of English writers in metaphysical
philosophy we come at length to the work that
has eclipsed every other, and given to such
inquiries whatever popularity they ever possessed, the Essay of Locke on the Human Understanding.
Neither the writings of Descartes, as I conceive,
nor perhaps those of Hobbes, so far as strictly
metaphysical, had excited much attention in England beyond the class of merely studious men. But the Essay on
Human Understanding was frequently reprinted within
a few years from its publication, and became the acknowledged code of English philosophy.[o] The assaults it

Side notes: Wilkins. | Locke on Human Understanding. | Its merits.

nomine aliquo prædicamentali, et omnes
particulas esse vere casus seu modos no-
tionum nominalium. p. 120. He does
not seem to have arrived at this conclusion by etymological analysis, but by his
own logical theories.

The verb-substantive, he says, is equivalent to *ita*. Thus, Petrus est in domo
means, Petrus—ita—in domo. That is,
it expresses an idea of apposition or
conformity between a subject and predicate. This is a theory to which a man
might be led by the habit of considering
propositions logically, and thus reducing
all verbs to the verb-substantive; and it
is not deficient, at least, in plausibility.

[a] Dalgarno, many years afterwards,
turned his attention to a subject of no

slight interest, even in mere philosophy,
the instruction of the deaf and dumb.
His Didascalocophus is perhaps the first
attempt to found this on the analysis of
language. But it is not so philosophical
as what has since been effected.

[o] It was abridged at Oxford, and used
by some tutors as early as 1695. But
the heads of the university came afterwards to a resolution to discourage the
reading of it. Stillingfleet, among many
others, wrote against the Essay, and
Locke, as is well known, answered the
bishop. I do not know that the latter
makes altogether so poor a figure as has
been taken for granted; but the defence
of Locke will seem in most instances satisfactory. Its success in public opinion

had to endure in the author's lifetime, being deemed to fail, were of service to its reputation; and considerably more than half a century was afterwards to elapse before any writer in our language (nor was the case very different in France, after the patronage accorded to it by Voltaire) could with much chance of success question any leading doctrine of its author. Several circumstances no doubt conspired with its intrinsic excellence to establish so paramount a rule in an age that boasted of peculiar independence of thinking, and full of intelligent and inquisitive spirits. The sympathy of an English public with Locke's tenets as to government and religion was among the chief of these; and the re-action that took place in a large portion of the reading classes towards the close of the eighteenth century turned in some measure the tide even in metaphysical disquisition. It then became fashionable sometimes to accuse Locke of preparing the way for scepticism; a charge which, if it had been truly applicable to some of his opinions, ought rather to have been made against the long line of earlier writers with whom he held them in common; sometimes, with more pretence, to allege that he had conceded too much to materialism; sometimes to point out and exaggerate other faults and errors of his Essay, till we have seemed in danger of forgetting that it is perhaps the first, and still the most complete chart of the human mind which has been laid down, the most ample repertory of truths relating to our intellectual being, and the one book which we are still compelled to name as the most important in metaphysical science.[p]

contributed much to the renown of his work; for Stillingfleet, though not at all conspicuous as a philosopher, enjoyed a great deal of reputation, and the world can seldom understand why a man who excels in one province of literature should fail in another.

[p] [The first endeavour completely to analyse the operations of the human understanding was made by Hobbes, in his Treatise of Human Nature: for, important as are the services of Descartes to psychology, he did not attempt to give a full scheme. Gassendi, in his different writings, especially in the Syntagma Philosophicum, seems to have had as extensive an object in view: but his investigation was neither so close, nor perhaps so complete, as that of our countryman. Yet even in this remarkable work of Hobbes, we find accounts of some principal faculties of the mind so brief and unsatisfactory, and so much wholly omitted, that Locke can hardly be denied the praise of having first gone painfully over the whole ground, and, as far as the merely intellectual part of man is concerned, explained in a great degree the various phænomena of his nature and the sources of his knowledge. Much allowance ought to be made by every candid reader for the defects of a book

Locke had not, it may be said, the luminous perspicacity of language we find in Descartes, and, when he does not soar too high, in Malebranche; but he had more judgment, more caution, more patience, more freedom from paradox, and from the sources of paradox, vanity and love of system, than either. We have no denial of sensation to brutes, no reference of mathematical truths to the will of God, no oscillation between the extremes of doubt and of positiveness, no bewildering mysticism. Certainly neither Gassendi nor even Hobbes could be compared with him; and it might be asked of the admirers of later philosophers, those of Berkeley, or Hume, or Hartley, or Reid, or Stewart, or Brown, without naming any on the continent of Europe, whether, in the extent or originality of their researches, any of these names ought to stand on a level with that of Locke. One of the greatest whom I have mentioned, and one who, though candid towards Locke, had no prejudice whatever in his favour, has extolled the first two books of the Essay on Human Understanding, which yet he deems in many respects inferior to the third and fourth, as "a precious accession to the theory of the human mind; as the richest contribution of well-observed and well-described facts which was ever bequeathed by a single individual; and as the indisputable, though not always acknowledged, source of some of the most refined conclusions with respect to the intellectual phænomena, which have been since brought to light by succeeding inquirers." [q]

which was written with so little aid from earlier inquirers, and displays throughout so many traces of an original mind. The bearings in our first voyages of discovery were not all laid down as correctly as at present. It is not pleasant to observe, that neither on the continent, nor, what is much worse, in Britain, has sufficient regard been paid to this consideration.—1847.]

[q] Stewart's Preliminary Dissertation to Encyclopædia Britannica, part ii.

[No one seems to have so much anticipated Locke, if we can wholly rely on the analysis of a work unpublished, and said to be now lost, as Father Paul Sarpi. This is a short treatise, entitled Arte di

ben Pensare, an extract from the analysis of which by Marco Foscarini is given in Sarpi's Life, by Bianchi Giovini, vol. i. p. 81. We have here not only the derivation of ideas from sense, but from reflection; the same theory as to substance, the formation of genera and species, the association of ideas, the same views as to axioms and syllogisms. But as the Italian who has given us this representation of Father Paul's philosophy had Locke before him, and does not quote his own author's words, we may suspect that he has somewhat exaggerated the resemblance. I do not think that any nation is more prone to claim every feather from the wings of other birds.—1847.]

106. It would be an unnecessary prolixity to offer in this place an analysis of so well-known a book as the Essay on the Human Understanding. Few have turned their attention to metaphysical inquiries without reading it. It has however no inconsiderable faults, which, though much over-balanced, are not to be passed over in a general eulogy. The style of Locke is wanting in philosophical precision ; it is a good model of the English language ; but too idiomatic and colloquial, too indefinite and figurative, for the abstruse subjects with which he has to deal. We miss in every page the translucent simplicity of his great French predecessors. This seems to have been owing, in a considerable degree, to an excessive desire of popularising the subject, and shunning the technical pedantry which had repelled the world from intellectual philosophy. Locke displays in all his writings a respect which can hardly be too great, for men of sound understanding unprejudiced by authority, mingled with a scorn, perhaps a little exaggerated, of the gown-men or learned world ; little suspecting that the same appeal to the people, the same policy of setting up equivocal words and loose notions, called the common sense of mankind, to discomfit subtle reasoning, would afterwards be turned against himself, as it was, very unfairly and unsparingly, by Reid and Beattie. Hence he falls a little into a laxity of phrase, not unusual, and not always important, in popular and practical discourse, but an inevitable source of confusion in the very abstract speculations which his Essay contains. And it may perhaps be suspected, without disparagement to his great powers, that he did not always preserve the utmost distinctness of conception, and was liable, as almost every other metaphysician has been, to be entangled in the ambiguities of language.

Its defects.

107. The leading doctrine of Locke, as is well known, is the derivation of all our *simple* ideas from sensation and from reflection. The former present, comparatively, no great difficulty ; but he is not very clear or consistent about the latter. He seems in general to limit the word to the various operations of our own minds in thinking, believing, willing, and so forth. This, as has been shown for-

Origin of ideas, according to Locke.

merly, is taken from, or at least coincident with, the
theory of Gassendi in his Syntagma Philosophicum.   It
is highly probable that Locke was acquainted with that
work; if not immediately, yet through the account of
the philosophy of Gassendi, published in English by
Dr. Charleton, in 1663, which I have not seen, or through
the excellent and copious abridgment of the Syntagma
by Bernier.   But he does not strictly confine his ideas
of reflection to this class.   Duration is certainly no mode
of thinking; yet the idea of duration is reckoned by
Locke among those with which we are furnished by
reflection.   The same may perhaps be said, though I do
not know that he expresses himself with equal clearness,
as to his account of several other ideas, which cannot be
deduced from external sensation, nor yet can be reckoned
modifications or operations of the soul itself; such as
number, power, existence.[r]

[r] [Upon more attentive consideration
of all the passages wherein Locke speaks
of ideas derived from reflection, I entertain no doubt but that Stewart is right,
and some of Locke's opponents in the
wrong.   He evidently meant that by
reflecting on the operations of our own
minds, as well as on our bodily sensations,
divers new simple ideas are suggested to
us, which are not in themselves either
such operations or such sensations.   These
"simple ideas convey themselves into the
mind by all the ways of sensation and
reflection;" and he enumerates pleasure
and pain, power, existence, unity; to
which he afterwards adds duration.   "Reflection on the appearance of several
ideas, one after another, in our minds, is
that which furnishes us with the idea of
succession.   And the distance between
any parts of that succession, or between
the appearance of new ideas in our minds,
is that we call duration."   B. ii. ch. 14,
§ 3.   So of number, or unity, which he
takes for the basis of the idea of number.
"Amongst all the ideas we have, as there
is none suggested to the mind by more
ways, so is there none more simple than
that of unity, or one; it has no shadow of
variety or composition in it; every object our senses are employed about, every
idea in our understandings, every thought
of our minds, brings this idea along with
it."   ch. x. § 1.   Thus we have proofs,
and more might easily be alleged, that
Locke really admitted the understanding
to be so far the source of new simple
ideas, that several of primary importance
arise in our minds, on the *suggestion* of
the senses, or of our observing the inward
operations of our minds, which are not
strictly to be classed themselves as suggestions, or as acts of consciousness.   And
when we remember also, that the power
of the understanding to compound simple
ideas is a leading part of his system, and
also that certain ideas, which others take
for simple, are reckoned by him, whether
rightly or no, to be complex, we may be
forced to admit that the outcry raised
against Locke as a teacher of the sensualist school has been chiefly founded on
inattention to his language, and to some
inaccuracy in it.   Stewart had already
stated the true doctrine as to ideas of reflection.   "In such cases all that can be
said is, that the exercise of a particular
faculty furnishes the occasion on which
certain simple notions are, by the laws
of our constitution, presented to our
thoughts; nor does it seem possible for
us to trace the origin of a particular notion any farther, than to ascertain what
the nature of the occasion was, which, in
the first instance, introduced it to our
acquaintance."   Philos. Essays, I. chap.
ii.   It is true, that he proceeds to impute
a different theory to Locke; namely,

108. Stewart has been so much struck by this inde- Vague use
finiteness, with which the phrase "ideas of of the word
reflection" has been used in the Essay on the idea.
Human Understanding, that he "does not think,
notwithstanding some casual expressions which may seem
to favour the contrary supposition, that Locke would
have hesitated for a moment to admit with Cudworth
and Price, that the understanding is the source of new
ideas." [*] And though some might object that this is too
much in opposition, not to casual expressions, but to
the whole tenour of Locke's Essay, his language con-

that consciousness is exclusively the source of all our knowledge : which he takes to mean that all our original ideas may be classed under acts of consciousness, as well as suggested by it. But in his Dissertation, we have seen that he takes a more favourable view of the Essay on the Human Understanding in this great question of the origin of our ideas, and, as it now appears to me, beyond dispute a more true one. The want of precision, so unhappily characteristic of Locke, has led to this misapprehension of his meaning. But surely no one can believe, hardly the most depreciating critic of Locke at Paris or Oxford, that he took duration and number for actual operations of the mind, such as doubting or comparing. Price had long since admitted that Locke had no other meaning than that our ideas are derived, immediately or ultimately, from sensation or reflection, or, in other words, "that they furnish us with all the subjects, materials, and occasions of knowledge, comparison, and internal perception. This however by no means renders them in any proper sense the source of all our ideas." Price's Dissertations on Morals, p. 16.

Cousin enumerates, as simple ideas not derived from sensation or reflection, space, duration, infinity, identity, substance, cause, and right. Locke would have replied that the idea of space, as mere definite extension, was derived from sensation, and that of space generally, or what he has called expansion, was not simple, but complex ; that those of duration, cause (or power), and identity, were furnished by reflection; that the idea of right is not simple, and that those

of substance and infinity are hardly formed by the mind at all. He would add existence and unity to the list, both, according to him, derived from reflection.

M. Cousin has by no means done justice to Locke as to the idea of *cause*. "On sait que Locke, après avoir affirmé dans un chapitre sur l'idée de cause et d'effet, que cette idée nous est donnée par la sensation, s'avise, dans un chapitre différent sur la puissance, d'une toute autre origine, bien qu'il s'agisse, au fond, de la même idée, il trouve cette origine nouvelle dans la réflexion appliquée à la volonté," &c. Fragmens Philosophiques, p. 83. Now, in the first place, the chapter on Power, in the Essay on the Human Understanding, B. ii. ch. 21, comes before and not after that on Cause and Effect, ch. 26. But it is more important to observe that in the latter chapter, and at the close of the 25th, Locke distinctly says that the idea is " derived from the two fountains of all our knowledge, sensation and reflection," and " that this relation, how comprehensive soever, terminates at last in them." It is also to be kept in mind that he is here speaking of physical causes ; but in his chapter on Power, of efficient ones, and principally of the human mind ; intimating also his opinion, that matter is destitute of active power, that is, of efficient causation. The form *on sait* is, as *on sait*, a common mode of introducing any questionable position. It does not follow from this that Locke's expressions in the 26th chapter, on Cause and Effect, are altogether the best ; but they must be considered in connexion with his long chapter on Power.—1847.]

[*] Prelim. Dissertation.

cerning substance almost bears it out.   Most of the perplexity which has arisen on this subject, the combats of
some metaphysicians with Locke, the portentous errors
into which others have been led by want of attention
to his language, may be referred to the equivocal meaning of the word idea.   The Cartesians understood by
this whatever is the object of thought, including an intellection as well as an imagination. · By an intellection
they meant that which the mind conceives to exist,
and to be the subject of knowledge, though it may
be unimaginable and incomprehensible.   Gassendi and
Locke (at least in this part of his Essay) limit the word
idea to something which the mind sees and grasps as
immediately present to it.   " That," as Locke not very
well expresses it, " which the mind is applied about
while thinking being the ideas that are there."   Hence
he speaks with some ridicule of " men who persuade
themselves that they have clear comprehensive ideas of
infinity."   Such men can hardly have existed ; but it is
by annexing the epithets clear and comprehensive, that
he shows the dispute to be merely verbal.   For that we
know the existence of infinites as objectively real, and
can reason upon them, Locke would not have denied ;
and it is this knowledge to which others gave the name
of idea.

109. The different manner in which this all-important
word was understood by philosophers is strikingly shown
when they make use of the same illustration.   Arnauld,
if he is author of L'Art de Penser, mentions the idea of
a chiliagon, or figure of 1000 sides, as an instance of the
distinction between that which we imagine and that
which we conceive or understand.   Locke has employed
the same instance to exemplify the difference between
clear and obscure ideas.   According to the former, we
do not imagine a figure with 1000 sides at all ; according
to the latter, we form a confused image of it.   We have
an idea of such a figure, it is agreed by both ; but in
the sense of Arnauld, it is an idea of the understanding
alone ; in the sense of Locke, it is an idea of sensation,
framed, like other complex ideas, by putting together
those we have formerly received, though we may never
have seen the precise figure.   That the word suggests
to the mind an image of a polygon with many sides is

indubitable; but it is urged by the Cartesians, that as we are wholly incapable of distinguishing the exact number, we cannot be said to have, in Locke's sense of the word, any idea, even an indistinct one, of a figure with 1000 sides : since all we do imagine is a polygon. And it is evident that in geometry we do not reason from the properties of the image, but from those of a figure which the understanding apprehends.   Locke, however, who generally preferred a popular meaning to one more metaphysically exact, thought it enough to call this a confused idea.   He was not, I believe, conversant with any but elementary geometry.   Had he reflected upon that which in his age had made such a wonderful beginning, or even upon the fundamental principles of it, which might be found in Euclid, the theory of infinitesimal quantities, he must, one would suppose, have been more puzzled to apply his narrow definition of an idea.   For what image can we form of a differential, which can pretend to represent it in any other sense than as $d\,x$ represents it, by suggestion, not by resemblance?

110. The case is however much worse when Locke deviates, as in the third and fourth books he constantly does, from this sense that he has put on the word idea, and takes it either in the Cartesian meaning, or in one still more general and popular.   Thus, in the excellent chapter on the abuse of words, he insists upon the advantage of using none without clear and distinct ideas; he who does not this " only making a noise without any sense or signification."   ` If we combine this position with that in the second book, that we have no clear and distinct idea of a figure with 1000 sides, it follows with all the force of syllogism, that we should not argue about a figure of 1000 sides at all, nor, by parity of reason, about many other things of far higher importance.   It will be found, I incline to think, that the large use of the word idea for that about which we have some knowledge, without limiting it to what can be imagined, pervades the third and fourth books.   Stewart has ingeniously conjectured that they were written before the second, and probably before the mind of Locke had been much turned to the psychological analysis which that contains.   It is, however, certain that

K 2

in the Treatise upon the Conduct of the Understanding, which was not published till after the Essay, he uses the word idea with full as much latitude as in the third and fourth books of the latter. We cannot, upon the whole, help admitting that the story of a lady who, after the perusal of the Essay on the Human Understanding, laid it down with a remark, that the book would be perfectly charming were it not for the frequent recurrence of one very hard word, *idea*, though told, possibly, in ridicule of the fair philosopher, pretty well represents the state of mind in which many at first have found themselves.[t]

111. Locke, as I have just intimated, seems to have possessed but a slight knowledge of geometry —a science which, both from the clearness of the illustrations it affords, and from its admitted efficacy in rendering the logical powers acute and cautious, may be reckoned, without excepting physiology, the most valuable of all to the metaphysician. But it did not require any geometrical knowledge, strictly so called, to avoid one material error into which he has fallen ; and which I mention the rather, because even Descartes, in one place, has said something of the same kind ; and I have met with it not only in Norris very distinctly and positively, but, more or less, in many or most of those who have treated of the metaphysics or abstract principles of geometry. " I doubt not," says Locke,[u] " but it will be easily granted that the know-

An error as to geometrical figure.

---

[t] [The character of Locke's philosophical style, as given by a living philosopher, by no means favourable to him, is perhaps too near the truth. " In his *language*, Locke is, of all philosophers, the most figurative, ambiguous, vacillating, various, and even contradictory, as has been noticed by Reid and Stewart, and by Brown himself; indeed, we believe, by every author who has had occasion to comment on this philosopher. The opinions of such a writer are not, therefore, to be assumed from isolated and casual expressions, which themselves require to be interpreted on the general analogy of his system." Edinb. Rev. (Sir William Hamilton) vol. lii. p. 189. I am happy to cite another late writer of high authority, in favour of the *general* character of Locke as a philosopher. " Few among the great names in philosophy," says Mr. Mill, " have met with a harder measure of justice from the present generation than Locke, the unquestioned founder of the analytical philosophy of mind." Perhaps Descartes and Hobbes, not to mention Gassendi, might contest the palm as *founders* of psychological analysis, but Mr. Mill justly gives to Locke the preference over Hobbes, who has been sometimes overrated of late, "not only in sober judgment, but even in profundity and original genius." System of Logic, vol. i. p. 150. —1847.]

[u] B. iv. c. 8.

ledge we have of mathematical truths is not only certain but real knowledge, and not the bare empty vision of vain insignificant chimeras of the brain; and yet if we well consider, we shall find that it is only of our own ideas.   The mathematician considers the truth and properties belonging to a rectangle or circle only as they are in idea in his own mind; for it is possible he never found either of them existing mathematically, that is, precisely true, in his life. . . . . All the discourses of the mathematicians about the squaring of a circle, conic sections, or any other part of mathematics, concern not the existence of any of those figures; but their demonstrations, which depend on their ideas, are the same, whether there be any square or circle in the world or no."   And the inference he draws from this is, that moral as well as mathematical ideas, being archetypes themselves, and so adequate and complete ideas, all the agreement or disagreement which he shall find in them will produce real knowledge, as well as in mathematical figures.

112. It is not perhaps necessary to inquire how far, upon the hypothesis of Berkeley, this notion of mathematical figures, as mere creations of the mind, could be sustained.   But on the supposition of the objectivity of space, as truly existing without us, which Locke undoubtedly assumes, it is certain that the passage just quoted is entirely erroneous, and that it involves a confusion between the geometrical figure itself and its delineation to the eye.   A geometrical figure is a portion of space contained in boundaries, determined by given relations.   It exists in the infinite round about us, as the statue exists in the block.[x]   No one can doubt, if he turns his mind to the subject, that every point in space is equidistant, in all directions, from certain other points.   Draw a line through all these, and you have the circumference of a circle; but the circle itself and its circumference

---

[x] Michael Angelo has well conveyed this idea in four lines, which I quote from Corniani :—

Non ha l' ottimo artista alcun concetto,
Che un marmo solo in se non circonscriva
Col suo soverchio, e solo a quello arriva
La mano che obbedisce all' intelletto.

The geometer uses not the same obedient hand, but he equally feels and perceives the reality of that figure which the broad infinite around him comprehends *col suo soverchio*.

[Cicero has a similar expression :— Quasi non in omni marmore necesse sit inesse vel Praxitelia capita ! illa enim ipsa efficiuntur detractione.   De Divinatione, ii. 21.—1842.]

exist before the latter is delineated. Thus the orbit of a planet is not a regular geometrical figure, because certain forces disturb it. But this disturbance means only a deviation from a line which exists really in space, and which the planet would actually describe if there were nothing in the universe but itself and the centre of attraction. The expression, therefore, of Locke, " whether there be any square or circle existing in the world or no," is highly inaccurate, the latter alternative being an absurdity. All possible figures, and that " in number numberless," exist every where ; nor can we evade the perplexities into which the geometry of infinites throws our imagination, by considering them as mere beings of reason, the creatures of the geometer, which I believe some are half disposed to do, nor by substituting the vague and unphilosophical notion of indefinitude for a positive objective infinity.[y]

[y] [The confusion, as it appears to me, between sensible and real figure in geometry, I have found much more general in philosophical writers than I was aware of when this passage was first committed to the press. Thus M. Cousin: " Il n'existe, dans la nature, que des figures imparfaites, et la géométrie a pour condition d'opérer sur des figures parfaites, sur le triangle parfait, le cercle parfait, &c. ; c'est à dire, sur des figures qui n'ont pas d'existence réelle, et qui sont des pures conceptions de l'esprit." Hist. de la Philos., vol. ii. p. 311. If by figure we mean only visible circumference, this is very true. But the geometer generally reasons, not upon the boundaries, but upon the extension, superficial or solid, comprehended within them ; and to this extension itself we usually give the name of figure. Again, " It is not true," says Mr. Mill, " that a circle exists, or can be described, which has all its radii exactly equal." System of Logic, vol. i. p. 200. Certainly such a circle cannot be described, but in every geometrical sense it really exists. Hence he asserts " the character of necessity, ascribed to mathematics, to be a mere illusion ; nothing exists conformable to the definitions, nor is even possible." P. 296. It follows, of course, that a straight line is impossible ; which is perfectly true, if it must be drawn with a ruler. But is it not surprising that so acute a writer as Mr. Mill can think anything impossible, in a metaphysical sense, which implies no contradiction, and is easily conceived? He must have used possible in a sense limited to human execution.

Another eminent reasoner has gone the full lengths of this paradox. " It has been rightly remarked by Dugald Stewart, that mathematical propositions are not properly true or false, in the same sense as any proposition respecting real fact is so called, and hence the truth, such as it is, of such propositions is necessary and eternal ; since it amounts only to this, that any complex notion which you have arbitrarily formed must be exactly conformable to itself." Whately's Elements of Logic, 3rd edit., p. 229. And thus a celebrated writer who began in that school, though he has since traversed the diameter of theology: " We are able to define the creations of our own minds, for they are what we make them ; but it were as easy to create what is real, as to define it." Newman's Sermons before the University of Oxford, p. 333.

The only meaning we can put on such assertions is, that geometry is a mere pastime of the mind, an exercise of logic, in which we have only to take care that we assign no other properties to the imaginary figures which answer to the syllogistic letters, A, B, and C, than

113. The distinction between ideas of mere sensation and those of intellection, between what the mind com-

such as are contained in their definition, without any objective truth whatever, or relation to a real external universe. The perplexities into which mathematicians have been thrown by the metaphysical difficulties of their science, must appear truly ludicrous, and such as they have manufactured for themselves. But the most singular circumstance of all is, that nature is regulated by these arbitrary definitions; and that the truths of geometry, *such as they are*, enable us to predict the return of Uranus or Neptune to the same place in the heavens after the present generation are in their graves. A comet leaves its perihelion, and pursues its path through the remote regions of space; the astronomer foretells its return by the laws of a geometrical figure, and if it come a few days only before the calculated moment, has recourse to the hypothesis of some resistance which has diminished its orbit; so sure is he that the projectile force, and that of gravity, act in lines geometrically straight.

The source of this paradox appears to be a too hasty and rather inaccurate assumption, that geometry depends upon definitions. But though we cannot argue except according to our definitions, the real subject of the science is not those terms, but the properties of the things defined. We conceive a perfect circle to be not only a possible but a real figure; that its radii are equal, belongs to the idea, not to the words by which we define it. Men might reason by themselves on geometry without any definitions; or, if they could not, the truths of the science would be the same.

The universal and necessary belief of mankind is, that we are placed in the midst of an unbounded ocean of space. On all sides of us, and in three dimensions, this is spread around. We cannot conceive it to be annihilated, or to have had a beginning. Innumerable objects of our senses, themselves extended, that is, occupying portions of this space, but portions not always the same, float within it. And as we find other properties than mere extension in these objects, by which properties alone they are distinguishable from the surrounding space, we denomi-

nate them bodies, or material substances. Considered in its distinction from this space, their own proper extension has boundaries by which they come under the relation of figure; and thus all bodies are figured. But we do not necessarily limit this word to material substances. The mind is not only perfectly capable of considering geometrical figures, that is, particular portions of the continuous extension which we call absolute space, by themselves, as measured by the mutual distances of their boundaries, but is intuitively certain that such figures are real, that extension is divisible into parts, and that there must be everywhere in the surrounding expanse triangles and circles mathematically exact, though any diagram which we can delineate will be more or less incorrect. "Space," says Sir John Herschel (if we may name him), "in its ultimate analysis, is nothing but an assemblage of distances and directions." Quarterly Review, June, 1841, quoted in Mill's Logic, i. 324. This is very forcibly expressed, if not with absolute precision; for distance is perhaps, in strictness, rather the measure of space than space itself. It is suggested by every extended body, the boundaries whereof must be distant one from another, and it is suggested also by the separation of these bodies, which, when not in contact, are perceived to have intervals between them. But these intervals are not necessarily filled by other bodies, nor even by light; as when we perceive stars, and estimate their distances from one another, in a moonless night. The mere ideas of distance and direction seem to be simple, or rather modes of the simple idea extension; and for this reason no definition can be given of a straight line. It is the measure of distance itself; which the mind intuitively apprehends to be but one, and that the shortest line which can be drawn.

"The only clear notion," says Herschel, "we can form of straightness, is uniformity of direction." And as the line itself is only imaginary, or, if it be drawn, is but the representative of distance or length, it cannot have, as such, any other dimension. Though we know

prehends, and what it conceives without comprehending, is the point of divergence between the two sects of psy-

that a material line must have breadth, it is not a mere abstraction of the geometer to say, that the distance of an object from the eye has no breadth, but it would be absurd to say the contrary.

The definition of a mathematical figure involves only its possibility. But our knowledge of extension itself, as objectively real, renders all figures true beings, not *entia rationis*, but actual beings, portions of one infinite continuous extension. They exist in space, to repeat the metaphor (which indeed is no metaphor, but an instance), as the statue exists in the block. Extension, perhaps, and figure, are rather the conditions under which bodies, whatever else they may be, are presented to our senses, than, in perfect strictness of expression, the essentials of body itself. They have been called by Stewart the mathematical properties of matter. Certain it is that they remain when the body is displaced; and would remain were it annihilated. And it is with the relation of bodies to space absolute that the geometer has to deal; never, in his pure science, with their material properties.

What, then, is the meaning of what we sometimes read, that there is no such thing as a circle or a triangle in nature? If we are to understand the physical universe, the material world, which is the common sense, this may perhaps be true; but what, then, has the geometer to do with nature? If we include absolute space under the word nature, I must entirely deny the assertion. Can we doubt that portions of space, or points, exist in every direction at the same distance from any other assignable point or portion of space? I cannot draw a radius precisely a foot long; but I can draw a line more than eleven inches in length, and can produce this till it is more than twelve. At some point or other it has been exactly the length of a foot. The want of precise uniformity of direction may be overcome in the same way; there is a series of points along which the line might have been directed, so as to be perfectly uniform; just as in the orbit of a planet round the sun, disturbed as it is by the attraction of a third body

at every point, there is yet at every point a line, called the instantaneous ellipse, along which the path of the body might by possibility have proceeded in a geometrical curve. Let the mind once fix itself on the idea of continuous extension, and its divisibility into parts mathematically equal, or in mathematical ratios, must appear necessary.

Geometry, then, is not a science of reasoning upon definitions, such as we please to conceive, but on the relations of space; of space, an objective being, according at least to human conceptions, space, the bosom of nature, that which alone makes all things sensibly without us; made known to us by a primary law of the understanding, as some hold; by experience of sensation, or inference from it, as others maintain; but necessary, eternal, the basis of such demonstration as no other science possesses; because in no other do we perceive an absolute impossibility, an impossibility paramount, speaking reverently, to the Creator's will, that the *premises* of our reasoning might have been different from what they are. The definitions of geometrical figures no more constitute their essence than those of a plant or a mineral. Whether geometrical *reasoning* is built on the relations of parts of space, merely as defined in words, is another question; it certainly appears to me that definitions supply only the terms of the proposition, and that without a knowledge, verbal or implied, of the axioms, we could not deduce any conclusions at all. But this affects only the logic of the theorem, the process by which the relations of space are unfolded to the human understanding. I cannot for a moment believe that the distinguished philosopher, who has strenuously argued for the deduction of geometry from definitions, meant any more than to oppose them to axioms. That they are purely arbitrary, that they are the creatures of the mind, like harpies and chimæras, he could hardly have thought, being himself habituated to geometrical studies. But the language of Stewart is not sufficiently guarded; and he has served as an authority to those who have uttered so singular a paradox. " From what principle," says

chology which still exist in the world. Nothing is in the intellect which has not before been in the sense,

Stewart, "are the various properties of the circle derived, but from the definition of a circle? from what principle the properties of the parabola or ellipse, but from the definitions of these curves? A similar observation may be extended to all the other theorems which the mathematician demonstrates." Vol. ii. p. 41. The properties of a circle or the other curves, we answer, are derived from that leading property which we express in the definition. But surely we can make use of no definition which does not declare a real property. We might impose a name on a quadrilateral figure with equal angles and sides not parallel; but could we draw an inference from it? And why could we not, but because we should be restrained by its incompatibility with our necessary conceptions of the relations of space? It is these primary conceptions to which our definitions must conform. Definitions of figure, at least in all but the most familiar, are indispensable, in order to make us apprehend particular relations of distance, and to keep our reasonings clear from confusion; but this is only the common province of language. In this I have the satisfaction of finding myself supported by the authority of Dr. Whewell. "Supposing," he observes in his Thoughts on the Study of the Mathematics, "we could get rid of geometrical axioms altogether, and deduce our reasoning from definitions alone, it must be allowed, I think, that still our geometrical propositions would probably depend, not on the definitions, but on the act of mind by which we fix upon such definitions; in short, on our conception of *space*. The axiom, that two straight lines cannot enclose space, is a self-evident truth, and founded upon our faculty of apprehending the properties of space, and of conceiving a straight line. . . . We should present a false view of the nature of geometrical truth if we were to represent it as resting upon definitions, and should overlook or deny the faculty of the mind, and the intellectual process which is implied in our fixing upon such definitions. The foundation of all the properties of straight lines is certainly not the definition, but the conception of

a straight line, and in the same manner the foundation of all geometrical truth resides in our general conceptions of space." P. 151.

That mathematical truths (a position of Stewart commended by Whately) are not properly called matters of fact, is no new distinction. They are not γενόμενα; they have no being in time, as matters of fact have; they are ὄντα, beings of a higher order than any facts, but still realities, and, as some philosophers have held, more truly real than any created essence. But Archbishop Whately is a nominalist of the school of Hobbes. Mr. Mill, who is an avowed conceptualist, has said: "Every proposition which conveys real information, asserts a matter of fact dependent on the laws of nature, and not upon artificial classification." Vol. i. p. 237. But here he must use matter of fact in a loose sense; for he would certainly admit mathematical theorems to convey real information; though I do not agree with him that they are, in propriety of language, dependent on the laws of nature. He observes on the archbishop's position, that the object of reasoning is to expand the assertions wrapped up in those with which we set out, that "it is not easy to see how such a science as geometry can be said to be wrapped up in a few definitions and axioms." P. 297. Whether this be a sufficient answer to the archbishop or no, it shows that Mr. Mill considers mathematical propositions to convey real science.

Two opposite errors are often found in modern writers on the metaphysics of geometry; the one, that which has just been discussed, the denial of absolute reality to mathematical truths; the other wholly opposite, yet which equally destroys their prerogative; I mean the theory that they are only established by induction. As in the first they are no facts in any sense, not real truths, so in the other they are mere facts. But, indeed, both these opinions, divergent as they seem, emanate from the ultra-nominalist school, and they sometimes are combined in the same writer. Mr. Mill and Mr. De Morgan have lent their great authority to the second doctrine, which

said the Aristotelian schoolmen.   Every idea has its original in the senses, repeated the disciple of Epicurus,

was revived from Hobbes, fifty years since, by Dr. Beddoes, in a tract on Demonstrative Evidence, which I have heard attributed, in part, to Professor Leslie, a supporter of the same theory. Sir William Hamilton exclaims upon the position of two writers in the suite of Archbishop Whately, that it is by induction all axioms are known; such as, ' A whole is greater than its parts.' " Is such the Oxford metaphysics?" Edinb. Rev. vol. lvii. p. 232. But though the assertion seems more monstrous, when applied to such an axiom as this, it is substantially found in many writers of deserved fame; nor is it either a metaphysics of Oxford growth, or very likely to be well received there. The Oxford error at present, that at least of the dominant school, seems to be the very reverse; a strong tendency to absolute Platonic realism. This has had, cause or effect, something to do with the apotheosis of the *Church*, which implies reality, a step to personality.

It seems to follow from this inductive theory, that we believe two straight lines not to include a space, because we have never seen them do so, or heard of any one who has; and as mere induction is confessed to be no basis of certain truth, we must admit mathematical demonstration to differ only in degree of positive evidence from probability. As the passage in my text to which this note refers bears no relation to this second opinion, I shall not dwell upon it farther than to remark, that it seems strange to hear that two straight lines are only proved by observation not to include a space, when we are told in the same breath that no straight lines exist, and consequently that any which we may take for straight would be found, on a more accurate examination, to include a space between them. But, reverting to the subject of the former part of this note, it may be observed, that our conception that two straight lines cannot include a space is a homage to the reality of geometrical figure, for experience has not given it; all we learn from experience is, that the nearer to straightness two lines are drawn, the less space they include; and even here the reasoning is in the inverse order,

the less space they include, the more they approach to straight, that is the nearer to uniformity is their direction.

In all this I have assumed the reality of space, according to the usual apprehension of mankind. With the transcendental problem, raised by the Kantian school, it seems unnecessary to meddle. We know at least that we acknowledge the objectivity of space by a condition of our understandings; we know that others with whom we converse have the like conceptions of it; we have every reason to believe that inferior animals judge of extension, distance, and direction, by sensations and inferences analogous to our own; we predict the future, in calculating the motions of heavenly and terrestrial bodies, on the assumption that space is no fiction of the brain, its portions and measured distances no creations of an arbitrary definition. Locke, I am aware, in one of the miscellaneous papers published by Lord King (Life of Locke, vol. ii. p. 175), bearing the date 1677, says: " Space in itself seems to be nothing but a capacity or possibility for extended beings or bodies to be or exist;" and, " The space where a real globe of a foot diameter exists, though we imagine it to be really something, to have a real existence before and after its [the globe's] existence, there in truth is really nothing." And finally, " though it be true that the black lines drawn on a rule have the relation one to another of an inch distance, they being real sensible things; and though it be also true that I, knowing the idea of an inch, can imagine that length without imagining body, as well as I can imagine a figure without imagining body, yet it is no more true that there is any real distance in that which we call imaginary space, than that there is any real figure there." P. 185.

I confess myself wholly at a loss how to reconcile such notions of space and distance, not only with geometry but dynamics; the idea of velocity involving that of mere extension in a straight line, without the conception, necessarily implied, of any body except the moving one. But it is worthy of remark, that Locke appears to have modified his doctrine here delivered, before he wrote the Essay

Gassendi.   Locke indeed, as Gassendi had done before him, assigned another origin to one class of ideas ; but

on the Human Understanding ; where he argues at length, in language adapted to the common belief of the reality of space, and once only observes that some may " take it to be only a relation resulting from the existence of other beings at a distance, while others understand the words of Solomon and St. Paul in a literal sense " (b. ii. c. 13, § 27) ; by which singular reference to Scripture he may perhaps intimate that he does not perceive the force of the metaphysical argument. I think it not impossible that the reading of Newton, who had so emphatically pronounced himself for the real existence of absolute space, had so far an effect upon the mind of Locke, that he did not commit himself to an opposite hypothesis. Except with a very few speculative men, I believe the conviction, that space exists truly and independently around us, to be universal in mankind.

Locke was a philosopher, equally bold in following up his own inquiries, and cautious in committing them, except as mere conjectures, to the public. Perhaps an instance might be given from the remarkable anticipation of the theory of Boscovich as to the nature of matter, which Stewart has sagaciously inferred from a passage in the Essay on the Human Understanding. But if we may trust an anecdote in the Bibliothèque Raisonnée, vol. iv. p. 350, on the authority of Coste, the French translator of that work, Newton conceived the idea of Boscovich's theory; and suggested it to Locke. The quotation is in the words of the translator :—

" Ici M. Locke excite notre curiosité sans vouloir la satisfaire. Bien des gens s'étant imaginés qu'il m'avait communiqué cette manière d'expliquer la création de la matière, me prièrent, peu de temps après que ma traduction eut vu le jour, de leur en faire part ; mais je fus obligé de leur avouer que M. L. m'en avait fait un secret à moi-même. Enfin, longtemps après sa mort, M. le Chevalier Newton, à qui je parlais, par hasard, de cet endroit du livre de M. Locke, me découvrit tout le mystère. Souriant, il me dit d'abord, que c'était lui-même qui avait imaginé cette manière d'expliquer

la création de la matière ; que la pensée lui en était venue dans l'esprit, un jour qu'il vint à tomber sur cette question avec M. L. et un seigneur Anglais plein de vie, et qui n'est pas moins illustre par l'étendue de ses lumières que par sa naissance. Et voici comment il leur expliqua sa pensée. ' On pouvait,' dit-il, ' se former, en quelque manière, une idée de la création de la matière, en supposant que Dieu eût empêché par sa puissance, que rien ne pût entrer dans une certaine portion de l'espace pur, que, de sa nature, est pénétrable, éternel, nécessaire, infini ; car dès-là cette portion d'espace aurait l'impénétrabilité, l'une des qualités essentielles à la matière. Et comme l'espace pur est absolument uniforme, on n'a qu'à supposer que Dieu aurait communiqué cette espèce d'impénétrabilité à une autre pareille portion de l'espace, et cela nous donnerait, en quelque sorte, une idée de la mobilité de la matière, autre qualité qui lui est aussi très-essentielle.' Nous voilà maintenant délivrés de chercher ce que M. L. avait trouvé bon de cacher à ses lecteurs." Bibl. Raisonnée, vol. iv. p. 349.

It is unnecessary to observe what honour the conjecture of Stewart does to his sagacity ; for he was not very likely to have fallen on this passage in an old review little read, nor was he a man to conceal the obligation, had he done so. The theory of Boscovich, or, as we may perhaps now say, of Newton, has been lately supported, with abundance of new illustration, by the greatest genius in philosophical discovery whom this age and country can boast. I will conclude with throwing out a suggestion, whether, on the hypothesis that matter is only a combination of forces, attractive or repulsive, and varying in different substances or bodies, as they are vulgarly called, inasmuch as all forces are capable of being mathematically expressed, there is not a proper formula belonging to each body, though of course not assignable by us, which might be called its equation, and which, if known, would be the definition of its essence, as strictly as that of a geometrical figure.—1847.]

these were few in number, and in the next century two
writers of considerable influence, Hartley and Condillac,
attempted to resolve them all into sensation. The ancient
school of the Platonists, and even that of Descartes, who
had distinguished innate ideas, or at least those spontaneously suggesting themselves on occasion of visible
objects, from those strictly belonging to sense, lost
ground both in France and England ; nor had Leibnitz,
who was deemed an enemy to some of our great English
names, sufficient weight to restore it. In the hands of
some who followed in both countries, the worst phrases
of Locke were preferred to the best ; whatever could be
turned to the account of pyrrhonism, materialism, or
atheism, made a figure in the Epicurean system of a
popular philosophy.* The German metaphysicians from
the time of Kant deserve at least the credit of having
successfully withstood this coarse sensualism, though
they may have borrowed much that their disciples take
for original, and added much that is hardly better than
what they have overthrown. France has also made
a rapid return since the beginning of this century,
and with more soundness of judgment than Germany,
towards the doctrines of the Cartesian school. Yet the

* ["Locke," says M. Cousin, "has certainly not confounded sensation with
the faculties of the mind; he expressly
distinguishes them, but he makes the
latter play a secondary and insignificant
part, and concenters their action on sensible *data;* it was but a step from thence
to confound them with sensibility ; and
we have here the feeble germ of a future
theory, that of transformed sensation, of
sensation as the only principle of all the
operations of the mind. Locke, without
knowing or designing it, has opened the
road to this exclusive doctrine, by adding
nothing to sensation but faculties whose
whole business is to exercise themselves
upon it, with no peculiar or original
power." Hist. de la Philos., vol. ii. p. 137.
If the powers of combining, comparing,
and generalising the ideas originally derived from sense are not to be called peculiar and original, this charge might be
sustained. But though Locke had not
the same views of the active and self-ori-
ginated powers of the mind which have
been taken by others, if he derived some

ideas from sense to which a different
source has been assigned, it seems too
much to say that he makes the faculties
play a secondary and insignificant part ;
when the part he attributes to them is
that of giving us all our knowledge beyond that of mere simple sense ; and, to
use his own analogy, being to sensation
what the words of a language, in all their
combinations, are to the letters which
compose them. M. Cousin, and the other
antagonists of Locke, will not contend
that we could have had any knowledge of
geometry or arithmetic without sensation ; and Locke has never supposed that
we could have so much as put two ideas
of extension or number together without
the active powers of the mind. In this
point I see no other difference between
the two schools, than that one derives a
few ideas from sense, which the other
cannot trace to that source ; and this is
hardly sufficient to warrant the depreciation of Locke as a false and dangerous
guide in philosophy.—1847.]

opposite philosophy to that which never rises above sensible images is exposed to a danger of its own; it is one which the infirmity of the human faculties renders perpetually at hand; few there are who in reasoning on subjects where we cannot attain what Locke has called "positive comprehensive ideas" are secure from falling into mere nonsense and repugnancy. In that part of physics which is simply conversant with quantity, this danger is probably not great, but in all such inquiries as are sometimes called transcendental, it has perpetually shipwrecked the adventurous navigator.

114. In the language and probably the notions of Locke as to the nature of the soul there is an indistinctness more worthy of the Aristotelian schoolmen than of one conversant with the Cartesian philosophy. "Bodies," he says, "manifestly produce ideas in us by impulse, the only way which we can conceive bodies to operate in. If, then, external objects be not united to our minds, when they produce ideas in it, and yet we perceive these original qualities in such of them as singly fall under our senses, it is evident that some motion must be thence continued by our nerves, or animal spirits, by some parts of our bodies to the brain, or the seat of sensation, there to produce in our minds the particular ideas we have of them. And since the extension, figure, number, and motion of bodies of an observable bigness may be perceived at a distance by the sight, it is evident some singly imperceptible bodies must come from them to the eyes, and thereby convey to the brain some motion which produces those ideas which we have of them in us." He so far retracts his first position afterwards as to admit, "in consequence of what Mr. Newton has shown in the Principia on the gravitation of matter towards matter," that God not only can put into bodies powers and ways of operation above what can be explained from what we know of matter, but that he has actually done so. And he promises to correct the former passage, which however he has never performed. In fact, he seems, by the use of phrases which recur too often to be thought merely figurative, to have supposed that something in the brain comes into local contact with the mind. He was here unable to divest himself, any more than the schoolmen had

His notions as to the soul,

done, of the notion that there is a proper action of the
body on the soul in perception. The Cartesians had
brought in the theory of occasional causes and other
solutions of the phænomena, so as to avoid what seems
so irreconcilable with an immaterial principle. No one
is so lavish of a cerebral instrumentality in mental
images as Malebranche; he seems at every moment on
the verge of materialism; he coquets, as it were, with
an Epicurean physiology; but, if I may be allowed to
continue the metaphor, he perceives the moment where
to stop, and retires, like a dexterous fair one, with un-
smirched honour to his immateriality. It cannot be said
that Locke is equally successful.

115. In another and a well-known passage he has
and its im-
materiality. thrown out a doubt whether God might not
superadd the faculty of thinking to matter;
and, though he thinks it probable that this has not been
the case, leaves it at last a debateable question, wherein
nothing else than presumptions are to be had. Yet he
has strongly argued against the possibility of a material
Deity upon reasons derived from the nature of matter.
Locke almost appears to have taken the union of a
thinking being with matter for the thinking of matter
itself. What is there, Stillingfleet well asks, like self-
consciousness in matter? "Nothing at all," Locke replies, "in matter as matter. But that God cannot
bestow on some parcels of matter a power of thinking,
and with it self-consciousness, will never be proved by
asking how it is possible to apprehend that mere body
should perceive that it doth perceive." But if that we
call mind, and of which we are self-conscious, were thus
superadded to matter, would it the less be something
real? In what sense can it be compared to an accident
or quality? It has been justly observed that we are
much more certain of the independent existence of mind
than of that of matter. But that, by the constitution of
our nature, a definite organisation, or what will be generally thought the preferable hypothesis, an organic mole-
cule, should be a necessary concomitant of this immaterial principle, does not involve any absurdity at all,
whatever want of evidence may be objected to it.

116. It is remarkable that, in the controversy with
Stillingfleet on this passage, Locke seems to take for

granted that there is no immaterial principle in brutes; and as he had too much plain sense to adopt the Cartesian theory of their insensibility, he draws the most plausible argument for the possibility of thought in matter by the admitted fact of sensation and voluntary motion in these animal organisations. " It is not doubted but that the properties of a rose, a peach, or an elephant, superadded to matter, change not the properties of matter, but matter is in these things matter still." Few perhaps at present who believe in the immateriality of the human soul would deny the same to an elephant; but it must be owned that the discoveries of zoology have pushed this to consequences which some might not readily adopt. The spiritual being of a sponge revolts a little our prejudices; yet there is no resting-place, and we must admit this, or be content to sink ourselves into a mass of medullary fibre. Brutes have been as slowly emancipated in philosophy as some classes of mankind have been in civil polity; their souls, we see, were almost universally disputed to them at the end of the seventeenth century, even by those who did not absolutely bring them down to machinery. Even within the recollection of many it was common to deny them any kind of reasoning faculty, and to solve their most sagacious actions by the vague word instinct. We have come of late years to think better of our humble companions; and, as usual in similar cases, the predominant bias, at least with foreign naturalists, seems rather too much of a levelling character.

117. No quality more remarkably distinguishes Locke than his love of truth. He is of no sect or party, has no oblique design, such as we so frequently perceive, of sustaining some tenet *His love of truth and originality.* which he suppresses, no submissiveness to the opinions of others, nor, what very few lay aside, to his own. Without having adopted certain dominant ideas, like Descartes and Malebranche, he follows with inflexible impartiality and unwearied patience the long process of analysis to which he has subjected the human mind. No great writer has been more exempt from vanity, in which he is very advantageously contrasted with Bacon and Descartes; but he is sometimes a little sharp and contemptuous of his predecessors. The originality of Locke

is real and unaffected ; not that he has derived nothing
from others, which would be a great reproach to himself
or to them, but in whatever he has in common with
other philosophers there is always a tinge of his own
thoughts, a modification of the particular tenet, or at
least a peculiarity of language which renders it not very
easy of detection.   " It was not to be expected," says
Stewart, " that in a work so composed by snatches, to
borrow a phrase of the author, he should be able accurately to draw the line between his own ideas and the
hints for which he was indebted to others.   To those
who are well acquainted with his speculations it must
appear evident that he had studied diligently the metaphysical writings both of Hobbes and Gassendi, and
that he was no stranger to the Essays of Montaigne, to
the philosophical works of Bacon, and to Malebranche's
Inquiry after Truth.   That he was familiarly conversant
with the Cartesian system may be presumed from what
we are told by his biographer, that it was this which
first inspired him with a disgust at the jargon of the
schools, and led him into that train of thinking which
he afterwards prosecuted so successfully.   I do not,
however, recollect that he has anywhere in his Essay
mentioned the name of any one of those authors.   It is
probable that when he sat down to write he found the
result of his youthful reading so completely identified
with the fruits of his subsequent reflections, that it was
impossible for him to attempt a separation of the one
from the other, and that he was thus occasionally led to
mistake the treasures of memory for those of invention.
That this was really the case may be further presumed
from the peculiar and original cast of his phraseology,
which, though in general careless and unpolished, has
always the merit of that characteristical unity and raciness of style which demonstrate that while he was
writing he conceived himself to be drawing only from
his own resources."[a]

118. The writer, however, whom we have just quoted
Defended in has not quite done justice to the originality of
two cases. Locke in more than one instance.   Thus on
this very passage we find a note in these words :—

---

[a] **Preliminary Dissertation.**

" Mr. Addison has remarked that Malebranche had the start of Locke by several years in his notions on the subject of duration. Some other coincidences not less remarkable might be easily pointed out in the opinions of the English and of the French philosopher." I am not prepared to dispute, nor do I doubt, the truth of the latter sentence. But with respect to the notions of Malebranche and Locke on duration, it must be said, that they are neither the same, nor has Addison asserted them to be so.[b] The one threw out an hypothesis with no attempt at proof; the other offered an explanation of the phænomena. What Locke has advanced as to our getting the idea of duration by reflecting on the succession of our ideas seems to be truly his own. Whether it be entirely the right explanation, is another question. It rather appears to me that the internal sense, as we may not improperly call it, of duration belongs separately to each idea, and is rather lost than suggested by their succession. Duration is best perceived when we are able to detain an idea for some time without change, as in watching the motion of a pendulum. And though it is impossible for the mind to continue in this state of immobility more perhaps than about a second or two, this is sufficient to give us an idea of duration as the necessary condition of existence. Whether this be an objective or merely a subjective necessity, is an abstruse question, which our sensations do not enable us to decide. But Locke appears to have looked rather at the measure of duration, by which we divide it into portions, than at the mere simplicity of the idea itself. Such a measure, it is certain, can only be obtained through the medium of a succession in our ideas.

119. It has been also remarked by Stewart that Locke claims a discovery due rather to Descartes, namely, the impossibility of defining simple ideas. Descartes, however, as well as the authors of the Port-Royal Logic, merely says that words already as clear as we can make them, do not require, or even admit of definition. But I do not perceive that he has made the distinction we find in the Essay on the Human Understanding, that the names of simple ideas are not capable of any defini-

b Spectator, No. 94.

tion, while the names of all complex ideas are so. " It has not, that I know," Locke says, " been observed by anybody what words are, and what words are not, capable of being defined." The passage which I have quoted in another place from Descartes' posthumous dialogue, even if it went to this length, was unknown to Locke ; yet he might have acknowledged that he had been in some measure anticipated in other observations by that philosopher.

120. The first book of the Essay on the Human Understanding is directed, as is well known, against the doctrine of innate ideas, or innate principles in the mind. This has been often censured, as combating in some places a tenet which no one would support, and as, in other passages, breaking in upon moral distinctions themselves, by disputing the universality of their acknowledgment. With respect to the former charge, it is not perhaps easy for us to determine what might be the crude and confused notions, or at least language, of many who held the theory of innate ideas. It is by no means evident that Locke had Descartes chiefly or even at all in his view. Lord Herbert, whom he distinctly answers, and many others, especially the Platonists, had dwelt upon innate ideas in far stronger terms than the great French metaphysician, if indeed he can be said to have maintained them at all. The latter and more important accusation rests upon no other pretext than that Locke must be reckoned among those who have not admitted a moral faculty of discerning right from wrong to be a part of our constitution. But that there is a law of nature imposed by the Supreme Being, and consequently universal, has been so repeatedly asserted in his writings, that it would imply great inattention to question it. Stewart has justly vindicated Locke in this respect from some hasty and indefinite charges of Beattie ;[c] but I must venture to think that he goes much too far when he attempts to identify the doctrines of the Essay with those of Shaftesbury. These two philosophers were in opposite schools as to the test

His view of innate ideas.

---

[c] [To the passages quoted by Stewart (First Dissertation, p. 29) we may add a letter since published, of Locke to Mr. Tyrrell, wherein he most explicitly declares his belief, " that there is a law of nature knowable by the light of nature." King's Life of Locke, vol. i. p. 366.— 1847.]

of moral sentiments. Locke seems always to adopt what is called the selfish system in morals, resolving all morality into religion, and all religion into a regard to our own interest. And he seems to have paid less attention to the emotions than to the intellectual powers of the soul.

121. It would by no means be difficult to controvert other tenets of this great man. But the obliga- General praise. tions we owe to him for the Essay on the Human Understanding are never to be forgotten. It is truly the first real chart of the coasts; wherein some may be laid down incorrectly, but the general relations of all are perceived. And we who find some things to censure in Locke have perhaps learned how to censure them from himself; we have thrown off so many false notions and films of prejudice by his help that we are become capable of judging our master. This is what has been the fate of all who have pushed onward the landmarks of science; they have made that easy for inferior men which was painfully laboured through by themselves. Among many excellent things in the Essay on Human Understanding none are more admirable than much of the third book on the nature of words, especially the three chapters on their imperfection and abuse.[d] In earlier treatises of logic, at least in that of Port-Royal, some of this might be found; but nowhere are verbal fallacies, and above all, the sources from which they spring, so fully and conclusively exposed.[e]

d [In former editions I had said " the whole third book," which Mr. Mill calls " that immortal third book." But we must except the sixth chapter on the names of substances, in which Locke's reasoning against the real distinction of species in the three kingdoms of nature is full of false assumptions, and cannot be maintained at all in the present state of natural history. He asks, ch. vi. § 13, " What are the alterations may or may not be in a horse or lead, without making either of them to be of another species?" The answer is obvious, that an animal engendered between a horse and mare, is a horse, and no other; and that any alteration in the atomic weight of lead would make it a different species. " I once saw a creature," says Locke, " that was the issue of a cat and a rat, and had the plain marks of both about it." This cannot be true; but if it were? Are there, therefore, no mere cats and mere rats?—1847.]

e [A highly-distinguished philosopher, M. Cousin, has devoted nearly a volume to the refutation of Locke, discussing almost every chapter in the second and fourth books of the Essay on Human Understanding. In many of these treatises I cannot by any means go along with the able writer; and regret that he has taken so little pains to distinguish real from verbal differences of opinion, but has, on the contrary, had nothing so much at heart as to depreciate the glory of one whom Europe has long reckoned among the founders of metaphysical science. It may have been wrong in Locke to employ

122. The same praiseworthy diligence in hunting error to its lurking-places distinguishes the short

the word *idea* in different senses. But, as undoubtedly he did not always mean by it an image in the mind, what can be less fair than such passages as the following? " Eh bien! songez y, vous n'avez de connaissance légitime de la pensée, de la volonté, de la sensibilité, qu'à la condition que les idées que vous en ayez vous les représentent; et ces idées doivent être des images, et par conséquent des images matérielles. Jugez dans quelle abîme d'absurdités nous voilà tombés. Pour connaître la pensée et la volonté qui sont immatérielles, il faut que nous en ayons une image matérielle qui leur ressemble." (Cours de l'Hist. de la Philos., vol. ii. p. 348, ed. 1829.) It ought surely to have occurred that, in proportion to the absurdity of such a proposition, was the want of likelihood that a mind eminently cautious and reflective should have embraced it.

It is not possible in a note to remark on the many passages wherein M. Cousin has dealt no fair measure to our illustrious metaphysician. But one I will not pass over. He quotes Locke for the words: " A l'égard des esprits (nos âmes, les intelligences) [interpolation by M. Cousin himself], nous ne pouvons pas plus connaître qu'il y a des esprits finis réellement existans, par les idées que nous en avons, que nous ne pouvons connaître qu'il y a des fées ou des centaures par les idées que nous nous en formons." Voilà bien, ce me semble, le scepticisme absolu; et vous pensez peut-être que la conclusion dernière de Locke sera qu'il n'y a aucune connoissance des esprits finis, par conséquent de notre âme, par conséquent encore d'aucune des facultés de notre âme; car l'objection est aussi valable contre les phénomènes de l'âme que contre la substance. C'est là où il aurait dû aboutir; mais il ne l'ose, parce qu'il n'y a pas un philosophe à la fois plus sage et plus inconsistant que Locke. Que fait-il, Messieurs? Dans le péril où le pousse la philosophie, il abandonne sa philosophie et toute philosophie, et il en appelle au christianisme, à la révélation, à la foi; et par foi, par révélation, il n'entend pas une foi, une révélation philosophique; cette interprétation n'appartient

pas au temps de Locke; il entend la foi et la révélation dans le sens propre de la théologie la plus orthodoxe; et il conclut ainsi: " Par conséquent, sur l'existence de l'esprit nous devons nous contenter de l'évidence de la foi." P. 350. Who could suppose that all this imputation of unlimited scepticism, not less than that of Hume, since it amounts to a doubt of the existence of our own minds, is founded on M. Cousin's misunderstanding of the word *spirit*? By spirits, or finite spirits, Locke did not mean our own minds, but created intelligences, differing from human, as the word was constantly used in theological metaphysics. The sense of the passage to which M. Cousin refers is so clear, that no English reader could misconceive it; probably he was led wrong by a translation in which he found the word *esprit*.

But I really cannot imagine any translation to be so unfaithful as to remove from M. Cousin the blame of extreme carelessness. The words of Locke are, " Concerning finite spirits, as well as several other things, we must content ourselves with the evidence of faith." B. iv. ch. 11. But at the beginning of the same chapter he says, " The knowledge of our own being we have by intuition." And in the preceding, the tenth chapter, more fully: " I think it is beyond question that man has a clear perception of his own being: he knows certainly that he exists, and that he is something. He that can doubt whether he be anything or no, I speak not to, no more than I would argue with pure nothing, or endeavour to convince non-entity that it were something." Compare this with M. Cousin's representation.

The name of Locke is part of our literary inheritance, which, as Englishmen, we cannot sacrifice. If, indeed, the university at which he was educated cannot discover that he is, perhaps, her chief boast, if a declaimer from that quarter presumes to speak of " the sophist Locke," we may console ourselves by recollecting how little influence such a local party is likely to obtain over the literary world. But the fame of M. Cousin is so conspicuous, that his prejudices readily

treatise on the Conduct of the Understanding; which having been originally designed as an additional chapter to the Essay,[f] is as it were the ethical application of its theory, and ought always to be read with it, if indeed, for the sake of its practical utility, it should not come sooner into the course of education. Aristotle himself, and the whole of his dialectical school, had pointed out many of the sophisms against which we should guard our reasoning faculties ; but these are chiefly such as others attempt to put upon us in dispute. There are more dangerous fallacies by which we cheat ourselves ; prejudice, partiality, self-interest, vanity, inattention, and indifference to truth. Locke, who was as exempt from these as almost any man who has turned his mind to so many subjects where their influence is to be suspected, has dwelled on the moral discipline of the intellect in this treatise better, as I conceive, than any of his predecessors, though we have already seen, and it might appear far more at length to those who should have recourse to the books, that Arnauld and Malebranche, besides other French philosophers of the age, had not been remiss in this indispensable part of logic.

123. Locke throughout this treatise labours to secure the inquirer from that previous persuasion of his own opinion, which generally renders all his pretended investigations of its truth little more than illusive and nugatory. But the indifferency which he recommends to everything except truth itself, so that we should not even wish anything to be true before we have examined whether it be so, seems to involve the impossible hypothesis that man is but a purely reasoning being. It is vain to press the recommendation of freedom from prejudice so far ; since we cannot but conceive some propositions to be more connected with our welfare than others, and consequently to desire their truth. These exaggerations lay a fundamental condition of honest inquiry open to the sneers of its adversaries ; and it is sufficient, because nothing more is really attainable, first to dispossess ourselves of the notion that our interests

become the prejudices of many, and his misrepresentations pass with many for unanswerable criticisms.—1847.]

[f] See a letter to Molyneux, dated April, 1697. Locke's Works (fol. 1759), vol. iii. p. 539.

are concerned where they are not, and next, even when we cannot but wish one result of our inquiries rather than another, to be the more unremitting in our endeavours to exclude this bias from our reasoning.

124. I cannot think any parent or instructor justified in neglecting to put this little treatise in the hands of a boy about the time when the reasoning faculties become developed. It will give him a sober and serious, not flippant or self-conceited, independency of thinking; and while it teaches how to distrust ourselves and to watch those prejudices which necessarily grow up from one cause or another, will inspire a reasonable confidence in what he has well considered, by taking off a little of that deference to authority, which is the more to be regretted in its excess, that, like its cousin-german, party-spirit, it is frequently united to loyalty of heart and the generous enthusiasm of youth.

CHAPTER IV.

HISTORY OF MORAL AND POLITICAL PHILOSOPHY AND OF JURISPRUDENCE, FROM 1650 TO 1700.

~~~~~~~~~~~~~~~

Sect. I.—On Moral Philosophy.

Pascal's Provincial Letters — Taylor — Cudworth — Spinosa — Cumberland's Law of Nature — Puffendorf's Treatise on the same Subject — Rochefoucault and La Bruyère — Locke on Education — Fenelon.

1. The casuistical writers of the Roman church, and especially of the Jesuit order, belong to earlier periods; for little room was left for any thing but popular compilations from large works of vast labour and accredited authority. But the false principles imputed to the latter school now raised a louder cry than before. Implacable and unsparing enemies, as well as ambitious intriguers themselves, they were encountered by a host of those who envied, feared, and hated them. Among those none were such willing or able accusers as the Jansenists whom they persecuted. Pascal, by his Provincial Letters, did more to ruin the name of Jesuit than all the controversies of Protestantism, or all the fulminations of the parliament of Paris. A letter of Antony Arnauld, published in 1655, wherein he declared that he could not find in Jansenius the propositions condemned by the pope, and laid himself open to censure by some of his own, provoked the Sorbonne, of which he was a member, to exclude him from the faculty of theology. Before this resolution was taken, Pascal came forward in defence of his friend, under a fictitious name, in the first of what have been always called Lettres Provinciales, but more accurately, Lettres écrites par Louis de Montalte à un Provincial de ses Amis. In the first four of them he discusses the thorny problems of Jansenism, aiming

chiefly to show that St. Thomas Aquinas had maintained the same doctrine on efficacious grace which his disciples the Dominicans now rejected from another quarter. But he passed from hence to a theme more generally intelligible and interesting, the false morality of the Jesuit casuists. He has accumulated so long a list of scandalous decisions, and dwelled upon them with so much wit and spirit, and yet with so serious a severity, that the order of Loyola became a by-word with mankind. I do not agree with those who think the Provincial Letters a greater proof of the genius of Pascal than his Thoughts, in spite of the many weaknesses in reasoning which these display. The former are at present, finely written as all confess them to be, too much filled with obsolete controversy, they quote books too much forgotten, they have too little bearing on any permanent sympathies, to be read with much interest or pleasure.

2. The Jesuits had, unfortunately for themselves, no writers at that time of sufficient ability to defend them; and being disliked by many who were not Jansenists, could make little stand against their adversaries, till public opinion had already taken its line. They have since not failed to charge Pascal with extreme misrepresentation of their eminent casuists, Escobar, Busenbaum, and many others, so that some later disciples of their school have ventured to call the Provincial Letters the immortal liars (les immortelles menteuses). It has been insinuated, since Pascal's veracity is hard to attack, that he was deceived by those from whom he borrowed his quotations. But he has himself declared, in a remarkable passage, not only that, far from repenting of these letters, he would make them yet stronger if it were to be done again, but that, although he had not read all the books he has quoted, else he must have spent great part of his life in reading bad books, yet he had read Escobar twice through; and with respect to the rest, he had not quoted a single passage without having seen it in the book, and examined the context before and after, that he might not confound an objection with an answer, which would have been reprehensible and unjust: it is therefore impossible to save the honour of Pascal, if his quotations are not

Their truth questioned by some.

* Œuvres de Pascal, vol. i. p. 400.

fair.   Nor did he stand alone in his imputations on the Jesuit casuistry.   A book, called Morale des Jésuites, by Nicolas Perrault, published at Mons in 1667, goes over the same ground with less pleasantry, but not less learning.

3. The most extensive and learned work on casuistry which has appeared in the English language is the Ductor Dubitantium of Jeremy Taylor, published in 1660.   This, as its title shows, *Taylor's Ductor Dubitantium.* treats of subjective morality, or the guidance of the conscience.   But this cannot be much discussed without establishing some principles of objective right and wrong, some standard by which the conscience is to be ruled.   "The whole measure and rule of conscience," according to Taylor, " is the law of God, or God's will signified to us by nature or revelation; and by the several manners and times and parts of its communication it hath obtained several names ;—the law of nature— the consent of nations—right reason—the Decalogue— the sermon of Christ—the canons of the apostles—the laws ecclesiastical and civil of princes and governors— fame or the public reputation of things, expressed by proverbs and other instances and manners of public honesty. ... These being the full measures of right and wrong, of lawful and unlawful, will be the rule of conscience and the subject of the present book."

4. The heterogeneous combination of things so different in nature and authority, as if they were *Its character and defects.* all expressions of the law of God, does not augur well for the distinctness of Taylor's moral philosophy, and would be disadvantageously compared with the Ecclesiastical Polity of Hooker.   Nor are we deceived in the anticipations we might draw. With many of Taylor's excellences, his vast fertility and his frequent acuteness, the Ductor Dubitantium exhibits his characteristic defects; the waste of quotations is even greater than in his other writings, and his own exuberance of mind degenerates into an intolerable prolixity.   His solution of moral difficulties is often unsatisfactory; after an accumulation of arguments and authorities we have the disappointment to perceive that the knot is neither untied nor cut; there seems a want of close investigation of principles, a frequent confusion and

obscurity, which Taylor's two chief faults, excessive display of erudition and redundancy of language, conspire to produce. Paley is no doubt often superficial, and sometimes mistaken ; yet in clearness, in conciseness, in freedom from impertinent reference to authority, he is far superior to Taylor.

5. Taylor seems too much inclined to side with those who resolve all right and wrong into the positive will of God. The law of nature he defines to be " the universal law of the world, or of mankind, to which we are inclined by nature, invited by consent, prompted by reason, but which is bound upon us only by the command of God." Though in the strict meaning of the word, law, this may be truly said, it was surely required, considering the large sense which that word has obtained as coincident with moral right, that a fuller explanation should be given than Taylor has even intimated, lest the goodness of the Deity should seem something arbitrary and precarious. And though, in maintaining, against most of the scholastic metaphysicians, that God can dispense with the precepts of the Decalogue, he may be substantially right, yet his reasons seem by no means the clearest and most satisfactory that might be assigned. It may be added, that in his prolix rules concerning what he calls a probable conscience, he comes very near to the much decried theories of the Jesuits. There was indeed a vein of subtilty in Taylor's understanding which was not always without influence on his candour.

6. A treatise concerning eternal and immutable mora-
Cudworth's lity, by Cudworth, was first published in 1731.
immutable This may be almost reckoned a portion of his
morality. Intellectual System, the object being what he has declared to be one of those which he had there in view. This was to prove that moral differences of right and wrong are antecedent to any divine law. He wrote therefore not only against the Calvinistic school, but in some measure against Taylor, though he abstains from mentioning any recent author except Descartes, who had gone far in referring all moral distinctions to the arbitrary will of God. Cudworth's reasoning is by no means satisfactory, and rests too much on the dogmatic metaphysics which were going out of use. The nature

or essence of nothing, he maintains, can depend upon the will of God alone, which is the efficient, but not the formal, cause of all things ; a distinction not very intelligible, but on which he seems to build his theory.[b] For, though admitting that moral relations have no objective existence out of the mind, he holds that they have a positive essence, and therefore are not nothing ; whence it follows that they must be independent of will. He pours out much ancient learning, though not so lavishly as in the Intellectual System.

7. The urgent necessity of contracting my sails in this last period, far the most abundant as it is in the variety and extent of its literature, re- Nicole—La Placette. strains me from more than a bare mention of several works not undeserving of regard. The Essais de Morale of Nicole are less read than esteemed, says a late biographer.[c] Voltaire however prophesied that they would not perish. " The chapter, especially," he proceeds, " on the means of preserving peace among men is a master-piece to which nothing equal has been left to us by antiquity."[d] These Essays are properly contained in six volumes ; but so many other pieces are added in some editions that the collection under that title is very long. La Placette, minister of a French church at Copenhagen, has been called the Protestant Nicole. His Essais de Morale, in 1692 and other years, are full of a solid morality, rather strict in casuistry, and apparently not deficient in observation, and analytical views of human nature. They were much esteemed in their own age. Works of this kind treat so very closely on the department of practical religion that it is sometimes difficult to separate them on any fixed principle. A less homiletical form, a comparative absence of Scriptural quotation, a more reasoning and observing mode of dealing with the subject, are the chief distinctions. But in the sermons of Barrow and some others we find a great deal of what may be justly called moral philosophy.

8. A book by Sharrock, De Officiis secundum Rationis Humanæ Dictata, 1660, is occasionally quoted, Other writers. and seems to be of a philosophical nature.[e]

b P. 15.   c Biog. Univ.
d Siècle de Louis XIV.
e Cumberland (in præfatione) De Legibus Naturæ.

Velthuysen, a Dutch minister, was of more reputation.
His name was rather obnoxious to the orthodox, since he
was a strenuous advocate of toleration, a Cartesian in
philosophy, and inclined to judge for himself. His chief
works are De Principiis Justi et Decori, and De Natu-
rali Pudore.[f] But we must now pass on to those who
have exercised a greater influence in moral philosophy,
Cumberland and Puffendorf, after giving a short consideration to Spinosa.

9. The moral system, if so it may be called, of Spinosa,
Moral has been developed by him in the fourth and
System of fifth parts of his Ethics. We are not deceived
Spinosa. in what might naturally be expected from the
unhesitating adherence of Spinosa to a rigorous line of
reasoning, that his ethical scheme would offer nothing inconsistent with the fundamental pantheism of his philosophy. In nature itself, he maintains as before, there is
neither perfection nor imperfection, neither good nor evil ;
but these are modes of speaking, adopted to express the
relations of things as they appear to our minds. Whatever contains more positive attributes capable of being
apprehended by us than another contains, is more perfect
than it. Whatever we know to be useful to ourselves,
that is good ; and whatever impedes our attainment of
good, is evil. By this utility Spinosa does not understand happiness, if by that is meant pleasurable sensation,
but the extension of our mental and bodily capacities.
The passions restrain and overpower these capacities ;
and coming from without, that is, from the body, render
the mind a less powerful agent than it seems to be. It
is only, we may remember, in a popular sense, and
subject to his own definitions, that Spinosa acknowledges
the mind to be an agent at all ; it is merely so, in so far
as its causes of action cannot be referred by us to any
thing external. No passion can be restrained except by
a stronger passion. Hence even a knowledge of what
is really good or evil for us can of itself restrain no
passion ; but only as it is associated with a perception
of joy and sorrow, which is a mode of passion. This
perception is necessarily accompanied by desire or aversion ; but they may often be so weak as to be controlled
by other sentiments of the same class inspired by con-

<hr>

f Biogr. Univ.   Barbeyrac's notes on Puffendorf, passim.

flicting passions. This is the cause of the weakness and inconstancy of many, and he alone is wise and virtuous who steadily pursues what is useful to himself; that is, what reason points out as the best means of preserving his well-being and extending his capacities. Nothing is absolutely good, nothing therefore is principally sought by a virtuous man, but knowledge, not of things external, which gives us only inadequate ideas, but of God. Other things are good or evil to us so far as they suit our nature or contradict it; and so far as men act by reason, they must agree in seeking what is conformable to their nature. And those who agree with us in living by reason, are themselves of all things most suitable to our nature; so that the society of such men is most to be desired; and to enlarge that society by rendering men virtuous, and by promoting their advantage when they are so, is most useful to ourselves. For the good of such as pursue virtue may be enjoyed by all, and does not obstruct our own. Whatever conduces to the common society of mankind and promotes concord among them is useful to all; and whatever has an opposite tendency is pernicious. The passions are sometimes incapable of excess, but of this the only instances are joy and cheerfulness; more frequently they become pernicious by being indulged, and in some cases, such as hatred, can never be useful. We should therefore, for our own sakes, meet the hatred and malevolence of others with love and liberality. Spinosa dwells much on the preference due to a social above a solitary life, to cheerfulness above austerity, and alludes frequently to the current theological ethics with censure.

10. The fourth part of the Ethics is entitled On Human Slavery, meaning the subjugation of the reason to the passions; the fifth, On Human Liberty, is designed to show, as had been partly done in the former, how the mind or intellectual man is to preserve its supremacy. This is to be effected, not by the extinction, which is impossible, but the moderation of the passions; and the secret of doing this, according to Spinosa, is to contemplate such things as are naturally associated with affections of no great violence. We find that when we look at things simply in themselves, and not in their necessary relations, they affect us more powerfully; whence

it may be inferred that we shall weaken the passion by viewing them as parts of a necessary series. We promote the same end by considering the object of the passion in many different relations, and in general by enlarging the sphere of our knowledge concerning it. Hence the more adequate ideas we attain of things that affect us, the less we shall be overcome by the passion they excite. But most of all it should be our endeavour to refer all things to the idea of God. The more we understand ourselves and our passions, the more we shall love God ; for the more we understand anything, the more pleasure we have in contemplating it ; and we shall associate the idea of God with this pleasurable contemplation, which is the essence of love. The love of God should be the chief employment of the mind. But God has no passions ; therefore he who desires that God should love him, desires in fact that he should cease to be God. And the more we believe others to be united in the same love of God, the more we shall love him ourselves.

11. The great aim of the mind, and the greatest degree of virtue, is the knowledge of things in their essence. This knowledge is the perfection of human nature ; it is accompanied with the greatest joy and contentment ; it leads to a love of God, intellectual, not imaginative, eternal, because not springing from passions that perish with the body, being itself a portion of that infinite love with which God intellectually loves himself. In this love towards God our chief felicity consists, which is not the reward of virtue, but virtue itself ; nor is any one happy because he has overcome the passions, but it is by being happy, that is, by enjoying the fulness of divine love, that he has become capable of overcoming them.

12. These extraordinary effusions confirm what has been hinted in another place, that Spinosa, in the midst of his atheism, seemed often to hover over the regions of mystical theology. This last book of the Ethics speaks, as is evident, the very language of Quietism. In Spinosa himself it is not easy to understand the meaning ; his sincerity ought not, I think, to be called in question ; and this enthusiasm may be set down to the rapture of the imagination expatiating in the enchanting wilderness of its creation. But the possibility of combining such

a tone of contemplative devotion with the systematic denial of a Supreme Being, in any personal sense, may put us on our guard against the tendency of mysticism, which may again, as it has frequently, degenerate into a similar chaos.

13. The science of ethics, in the third quarter of the seventeenth century, seemed to be cultivated by three very divergent schools—by that of the theologians, who went no farther than revelation, or at least than the positive law of God, for moral distinctions—by that of the Platonic philosophers, who sought them in eternal and intrinsic relations ; and that of Hobbes and Spinosa, who reduced them all to selfish prudence.   A fourth theory, which, in some of its modifications, has greatly prevailed in the last two centuries, may be referred to Richard Cumberland, afterwards Bishop of Peterborough.   His famous work, De Legibus Naturæ Disquisitio Philosophica, was published in 1672.   It is contained in nine chapters, besides the preface or prolegomena. *margin: Cumberland's De Legibus Naturæ.*

14. Cumberland begins by mentioning Grotius, Selden, and one or two more who have investigated the laws of nature *à posteriori*, that is, by the testimony of authors and the consent of nations. But as some objections may be started against this mode of proof, which, though he does not hold them to be valid, are likely to have some effect, he prefers another line of demonstration, deducing the laws of nature, as effects, from their real causes in the constitution of nature itself.   The Platonic theory of innate moral ideas, sufficient to establish natural law, he does not admit.   "For myself at least I may say, that I have not been so fortunate as to arrive at the knowledge of this law by so compendious a road."   He deems it, therefore, necessary to begin with what we learn by daily use and experience, assuming nothing but the physical laws of motion shown by mathematicians, and the derivation of all their operations from the will of a First Cause. *margin: Analysis of prolegomena.*

15. By diligent observation of all propositions which can be justly reckoned general moral laws of nature, he finds that they may be reduced to one, the pursuit of the common good of all rational agents, which tends to our own good as part of the whole ; as its opposite tends not

only to the misery of the whole system, but to our own.[g]
This tendency, he takes care to tell us, though he uses
the present tense (conducit), has respect to the most
remote consequences, and is so understood by him. The
means which serve to this end, the general good, may be
treated as theorems in a geometrical method.[h] Cumberland, as we have seen in Spinosa, was captivated by the
apparent security of this road to truth.

16. This scheme, he observes, may at first sight want
the two requisites of a law, a legislator and a sanction.
But whatever is naturally assented to by our minds must
spring from the author of nature. God is proved to be
the author of every proposition which is proved to be
true by the constitution of nature, which has him for its
author.[i] Nor is a sanction wanting in the rewards, that
is, the happiness which attends the observance of the
law of nature, and in the opposite effects of its neglect;
and in a lax sense, though not that of the jurists, reward
as well as punishment may be included in the word
sanction.[k] But benevolence, that is, love and desire of
good towards all rational beings, includes piety towards
God, the greatest of them all, as well as humanity.[m]
Cumberland altogether abstains from arguments founded
on revelation, and is perhaps the first writer on natural
law who has done so, for they may even be found in
Hobbes. And I think that he may be reckoned the
founder of what is awkwardly and invidiously called the
utilitarian school; for though similar expressions about
the common good may sometimes be found in the ancients,
it does not seem to have been the basis of any ethical
system.

17. This common good, not any minute particle of it,
as the benefit of a single man, is the great end of the
legislator and of him who obeys his will. And such
human actions as by their natural tendency promote the
common good may be called naturally good, more than
those which tend only to the good of any one man, by
how much the whole is greater than this small part.
And whatever is directed in the shortest way to this
end may be called right, as a right line is the shortest
of all. And as the whole system of the universe, when

[g] Prolegomena, sect. 9.　　[h] Sect. 12.　　[i] Sect. 13.
[k] Sect. 14.　　[m] Sect. 15.

all things are arranged so as to produce happiness, is beautiful, being aptly disposed to its end, which is the definition of beauty, so particular actions contributing to this general harmony may be called beautiful and becoming."

18. Cumberland acutely remarks, in answer to the objection to the practice of virtue from the evils which fall on good men, and the success of the wicked, that no good or evil is to be considered, in this point of view, which arises from mere necessity, or external causes, and not from our virtue or vice itself. He then shows that a regard for piety and peace, for mutual intercourse, and civil and domestic polity, tends to the happiness of every one; and in reckoning the good consequences of virtuous behaviour we are not only to estimate the pleasure intimately connected with it, which the love of God and of good men produces, but the contingent benefits we obtain by civil society, which we promote by such conduct.° And we see that in all nations there is some regard to good faith and the distribution of property, some respect to the obligation of oaths, some attachments to relations and friends. All men, therefore, acknowledge, and to a certain extent perform, those things which really tend to the common good. And though crime and violence sometimes prevail, yet these are like diseases in the body which it shakes off; or if, like them, they prove sometimes mortal to a single community, yet human society is immortal; and the conservative principles of common good have in the end far more efficacy than those which dissolve and destroy states.

19. We may reckon the happiness consequent on virtue as a true sanction of natural law annexed to it by its author, and thus fulfilling the necessary conditions of its definition. And though some have laid less stress on these sanctions, and deemed virtue its own reward, and gratitude to God and man its best motive, yet the consent of nations and common experience show us that the observance of the first end, which is the common good, will not be maintained without remuneration or penal consequences.

20. By this single principle of common good we sim-

[a] Prolegomena, sect. 16.   ° Sect. 20.

plify the method of natural law, and arrange its secondary precepts in such subordination as best conduces to the general end.   Hence moral rules give way in particular cases, when they come in collision with others of more extensive importance.   For all ideas of right or virtue imply a relation to the system and nature of all rational beings.   And the principles thus deduced as to moral conduct are generally applicable to political societies, which in their two leading institutions, the division of property and the coercive power of the magistrate, follow the steps of natural law, and adopt these rules of polity, because they perceive them to promote the common weal.

21. From all intermixture of Scriptural authority Cumberland proposes to abstain, building only on reason and experience, since we believe the Scriptures to proceed from God because they illustrate and promote the law of nature. He seems to have been the first Christian writer who sought to establish systematically the principles of moral right independently of revelation. They are, indeed, taken for granted by many, especially those who adopted the Platonic language ; or the schoolmen may have demonstrated them by arguments derived from reason, but seldom, if ever, without some collateral reference to theological authority. In this respect, therefore, Cumberland may be deemed to make an epoch in the history of ethical philosophy, though Puffendorf, whose work was published the same year, may have nearly equal claims to it. If we compare the Treatise on the Laws of Nature with the Ductor Dubitantium of Taylor, written a very few years before, we shall find ourselves in a new world of moral reasoning. The schoolmen and fathers, the canonists and casuists, have vanished like ghosts at the first daylight ; the continual appeal is to experience, and never to authority ; or if authority can be said to appear at all in the pages of Cumberland, it is that of the great apostles of experimental philosophy, Descartes or Huygens, or Harvey or Willis. His mind, liberal and comprehensive as well as acute, had been forcibly impressed with the discoveries of his own age, both in mathematical science and in what is now more strictly called physiology. From this armoury he chose his weapons, and employed them, in some instances, with

great sagacity and depth of thought.   From the brilliant success also of the modern analysis, as well as from the natural prejudice in favour of a mathematical method, which arises from the acknowledged superiority of that science in the determination of its proper truths, he was led to expect more from the use of similar processes in moral reasoning than we have found justified by experience.   And this analogy had probably some effect on one of the chief errors of his ethical system, the reduction, at least in theory, of the morality of actions to definite calculation.

22. The prolegomena or preface to Cumberland's treatise contains that statement of his system with which we have been hitherto concerned, and which the whole volume does but expand. His theory expanded afterwards. His manner of reasoning is diffuse, abounding in repetitions, and often excursive; we cannot avoid perceiving that he labours long on propositions which no adversary would dispute, or on which the dispute could be little else than one of verbal definition.   This however is almost the universal failing of preceding philosophers, and was only put an end to, if it can be said yet to have ceased, by the sharper logic of controversy which a more general regard to metaphysical inquiries, and a juster sense of the value of words, brought into use.

23. The question between Cumberland and his adversaries, that is, the school of Hobbes, is stated to be, whether certain propositions of immutable truth, directing the voluntary actions of men in choosing good and avoiding evil, and imposing an obligation upon them, independently of civil laws, are necessarily suggested to the mind by the nature of things and by that of mankind.   And the affirmative of this question he undertakes to prove from a consideration of the nature of both: from which many particular rules might be deduced, but above all that which comprehends all the rest, and is the basis of his theory; namely, that the greatest possible benevolence (not a mere languid desire, but an energetic principle) of every rational agent towards all the rest constitutes the happiest condition of each and of all, so far as depends on their own power, and is necessarily required for their greatest happiness;

whence the common good is the supreme law. That God is the author of this law appears evident from his being the author of all nature and of all the physical laws according to which impressions are made on our minds.

24. It is easy to observe by daily experience that we have the power of doing good to others, and that no men are so happy or so secure as they who most exert this. And this may be proved synthetically and in that more rigorous method which he affects, though it now and then leads the reader away from the simplest argument, by considering our own faculties of speech and language, the capacities of the hand and countenance, the skill we possess in sciences and in useful arts ; all of which conduce to the social life of mankind and to their mutual co-operation and benefit. Whatever preserves and perfects the nature of anything, that is to be called good, and the opposite evil ; so that Hobbes has crudely asserted good to respect only the agent desiring it, and consequently to be variable. In this it will be seen that the dispute is chiefly verbal.

25. Two corollaries of great importance in the theory of ethics spring from a consideration of our physical powers. The first is, that, inasmuch as they are limited by their nature, we should never seek to transgress their bounds, but distinguish, as the Stoics did, things within our reach, $\tau\grave{a}$ $\dot{\epsilon}\phi'$ $\dot{\eta}\mu\hat{\iota}\nu$, from those beyond it, $\tau\grave{a}$ $o\mathring{v}\kappa$ $\dot{\epsilon}\phi'$ $\dot{\eta}\mu\hat{\iota}\nu$, thus relieving our minds from anxious passions, and turning them to the prudent use of the means assigned to us. The other is one which applies more closely to his general principle of morals ; that, as all we can do in respect of others, and all the enjoyment we or they can have of particular things, is limited to certain persons, as well as by space and time, we perceive the necessity of distribution, both as to things, from which spring the rights of property, and as to persons, by which our benevolence, though a general rule in itself, is practically directed towards individuals. For the conservation of an aggregate whole is the same as that of its divided parts, that is, of single persons, which requires a distributive exercise of the powers of each. Hence property and dominion, or *meum* and *tuum*, in the most general sense, are consequences from the general law of nature. Without a support from that law, according to Cumber-

land, without a positive tendency to the good of all rational agents, we should have no right even to things necessary for our preservation; nor have we that right, if a greater evil would be incurred by our preservation than by our destruction. It may be added, as a more universal reflection, that, as all which we see in nature is so framed as to persevere in its appointed state, and as the human body is endowed with the power of throwing off whatever is noxious and threatens the integrity of its condition, we may judge from this that the conservation of mankind in its best state must be the design of nature, and that their own voluntary actions conducing to that end must be such as the Author of nature commands and approves.

26. Cumberland next endeavours, by an enlarged analysis of the mental and bodily structure of mankind, to evince their aptitude for the social virtues, that is, for the general benevolence which is the primary law of nature. We have the power of knowing these by our rational faculty, which is the judge of right and wrong, that is, of what is conformable to the great law; and by the other faculties of the mind, as well as by the use of language, we generalise and reduce to propositions the determinations of reason. We have also the power of comparison, and of perceiving analogies, by means of which we estimate degrees of good. And if we are careful to guard against deciding without clear and adequate apprehensions of things, our reason will not mislead us. The observance of something like this general law of nature by inferior animals, which rarely, as Cumberland supposes, attack those of the same species, and in certain instances live together, as if by a compact for mutual aid; the peculiar contrivances in the human body which seem designed for the maintenance of society; the possession of speech, the pathognomic countenance, the efficiency of the hand, a longevity beyond the lower animals, the duration of the sexual appetite throughout the year, with several other arguments derived from anatomy, are urged throughout this chapter against the unsocial theory of Hobbes.

27. Natural good is defined by Cumberland with more latitude than has been used by Paley and by those of a later school, who confine it to happiness or pleasurable

perception. Whatever conduces to the preservation of an intelligent being, or to the perfection of his powers, he accounts to be good, without regard to enjoyment. And for this he appeals to experience, since we desire existence, as well as the extension of our powers of action, for their own sakes. It is of great importance to acquire a clear notion of what is truly good, that is, of what serves most to the happiness and perfection of every one; since all the secondary laws of nature, that is, the rules of particular virtues, derive their authority from this effect. These rules may be compared one with another as to the probability as well as the value of their effects upon the general good; and he anticipates greater advantage from the employment of mathematical reasoning and even analytical forms in moral philosophy than the different nature of the subjects would justify, even if the fundamental principle of converting the theory of ethics into calculation could be allowed.[p]

28. A law of nature, meaning one subordinate to the great principle of benevolence, is defined by Cumberland to be a proposition manifested by the nature of things to the mind according to the will of the First Cause, and pointing out an action tending to the good of rational beings, from the performance of which an adequate reward, or from the neglect of which a punishment, will ensue by the nature of such rational beings. Every part of this definition he proves with exceeding prolixity in the longest chapter, namely, the fifth, of his treatise; but we have already seen the foundations of his theory upon which it rests. It will be evident to the reader of this chapter that both Butler and Paley have been largely indebted to Cumberland.[q] Natural obligation he defines thus: No other necessity determines the will to act than that of avoiding evil and of seeking good, so far as appears to be in our power.[r] Moral obligation is more limited, and is differently de-

[p] Ea quippe tota (disciplina morum) versatur in æstimandis rationibus virium humanarum ad commune bonum entium rationalium quicquam facientium, quæ quidem variant in omni casuum possibilium varietate. Cap. ii. sect. 9. The same is laid down in several other passages. By *rationibus* we must understand *ratios*; which brings out the calculating theory in the strongest light.

[q] A great part of the second and third chapters of Butler's Analogy will be found in Cumberland. See cap. v. sect. 22.

[r] Non alia necessitas voluntatem ad agendum determinat, quam malum in quantum tale esse nobis constat fugiendi, bonumque quatenus nobis apparet prosequendi. Cap. v. sect. 7.

fined.[*] But the main point, as he justly observes, of the controversy is the connection between the tendency of each man's actions, taking them collectively through his life, to the good of the whole, and that to his own greatest happiness and perfection. This he undertakes to show, premising that it is twofold; consisting immediately in the pleasure attached to virtue, and ultimately in the rewards which it obtains from God and from man. God, as a rational being, cannot be supposed to act without an end, or to have a greater end than the general good; that is, the happiness and perfection of his creatures.[t] And his will may not only be shown à priori, by the consideration of his essence and attributes, but by the effects of virtue and vice in the order of nature which he has established. The rewards and punishments which follow at the hands of men are equally obvious; and whether we regard men as God's instruments, or as voluntary agents, demonstrate that virtue is the highest prudence. These arguments are urged rather tediously, and in such a manner as not to encounter all the difficulties which it is desirable to overcome.

29. Two objections might be alleged against this kind of proof: that the rewards and punishments of moral actions are too uncertain to be accounted clear proofs of the will of God, and consequently of their natural obligation; and that by laying so much stress upon them we make private happiness the measure of good. These he endeavours to repel. The contingency of a future consequence has a determinate value, which, if it more than compensates, for good or evil, the evil or good of a present action, ought to be deemed a proof given by the Author of nature that reward or punishment are annexed to the action, as much as if they were its necessary consequences.[u] This argument, perhaps sophistical, is an instance of the calculating method affected by Cumberland, and which we may presume, from the then recent application of analysis to probability, he was the first to adopt on such an occasion. Paley is sometimes fond of a similar process. But after these mathematical reasonings, he dwells, as before, on the beneficial effects of virtue, and concludes that many of them are so uniform as to leave no doubt as to the intention of the Creator.

[*] Sect. 27.   [t] Sect. 19.   [u] Sect. 37.

Against the charge of postponing the public good to that of the agent, he protests that it is wholly contrary to his principle, which permits no one to preserve his life, or what is necessary for it, at the expense of a greater good to the whole.[x]   But his explication of the question ends in repeating that no single man's greatest felicity can by the nature of things be inconsistent with that of all; and that every such hypothesis is to be rejected as an impossible condition of the problem.   It seems doubtful whether Cumberland uses always the same language on the question whether private happiness is the final motive of action, which in this part of the chapter he wholly denies.

30. From the establishment of this primary law of universal benevolence Cumberland next deduces the chief secondary principles, which are commonly called the moral virtues.   And among these he gives the first place to justice, which he seems to consider, by too lax an use of terms, or too imperfect an analogy, as comprehending the social duties of liberality, courtesy, and domestic affection.   The right of property, which is the foundation of justice, he rests entirely on its necessity for the common good; whatever is required for that prime end of moral action being itself obligatory on moral agents, they are bound to establish and to maintain separate rights.   And all right so wholly depends on this instrumentality to good, that the rightful sovereignty of God over his creatures is not founded on that relation which he bears to them as their Maker, much less on his mere power, but on his wisdom and goodness, through which his omnipotence works only for their happiness.   But this happiness can only be attained by means of an absolute right over them in their Maker, which is therefore to be reckoned a natural law.

31. The good of all rational beings is a complex whole, being nothing but the aggregate of good enjoyed by each.   We can only act in our proper spheres, labouring to do good.   But this labour will be fruitless, or rather mischievous, if we do not keep in mind the

---

[x] Sua cujusque felicitas est pars valde exigua finis illius, quem vir verè rationalis prosequitur, et ad totum finem, scilicet commune bonum, cui a natura seu a Deo intertexitur, eam tantum habet rationem quam habet unus homo ad aggregatum ex omnibus rationalibus, quae minor est quam habet unica arenula ad molem universi corporis.   Sect. 23 and sect. 28.

higher gradations which terminate in universal benevolence.   No man must seek his own advantage otherwise
than that of his family permits; or provide for his family to the detriment of his country; or promote the
good of his country at the expense of mankind; or
serve mankind, if it were possible, without regard to the
majesty of God.[y]   It is indeed sufficient that the mind
should acknowledge and recollect this principle of conduct, without having it present on every single occasion.   But where moral difficulties arise, Cumberland
contends that the general good is the only measure by
which we are to determine the lawfulness of actions,
or the preference due to one above another.

32. In conclusion he passes to political authority, deriving it from the same principle, and comments with
severity and success, though in the verbose style usual
to him, on the system of Hobbes.   It is, however,
worthy of remark, that he not only peremptorily declares the irresponsibility of the supreme magistrate in
all cases, but seems to give him a more arbitrary latitude in the choice of measures, so long as he does not
violate the chief negative precepts of the Decalogue,
than is consistent with his own fundamental rule of
always seeking the greatest good.   He endeavours to
throw upon Hobbes, as was not uncommon with the
latter's theological opponents, the imputation of encou-
raging rebellion while he seemed to support absolute
power; and observes with full as much truth that if
kings are bound by no natural law, the reason for their
institution, namely, the security of mankind, assigned
by the author of the Leviathan, falls to the ground.

33. I have gone rather at length into a kind of analysis of this treatise because it is now very
little read, and yet was of great importance in   Remarks on
the annals of ethical philosophy.   It was, if not   Cumberland's the-
a text-book in either of our universities, con-   ory.
cerning which I am not confident, the basis of the
system therein taught, and of the books which have had
most influence in this country.   Hutcheson, Law, Paley,
Priestley, Bentham, belong, no doubt some of them unconsciously, to the school founded by Cumberland.   Hutcheson adopted the principle of general benevolence as the

[y] Cap. viii. sect. 14, 15.

standard of virtue ; but by limiting the definition of good
to happiness alone, he simplified the scheme of Cumberland, who had included conservation and enlargement of
capacity in its definition. He rejected also what en-
cumbers the whole system of his predecessor, the including the Supreme Being among those rational agents
whose good we are bound to promote. The schoolmen,
as well as those whom they followed, deeming it necessary to predicate metaphysical infinity of all the divine
attributes, reckoned unalterable beatitude in the number.
Upon such a subject no wise man would like to dog-
matise. The difficulties on both sides are very great,
and perhaps among the most intricate to which the momentous problem concerning the cause of evil has given
rise. Cumberland, whose mind does not seem to have
been much framed to wrestle with mysteries, evades, in
his lax verbosity, what might perplex his readers.

34. In establishing the will of a supreme lawgiver as
essential to the law of nature, he is followed by the
bishop of Carlisle and Paley, as well as by the majority
of English moralists in the eighteenth century. But
while Paley deems the·recognition of a future state so
essential, that he even includes in the definition of
virtue that it is performed " for the sake of everlasting
happiness," Cumberland not only omits this erroneous
and almost paradoxical condition, but very slightly
alludes to another life, though he thinks it probable
from the stings of conscience and on other grounds ;
resting the whole argument on the certain consequences
of virtue and vice in the present, but guarding justly
against the supposition that any difference of happiness
in moral agents can affect the immediate question except
such as is the mere result of their own behaviour. If
any one had urged, like Paley, that unless we take a
future state into consideration, the result of calculating
our own advantage will either not always be in favour of
virtue, or in consequence of the violence of passion will
not always seem so, Cumberland would probably have
denied the former alternative, and replied to the other,
that we can only prove the truth of our theorems in
moral philosophy, and cannot compel men to adopt them.

35. Sir James Mackintosh, whose notice of Cumberland is rather too superficial, and hardly recognises his

influence on philosophy, observes that "the forms of scholastic argument serve more to encumber his style than to insure his exactness." [*] There is not however much of scholastic form in the treatise on the Laws of Nature, and this is expressly disclaimed in the preface. But he has, as we have intimated, a great deal too much of a mathematical line of argument which never illustrates his meaning, and has sometimes misled his judgment. We owe probably to his fondness for this specious illusion, I mean the application of reasonings upon quantity to moral subjects, the dangerous sophism that a direct calculation of the highest good, and that not relatively to particulars, but to all rational beings, is the measure of virtuous actions, the test by which we are to try our own conduct and that of others. And the intervention of general rules, by which Paley endeavoured to dilute and render palatable this calculating scheme of utility, seems no more to have occurred to Cumberland than it was adopted by Bentham.

36. Thus as Taylor's Ductor Dubitantium is nearly the last of a declining school, Cumberland's Law of Nature may be justly considered as the herald, especially in England, of a new ethical philosophy, of which the main characteristics were, first, that it stood complete in itself without the aid of revelation; secondly, that it appealed to no authority of earlier writers whatever, though it sometimes used them in illustration; thirdly, that it availed itself of observation and experience, alleging them generally, but abstaining from particular instances of either, and making, above all, no display of erudition; and fourthly, that it entered very little upon casuistry, leaving the application of principles to the reader.

37. In the same year, 1672, a work still more generally distinguished than that of Cumberland was published at Lund, in Sweden, by Samuel Puffendorf, a Saxon by birth, who filled the chair of moral philosophy in that recently-founded university. This large treatise, On the Law of Nature and Nations, in eight books, was abridged by the author, but not without some variations, in one perhaps more useful, On the Duties of a Man and a Citizen.

Puffendorf's Law of Nature and Nations.

[*] Dissertation on Ethical Philosophy, p. 48.

Both have been translated into French and English;
both were long studied in the foreign universities, and
even in our own. Puffendorf has been perhaps, in moral
philosophy, of greater authority than Grotius, with
whom he is frequently named in conjunction ; but this
is not the case in international jurisprudence.

38. Puffendorf, after a very diffuse and technical
Analysis of chapter on moral beings, or modes, proceeds
this work. to assert a demonstrative certainty in moral
science, but seems not to maintain an inherent right
and wrong in actions antecedent to all law, referring
the rule of morality altogether to the divine appointment. He ends however by admitting that man's
constitution being what it is, God could not without inconsistency have given him any other law than that
under which he lives.[a] We discern good from evil by
the understanding, which judgment when exercised on
our own actions is called conscience ; but he strongly
protests against any such jurisdiction of conscience, independent of reason and knowledge, as some have
asserted. This notion " was first introduced by the
schoolmen, and has been maintained in these latter ages
by the crafty casuists for the better securing of men's
minds and fortunes to their own fortune and advantage." [b]
Puffendorf was a good deal imbued with the Lutheran
bigotry which did no justice to any religion but its own.

39. Law alone creates obligation ; no one can be
obliged except towards a superior. But to compel and
to oblige being different things, it is required for this
latter that we should have received some great good at
the hands of a superior, or have voluntarily submitted
to his will. This seems to involve an antecedent moral
right, which Puffendorf's general theory denies.[c] Barbeyrac, his able and watchful commentator, derives obligation from our natural dependence on the supreme
authority of God, who can punish the disobedient and
reward others. In order to make laws obligatory, it is
necessary, according to Puffendorf, that we should know
both the law and the lawgiver's authority. Actions are
good or evil, as they conform more or less to law. And,
coming to consider the peculiar qualities of moral
actions, he introduces the distinction of perfect and im-

<hr>

[a] C. 2.   [b] C. 3.   [c] C. 6.

perfect rights, objecting to that of Grotius and the Roman lawyers, expletive and distributive justice.[d] This first book of Puffendorf is very diffuse; and some chapters are wholly omitted in the abridgment.

40. The natural state of man, such as in theory we may suppose, is one in which he was never placed, "thrown into the world at a venture, and then left entirely to himself with no larger endowments of body or mind than such as we now discover in men." This, however, he seems to think physically possible to have been, which I should incline to question. Man in a state of nature is subject to no earthly superior; but we must not infer thence that he is incapable of law, and has a right to every thing that is profitable to himself. But, after discussing the position of Hobbes that a state of nature is a state of war, he ends by admitting that the desire of peace is too weak and uncertain a security for its preservation among mankind.[e]

41. The law of nature he derives not from consent of nations, nor from personal utility, but from the condition of man. It is discoverable by reason; its obligation is from God. He denies that it is founded on the intrinsic honesty or turpitude of actions. It was free to God whether he would create an animal to whom the present law of nature should be applicable. But supposing all things human to remain constant, the law of nature, though owing its institution to the free will of God, remains unalterable. He therefore neither agrees wholly with those who deem of this law as of one arbitrary and mutable at God's pleasure, nor with those who look upon it as an image of his essential holiness and justice. For he doubts whether the law of nature is altogether conformed to the divine attributes as to a type; since we cannot acquire a right with respect to God; so that his justice must be of a different kind from ours. Common consent, again, is an insufficient basis of natural law, few men having searched into the foundations of their assent, even if we could find a more general consent than is the case. And here he expatiates, in the style of Montaigne's school, on the variety of moral opinions.[f] Puffendorf next attacks those who resolve right into self-interest. But unfortunately he only proves that men often

d C. 7.　　　　　e Lib. ii. c. 2.　　　　　f C. 3.

mistake their interest. " It is a great mistake to fancy it
will be profitable to you to take away either by fraud or
violence what another man has acquired by his labour;
since others have not only the power of resisting you,
but of taking the same freedom with your goods and
possessions." [g] This is evidently no answer to Hobbes
or Spinosa.

42. The nature of man, his wants, his powers of doing
mischief to others, his means of mutual assistance, show
that he cannot be supported in things necessary and convenient to him without society, so that others may promote his interests. Hence sociableness is a primary law
of nature, and all actions tending towards it are com-
manded, as the opposite are forbidden, by that law. In
this he agrees with Grotius; and, after he had become
acquainted with Cumberland's work, observes that the
fundamental law of that writer, to live for the common good and show benevolence towards all men,
does not differ from his own. He partly explains, and
partly answers, the theory of Hobbes. From Grotius he
dissents in denying that the law of nature would be
binding without religion, but does not think the soul's
immortality essential to it. [h] The best division of natural law is into duties towards ourselves and towards
others. But in the abridged work, the Duties of a Man
and a Citizen, he adds those towards God.

43. The former class of duties he illustrates with
much prolixity and needless quotation, [i] and passes to
the right of self-defence, which seems to be the debatable
frontier between the two classes of obligation. In this
chapter Puffendorf is free from the extreme scrupulous-
ness of Grotius; yet he differs from him, as well as from
Barbeyrac and Locke, in denying the right of attacking
the aggressor, where a stranger has been injured, unless
where we are bound to him by promise. [k]

44. All persons, as is evident, are bound to repair
wilful injury, and even that arising from their neglect;
but not where they have not been in fault. [m] Yet the civil
action *ob pauperiem*, for casual damage by a beast or
slave, which Grotius held to be merely of positive law,
and which our own (in the only applicable case) does
not recognise, Puffendorf thinks grounded on natural

[g] C. 3.　　[h] C. 3.　　[i] C. 4.　　[k] C. 5.　　[m] Lib. iii. c. 1.

right. He considers several questions of reparation, chiefly such as we find in Grotius. From these, after some intermediate disquisitions on moral duties, he comes to the more extensive province of casuistry, the obligation of promises.[n] These, for the most part, give perfect rights which may be enforced, though this is not universal; hence promises may themselves be called imperfect or perfect. The former, or *nuda pacta*, seem to be obligatory rather by the rules of veracity, and for the sake of maintaining confidence among men, than in strict justice; yet he endeavours to refute the opinion of a jurist who held *nuda pacta* to involve no obligation beyond a compensation for damage. Free consent and knowledge of the whole subject are required for the validity of a promise; hence drunkenness takes away its obligation.[o] Whether a minor is bound in conscience, though not in law, has been disputed; the Romish casuists all denying it unless he has received an advantage. La Placette, it seems, after the time of Puffendorf, though a very rigid moralist, confines the obligation to cases where the other party sustains any real damage by the non-performance. The world, in some instances at least, would exact more than the strictest casuists. Promises were invalidated, though not always mutual contracts, by error; and fraud in the other party annuls a contract. There can be no obligation, Puffendorf maintains, without a corresponding right; hence fear arising from the fault of the other party invalidates a promise. But those made to pirates or rebels, not being extorted by fear, are binding. Vows to God he deems not binding, unless accepted by him; but he thinks that we may presume their acceptance when they serve to define or specify an indeterminate duty.[p] Unlawful promises must not be performed by the party promising to commit an evil act, and as to performance of the other party's promise, he differs from Grotius in thinking it not binding. Barbeyrac concurs with Puffendorf, but Paley holds the contrary; and the common sentiments of mankind seem to be on that side.[q]

45. The obligations of veracity Puffendorf, after much needless prolixity on the nature of signs and words, deduces from a tacit contract among mankind, that words,

[n] C. 5. [o] C. 6. [p] C. 6. [q] C. 7.

or signs of intention, shall be used in a definite sense which others may understand.' He is rather fond of these imaginary compacts. The laxer casuists are in nothing more distinguishable from the more rigid than in the exceptions they allow to the general rule of veracity. Many, like Augustin and most of the fathers, have laid it down that all falsehood is unlawful; even some of the jurists, when treating of morality, had done the same. But Puffendorf gives considerable latitude to deviations from truth, by mental reserve, by ambiguous words, by direct falsehood. Barbeyrac, in a long note, goes a good deal farther, and indeed beyond any safe limit.' An oath, according to these writers, adds no peculiar obligation; another remarkable discrepancy between their system and that of the theological casuists. Oaths may be released by the party in favour of whom they are made; but it is necessary to observe whether the dispensing authority is really the obligee.

46. We now advance to a different part of moral philosophy, the rights of property. Puffendorf first inquires into the natural right of killing animals for food; but does not defend it very well, resting this right on the want of mutual obligation between man and brutes. The arguments from physiology, and the manifest propensity in mankind to devour animals, are much stronger. He censures cruelty towards animals, but hardly on clear grounds; the disregard of moral emotion, which belongs to his philosophy, prevents his judging it rightly.' Property itself in things he grounds on an express or tacit contract of mankind, while all was yet in common, that each should possess a separate portion. This covenant he supposes to have been gradually extended, as men perceived the advantage of separate possession, lands having been cultivated in common after severalty had

---

' L. iv. c. 1.

* Barbeyrac admits that several writers of authority since Puffendorf had maintained the strict obligation of veracity for its own sake; Thomasius, Buddæus, Noodt, and, above all, La Placette. His own notions are too much the other way, both according to the received standard of honourable and decorous character among men, and according to any sound theory of ethics. Lying, he says, as condemned in Scripture, always means fraud or injury to others. His doctrine is, that we are to speak the truth, or to be silent, or to feign and dissemble, according as our own lawful interest, or that of our neighbour, may demand it. This is surely as untenable one way as any paradox in Augustin or La Placette can be the other.

t C. 3.

been established in houses and movable goods; and he refutes those who maintain property to be coeval with mankind, and immediately founded on the law of nature.[u] Nothing can be the subject of property which is incapable of exclusive occupation; not therefore the ocean, though some narrow seas may be appropriated.[x] In the remainder of this fourth book he treats on a variety of subjects connected with property, which carry us over a wide field of natural and positive jurisprudence.

47. The fifth book of Puffendorf relates to price, and to all contracts onerous or lucrative, according to the distinction of the jurists, with the rules of their interpretation. It is a running criticism on the Roman law, comparing it with right reason and justice. Price he divides into proper and eminent; the first being what we call real value, or capacity of procuring things desirable by means of exchange; the second the money value. What is said on this subject would now seem commonplace and prolix; but it is rather interesting to observe the beginnings of political economy. Money, he thinks, was introduced by an agreement of civilized nations, as a measure of value. Puffendorf, of more enlarged views than Grotius, vindicates usury, which the other had given up; and mentions the evasions usually practised, such as the grant of an annuity for a limited term.

48. In the sixth book we have disquisitions on matrimony and the rights incident to it, on paternal and on herile power. Among other questions he raises one whether the husband has any natural dominion over the wife. This he thinks hard to prove, except as his sex gives him an advantage; but fitness to govern does not create a right. He has recourse therefore to his usual solution, her tacit or express promise of obedience. Polygamy he deems contrary to the law of nature, but not incest, except in the direct line. This is consonant to what had been the general determination of philosophers.[y] The right of parents he derives from the general duty of sociableness, which makes preservation of children necessary, and on the affection implanted in them by nature; also on a presumed consent of the children

---

[u] C. 4. Barbeyrac more wisely denies this assumed compact, and rests the right of property on individual occupancy.

[x] C. 5.
[y] L. vi. c. 1.

in return for their maintenance.[*] In a state of nature
this command belongs to the mother, unless she has
waived it by a matrimonial contract. In childhood,
the fruits of the child's labour belong to the father,
though the former seems to be capable of receiving
gifts. Fathers, as heads of families, have a kind of
sovereignty, distinct from the paternal, to which adult
children residing with them are submitted. But after
their emancipation by leaving their father's house, which
does not absolutely require his consent, they are bound
only to duty and reverence. The power of a master
over his servant is not by nature, nor by the law of war,
but originally by a contract founded on necessity. War
increased the number of those in servitude. A slave,
whatever Hobbes may say, is capable of being injured
by his master; but the laws of some nations give more
power to the latter than is warranted by those of nature.
Servitude implies only an obligation to perpetual labour
for a recompence (namely, at least maintenance); the
evil necessary to this condition has been much exaggerated by opinion.[*]

49. Puffendorf and Cumberland are the two great pro-
moters, if not founders, of that school in ethics,
which, abandoning the higher ground of both
philosophers and theologians, that of an intrinsic
fitness and propriety in actions. resolved them all into
their conduciveness towards good. Their *utile* indeed is
very different from what Cicero has so named, which is
merely personal, but it is different also from his *honestum*.
The sociableness of Puffendorf is perhaps much the same
with the general good of Cumberland, but is somewhat
less comprehensive and less clear. Paley, who had not
read a great deal. had certainly read Puffendorf; he has
borrowed from him several minor illustrations, such as
the equivocal promise of Timur (called by Paley Te-
mures) to the garrison of Sebastia, and the rules for division of profits in partnership. Their minds were in some
respects alike; both phlegmatic, honest, and sincere,
without warmth or fancy; yet there seems a more
thorough good-nature and kindliness of heart in our
countryman. Though an ennobled German, Puffendorf
had as little respect for the law of honour as Paley him-

Puffendorf and Paley compared.

self.　They do not, indeed, resemble each other in their modes of writing : one was very laborious, the other very indolent ; one sometimes misses his mark by circuity, the other by precipitance.　The quotations in Puffendorf are often as thickly strewed as in Grotius, though he takes less from the poets ; but he seems not to build upon their authority, which gives them still more the air of superfluity.　His theory, indeed, which assigns no weight to anything but a close geometrical deduction from axioms, is incompatible with much deference to authority ; and he sets aside the customs of mankind as unstable and arbitrary.　He has not taken much from Hobbes, whose principles are far from his, but a great deal from Grotius.　The leading difference between the treatises of these celebrated men is that, while the former contemplated the law that ought to be observed among independent communities as his primary object, to render which more evident he lays down the fundamental principles of private right or the law of nature, the latter, on the other hand, not only begins with natural law, but makes it the great theme of his inquiries.

50.　Few books have been more highly extolled or more severely blamed than the Thoughts or Maxims of the Duke of la Rochefoucault.　They Rochefoucault. have, indeed, the greatest advantages for popularity ; the production of a man less distinguished by his high rank than by his active participation in the factions of his country at a time when they reached the limits of civil war, and by his brilliancy among the accomplished courtiers of Louis XIV. ; concise and energetic in expression ; reduced to those short aphorisms which leave much to the reader's acuteness, and yet save his labour ; not often obscure, and never wearisome ; an evident generalization of long experience, without pedantry, without method, without deductive reasonings, yet wearing an appearance at least of profundity, they delight the intelligent though indolent man of the world, and must be read with some admiration by the philosopher.　Among the books in ancient and modern times which record the conclusions of observing men on the moral qualities of their fellows, a high place should be reserved for the Maxims of Rochefoucault.

51.　The censure that has so heavily fallen upon this

writer is founded on his proneness to assign a low and selfish motive to human actions, and even to those which are most usually denominated virtuous. It is impossible to dispute the partial truth of this charge. Yet it may be pleaded, that many of his maxims are not universal even in their enunciation ; and that, in others, where, for the sake of a more effective expression, the position seems general, we ought to understand it with such limitations as our experience may suggest. The society with which the Duke of la Rochefoucault was conversant could not elevate his notions of disinterested probity in man, or of unblemished purity in woman. Those who call themselves the world, it is easy to perceive, set aside, in their remarks on human nature, all the species but themselves, and sometimes generalize their maxims, to an amusing degree, from the manners and sentiments which have grown up in the atmosphere of a court or an aristocratic society. Rochefoucault was of far too reflecting a mind to be confounded with such mere worldlings ; yet he bears witness to the contracted observation and the precipitate inferences which an intercourse with a single class of society scarcely fails to generate. The causticity of Rochefoucault is always directed against the false virtues of mankind, but never touches the reality of moral truths, and leaves us less injured than the cold, heartless indifference to right which distils from the pages of Hobbes. Nor does he deal in those sweeping denials of goodness to human nature which are so frequently hazarded under the mask of religion. His maxims are not exempt from defects of a different kind ; they are sometimes refined to a degree of obscurity, and sometimes, under an epigrammatic turn, convey little more than a trivial {meaning. Perhaps, however, it would be just to say that one-third of the number deserve to be remembered, as at least partially true and useful ; and this is a large proportion, if we exclude all that are not in some measure original.

52. The Characters of La Bruyère, published in 1687,
La Bruyère. approach to the Maxims of La Rochefoucault by their refinement, their brevity, their general tendency to an unfavourable explanation of human conduct. This nevertheless is not so strongly marked, and

the picture of selfishness wants the darkest touches of his contemporary's colouring. La Bruyère had a model in antiquity, Theophrastus, whose short book of Characters he had himself translated, and prefixed to his own; a step not impolitic for his own glory, since the Greek writer, with no contemptible degree of merit, has been incomparably surpassed by his imitator. Many changes in the condition of society, the greater diversity of ranks and occupations in modern Europe, the influence of women over the other sex as well as their own varieties of character and manners, the effects of religion, learning, chivalry, royalty, have given a range to this very pleasing department of moral literature which no ancient could have compassed. Nor has Theophrastus taken much pains to search the springs of character; his delineations are bold and clear, but merely in outline; we see more of manners than of nature, and the former more in general classes than in portraiture. La Bruyère has often painted single persons; whether accurately or no, we cannot at this time determine, but with a felicity of description which at once renders the likeness probable, and suggests its application to those we ourselves have seen. His general reflections, like those of Rochefoucault, are brilliant with antithesis and epigrammatic conciseness; sometimes perhaps not quite just or quite perspicuous. But he pleases more on the whole, from his greater variety, his greater liveliness, and his gentler spirit of raillery. Nor does he forget to mingle the praise of some with his satire. But he is rather a bold writer for his age and his position in the court, and what looks like flattery may well have been ironical. Few have been more imitated, as well as more admired, than La Bruyère, who fills up the list of those whom France has boasted as most conspicuous for their knowledge of human nature. The others are Montaigne, Charron, Pascal, and Rochefoucault; but we might withdraw the second name without injustice.

53. Moral philosophy comprehends in its literature whatever has been written on the best theory and precepts of moral education, disregarding what is confined to erudition, though this may frequently be partially treated in works of the former

Education. Milton's Tractate.

class.   Education, notwithstanding its recognized importance, was miserably neglected in England, and
quite as much, perhaps, in every part of Europe.
Schools, kept by low-born, illiberal pedants, teaching
little, and that little ill, without regard to any judicious
discipline or moral culture, on the one hand, or, on the
other, a pretence of instruction at home under some
ignorant and servile tutor, seem to have been the alter-
natives of our juvenile gentry.   Milton raised his voice
against these faulty methods in his short Tractate on
Education.   This abounds with bursts of his elevated
spirit ; and sketches out a model of public colleges,
wherein the teaching should be more comprehensive,
more liberal, more accommodated to what he deems the
great aim of education than what was in use.   "That,"
he says, "I call a complete and generous education
which fits a man to perform justly, skilfully, and mag-
nanimously all the offices both private and public, of
peace and war."   But when Milton descends to specify
the course of studies he would recommend, it appears
singularly ill-chosen and impracticable, nearly confined
to ancient writers, even in mathematics and other subjects where they could not be sufficient, and likely to
leave the student very far from that aptitude for offices
of war and peace which he had held forth as the reward
of his diligence.

54. Locke, many years afterwards, turned his thoughts
to education with all the advantages that a
strong understanding and entire disinterested-
ness could give him ; but, as we should imagine, with some necessary deficiencies of experience,
though we hardly perceive much of them in his writings.
He looked on the methods usual in his age with severity,
or, some would say, with prejudice ; yet I know not by
what proof we can refute his testimony.   In his Treatise on Education, which may be reckoned an introduction to that on the Conduct of the Understanding, since
the latter is but a scheme of that education an adult
person should give himself, he has uttered, to say the
least, more good sense on the subject than will be found
in any preceding writer.   Locke was not like the pedants of his own or other ages, who think that to pour
their wordy book-learning into the memory is the true

*Locke on
Education.
Its merits.*

discipline of childhood. The culture of the intellectual and moral faculties in their most extensive sense, the health of the body, the accomplishments which common utility or social custom has rendered valuable, enter into his idea of the best model of education, conjointly at least with any knowledge that can be imparted by books. The ancients had written in the same spirit; in Xenophon, in Plato, in Aristotle, the noble conception which Milton has expressed, of forming the perfect man, is always predominant over mere literary instruction, if indeed the latter can be said to appear at all in their writings on this subject; but we had become the dupes of schoolmasters in our riper years, as we had been their slaves in our youth. Much has been written, and often well, since the days of Locke; but he is the chief source from which it has been ultimately derived; and though the Emile is more attractive in manner, it may be doubtful whether it is as rational and practicable as the Treatise on Education. If they have both the same defect, that their authors wanted sufficient observation of children, it is certain that the caution and sound judgment of Locke have rescued him better from error.

55. There are, indeed, from this or from other causes, several passages in the Treatise on Education and defects. to which we cannot give an unhesitating assent. Locke appears to have somewhat exaggerated the efficacy of education. This is an error on the right side in a work that aims at persuasion in a practical matter; but we are now looking at theoretical truth alone. "I think I may say," he begins, "that of all the men we meet with, nine parts of ten are what they are, good or evil, useful or not, by their education. It is this which makes the great difference in mankind. The little or almost insensible impressions on our tender infancies have very important and lasting consequences; and there 'tis as in the fountains of some rivers, where a gentle application of the hand turns the flexible waters into channels that make them take quite contrary courses; and by this little direction given them at first in the source, they receive different tendencies, and arrive at last at very remote and distant places." "I imagine," he adds soon afterwards, "the minds of

children as easily turned this or that way as water
itself." [b]

56. This passage is an instance of Locke's unfortunate
fondness for analogical parallels, which, as far as I have
observed, much more frequently obscure a philosophical
theorem than shed any light upon it. Nothing would
be easier than to confirm the contrary proposition by
such fanciful analogies from external nature. In itself,
the position is hyperbolical to extravagance. It is no
more disparagement to the uses of education, that it will
not produce the like effects upon every individual, than
it is to those of agriculture (I purposely use this sort of
idle analogy) that we do not reap the same quantity of
corn from every soil. Those who are conversant with
children on a large scale will, I believe, unanimously deny
this levelling efficacy of tuition. The variety of characters even in children of the same family, where the domestic associations of infancy have run in the same
trains, and where many physical congenialities may produce, and ordinarily do produce, a moral resemblance,
is of sufficiently frequent occurrence to prove that in
human beings there are intrinsic dissimilitudes, which
no education can essentially overcome. Among mere
theorists, however, this hypothesis seems to be popular.
And as many of these extend their notion of the plas-
ticity of human nature to the effects of government and
legislation, which is a sort of continuance of the same
controlling power, they are generally induced to disregard past experience of human affairs, because they
flatter themselves that under a more scientific administration, mankind will become something very different
from what they have been.

57. In the age of Locke, if we may confide in what he
tells us, the domestic education of children must have
been of the worst kind. "If we look," he says, "into
the common management of children, we shall have
reason to wonder, in the great dissoluteness of manners
which the world complains of, that there are any foot-
steps at all left of virtue. I desire to know what vice
can be named which parents and those about children

[b] Treatise on Education, § 2. "The
difference," he afterwards says, "to be
found in the manners and abilities of
men is owing more to their education
than to any thing else." § 32.

do not season them with, and drop into them the seeds of, as often as they are capable to receive them." The mode of treatment seems to have been passionate and often barbarous severity alternating with foolish indulgence. Their spirits were often broken down, and their ingenuousness destroyed, by the former; their habits of self-will and sensuality confirmed by the latter. This was the method pursued by parents; but the pedagogues of course confined themselves to their favourite scheme of instruction and reformation by punishment. Dugald Stewart has animadverted on the austerity of Locke's rules of education.[c] And this is certainly the case in some respects. He recommends that children should be taught to expect nothing because it will give them pleasure, but only what will be useful to them; a rule fit, in its rigid meaning, to destroy the pleasure of the present moment, in the only period of life that the present moment can be really enjoyed. No father himself, Locke neither knew how ill a parent can spare the love of his child, nor how ill a child can want the constant and practical sense of a parent's love. But if he was led too far by deprecating the mischievous indulgence he had sometimes witnessed, he made some amends by his censures on the prevalent discipline of stripes. Of this he speaks with the disapprobation natural to a mind already schooled in the habits of reason and virtue.[d] " I cannot think any correction useful to a child where the shame of suffering for having done amiss does not work more upon him than the pain." Esteem and disgrace are the rewards and punishments to which he principally looks. And surely this is a noble foundation for moral discipline. He also recommends that children should be much with their parents, and allowed all reasonable liberty. I cannot think that Stewart's phrase " hardness of character," which he accounts for by the early intercourse of Locke with the

[c] Preliminary Dissertation to Encyclop. Britann.

[d] " If severity carried to the highest pitch does prevail, and works a cure upon the present unruly distemper, it is often bringing in the room of it a worse and more dangerous disease by breaking the mind; and then, in the place of a disorderly young fellow, you have a low-spirited moped creature, who however with his unnatural sobriety he may please silly people, who commend tame inactive children, because they make no noise, nor give them any trouble; yet at last will probably prove as uncomfortable a thing to his friends, as he will be all his life an useless thing to himself and others." § 51.

Puritans, is justly applicable to anything that we know
of him ; and many more passages in this very treatise
might be adduced to prove his kindliness of disposition,
than will appear to any judicious person over-austere.
He found, in fact, everything wrong ; a false system of
reward and punishment, a false view of the objects of
education, a false selection of studies, false methods of
pursuing them.   Where so much was to be corrected, it
was perhaps natural to be too sanguine about the effects
of the remedy.

58. Of the old dispute as to public and private education he says, that both sides have their inconveniences,
but inclines to prefer the latter, influenced, as is evident, rather by disgust at the state of our schools than
by any general principle.* For he insists much on the
necessity of giving a boy a sufficient knowledge of what
he is to expect in the world.   " The longer he is kept
hoodwinked, the less he will see when he comes abroad
into open daylight, and be the more exposed to be a
prey to himself and others."   But this experience will,
as is daily seen, not be supplied by a tutor's lectures,
any more than by books ; nor can be given by any
course save a public education. Locke urges the necessity of having a tutor well-bred, and with knowledge
of the world, the ways, the humours, the follies, the
cheats, the faults of the age he is fallen into, and particularly of the country he lives in, as of far more importance than his scholarship.   " The only fence against
the world is a thorough knowledge of it: . . . He that
thinks not this of more moment to his son, and for
which he more needs a governor, than the languages
and learned sciences, forgets of how much more use it is
to judge right of men and manage his affairs wisely with
them, than to speak Greek and Latin, and argue in
mood and figure, or to have his head filled with the abstruse speculations of natural philosophy and metaphysics ; nay, than to be well versed in Greek and Roman
writers, though that be much better for a gentleman,
than to be a good Peripatetic or Cartesian ; because
these ancient authors observed and painted mankind
well, and give the best light into that kind of knowledge.
He that goes into the eastern parts of Asia will find

* § 70.

able and acceptable men without any of these; but without virtue, knowledge of the world, and civility, an accomplished and valuable man can be found nowhere."[f]

59. It is to be remembered, that the person whose education Locke undertakes to fashion is an English gentleman. Virtue, wisdom, breeding, and learning, are desirable for such a one in their order, but the last not so much as the rest.[g] It must be had, he says, but only as subservient to greater qualities. No objections have been more frequently raised against the scheme of Locke than on account of his depreciation of classical literature and of the study of the learned languages. This is not wholly true; Latin he reckons absolutely necessary for a gentleman, though it is absurd that those should learn Latin who are designed for trade, and never look again at a Latin book.[h] If he lays not so much stress on Greek as a gentleman's study, though he by no means would abandon it, it is because, in fact, most gentlemen, especially in his age, have done very well without it; and nothing can be deemed indispensable in education of a child, the want of which does not leave a manifest deficiency in the man. "No man," he observes, "can pass for a scholar who is ignorant of the Greek language. But I am not here considering of the education of a professed scholar, but of a gentleman."[i]

60. The peculiar methods recommended by Locke in learning languages, especially the Latin, appear to be of very doubtful utility, though some of them do not want strenuous supporters in the present day. Such are the method of interlinear translation, the learning of mere words without grammar, and above all the practice of talking Latin with a tutor who speaks it well—a phœnix whom he has not shown us where to find.[k] In general, he seems to underrate the difficulty of acquiring what even he would call a competent learning, and what is of more importance, and no rare mistake in those who write on this subject, to confound the acquisition of a language with the knowledge of its literature. The best ancient writers both in Greek and Latin furnish so much of wise reflection, of noble sentiment, of all that is beautiful and salutary, that no one who has had the

f § 94.   g § 138.   h § 189.   i § 195.   k § 165.

happiness to know and feel what they are, will desire to
see their study excluded or stinted in its just extent,
wherever the education of those who are to be the first
and best of the country is carried forward.   And though
by far the greater portion of mankind must, by the
very force of terms, remain in the ranks of intellectual
mediocrity, it is an ominous sign of any times when no
thought is taken for those who may rise beyond it.

61. In every other part of instruction, Locke has still
an eye to what is useful for a gentleman.   French he
justly thinks should be taught before Latin ; no geometry
is required by him beyond Euclid ; but he recommends
geography, history and chronology, drawing, and what
may be thought now as little necessary for a gentleman
as Homer, the jurisprudence of Grotius and Puffendorf.
He strongly urges the writing English well, though a
thing commonly neglected ; and after speaking with
contempt of the artificial systems of logic and rhetoric,
sends the pupil to Chillingworth for the best example of
reasoning, and to Tully for the best idea of eloquence.
"And let him read those things that are well writ in
English to perfect his style in the purity of our language." [m]

62. It would be to transcribe half this treatise, were
we to mention all the judicious and minute observations
on the management of children it contains.   Whatever
may have been Locke's opportunities, he certainly
availed himself of them to the utmost.   It is as far as
possible from a theoretical book ; and in many respects
the best of modern times, such as those of the Edgeworth
name, might pass for developments of his principles.
The patient attention to every circumstance, a peculiar
characteristic of the genius of Locke, is in none of his
works better displayed.   His rules for the health of
children, though sometimes trivial, since the subject has
been more regarded, his excellent advice as to checking
effeminacy and timorousness, his observations on their
curiosity, presumption, idleness, on their plays and re-
creations, bespeak an intense, though calm love of truth
and goodness ; a quality which few have possessed more
fully or known so well how to exert as this admirable
philosopher.

[m] § 188.

63. No one had condescended to spare any thoughts for female education, till Fenelon, in 1688, published his earliest work, Sur l'Education des Filles. This was the occasion of his appointment as preceptor to the grandchildren of Louis XIV.; for much of this treatise, and perhaps the most valuable part, is equally applicable to both sexes. It may be compared with that of Locke, written nearly at the same time, and bearing a great resemblance in its spirit. Both have the education of a polished and high-bred class, rather than of scholars, before them; and Fenelon rarely loses sight of his peculiar object, or gives any rule which is not capable of being practised in female education. In many respects he coincides with our English philosopher, and observes with him that a child learns much before he speaks, so that the cultivation of his moral qualities can hardly begin too soon. Both complain of the severity of parents, and deprecate the mode of bringing up by punishment. Both advise the exhibition of virtue and religion in pleasing lights, and censure the austere dogmatism with which they were inculcated, before the mind was sufficiently developed to apprehend them. But the characteristic sweetness of Fenelon's disposition is often shown in contrast with the somewhat stern inflexibility of Locke. His theory is uniformly indulgent; his method of education is a labour of love; a desire to render children happy for the time, as well as afterwards, runs through his book, and he may perhaps be considered the founder of that school which has endeavoured to dissipate the terrors and dry the tears of childhood. "I have seen," he says, " many children who have learned to read in play; we have only to read entertaining stories to them out of a book, and insensibly teach them the letters, they will soon desire to go for themselves to the source of their amusement." "Books should be given them well bound and gilt, with good engravings, clear types; for all that captivates the imagination facilitates study: the choice should be such as contain short and marvellous stories." These details are now trivial, but in the days of Fenelon they may have been otherwise.

64. In several passages he displays not only a judicious spirit, but an observation that must have been long

exercised. "Of all the qualities we perceive in children," he remarks, "there is only one that can be trusted as likely to be durable, which is sound judgment; it always grows with their growth, if it is well cultivated; but the grace of childhood is effaced; its vivacity is extinguished; even its sensibility is often lost, because their own passions and the intercourse of others insensibly harden the hearts of young persons who enter into the world." It is, therefore, a solid and just way of thinking which we should most value and most improve, and this not by any means less in girls than in the other sex, since their duties and the occupations they are called upon to fill do not less require it. Hence he not only deprecates an excessive taste for dress, but, with more originality, points out the danger of that extreme delicacy and refinement which incapacitate women for the ordinary affairs of life, and give them a contempt for a country life and rural economy.

65. It will be justly thought at present, that he discourages too much the acquisition of knowledge by women. "Keep their minds," he says in one place, "as much as you can within the usual limits, and let them understand that the modesty of their sex ought to shrink from science with almost as much delicacy as from vice." This seems, however, to be confined to science or philosophy in a strict sense; for he permits afterwards a larger compass of reading. Women should write a good hand, understand orthography and the four rules of arithmetic, which they will want in domestic affairs. To these he requires a close attention, and even recommends to women an acquaintance with some of the common forms and maxims of law. Greek, Roman, and French history, with the best travels, will be valuable, and keep them from seeking pernicious fictions. Books also of eloquence and poetry may be read with selection, taking care to avoid any that relate to love; music and painting may be taught with the same precaution. The Italian and Spanish languages are of no use but to enlarge their knowledge of dangerous books; Latin is better as the language of the church, but this he would recommend only for girls of good sense and discreet conduct, who will make no display of the acquisition.

SECT. II.—ON POLITICAL PHILOSOPHY.

Puffendorf — Spinosa — Harrington's Oceana — Locke on Government — Political
Economy.

66. IN the seventh book of Puffendorf's great work, he comes to political philosophy, towards which he had been gradually tending for some time; primary societies, or those of families, leading the way to the consideration of civil government. Grotius derives the origin of this from the natural sociableness of mankind. But this, as Puffendorf remarks, may be satisfied by the primary societies. The real cause was experience of the injuries which one man can inflict on another.[a] And, after a prolix disquisition, he concludes that civil society must have been constituted, first, by a covenant of a number of men, each with each, to form a commonwealth, and to be bound by the majority, in which primary covenant they must be unanimous, that is, every dissentient would retain his natural liberty; next, by a resolution or decree of the majority, that certain rulers shall govern the rest; and, lastly, by a second covenant between these rulers and the rest, one promising to take care of the public weal, and the other to obey lawful commands.[c] This covenant, as he attempts to show, exists even in a democracy, though it is less evident than in other forms. Hobbes had admitted the first of these covenants, but denied the second; Barbeyrac, the able commentator on Puffendorf, has done exactly the reverse. A state once formed may be conceived to exist as one person, with a single will, represented by that of the sovereign, wherever the sovereignty may be placed. This sovereignty is founded on the covenants, and is not conferred, except indirectly like every other human power, by God. Puffendorf here combats the opposite opinion, which churchmen were as prone to hold, it seems, in Germany as in England.[p]

67. The legislative, punitive, and judiciary powers, those of making war and peace, of appointing magistrates, and levying taxes, are so closely connected that

Puffendorf's theory of politics.

[a] L. vii. c. 1.   [c] C. 2.   [p] C. 3.

no one can be denied to the sovereign.   As to his right in ecclesiastical matters, Puffendorf leaves it for others to determine.⁹ He seems in this part of the work too favourable to unlimited monarchy, declaring himself against a mixed government.   The sovereign power must be irresponsible, and cannot be bound by the law which itself has given.   He even denies that all government is intended for the good of the governed—a position strangely inconsistent with his theory of a covenant —but he contends that, if it were, this end, the public good, may be more probably discerned by the prince than by the people.ʳ   Yet he admits that the exorbitances of a prince should be restrained by certain fundamental laws, and holds, that having accepted such, and ratified them by oath, he is not at liberty to break them ; arguing, with some apparent inconsistency, against those who maintain such limitations to be inconsistent with monarchy, and even recommending the institution of councils, without whose consent certain acts of the sovereign shall not be valid.   This can only be reconciled with his former declaration against a mixed sovereignty, by the distinction familiar to our own constitutional lawyers, between the joint acts of A. and B., and the acts of A. with B.'s consent.   But this is a little too technical and unreal for philosophical politics. Governments not reducible to one of the three simple forms he calls irregular ; such as the Roman republic or German empire.   But there may be systems of states, or aggregate communities, either subject to one king by different titles, or united by federation.   He inclines to deny that the majority can bind the minority in the latter case, and seems to take it for granted that some of the confederates can quit the league at pleasure.ˢ

68. Sovereignty over persons cannot be acquired, strictly speaking, by seizure or occupation, as in the case of lands, and requires, even after conquest, their consent to obey ; which will be given, in order to secure themselves from the other rights of war.   It is a problem whether, after an unjust conquest, the forced consent of the people can give a lawful title to sovereignty.   Puffendorf distinguishes between a monarchy and a republic thus unjustly subdued.   In the former

⁹ C. 4.   ʳ C. 6.   ˢ C. 5.

case, so long as the lawful heirs exist or preserve their claim, the duty of restitution continues. But in the latter, as the people may live as happily under a monarchy as under a republic, he thinks that an usurper has only to treat them well, without scruple as to his title. If he oppresses them, no course of years will make his title lawful, or bind them in conscience to obey, length of possession being only length of injury. If a sovereign has been justly divested of his power, the community becomes immediately free ; but if by unjust rebellion, his right continues till by silence he has appeared to abandon it.[t]

69. Every one will agree that a lawful ruler must not be opposed within the limits of his authority. But let us put the case that he should command what is unlawful, or maltreat his subjects. Whatever Hobbes may say, a subject may be injured by his sovereign. But we should bear minor injuries patiently, and in the worst cases avoid personal resistance. Those are not to be listened to who assert that a king, degenerating into a tyrant, may be resisted and punished by his people. He admits only a right of self-defence, if he manifestly becomes a public enemy : in all this he seems to go quite as far as Grotius himself. The next question is as to the right of invaders and usurpers to obedience. This, it will be observed, he had already in some measure discussed ; but Puffendorf is neither strict in method, nor free from repetitions. He labours much about the rights of the lawful prince, insisting upon them, where the subjects have promised allegiance to the usurper. This, he thinks, must be deemed temporary, until the legitimate sovereign has recovered his dominions. But what may be done towards promoting this end by such as have sworn fidelity to the actual ruler, he does not intimate.[u]

70. Civil laws are such as emanate from the supreme power, with respect to things left indifferent by the laws of God and nature. What chiefly belongs to them is the form and method of acquiring rights or obtaining redress for wrongs. If we give the law of nature all that belongs to it, and take away from the civilians what they have hitherto engrossed and promiscuously

treated, we shall bring the civil law to a much narrower
compass; not to say that at present whenever the latter
is deficient we must have recourse to the law of nature,
and that therefore in all commonwealths the natural
laws supply the defects of the civil.[x]   He argues against
Hobbes' tenet that the civil law cannot be contrary to
the law of nature; and that what shall be deemed theft,
murder, or adultery, depends on the former.   The subject is bound generally not to obey the unjust commands
of his sovereign; but in the case of war he thinks it, on
the whole, safest, considering the usual difficulties of
such questions, that the subject should serve, and throw
the responsibility before God on the prince.[y]   In this
problem of casuistry, common usage is wholly against
the stricter theory.

71. Punishment may be defined an evil inflicted by
authority upon view of antecedent transgression.[z]   Hence
exclusion, on political grounds, from public office, or
separation of the sick for the sake of the healthy, is not
punishment.   It does not belong to distributive justice,
nor is the magistrate bound to apportion it to the malignity of the offence, though this is usual.   Superior authority is necessary to punishment; and he differs from
Grotius by denying that we have a right to avenge the
injuries of those who have no claim upon us.   Punishment ought never to be inflicted without the prospect
of some advantage from it; either the correction of
the offender, or the prevention of his repeating the
offence.   But example he seems not to think a direct
end of punishment, though it should be regarded in its
infliction.   It is not necessary that all offences which
the law denounces should be actually punished, though
some jurists have questioned the right of pardon.
Punishments ought to be measured according to the
object of the crime, the injury to the commonwealth,
and the malice of the delinquent.   Hence offences
against God should be deemed most criminal, and next,
such as disturb the state; then whatever affect life, the
peace or honour of families, private property or reputation, following the scale of the Decalogue.   But
though all crimes do not require equal severity, an
exact proportion of penalties is not required.   Most of

[x] L. viii. c. 1.   [y] L. viii. c. 1.   [z] C. 3.

this chapter exhibits the vacillating, indistinct, and almost self-contradictory resolutions of difficulties so frequent in Puffendorf. He concludes by establishing a great truth, that no man can be justly punished for the offence of another; not even a community for the acts of their forefathers, notwithstanding their fictitious immortality.[a]

72. After some chapters on the law of nations, Puffendorf concludes with discussing the cessation of subjection. This may ordinarily be by voluntarily removing to another state with permission of the sovereign. And if no law or custom interferes, the subject has a right to do this at his discretion. The state has not a right to expel citizens without some offence. It loses all authority over a banished man. He concludes by considering the rare case of so great a diminution of the people, as to raise a doubt of their political identity.[b]

73. The political portion of this large work is not, as will appear, very fertile in original or sagacious reflection. A greater degree of both, though Politics of Spinosa. by no means accompanied with a sound theory, distinguishes the Political Treatise of Spinosa, one which must not be confounded with the Theologico-political Treatise, a very different work. In this he undertakes to show how a state under a regal or aristocratic government ought to be constituted so as to secure the tranquillity and freedom of the citizens. Whether Spinosa borrowed his theory on the origin of government from Hobbes, is perhaps hard to determine: he seems acquainted with the treatise De Cive; but the philosophical system of both was such as, in minds habituated like theirs to close reasoning, could not lead to any other result. Political theory, as Spinosa justly observes, is to be founded on our experience of human kind as it is, and on no visionary notions of an Utopia or golden age; and hence politicians of practical knowledge have written better on these subjects than philosophers. We must treat of men as liable to passions, prone more to revenge than to pity, eager to rule and to compel others to act like themselves, more pleased with having done harm to others than with procuring their own good. Hence no state wherein the public affairs are entrusted to any one's

[a] C. 3.   [b] C. 11, 12.

good faith can be secure of their due administration; but means should be devised that neither reason nor passion should induce those who govern to obstruct the public weal; it being indifferent by what motive men act if they can be brought to act for the common good.

74. Natural law is the same as natural power; it is that which the laws of nature, that is the order of the world, give to each individual. Nothing is forbidden by this law, except what no one desires, or what no one can perform. Thus no one is bound to keep the faith he has plighted any longer than he will, and than he judges it useful to himself; for he has not lost the power of breaking it, and power is right in natural law. But he may easily perceive that the power of one man in a state of nature is limited by that of all the rest, and in effect is reduced to nothing, all men being naturally enemies to each other; while, on the other hand, by uniting their force and establishing bounds by common consent to the natural powers of each, it becomes really more effective than while it was unlimited. This is the principle of civil government; and now the distinctions of just and unjust, right and wrong, begin to appear.

75. The right of the supreme magistrate is nothing but the collective rights of the citizens, that is, their powers. Neither he nor they in their natural state can do wrong; but after the institution of government, each citizen may do wrong by disobeying the magistrate; that, in fact, being the test of wrong. He has not to inquire whether the commands of the supreme power are just or unjust, pious or impious; that is, as to action, for the state has no jurisdiction over his judgment.

76. Two independent states are naturally enemies, and may make war on each other whenever they please. If they make peace or alliance, it is no longer binding than the cause, that is, hope or fear in the contracting parties, shall endure. All this is founded on the universal law of nature, the desire of preserving ourselves; which, whether men are conscious of it or no, animates all their actions. Spinosa in this, as in his other writings, is more fearless than Hobbes; and, though he sometimes may throw a light veil over his abjuration of moral and religious principle, it is frequently placed in a more prominent view than his English precursor in the same

system had deemed it secure to exhibit. Yet so slight is often the connexion between theoretical tenets and human practice, that Spinosa bore the character of a virtuous and benevolent man. In this treatise of politics, especially in the broad assertion that good faith is only to be preserved so long as it is advantageous, he leaves Machiavel and Hobbes at some distance, and may be reckoned the most phlegmatically impudent of the whole school.

77. The contract or fundamental laws, he proceeds, according to which the multitude transfers its right to a king or a senate, may unquestionably be broken, when it is advantageous to the whole to do so. But Spinosa denies to private citizens the right of judging concerning the public good in such a point, reserving, apparently, to the supreme magistrate an ultimate power of breaking the conditions upon which he was chosen. Notwithstanding this dangerous admission, he strongly protests against intrusting absolute power to any one man; and observes, in answer to the common argument of the stability of despotism, as in the instance of the Turkish monarchy, that if barbarism, slavery, and desolation are to be called peace, nothing can be more wretched than peace itself. Nor is this sole power of one man a thing so possible as we imagine; the kings who seem most despotic trusting the public safety and their own to counsellors and favourites, often the worst and weakest in the state.

78. He next proceeds to his scheme of a well-regulated monarchy, which is in some measure original His theory of and ingenious. The people are to be divided a monarchy. into families, by which he seems to mean something like the φρατρίαι of Attica. From each of these, councillors, fifty years of age, are to be chosen by the king, succeeding in a rotation quinquennial, or less, so as to form a numerous senate. This assembly is to be consulted upon all public affairs, and the king is to be guided by its unanimous opinion. In case, however, of disagreement, the different propositions being laid before the king, he may choose that of the minority, provided at least one hundred councillors have recommended it. The less remarkable provisions of this ideal polity it would be waste of time to mention; except that he

advises that all the citizens should be armed as a militia, and that the principal towns should be fortified, and consequently, as it seems, in their power.   A monarchy thus constituted would probably not degenerate into the despotic form.   Spinosa appeals to the ancient government of Aragon, as a proof of the possibility of carrying his theory into execution.

79. From this imaginary monarchy he comes to an aristocratical republic.   In this he seems to have taken Venice, the idol of theoretical politicians, as his primary model, but with such deviations as affect the whole scheme of government.   He objects to the supremacy of an elective doge, justly observing that the precautions adopted in the election of that magistrate show the danger of the office itself, which was rather retained in the aristocratical polity as an ancient institution than from any persuasion of its usefulness.   But the most remarkable discrepancy between the aristocracy of Spinosa and that of Venice is, that his great council, which ought, as he strongly urges, not to consist of less than 5000, the greatness of its number being the only safeguard against the close oligarchy of a few families, is not to be hereditary, but its vacancies to be filled up by self-election.   In this election, indeed, he considers the essence of aristocracy to consist, being, as is implied in its meaning, a government by the best, who can only be pronounced such by the choice of many.   It is singular that he never adverts to popular representation, of which he must have known examples.   Democracy, on the contrary, he defines to be a government where political power falls to men by chance of birth, or by some means which has rendered them citizens, and who can claim it as their right, without regard to the choice of others. And a democracy, according to Spinosa, may exist, if the law should limit this privilege of power to the seniors in age, or to the elder branches of families, or to those who pay a certain amount in taxation ; although the numbers enjoying it should be a smaller portion of the community than in an aristocracy of the form he has recommended. His treatise breaks off near the beginning of the chapters intended to delineate the best model of democracy, which he declares to be one wherein all persons, in their own power, and not infamous by crime, should have a share

in the public government.   I do not know that it can be inferred from the writings of Spinosa, nor is his authority, perhaps, sufficient to render the question of any interest, to which of the three plans devised by him as the best in their respective forms, he would have ascribed the preference.

80. The condition of France under Louis XIV. was not very tempting to speculators on political theory.   Whatever short remarks may be found in those excellent writers on other subjects who distinguish this period, we can select no one book that falls readily into this class.   For Télémaque we must find another place.   It is scarcely worth while to mention the political discourses on Tacitus, by Amelot de la Houssaye.   These are a tedious and pedantic running commentary on Tacitus, affecting to deduce general principles, but much unlike the short and poignant observations of Machiavel and Bacon.   A whole volume on the reign alone of Tiberius, and printed at Paris, is not likely to repay a reader's trouble; at least I have found nothing in it above the common level.   I have no acquaintance with the other political writings of Amelot de la Houssaye, one of those who thought they could make great discoveries by analysing the constitution of Venice and other states. *Amelot de la Houssaye.*

81. England, thrown at the commencement of this period upon the resources of her own invention to replace an ancient monarchy by something new, and rich at that time in reflecting as well as learned men, with an unshackled press, and a growing disdain of authority as opposed to argument, was the natural soil of political theory.   The earliest fruit was Sir James Harrington's Oceana, published in 1656.   This once famous book is a political allegory, partly suggested, perhaps, by the Dodona's Grove of Howell, or by Barclay's Argenis, and a few other fictions of the preceding age.   His Oceana represents England, the history of which is shadowed out with fictitious names.   But this is preliminary to the great object, the scheme of a new commonwealth, which, under the auspices of Olphaus Megaletor, the Lord Archon, meaning, of course, Cromwell, not as he was, but as he ought to have been, the author feigns to have been established.   The various *Harrington's Oceana.*

laws and constitutions of this polity occupy the whole work.

82. The leading principle of Harrington is that power depends on property; denying the common saying that knowledge or prudence is power. But this property must be in land, "because, as to property producing empire, it is required that it should have some certain root or foothold, which except in land it cannot have, being otherwise, as it were, upon the wing. Nevertheless, in such cities as subsist mostly by trade, and have little or no land, as Holland and Genoa, the balance of treasure may be equal to that of land."[c] The law fixing the balance of lands is called by him agrarian; and without an agrarian law he holds that no government, whether monarchical, aristocratic, or popular, has any long duration: this is rather paradoxical; but his distribution of lands varies according to the form of the commonwealth. In one best constituted the possession of lands is limited to 2000l. a-year; which, of course, in his time was a much greater estate than at present.

83. Harrington's general scheme of a good government is one "established upon an equal agrarian arising into the superstructure, or three orders, the senate debating and proposing, the people resolving, and the magistracy executing by an equal rotation through the suffrage of the people given by the ballot." His more particular form of polity, devised for his Oceana, it would be tedious to give in detail: the result is a moderate aristocracy; property, though under the control of his agrarian, which prevents its excess, having so great a share in the elections that it must predominate. But it is an aristocracy of what we should call the middle ranks, and might not be unfit for a small state. In general it may be said of Harrington that he is prolix, dull, pedantic, and seldom profound; but sometimes redeems himself by just observations. Like most theoretical politicians of that age, he had an excessive admiration for the republic of Venice.[d] His other political writings are in the same spirit as the Oceana, but still less interesting.

c P. 38, edit. 1771.

d " If I be worthy to give advice to a man that would study politics, let him understand Venice; he that understands Venice right, shall go nearest to judge, notwithstanding the difference that is in every policy, right of any government in the world." Harrington's Works, p. 292.

84. The manly republicanism of Harrington, though sometimes visionary and perhaps impracticable, *Patriarcha of Filmer.* shines by comparison with a very opposite theory, which, having been countenanced in the early part of the century by our clergy, revived with additional favour after the Restoration. This was maintained in the Patriarcha of Sir Robert Filmer, written, as it appears, in the reign of Charles I., but not published till 1680, at a time when very high notions of royal prerogative were as well received by one party as they were indignantly rejected by another. The object, as the author declares, was to prove that the first kings were fathers of families; that it is unnatural for the people to govern or to choose governors; that positive laws do not infringe the natural and fatherly power of kings. He refers the tenet of natural liberty and the popular origin of government to the schoolmen, allowing that all papists and the reformed divines have imbibed it, but denying that it is found in the fathers. He seems, however, to claim the credit of an original hypothesis; those who have vindicated the rights of kings in most points not having thought of this, but with one consent admitted the natural liberty and equality of mankind. It is certain, nevertheless, that the patriarchal theory of government as the basis of actual right was laid down as explicitly as by himself in what is called Bishop Overall's Convocation Book, at the beginning of the reign of James I. But this book had not been published when Filmer wrote. His arguments are singularly insufficient; he quotes nothing but a few irrelevant texts from Genesis; he seems not to have known at all the strength, whatever it may be, of his own case, and it is hardly possible to find a more trifling and feeble work. It had however the advantage of opportunity to be received by a party with approbation.

85. Algernon Sidney was the first who devoted his time to a refutation of this patriarchal theory, *Sidney's Discourses on Government.* propounded as it was, not as a plausible hypothesis to explain the origin of civil communities, but as a paramount title, by virtue of which all actual sovereigns, who were not manifest usurpers, were to reign with an unmitigated despotism. Sidney's Discourses on Government, not published till 1698, are

a diffuse reply to Filmer. They contain indeed many chapters full of historical learning and judicious reflection; yet the constant anxiety to refute that which needs no refutation renders them a little tedious. Sidney does not condemn a limited monarchy like the English, but his partiality is for a form of republic which would be deemed too aristocratical for our popular theories.

86. Locke, immediately after the Revolution, attacked Locke on the Patriarcha with more brevity, and laid Govern- down his own celebrated theory of government. ment. The fundamental principle of Filmer is, that paternal authority is naturally absolute. Adam received it from God, exercised it over his own children, and transmitted it to the eldest born for ever. This assumption Locke combats rather too diffusely, according to our notions. Filmer had not only to show this absolute monarchy of a lineal ancestor, but his power of transmitting it in course of primogeniture. Locke denies that there is any natural right of this kind, maintaining the equality of children. The incapacity of Filmer renders his discomfiture not difficult. Locke, as will be seen, acknowledges a certain *de facto* authority in fathers of families, and possibly he might have found, as indeed he seems to admit, considerable traces of a regard to primogeniture in the early ages of the world. It is the question of natural right with which he is here concerned; and as no proof of this had been offered, he had nothing to answer.

87. In the second part of Locke's Treatise on Civil Government, he proceeds to lay down what he holds to be the true principles upon which society is founded. A state of nature is a state of perfect freedom and equality; but within the bounds of the law of nature, which obliges every one, and renders a state of liberty no state of licence. And the execution of this law, in such a state, is put into every one's hands, so that he may punish transgressors against it, not merely by way of reparation for his own wrongs, but for those of others. "Every offence that can be committed in the state of nature may, in the state of nature, be punished equally, and as far forth, as it may in a commonwealth." And not only independent communities, but all men, as he thinks, till

they voluntarily enter into some society, are in a state of nature.[a]

88. Whoever declares by word or action a settled design against another's life, puts himself in a state of war against him, and exposes his own life to be taken away, either by the other party, or by any one who shall espouse his cause. And he who endeavours to obtain absolute power over another may be construed to have a design on his life, or at least to take away his property. Where laws prevail, they must determine the punishment of those who injure others; but if the law is silenced, it is hard to think but that the appeal to Heaven returns, and the aggressor may be treated as one in a state of war.[b]

89. Natural liberty is freedom from any superior power except the law of nature. Civil liberty is freedom from the dominion of any authority except that which a legislature, established by consent of the commonwealth, shall confirm. No man, according to Locke, can by his own consent enslave himself, or give power to another to take away his life. For slavery, in a strict sense, is but a continuance of the state of war between a conqueror and his captive.[c]

90. The excellent chapter on property which follows would be sufficient, if all Locke's other writings had perished, to leave him a high name in philosophy. Nothing can be more luminous than his deduction of the natural right of property from labour, not merely in gathering the fruits of the earth, or catching wild animals, but in the cultivation of land, for which occupancy is but the preliminary, and gives as it were an inchoate title. "As much land as a man tills, plants, improves, cultivates, and can use the product of, so much is his property. He by his labour does, as it were, inclose it from the common." Whatever is beyond the scanty limits of individual or family labour, has been appropriated under the authority of civil society. But labour is the primary basis of natural right. Nor can it be thought unreasonable that labour should confer an exclusive right, when it is remembered how much of every thing's value depends upon labour alone. "Whatever bread is more worth than acorns, wine than water,

[a] L. ii. c. 2   [b] C. 3.   [c] C. 4.

and cloth or silk than leaves, skins, or moss, that is wholly owing to labour and industry." The superiority in good sense and satisfactory elucidation of his principle, which Locke has manifested in this important chapter over Grotius and Puffendorf, will strike those who consult those writers, or look at the brief sketch of their theories in the foregoing pages. It is no less contrasted with the puerile rant of Rousseau against all territorial property. That property owes its origin to occupancy accompanied with labour, is now generally admitted; the care of cattle being of course to be considered as one species of labour, and requiring at least a temporary ownership of the soil.[h]

91. Locke, after acutely remarking that the common arguments for the power of a father over his children would extend equally to the mother, so that it should be called parental power, reverts to the train of reasoning in the first book of this treatise against the regal authority of fathers. What they possess is not derived from generation, but from the care they necessarily take of the infant child, and during his minority; the power then terminates, though reverence, support, and even compliance are still due. Children are also held in subordination to their parents by the institutions of property, which commonly make them dependent both as to maintenance and succession. But Locke, which is worthy to be remarked, inclines to derive the origin of civil government from the patriarchal authority; one not strictly coercive, yet voluntarily conceded by habit and family consent. " Thus the natural fathers of families, by an insensible change, became the politic monarchs of them too; and as they chanced to live long, and leave worthy and able heirs for several successions or otherwise, so they laid the foundations of hereditary or elective kingdoms."[i]

92. The necessity that man should not live alone, produced the primary society of husband and wife, parent and children, to which that of master and servant was early added; whether of freemen engaging their service for hire, or of slaves taken in just war, who are by the right of nature subject to the absolute dominion of the captor. Such a family may sometimes resemble a little

h C. 5.   i C. 6.

commonwealth by its numbers, but is essentially distinct from one, because its chief has no imperial power of life and death except over his slaves, nature having given him none over his children, though all men have a right to punish breaches of the law of nature in others according to the offence. But this natural power they quit and resign into the hands of the community, when civil society is instituted ; and it is in this union of the several rights of its members that the legislative right of the commonwealth consists, whether this be done by general consent at the first formation of government, or by the adhesion which any individual may give to one already established. By either of these ways men pass from a state of nature to one of political society, the magistrate having now that power to redress injuries which had previously been each man's right. Hence absolute monarchy, in Locke's opinion, is no form of civil government ; for there being no common authority to appeal to, the sovereign is still in a state of nature with regard to his subjects.[k]

93. A community is formed by the unanimous consent of any body of men ; but when thus become one body, the determination of the majority must bind the rest, else it would not be one. Unanimity, after a community is once formed, can no longer be required ; but this consent of men to form a civil society is that which alone did or could give beginning to any lawful government in the world. It is idle to object that we have no records of such an event ; for few commonwealths preserve the tradition of their own infancy ; and whatever we do know of the origin of particular states gives indications of this mode of union. Yet he again inclines to deduce the usual origin of civil societies from imitation of patriarchal authority, which having been recognised by each family in the arbitration of disputes and even punishment of offences, was transferred with more readiness to some one person, as the father and representative head of the infant community. He even admits that this authority might tacitly devolve upon the eldest son. Thus the first governments were monarchies, and those with no express limitations of power, till exposure of its abuse gave occasion to social laws, or to co-ordinate authority.

k C. 7.

In all this he follows Hooker, from the first book of whose Ecclesiastical Polity he quotes largely in his notes.[m]

94. A difficulty commonly raised against the theory of compact is, that all men being born under some government, they cannot be at liberty to erect a new one, or even to make choice whether they will obey or no. This objection Locke does not meet, like Hooker and the jurists, by supposing the agreement of a distant ancestor to oblige all his posterity. But explicitly acknowledging that nothing can bind freemen to obey any government save their own consent, he rests the evidence of a tacit consent on the enjoyment of land, or even on mere residence within the dominions of the community; every man being at liberty to relinquish his possessions, or change his residence, and either incorporate himself with another commonwealth, or, if he can find an opportunity, set up for himself in some unoccupied part of the world. But nothing can make a man irrevocably a member of one society, except his own voluntary declaration; such perhaps as the oath of allegiance, which Locke does not mention, ought to be reckoned.[n]

95. The majority having, in the first constitution of a state, the whole power, may retain it themselves, or delegate it to one or more persons.[o] And the supreme power is, in other words, the legislature, sacred and unalterable in the hands where the community have once placed it, without which no law can exist, and in which all obedience terminates. Yet this legislative authority itself is not absolute or arbitrary over the lives and fortunes of its subjects. It is the joint power of individuals surrendered to the state; but no man has power over his own life or his neighbour's property. The laws enacted by the legislature must be conformable to the will of God, or natural justice. Nor can it take any part of the subject's property without his own consent, or that of the majority. "For if any one shall claim a power to lay and levy taxes on the people by his own authority, and without such consent of the people, he thereby invades the fundamental law of property, and subverts the end of government. For what property have I in that which another may by right take, when he pleases, to himself?"

[m] C. 8.   [n] C. 8.   [o] C. 10.

Lastly, the legislative power is inalienable; being but delegated from the people, it cannot be transferred to others.ᵖ This is the part of Locke's treatise which has been open to most objection, and which in some measure seems to charge with usurpation all the established governments of Europe. It has been a theory fertile of great revolutions, and perhaps pregnant with more. In some part of this chapter also, though by no means in the most practical corollaries, the language of Hooker has led onward his more hardy disciple.

96. Though the legislative power is alone supreme in the constitution, it is yet subject to the people themselves, who may alter it whenever they find that it acts against the trust reposed in it; all power given in trust for a particular end being evidently forfeited when that end is manifestly disregarded or obstructed. But while the government subsists the legislature is alone sovereign, though it may be the usage to call a single executive magistrate sovereign, if he has also a share in legislation. Where this is not the case, the appellation is plainly improper. Locke has in this chapter a remarkable passage, one perhaps of the first declarations in favour of a change in the electoral system of England. "To what gross absurdities the following of custom, when reason has left it, may lead, we may be satisfied when we see the bare name of a town, of which there remains not so much as the ruins, where scarce so much housing as a sheep-cote or more inhabitants than a shepherd is to be found, send as many representatives to the grand assembly of law-makers as a whole county, numerous in people, and powerful in riches. This strangers stand amazed at, and every one must confess needs a remedy, though most think it hard to find one, because the constitution of the legislative being the original and supreme act of the society, antecedent to all positive laws in it, and depending wholly on the people, no inferior power can alter it." But Locke is less timid about a remedy, and suggests that the executive magistrate might regulate the number of representatives, not according to old custom but reason, which is not setting up a new legislature, but restoring an old one. "Whatsoever shall be done manifestly for the good of the people and the establishing

P C. 11.

the government on its true foundation, is, and always will be, just prerogative ;" ⁹ a maxim of too dangerous latitude for a constitutional monarchy.

97. Prerogative he defines to be "a power of acting according to discretion for the public good without the prescription of the law, and sometimes even against it." This, however, is not by any means a good definition in the eyes of a lawyer ; and the word, being merely technical, ought not to have been employed in so partial if not so incorrect a sense. Nor is it very precise to say, that in England the prerogative was always largest in the hands of our wisest and best princes, not only because the fact is otherwise, but because he confounds the legal prerogative with its actual exercise. This chapter is the most loosely reasoned of any in the treatise.ʳ

98. Conquest, in an unjust war, can give no right at all, unless robbers and pirates may acquire a right. Nor is any one bound by promises which unjust force extorts from him. If we are not strong enough to resist, we have no remedy save patience ; but our children may appeal to Heaven, and repeat their appeals till they recover their ancestral right, which was to be governed by such a legislation as themselves approve. He that appeals to Heaven must be sure that he has right on his side, and right too that is worth the trouble and cost of his appeal, as he will answer at a tribunal that cannot be deceived. Even just conquest gives no further right than to reparation of injury ; and the posterity of the vanquished, he seems to hold, can forfeit nothing by their parent's offence, so that they have always a right to throw off the yoke. The title of prescription, which has commonly been admitted to silence the complaints, if not to heal the wounds, of the injured, finds no favour with Locke.ˢ But hence it seems to follow that no state composed, as most have been, out of the spoils of conquest, can exercise a legitimate authority over the latest posterity of those it has incorporated. Wales, for instance, has an eternal right to shake off the yoke of England ; for what Locke says of consent to laws by representatives, is of little weight when these must be outnumbered in the general legislature of both countries ;

ᵠ C. 13.   ʳ C. 14.   ˢ C. 16.

and indeed the first question for the Cambro-Britons would be to determine whether they would form part of such a common legislation.

99. Usurpation, which is a kind of domestic conquest, gives no more right to obedience than unjust war; it is necessary that the people should both be at liberty to consent, and have actually consented to allow and confirm a power which the constitution of their commonwealth does not recognise.[t] But tyranny may exist without usurpation, whenever the power reposed in any one's hands for the people's benefit is abused to their impoverishment or slavery. Force may never be opposed but to unjust and unlawful force: in any other case, it is condemned before God and man. The king's person is in some countries sacred by law; but this, as Locke thinks, does not extend to the case where, by putting himself in a state of war with his people, he dissolves the government.[u] A prince dissolves the government by ruling against law, by hindering the regular assembly of the legislature, by changing the form of election, or by rendering the people subject to a foreign power. He dissolves it also by neglecting or abandoning it, so that the laws cannot be put into execution. The government is also dissolved by breach of trust in either the legislature or the prince; by the former when it usurps an arbitrary power over the lives, liberties, and fortunes of the subject; by the latter, when he endeavours to corrupt the representatives or to influence the choice of the electors. If it be objected that no government will be able long to subsist, if the people may set up a new legislature whenever they take offence at the old one, he replies that mankind are too slow and averse to quit their old institutions for this danger to be apprehended. Much will be endured from rulers without mutiny or murmur. Nor is anything more likely to restrain governments than this doctrine of the right of resistance. It is as reasonable to tell men they should not defend themselves against robbers, because it may occasion disorder, as to use the same argument for passive obedience to illegal dominion. And he observes, after quoting some other writers, that Hooker alone might be enough to satisfy those who rely on him for their ecclesiastical polity.[x]

t C. 17.   u C. 18.   x C. 19.

100. Such is, in substance, the celebrated treatise of
Locke on civil government, which, with the
favour of political circumstances, and the authority of his name, became the creed of a
numerous party at home; while silently spreading the
fibres from its root over Europe and America, it prepared the way for theories of political society, hardly
bolder in their announcement, but expressed with more
passionate ardour, from which the great revolutions of
the last and present age have sprung. But as we do not
launch our bark upon a stormy sea, we shall merely
observe that neither the Revolution of 1688, nor the administration of William III., could have borne the test
by which Locke has tried the legitimacy of government.
There was certainly no appeal to the people in the former, nor would it have been convenient for the latter to
have had the maxim established, that an attempt to corrupt the legislature entails a forfeiture of the intrusted
power. Whether the opinion of Locke, that mankind
are slow to political change, be conformable to an enlarged experience, must be judged by every one according to his reading and observation; it is at least very
different from that which Hooker, to whom he defers so
greatly in most of his doctrine, has uttered in the very
first sentence of his Ecclesiastical Polity. For my own
part I must confess, that in these latter chapters of Locke
on Government I see, what sometimes appears in his
other writings, that the influence of temporary circumstances on a mind a little too susceptible of passion and
resentment, had prevented that calm and patient examination of all the bearings of this extensive subject which
true philosophy requires.

101. But whatever may be our judgment of this work,
it is equally true that it opened a new era of political
opinion in Europe. The earlier writings on the side of
popular sovereignty, whether those of Buchanan and
Languet, of the Jesuits, or of the English republicans,
had been either too closely dependent on temporary
circumstances, or too much bound up with odious and
unsuccessful factions, to sink very deep into the hearts
of mankind. Their adversaries, with the countenance
of every government on their side, kept possession of
the field; and no later jurist, nor theologian, nor philo-

sopher on the Continent, while they generally followed
their predecessors in deriving the origin of civil society
from compact, ventured to moot the delicate problem of
resistance to tyranny, or of the right to reform a constitution, except in the most cautious and indefinite language.   We have seen this already in Grotius and
Puffendorf.   But the success of the English Revolution,
the necessity which the powers allied against France
found of maintaining the title of William, the peculiar
interest of Holland and Hanover (states at that time
very strong in the literary world) in our new scheme of
government, gave a weight and authority to principles
which, without some such application, it might still
have been thought seditious to propound.   Locke too,
long an exile in Holland, was intimate with Le Clerc,
who exerted a considerable influence over the Protestant
part of Europe.   Barbeyrac, some time afterwards, trod
nearly in the same steps, and without going all the
lengths of Locke, did not fail to take a very different
tone from the two older writers upon whom he has com-
mented.

102. It was very natural that the French Protestants,
among whom traditions of a turn of thinking
not the most favourable to kings may have
been preserved, should, in the hour of severe
persecution, mutiny in words and writings
against the despotism that oppressed them.   Such, it
appears, had been the language of those exiles, as it is of
all exiles, when an anonymous tract, entitled Avis aux
Refugiéz, was published with the date of Amsterdam, in
1690.   This, under pretext of giving advice, in the
event of their being permitted to return home, that they
should get rid of their spirit of satire, and of their
republican theories, is a bitter and able attack on those
who had taken refuge in Holland.   It asserts the principle of passive obedience, extolling also the King of
France and his government, and censuring the English
Revolution.   Public rumour ascribed this to Bayle; it
has usually passed for his, and is even inserted in the
collection of his miscellaneous works.   Some, however,
have ascribed it to Pelisson, and others to Larroque;
one already, and the other soon after, proselytes to the
church of Rome.   Basnage thought it written by the

Avis aux
Refugiéz,
perhaps by
Bayle.

latter, and published by Bayle, to whom he ascribed the preface. This is apparently in a totally opposite strain, but not without strong suspicion of irony or ill faith. The style and manner of the whole appear to suggest Bayle; and though the supposition is very discreditable to his memory, the weight of presumption seems much to incline that way.

103. The separation of political economy from the
Political economists. general science which regards the well-being of communities, was not so strictly made by the earlier philosophers as in modern times. It does not follow that national wealth engaged none of their attention. Few, on the contrary, of those who have taken comprehensive views could have failed to regard it. In Bodin, Botero, Bacon, Hobbes, Puffendorf, we have already seen proofs of this. These may be said to have discussed the subject, not systematically, nor always with thorough knowledge, but with acuteness and in a philosophical tone. Others there were of a more limited range, whose habits of life and experience led them to particular departments of economical inquiry, especially as to commerce, the precious metals, and the laws affecting them. The Italians led the way; Serra has been mentioned in the last period, and a few more might find a place in this. De Witt's Interest of Holland can hardly be reckoned among economical writings; and it is said by Morhof, that the Dutch were not fond of promulgating their commercial knowledge;[y] little at least was contributed from that country, even at a later period, towards the theory of becoming rich. But England now took a large share in this new literature. Free, inquisitive, thriving rapidly in commerce, so that her progress even in the nineteenth century has hardly been in a greater ratio than before and after the middle of the seventeenth, if we may trust the statements of contemporaries, she produced some writers who, though few of them merit the name of philosophers, yet may not here be overlooked, on account of their influence, their reputation, or their position as links in the chain of science.

104. The first of these was Thomas Mun, an intelli-

---

[y] Polyhistor, part iii. lib. iii. § 3.

gent merchant in the earlier part of the century, whose posthumous treatise, England's Treasure by Foreign Trade, was published in 1664, but seems to have been written soon after the accession of Charles I.[a] Mun is generally reckoned the founder of what has been called the mercantile system. His main position is that " the ordinary means to increase our wealth and treasure is by foreign trade, wherein we must ever observe this rule, to sell more to strangers yearly than we consume of theirs in value."[a] We must therefore sell as cheap as possible; it was by underselling the Venetians of late years, that we had exported a great deal of cloth to Turkey.[b] It is singular that Mun should not have perceived the difficulty of selling very cheap the productions of a country's labour, whose gold and silver were in great abundance. He was, however, too good a merchant not to acknowledge the inefficacy and impolicy of restraining by law the exportation of coin, which is often a means of increasing our treasure in the long run; advising instead a due regard to the balance of trade, or general surplus of exported goods, by which we shall infallibly obtain a stock of gold and silver. These notions have long since been covered with ridicule; and it is plain that, in a merely economical view, they must always be delusive. Mun, however, looked to the accumulation of a portion of this imported treasure by the state; a resource in critical emergencies which we have now learned to despise since others have been at hand, but which in reality had made a great difference in the events of war, and changed the balance of power between many commonwealths. Mun was followed, about 1670, by Sir Josiah Child, in a discourse on Trade, written on the same principles of the mercantile system, but more copious and varied. The chief aim of Child is to effect a reduction of the legal interest of money from six to four per cent., drawing an erroneous inference from the increase of wealth which had followed similar enactments.

Mun on foreign trade.

Child on Trade.

105. Among the many difficulties with which the

---

[a] Mr. M'Culloch says (Introductory Discourse to Smith's Wealth of Nations) it had most probably been written about 1635 or 1640. I remarked some things which serve to carry it up a little higher. [a] P. 11 (edit. 1664). [b] P. 18.

government of William III. had to contend, one of the
most embarrassing was the scarcity of the precious metals and depreciated condition of the
coin.   This opened the whole field of controversy in
that province of political economy ; and the bold spirit
of inquiry, unshackled by prejudice in favour of ancient
custom, which in all respects was characteristic of that
age, began to work by reasonings on general theorems,
instead of collecting insulated and inconclusive details.
Locke stood forward on this, as on so many subjects,
with his masculine sense and habitual closeness of
thinking.   His " Considerations of the Consequences of
lowering Interest, and raising the Value of Money "
were published in 1691.   Two further treatises are in
answer to the pamphlets of Lowndes.   These economical
writings of Locke are not in all points conformable to
the modern principles of the science.   He seems to
incline rather too much towards the mercantile theory,
and to lay too much stress on the possession of the precious metals.   From his excellent sense, however, as
well as from some expressions, I should conceive that
he only considers them, as they doubtless are, a portion
of the exchangeable wealth of the nation, and by their
inconsumable nature, as well as by the constancy of the
demand for them, one of the most important.   " Riches
do not consist," he says, " in having more gold and
silver, but in having more in proportion than the rest of
the world or than our neighbours, whereby we are
enabled to procure to ourselves a greater plenty of the
conveniences of life."

106. Locke had the sagacity to perceive the impossibility of regulating the interest of money by law.   It
was an empirical proposition at that time, as we have
just seen, of Sir Josiah Child, to render loans more easy
to the borrower by reducing the legal rate to four per
cent.   The whole drift of his reasoning is against any
limitation, though, from fear of appearing too paradoxical, he does not arrive at that inference.   For the
reasons he gives in favour of a legal limit of interest,
namely, that courts of law may have some rule where
nothing is stipulated in the contract, and that a few
money lenders in the metropolis may not have the
monopoly of all loans in England, are, especially the

first, so trifling, that he could not have relied upon them; and indeed he admits that, in other circumstances, there would be no danger from the second. But his prudence having restrained him from speaking out, a famous writer almost a century afterwards came forward to assert a paradox, which he loved the better for seeming such, and finally to convince the thinking part of mankind.

107. Laws fixing the value of silver Locke perceived to be nugatory, and is averse to prohibiting its exportation. The value of money, he maintains, does not depend on the rate of interest, but on its plenty relatively to commodities. Hence the rate of interest, he thinks, but perhaps erroneously, does not govern the price of land; arguing from the higher rate of land relatively to money, that is, the worse interest it gave, in the reigns of Elizabeth and James, than in his own time. But one of Locke's positions, if generally received, would alone have sufficed to lower the value of land. "It is in vain," he says, "in a country whose great fund is land, to hope to lay the public charges of the government on anything else; there at last it will terminate." The legislature soon proceeded to act on this mistaken theory in the annual land-tax; an impost of tremendous severity at that time, the gross unfairness, however, of which has been compensated in later times by the taxes on personal succession.

108. In such a monetary crisis as that of his time, Locke was naturally obliged to consider the usual resource of raising the denomination of the coin. This, he truly says, would be to rob all creditors of such a proportion of their debts. It is probable that his influence, which was very considerable, may have put a stop to the scheme. He contends in his Further Considerations, in answer to a tract by Lowndes, that clipped money should go only by weight. This seems to have been agreed by both parties; but Lowndes thought the loss should be defrayed by a tax, Locke that it should fall on the holders. Honourably for the government, the former opinion prevailed.

109. The Italians were the first who laid anything like a foundation for statistics or political arithmetic; that which is to the political economist   Statistical tracts.

what general history is to the philosopher. But their numerical reckonings of population, houses, value of lands or stock, and the like, though very curious, and sometimes taken from public documents, were not always more than conjectural, nor are they so full and minute as the spirit of calculation demands. England here again took the lead in Graunt's Observations on the Bills of Mortality, 1661, in Petty's Political Arithmetic (posthumous in 1691), and other treatises of the same ingenious and philosophical person, and, we may add, in the Observations of Gregory King on the Natural and Political State of England ; for though these were not published till near the end of the eighteenth century, the manuscripts had fallen into the hands of Dr. Charles Davenant, who has made extracts from them in his own valuable contributions to political arithmetic. King seems to have possessed a sagacity which has sometimes brought his conjectures nearer to the mark, than from the imperfection of his data it was reasonable to expect. Yet he supposes that the population of England, which he estimated, perhaps rightly, at five millions and a half, would not reach the double of that number before A.D. 2300. Sir William Petty, with a mind capable of just and novel theories, was struck by the necessary consequences of an uniformly progressive population. Though the rate of movement seemed to him, as in truth it then was, much slower than we have latterly found it, he clearly saw that its continuance would in an ascertainable length of time overload the world. " And then, according to the prediction of the Scriptures, there must be wars and great slaughter." He conceived that, in the ordinary course of things, the population of a country would be doubled in two hundred years ; but the whole conditions of the problem were far less understood than at present. Davenant's Essay on Ways and Means, 1693, gained him a high reputation, which he endeavoured to augment by many subsequent works, some falling within the seventeenth century. He was a man of more enlarged reading than his predecessors, with the exception of Petty, and of close attention to the statistical documents which were now more copiously published than before ; but he seldom launches into any extensive theory, confining himself rather to the accumulation of facts and to the immediate inferences, generally for temporary purposes, which they supplied.

Sect. III.—On Jurisprudence.

110. In 1667, a short book was published at Frankfort, by a young man of twenty-two years, entitled Methodi Novæ discendæ docendæque Jurisprudentiæ. The science which of all others had been deemed to require the most protracted labour, the ripest judgment, the most experienced discrimination, was, as it were, invaded by a boy, but by one who had the genius of an Alexander, and for whom the glories of an Alexander were reserved. This is the first production of Leibnitz; and it is probably in many points of view the most remarkable work that has prematurely united erudition and solidity. We admire in it the vast range of learning (for though he could not have read all the books he names, there is evidence of his acquaintance with a great number, and at least with a well-filled chart of literature), the originality of some ideas, the commanding and comprehensive views he embraces, the philosophical spirit, the compressed style in which it is written, the entire absence of juvenility, of ostentatious paradox,[c] of imagination, ardour, and enthusiasm, which, though Leibnitz did not always want them, would have been wholly misplaced on such a subject. Faults have been censured in this early performance, and the author declared himself afterwards dissatisfied with it.[d]

Works of Leibnitz on Roman law.

---

[c] I use the epithet ostentatious, because some of his original theories are a little paradoxical; thus he has a singular notion that the right of bequeathing property by testament is derived from the immortality of the soul; the living heirs being, as it were, the attorneys of those we suppose to be dead. Quia mortui revera adhuc vivunt, ideo manent domini rerum, quos vero hæredes reliquerunt, concipiendi sunt ut procuratores in rem suam. In our own discussions on the law of entail, I am not aware that this argument has ever been explicitly urged, though the advocates of perpetual control seem to have none better.

[d] This tract, and all the other works of Leibnitz on Jurisprudence, will be found in the fourth volume of his works by Dutens. An analysis by Bon, professor of law at Turin, is prefixed to the Methodi Novæ, and he has pointed out

111. Leibnitz was a passionate admirer of the Roman jurisprudence; he held the great lawyers of antiquity second only to the best geometers for strong, and subtle, and profound reasoning; not even acknowledging, to any considerable degree, the contradictions (antinomiæ juris) which had perplexed their disciples in later times, and on which many volumes had been written. But the arrangement of Justinian he entirely disapproved; and in another work, Corporis Juris reconcinnandi Ratio, published in 1668, he pointed out the necessity and what he deemed the best method of a new distribution. This appears to be not quite like what he had previously sketched, and which was rather a philosophical than a very convenient method;° in this new arrangement he proposes to retain the texts of the Corpus Juris Civilis, but in a form rather like that of the Pandects than of the Institutes; to the latter of which, followed as it has been among us by Hale and Blackstone, he was very averse.

112. There was only one man in the world who could have left so noble a science' as philosophical jurisprudence for pursuits of a still more exalted nature, and for which he was still more fitted; and that man was Leibnitz himself. He passed onward to reap the golden harvests of other fields. Yet the study of law has owed much to him; he did much to unite it with moral philosophy on the one hand, and with history on the other; a great master of both, he exacted perhaps a more comprehensive course of legal studies than the capacity of ordinary lawyers could grasp. In England also, its conduciveness to professional excellence might be hard to prove. It is however certain that, in Germany at least, philology, history, and philosophy have more or less since the time of Leibnitz marched together under the robe of law. " He did but pass over that

---

a few errors. Leibnitz says in a letter about 1676, that his book was effusus potius quam scriptus, in itinere, sine libris, &c., and that it contained some things he no longer would have said, though there were others of which he did not repent. Lerminier, Hist. du Droit, p. 150.

° In his Methodi Novæ he divides law, in the didactic part, according to the several sources of rights; namely. 1. Nature, which gives us right over res nullius, things where there is no prior property. 2. Succession. 3. Possession. 4. Contract. 5. Injury, which gives right to reparation.

kingdom," says Lerminier, " and he has reformed and enlarged it." [f]

113. James Godefroy was thirty years engaged on an edition of the Theodosian Code, published several years after his death, in 1665. It is by far the best edition of that body of laws, and retains a standard value in the historical department of jurisprudence. Domat, a French lawyer, and one of the Port-Royal connexion, in his Loix Civiles dans leur Ordre Naturel, the first of five volumes of which appeared in 1689, carried into effect the project of Leibnitz, by re-arranging the laws of Justinian, which, especially the Pandects, are well known to be confusedly distributed, in a more regular method, prefixing a book of his own on the nature and spirit of law in general. This appears to be an useful digest or abridgment, something like those made by Viner and earlier writers of our own text-books, but perhaps with more compression and choice ; two editions of an English translation were published. Domat's Public Law, which might, perhaps, in our language, have been called constitutional, since we generally confine the epithet public to the law of nations, forms a second part of the same work, and contains a more extensive system, wherein theological morality, ecclesiastical ordinances, and the fundamental laws of the French monarchy are reduced into method. Domat is much extolled by his countrymen ; but in philosophical jurisprudence, he seems to display little force or originality. Gravina, who obtained a high name in this literature at the beginning of the next century, was known merely as a professor at the close of this ; but a Dutch jurist, Gerard Noodt, may deserve mention for his treatise on Usury, in 1698, wherein he both endeavours to prove its natural and religious lawfulness, and traces its history through the Roman law. Several other works of Noodt on subjects of historical jurisprudence seem to fall within this century, though I do not find their exact dates of publication.

114. Grotius was the acknowledged master of all who

f Biogr. Univ.; Lerminier, Hist. du Droit, p. 142.

studied the theory of international right. It was, perhaps, the design of Puffendorf, as we may conjecture by the title' of his great work on the

Law of
Nations.—
Puffendorf.

Law of Nature and Nations, to range over the
latter field with as assiduous diligence as the former.
But from the length of his prolix labour on natural law
and the rights of sovereigns, he has not more than one
twentieth of the whole volume to spare for international
questions; and this is in great measure copied or abridged
from Grotius. In some instances he disagrees with his
master. Puffendorf singularly denies that compacts made
during war are binding by the law of nature, but for
weak and unintelligible reasons.[g] Treaties of peace
extorted by unjust force, he denies with more reason to
be binding; though Grotius had held the contrary.[h]
The inferior writers on the law of nations, or those
who, like Wicquefort, in his Ambassador, confined themselves to merely conventional usages, it is needless to
mention.

[g] B. viii. chap. 7.   [h] Chap. 8.

CHAPTER V.

HISTORY OF POETRY, FROM 1650 TO 1700.

SECT. I.—ON ITALIAN POETRY.

Filicaja — Guidi — Menzini — Arcadian Society.

1. THE imitators of Marini, full of extravagant metaphors, and the false thoughts usually called
concetti, were in their vigour at the commencement of this period. But their names are now
obscure, and have been overwhelmed by the
change of public taste, which has condemned and proscribed what it once most applauded. This change
came on long before the close of the century, though
not so decidedly but that some traces of the former
manner are discoverable in the majority of popular
writers. The general characteristics, however, of Italian
poetry were now a more masculine tone ; a wider reach
of topics, and a selection of the most noble ; an abandonment, except in the lighter lyrics, of amatory strains,
and especially of such as were languishing and queru-
lous ; an anticipation, in short, as far as the circumstances of the age would permit, of that severe and
elevated style which has been most affected for the last
fifty years. It would be futile to seek an explanation
of this manlier spirit in any social or political causes ;
never had Italy in these respects been so lifeless ; but
the world of poets is often not the world around them,
and their stream of living waters may flow, like that of
Arethusa, without imbibing much from the surrounding
brine. Chiabrera had led the way by the Pindaric
majesty of his odes, and had disciples of at least equal
name with himself.

Improved tone of Italian poetry.

2. Florence was the mother of one who did most to invigorate Italian poetry, Vincenzo Filicaja; a man gifted with a serious, pure, and noble spirit, from which congenial thoughts spontaneously arose, and with an imagination rather vigorous than fertile. The siege of Vienna in 1683, and its glorious deliverance by Sobieski, are the subjects of six odes. The third of these, addressed to the King of Poland himself, is generally most esteemed, though I do not perceive that the first or second are inferior. His ode to Rome, on Christina's taking up her residence there, is in many parts highly poetical; but the flattery of representing this event as sufficient to restore the eternal city from decay is too gross. It is not on the whole so successful as those on the siege of Vienna. A better is that addressed to Florence, on leaving it for a rural solitude, in consequence of his poverty and the neglect he had experienced. It breathes an injured spirit, something like the Complaint of Cowley, with which posterity are sure to sympathise. The sonnet of Filicaja, "Italia mia," is known by every one who cares for this poetry at all. This sonnet is conspicuous for its depth of feeling, for the spirit of its commencement, and above all, for the noble lines with which it ends; but there are surely awkward and feeble expressions in the intermediate part. *Armenti* for regiments of dragoons could only be excused by frequent usage in poetry, which, I presume, is not the case, though we find the same word in one of Filicaja's odes. A foreigner may venture upon this kind of criticism.

3. Filicaja was formed in the school of Chiabrera; but with his pomp of sound and boldness of imagery he is animated by a deeper sense both of religion and patriotism. We perceive more the language of the heart; the man speaks in his genuine character, not with assumed and mercenary sensibility, like that of Pindar and Chiabrera. His genius is greater than his skill; he abandons himself to an impetuosity which he cannot sustain, forgetful of the economy of strength and breath, as necessary for a poet as a race-horse. He has rarely or never any conceits or frivolous thoughts, but the expression is sometimes rather feeble. There is a general want of sunshine in Filicaja's poetry; unprosperous

himself, he views nothing with a worldly eye; his notes of triumph are without brilliancy, his predictions of success are without joy. He seems also deficient in the charms of grace and felicity. But his poetry is always the effusion of a fine soul; we venerate and love Filicaja as a man, but we also acknowledge that he was a real poet.

4. Guidi, a native of Pavia, raised himself to the highest point that any lyric poet of Italy has attained. His odes are written at Rome from about the year 1685 to the end of the century. Compared with Chiabrera, or even Filicaja, he may be allowed the superiority; if he never rises to a higher pitch than the latter, if he has never chosen subjects so animating, if he has never displayed so much depth and truth of feeling, his enthusiasm is more constant, his imagination more creative, his power of language more extensive and more felicitous. "He falls sometimes," says Corniani, "into extravagance, but never into affectation. . . . . His peculiar excellence is poetical expression, always brilliant with a light of his own. The magic of his language used to excite a lively movement among the hearers when he recited his verses in the Arcadian society." Corniani adds that he is sometimes exuberant in words and hyperbolical in images.[i]

5. The ode of Guidi on Fortune appears to me at least equal to any in the Italian language. If it has been suggested by that of Celio Magno, entitled Iddio, the resemblance does not deserve the name of imitation; a nobleness of thought, imagery, and language prevails throughout. But this is the character of all his odes. He chose better subjects than Chiabrera; for the ruins of Rome are more glorious than the living house of Medici. He resembles him, indeed, rather than any other poet, so that it might not always be easy to discern one from the other in a single stanza; but Guidi is a bolder, a more imaginative, a more enthusiastic poet. Both adorn and amplify a little to excess; and it may be imputed to Guidi that he has abused an advantage which his native language afforded. The Italian is rich in words, where the sound so well answers to the meaning, that it is hardly possible to hear them without an

Guidi.

i Vol. viii. p. 224.

associated sentiment; their effect is closely analogous to musical expression. Such are the adjectives denoting mental elevation, as *superbo, altiero, audace, gagliardo, indomito, maestoso*. These recur in the poems of Guidi with every noun that will admit of them; but sometimes the artifice is a little too transparent, and though the meaning is not sacrificed to sound, we feel that it is too much enveloped in it, and are not quite pleased that a great poet should rely so much on a resource which the most mechanical slave of music can employ.

6. The odes of Benedetto Menzini are elegant and in
Menzini. poetical language, but such as does not seem very original, nor do they strike us by much vigour or animation of thought. The allusions to mythology, which we never find in Filicaja, and rarely in Guidi, are too frequent. Some of these odes are of considerable beauty, among which we may distinguish that addressed to Magalotti, beginning, " Un verde ramuscello in piaggia aprica." Menzini was far from confining himself to this species of poetry; he was better known in others. As an Anacreontic poet he stands, I believe, only below Chiabrera and Redi. His satires have been preferred by some to those of Ariosto; but neither Corniani nor Salfi acquiesce in this praise. Their style is a mixture of obsolete phrases from Dante with the idioms of the Florentine populace; and, though spirited in substance, they are rather full of commonplace invective. Menzini strikes boldly at priests and governments, and, what was dangerous to Orpheus, at the whole sex of women. His Art of Poetry, in five books, published in 1681, deserves some praise. As his atrabilious humour prompted, he inveighs against the corruption of contemporary literature, especially on the stage, ridiculing also the Pindaric pomp that some affected, not perhaps without allusion to his enemy Guidi. His own style is pointed, animated, sometimes poetical, where didactic verse will admit of such ornament, but a little too diffuse and minute in criticism.

7. These three are the great restorers of Italian poetry
Salvator Rosa— Redi. after the usurpation of false taste. And it is to be observed that they introduced a new manner, very different from that of the sixteenth century. Several others deserve to be mentioned,

though we can only do so briefly.   The Satires of Salvator Rosa, full of force and vehemence, more vigorous than elegant, are such as his ardent genius and rather savage temper would lead us to expect.   A far superior poet was a man not less eminent than Salvator, the philosophical and every way accomplished Redi.   Few have done so much in any part of science who have also shone so brightly in the walks of taste.   The sonnets of Redi are esteemed; but his famous dithyrambic, Bacco in Toscana, is admitted to be the first poem of that kind in modern language, and is as worthy of Monte Pulciano wine as the wine is worthy of it.

8. Maggi and Lemene bore an honourable part in the restoration of poetry, though neither of them is reckoned altogether to have purified himself *Other poets.* from the infection of the preceding age.   The sonnet of Pastorini on the imagined resistance of Genoa to the oppression of Louis XIV. in 1684, though not borne out by historical truth, is one of those breathings of Italian nationality which we always admire, and which had now become more common than for a century before.   It must be confessed, in general, that when the protestations of a people against tyranny become loud enough to be heard, we may suspect that the tyranny has been relaxed.

9. Rome was to poetry in this age what Florence had once been, though Rome had hitherto done less for the Italian muses than any other great city. *Christina's patronage of letters.* Nor was this so much due to her bishops and cardinals, as to a stranger and a woman.   Christina finally took up her abode there in 1688.   Her palace became the resort of all the learning and genius she could assemble round her; a literary academy was established, and her revenue was liberally dispensed in pensions.   If Filicaja and Guidi, both sharers of her bounty, have exaggerated her praises, much may be pardoned to gratitude, and much also to the natural admiration which those who look up to power must feel for those who have renounced it.   Christina died in 1690, and her own academy could last no longer; but a phoenix sprang at once from its ashes.   Crescimbeni, then young, has the credit of having planned the Society of Arcadians, *Society of Arcadians.* which began in 1690, and has eclipsed in cele-

brity most of the earlier academies of Italy. Fourteen, says Corniani, were the original founders of this society; among whom were Crescimbeni, and Gravina, and Zappi. In course of time the Arcadians vastly increased, and established colonies in the chief cities of Italy. They determined to assume every one a pastoral name and a Greek birthplace, to hold their meetings in some verdant meadow, and to mingle with all their compositions, as far as possible, images from pastoral life; images always agreeable, because they recall the times of primitive innocence. This poetical tribe adopted as their device the pipe of seven reeds bound with laurel, and their president or director was denominated general shepherd or keeper (custode generale).[k] The fantastical part of the Arcadian society was common to them with all similar institutions; and mankind has generally required some ceremonial follies to keep alive the wholesome spirit of association. Their solid aim was to purify the national taste. Much had been already done, and in great measure by their own members, Menzini and Guidi; but their influence, which was of course more felt in the next century, has always been reckoned both important and auspicious to Italian literature.

SECT. II.—ON FRENCH POETRY.

La Fontaine—Boileau—Minor French Poets.

10. WE must pass over Spain and Portugal as absolutely destitute of any name which requires comme-
La Fontaine. moration. In France it was very different; if some earlier periods had been not less rich in the number of versifiers, none had produced poets who have descended with so much renown to posterity. The most popular of these was La Fontaine. Few writers have left such a number of verses which, in the phrase of his country, have made their fortune, and been like ready money, always at hand for prompt quotation. His lines have at once a proverbial truth and a humour of ex-

k Corniani, viii. 301; Tiraboschi, xi. 43; Crescimbeni, Storia d'Arcadia (reprinted by Mathias).

pression which render them constantly applicable. This is chiefly true of his Fables; for his Tales, though no one will deny that they are lively enough, are not reckoned so well written, nor do they supply so much for general use.

11. The models of La Fontaine's style were partly the ancient fabulists whom he copied, for he pre-   Character tends to no originality; partly the old French   of his poets, especially Marot. From the one he took   Fables. the real gold of his fables themselves; from the other he caught a peculiar archness and vivacity, which some of them had possessed, perhaps, in no less degree, but which becomes more captivating from his intermixture of a solid and serious wisdom. For notwithstanding the common anecdotes (sometimes, as we may suspect, rather exaggerated) of La Fontaine's simplicity, he was evidently a man who had thought and observed much about human nature, and knew a little more of the world than he cared to let the world perceive. Many of his fables are admirable; the grace of the poetry, the happy inspiration that seems to have dictated the turns of expression, place him in the first rank among fabulists. Yet the praise of La Fontaine should not be indiscriminate. It is said that he gave the preference to Phædrus and Æsop above himself; and some have thought that in this he could not have been sincere. It was at least a proof of his modesty. But though we cannot think of putting Phædrus on a level with La Fontaine, were it only for this reason, that in a work designed for the general reader (and surely fables are of this description), the qualities that please the many are to be valued above those that please the few, yet it is true that the French poet might envy some talents of the Roman. Phædrus, a writer scarcely prized enough, because he is an early school-book, has a perfection of elegant beauty which very few have rivalled. No word is out of its place, none is redundant, or could be changed for a better; his perspicuity and ease make everything appear unpremeditated, yet everything is wrought by consummate art. In many fables of La Fontaine this is not the case; he beats round the subject, and misses often before he hits. Much, whatever La Harpe may assert to the contrary, could be retrenched; in much the exigencies of rhyme

and metre are too manifest.[m] He has, on the other hand, far more humour than Phædrus; and, whether it be praise or not, thinks less of his fable and more of its moral. One pleases by enlivening; the other pleases but does not enliven; one has more felicity, the other more skill; but in such skill there is felicity.

12. The first seven satires of Boileau appeared in 1666; and these, though much inferior to his later productions, are characterised by La Harpe as the earliest poetry in the French language where the mechanism of its verse was fully understood, where the style was always pure and elegant, where the ear was uniformly gratified. The Art of Poetry was published in 1673, the Lutrin in 1674; the Epistles followed at various periods. Their elaborate though equable strain, in a kind of poetry which, never requiring high flights of fancy, escapes the censure of mediocrity and monotony which might sometimes fall upon it, generally excites more admiration in those who have been accustomed to the numerous defects of less finished poets, than it retains in a later age, when others have learned to emulate and preserve the same uniformity. The fame of Pope was transcendant for this reason; and Boileau is the analogue of Pope in French literature.

13. The Art of Poetry has been the model of the Essay on Criticism; few poems more resemble each other. I will not weigh in opposite scales two compositions, of which one claims an advantage from its having been the original, the other from the youth of its author. Both are uncommon efforts of critical good sense; and both are distinguished by their short and pointed language, which remains in the memory. Boileau has very well incorporated the thoughts of Horace with

Boileau. His epistles. (margin)

His Art of Poetry. (margin)

---

[m] Let us take, for example, the first lines of L'Homme et la Couleuvre.

Un homme vit une couleuvre.
Ah méchante, dit-il, je m'en vais faire un œuvre
Agréable à tout l'univers !
A ces mots l'animal pervers
(C'est le serpent que je veux dire,
Et non l'homme, on pourroit aisément s'y tromper)
A ces mots le serpent se laissant attraper
Est pris, mis en un sac; et, ce qui fut le pire,
On résolut sa mort, *fût il coupable ou non.*

None of these lines appear to me very happy; but there can be no doubt about that in italics, which spoils the effect of the preceding, and is feebly redundant. The last words are almost equally bad; no question could arise about the serpent's guilt, which had been assumed before. But these petty blemishes are abundantly redeemed by the rest of the fable, which is beautiful in choice of thoughts and language, and may be classed with the best in the collection.

his own, and given them a skilful adaptation to his own times. He was a bolder critic of his contemporaries than Pope. He took up arms against those who shared the public favour, and were placed by half Paris among great dramatists and poets, Pradon, Desmarests, Breboeuf. This was not true of the heroes of the Dunciad. His scorn was always bitter, and probably sometimes unjust; yet posterity has ratified almost all his judgments. False taste, it should be remembered, had long infected the poetry of Europe; some steps had been lately taken to repress it; but extravagance, affectation, and excess of refinement are weeds that can only be eradicated by a thorough cleansing of the soil, by a process of burning and paring, which leaves not a seed of them in the public mind. And when we consider the gross blemishes of this description that deform the earlier poetry of France, as of other nations, we cannot blame the severity of Boileau, though he may occasionally have condemned in the mass what contained some intermixture of real excellence. We have become of late years in England so enamoured of the beauties of our old writers (and certainly they are of a superior kind) that we are sometimes more than a little blind to their faults.

14. By writing satires, epistles, and an Art of Poetry, Boileau has challenged an obvious comparison with Horace. Yet they are very unlike; one easy, colloquial, abandoning himself to every change that arises in his mind, the other uniform as a regiment under arms, always equal, always laboured, incapable of a bold neglect. Poetry seems to have been the delight of one, the task of the other. The pain that Boileau must have felt in writing communicates itself in some measure to the reader; we are fearful of losing some point, of passing over some epithet without sufficiently perceiving its selection; it is as with those pictures, which are to be viewed long and attentively, till our admiration of detached proofs of skill becomes wearisome by repetition.

15. The Lutrin is the most popular of the poems of Boileau. Its subject is ill chosen; neither interest nor variety could be given to it. Tassoni and Pope have the advantage in this respect; if their leading theme is trifling, we lose sight of it in the gay

liveliness of description and episode. In Boileau, after we have once been told that the canons of a church spend their lives in sleep and eating, we have no more to learn, and grow tired of keeping company with a race so stupid and sensual. But the poignant wit and satire, the elegance and correctness of numberless couplets, as well as the ingenious adaptation of classical passages, redeem this poem, and confirm its high place in the mock-heroic line.

16. The great deficiency of Boileau is in sensibility.
General character of his poetry. Far below Pope or even Dryden in this essential quality, which the moral epistle or satire not only admits but requires, he rarely quits two paths, those of reason and of raillery. His tone on moral subjects is firm and severe, but not very noble; a trait of pathos, a single touch of pity or tenderness, will rarely be found. This of itself serves to give a dryness to his poetry; and it may be doubtful, though most have read Boileau, whether many have read him twice.

17. The pompous tone of Ronsard and Du Bartas had
Lyric poetry lighter than before. become ridiculous in the reign of Louis XIV. Even that of Malherbe was too elevated for the public taste; none at least imitated that writer, though the critics had set the example of admiring him. Boileau, who had done much to turn away the world from imagination to plain sense, once attempted to emulate the grandiloquent strains of Pindar in an ode on the taking of Namur, but with no such success as could encourage himself or others to repeat the experiment. Yet there was no want of gravity or elevation in the prose writers of France, nor in the tragedies of Racine. But the French language is not very well adapted for the higher kind of lyric poetry, while it suits admirably the lighter forms of song and epigram. And their poets, in this age, were almost entirely men living at Paris, either in the court, or at least in a refined society, the most adverse of all to the poetical character. The influence of wit and politeness is generally directed towards rendering enthusiasm or warmth of fancy ridiculous; and without these no great energy of genius can be displayed. But in their proper department several poets of considerable merit appeared.

18. Benserade was called peculiarly the poet of the court; for twenty years it was his business to compose verses for the ballets represented before the king. His skill and tact were shown in delicate contrivances to make those who supported the characters of gods and goddesses, in these fictions, being the nobles and ladies of the court, betray their real inclinations, and sometimes their gallantries. He even presumed to shadow in this manner the passion of Louis for Mademoiselle La Valière, before it was publicly acknowledged. Benserade must have had no small ingenuity and adroitness; but his verses did not survive those who called them forth. In a different school, not essentially, perhaps, much more vicious than the court, but more careless of appearances, and rather proud of an immorality which it had no interest to conceal, that of Ninon l'Enclos, several of higher reputation grew up; Chapelle (whose real name was L'Huillier), La Fare, Bachaumont, Lainezer, and Chaulieu. The first, perhaps, and certainly the last of these, are worthy to be remembered. La Harpe has said that Chaulieu alone retains a claim to be read in a style where Voltaire has so much left all others behind, that no comparison with him can ever be admitted. Chaulieu was an original genius : his poetry has a marked character, being a happy mixture of a gentle and peaceable philosophy with a lively imagination. His verses flow from his soul ; and though often negligent through indolence, are never in bad taste or affected. Harmony of versification, grace and gaiety, with a voluptuous and Epicurean, but mild and benevolent, turn of thought, belong to Chaulieu ; and these are qualities which do not fail to attract the majority of readers.[n]

Benserade.

Chaulieu.

19. It is rather singular that a style so uncongenial to the spirit of that age as pastoral poetry appears was quite as much cultivated as before. But it is still true that the spirit of the age gained the victory, and drove the shepherds from their shady bowers, though without substituting anything more rational in the fairy tales which superseded the pastoral romance. At the middle of the century, and partially till near its close,

Pastoral poetry.

[n] La Harpe ; Bouterwek. vi. 127 ; Biogr. Univ.

the style of D'Urfé and Scudery retained its popularity.
Segrais. Three poets of the age of Louis were known in
pastoral : Segrais, Madame Deshoulières, and
Fontenelle. The first belongs most to the genuine school
of modern pastoral ; he is elegant, romantic, full of com-
plaining love ; the Spanish and French romances had
been his model in invention, as Virgil was in style. La
Harpe allows him nature, sweetness, and sentiment ; but
he cannot emulate the vivid colouring of Virgil, and the
language of his shepherds, though simple, wants elegance
and harmony. The tone of his pastorals seems rather
Deshou- insipid, though La Harpe has quoted some
lières. pleasing lines. Madame Deshoulières, with a
purer style than Segrais, according to the same critic,
has less genius. Others have thought her Idylls the best
in the language.[o] But these seem to be merely trivial
moralities addressed to flowers, brooks, and sheep, sometimes expressed in a manner both ingenious and natural,
but on the whole too feeble to give much pleasure.
Bouterwek observes that her poetry is to be considered
as that of a woman, and that its pastoral morality would
be somewhat childish in the mouth of man ; whether
this says more for the lady, or against her sex, I must
leave to the reader. She has occasionally some very
pleasing and even poetical passages.[p] The third among
Fontenelle. these poets of the pipe is Fontenelle. But his
pastorals, as Bouterwek says, are too artificial
for the ancient school, and too cold for the romantic. La
Harpe blames, besides this general fault, the negligence
and prosaic phrases of his style. The best is that entitled
Ismene. It is, in fact, a poem for the world ; yet as love
and its artifices are found everywhere, we cannot censure
any passage as absolutely unfit for pastoral, save a certain
refinement which belonged to the author in everything,
and which interferes with our sense of rural simplicity.

20. In the superior walks of poetry France had nothing
Bad epic of which she has been inclined to boast. Chape-
poems. lain, a man of some credit as a critic, produced
his long-laboured epic, La Pucelle, in 1656, which is
only remembered by the insulting ridicule of Boileau. A
similar fate has fallen on the Clovis of Desmarests, pub-

[o] Biogr. Univ.   [p] Bouterwek, vi. 152.

lished in 1684, though the German historian of literature
has extolled the richness of imagination it shows, and
observed that if those who saw nothing but a fantastic
writer in Desmarests had possessed as much fancy, the
national poetry would have been of a higher character.[q]
Breboeuf's translation of the Pharsalia is spirited, but
very extravagant.

21. The literature of Germany was now more corrupted
by bad taste than ever. A second Silesian school, German
but much inferior to that of Opitz, was founded poetry.
by Hoffmanswaldau and Lohenstein. The first had great
facility, and imitated Ovid and Marini with some success.
The second, with worse taste, always tumid and striving
at something elevated, so that the Lohenstein swell became a byword with later critics, is superior to Hoffmanswaldau in richness of fancy, in poetical invention,
and in warmth of feeling for all that is noble and great.
About the end of the century arose a new style, known
by the unhappy name spiritless (geistlos), which, avoiding the tone of Lohenstein, became wholly tame and
flat.[r]

Sect. III.—On English Poetry.

Waller—Butler—Milton—Dryden—The Minor Poets.

22. We might have placed Waller in the former division
of the seventeenth century with no more impro- Waller.
priety than we might have reserved Cowley for
the latter; both belong by the date of their writings to
the two periods. And, perhaps, the poetry of Waller
bears rather the stamp of the first Charles's age than of
that which ensued. His reputation was great, and somewhat more durable than that of similar poets has generally been; he did not witness its decay in his own
protracted life, nor was it much diminished at the beginning of the next century. Nor was this wholly undeserved. Waller has a more uniform elegance, a more
sure facility and happiness of expression, and, above all,

[q] Bouterwek, vi. 157.   Eichhorn, Geschichte der Cultur, iv.
[r] Id., vol. x. p. 288; Heinsius, iv. 287;   776.

a greater exemption from glaring faults, such as pedantry, extravagance, conceit, quaintness, obscurity, ungrammatical and unmeaning constructions, than any of the Caroline era with whom he would naturally be compared. We have only to open Carew or Lovelace to perceive the difference; not that Waller is wholly without some of these faults, but that they are much less frequent. If others may have brighter passages of fancy or sentiment, which is not difficult, he husbands better his resources, and though left behind in the beginning of the race, comes sooner to the goal. His Panegyric on Cromwell was celebrated. " Such a series of verses," it is said by Johnson, " had rarely appeared before in the English language. Of these lines some are grand, some are graceful, and all are musical. There is now and then a feeble verse, or a trifling thought; but its great fault is the choice of its hero." It may not be the opinion of all that Cromwell's actions were of that obscure and pitiful character which the majesty of song rejects, and Johnson has before observed, that Waller's choice of encomiastic topics in this poem is very judicious. Yet his deficiency in poetical vigour will surely be traced in this composition; if he rarely sinks, he never rises very high; and we find much good sense and selection, much skill in the mechanism of language and metre, without ardour and without imagination. In his amorous poetry he has little passion or sensibility; but he is never free and petulant, never tedious, and never absurd. His praise consists much in negations; but in a comparative estimate perhaps negations ought to count for a good deal.

23. Hudibras was incomparably more popular than Paradise Lost; no poem in our language rose at once to greater reputation. Nor can this be called ephemeral, like that of most political poetry. For at least half a century after its publication it was generally read, and perpetually quoted. The wit of Butler has still preserved many lines; but Hudibras now attracts comparatively few readers. The eulogies of Johnson seem rather adapted to what he remembered to have been the fame of Butler than to the feelings of the surrounding generation; and since his time new sources of amusement have sprung up, and writers of a more intelligible pleasantry have superseded those of the seven-

teenth century. In the fiction of Hudibras there was never much to divert the reader, and there is still less left at present. But what has been censured as a fault, the length of dialogue, which puts the fiction out of sight, is in fact the source of all the pleasure that the work affords. The sense of Butler is masculine, his wit inexhaustible, and it is supplied from every source of reading and observation. But these sources are often so unknown to the reader that the wit loses its effect through the obscurity of its allusions, and he yields to the bane of wit, a purblind mole-like pedantry. His versification is sometimes spirited, and his rhymes humorous; yet he wants that ease and flow which we require in light poetry.

24. The subject of Paradise Lost is the finest that has ever been chosen for heroic poetry; it is also managed by Milton with remarkable skill. The Iliad wants completeness; it has an unity of its own, but it is the unity of a part where we miss the relation to a whole. The Odyssey is not imperfect in this point of view; but the subject is hardly extensive enough for a legitimate epic. The Æneid is spread over too long a space, and perhaps the latter books, by the diversity of scene and subject, lose part of that intimate connexion with the former which an epic poem requires. The Pharsalia is open to the same criticism as the Iliad. The Thebaid is not deficient in unity or greatness of action; but it is one that possesses no sort of interest in our eyes. Tasso is far superior, both in choice and management of his subject, to most of these. Yet the Fall of Man has a more general interest than the Crusade. *Paradise Lost—Choice of subject.*

25. It must be owned, nevertheless, that a religious epic labours under some disadvantages; in proportion as it attracts those who hold the same tenets with the author, it is regarded by those who dissent from him with indifference or aversion. It is said that the discovery of Milton's Arianism, in this rigid generation, has already impaired the sale of Paradise Lost. It is also difficult to enlarge or adorn such a story by fiction. Milton has done much in this way; yet he was partly restrained by the necessity of conforming to Scripture. *Open to some difficulties.*

26. The ordonnance or composition of the Paradise
Its arrange- Lost is admirable; and here we perceive the
ment. advantage which Milton's great familiarity with
the Greek theatre, and his own original scheme of the
poem, had given him. Every part succeeds in an order,
noble, clear, and natural. It might have been wished
indeed that the vision of the eleventh book had not been
changed into the colder narrative of the twelfth. But
what can be more majestic than the first two books
which open this great drama? It is true that they
rather serve to confirm the sneer of Dryden that Satan
is Milton's hero; since they develop a plan of action in
that potentate, which is ultimately successful; the
triumph that he and his host must experience in the
fall of man being hardly compensated by their temporary
conversion into serpents; a fiction rather too grotesque.
But it is, perhaps, only pedantry to talk about the hero,
as if a high personage were absolutely required in an
epic poem to predominate over the rest. The conception of Satan is doubtless the first effort of Milton's
genius. Dante could not have ventured to spare so
much lustre for a ruined archangel, in an age when
nothing less than horns and a tail were the orthodox
creed.*

---

* Coleridge has a fine passage which I cannot resist my desire to transcribe. " The character of Satan is pride and sensual indulgence, finding in itself the motive of action. It is the character so often seen in little on the political stage. It exhibits all the restlessness, temerity, and cunning which have marked the mighty hunters of mankind from Nimrod to Napoleon. The common fascination of man is that these great men, as they are called, must act from some great motive. Milton has carefully marked in his Satan the intense selfishness, the alcohol of egotism, which would rather reign in hell than serve in heaven. To place this lust of self in opposition to denial of self or duty, and to show what exertions it would make, and what pains endure, to accomplish its end, is Milton's particular object in the character of Satan. But around this character he has thrown a singularity of daring, a grandeur of sufferance, and a ruined splen-

dour, which constitute the very height of poetic sublimity." Coleridge's Remains, p. 176.

In reading such a paragraph as this, we are struck with the vast improvement of the highest criticism, the philosophy of æsthetics, since the days of Addison. His papers in the Spectator on Paradise Lost were perhaps superior to any criticism that had been written in our language; and we must always acknowledge their good sense, their judiciousness, and the vast service they did to our literature, in settling the Paradise Lost on its proper level. But how little they satisfy us, even in treating of the *natura naturata,* the poem itself! and how little conception they show of the *natura naturans,* the individual genius of the author! Even in the periodical criticism of the present day, in the midst of much that is affected, much that is precipitate, much that is written for mere display, we find occasional reflections of a pro-

27. Milton has displayed great skill in the delineations of Adam and Eve ; he does not dress them up, Characters of Adam and Eve. after the fashion of orthodox theology, which had no spell to bind his free spirit, in the fancied robes of primitive righteousness.   South, in one of his sermons, has drawn a picture of unfallen man, which is even poetical; but it might be asked by the reader, Why then did he fall ?   The first pair of Milton are innocent of course, but not less frail than their posterity ; nor, except one circumstance, which seems rather physical intoxication than anything else, do we find any sign of depravity superinduced upon their transgression. It might even be made a question for profound theologians whether Eve, by taking amiss what Adam had said, and by self-conceit, did not sin before she tasted the fatal apple.   The necessary paucity of actors in Paradise Lost is perhaps the apology of Sin and Death ; they will not bear exact criticism, yet we do not wish them away.

28. The comparison of Milton with Homer has been founded on the acknowledged pre-eminence of He owes less to Homer than the tragedians. each in his own language, and on the lax application of the word epic to their great poems. But there was not much in common either between their genius or its products ; and Milton has taken less in direct imitation from Homer than from several other poets.   His favourites had rather been Sophocles and Euripides ; to them he owes the structure of his blank verse, his swell and dignity of style, his grave enunciation of moral and abstract sentiment, his tone of description, neither condensed like that of Dante, nor spread out with the diffuseness of the other Italians and of Homer himself.   Next to these Greek tragedians, Virgil seems to have been his model ; with the minor Latin poets, except Ovid, he does not, I think, show

---

fundity and discrimination which we should seek in vain through Dryden or Addison, or the two Wartons, or even Johnson, though much superior to the rest.   Hurd has perhaps the merit of being the first who in this country aimed at philosophical criticism; he had great ingenuity, a good deal of reading, and a facility in applying it; but he did not feel very deeply, was somewhat of a coxcomb, and having always before his eyes a model neither good in itself, nor made for him to emulate, he assumes a dogmatic arrogance, which, as it always offends the reader, so for the most part stands in the way of the author's own search for truth.

any great familiarity; and though abundantly conversant with Ariosto, Tasso, and Marini, we cannot say that they influenced his manner, which, unlike theirs, is severe and stately, never light, nor, in the sense we should apply the words to them, rapid and animated.'

29. To Dante, however, he bears a much greater likeness. He has in common with that poet an uniform seriousness, for the brighter colouring of both is but the smile of a pensive mind, a fondness for argumentative speech, and for the same strain of argument. This indeed proceeds in part from the general similarity, the religious and even theological cast of their subjects; I advert particularly to the last part of Dante's poem. We may almost say, when we look to the resemblance of their prose writings, in the proud sense of being born for some great achievement, which breathes through the Vita Nuova, as it does through Milton's earlier treatises, that they were twin spirits, and that each might have animated the other's body, that each would, as it were, have been the other, if he had lived in the other's age. As it is, I incline to prefer Milton, that is, the Paradise Lost, both because the subject is more extensive, and because the resources of his genius are more multifarious. Dante sins more against good taste, but only perhaps because there was no good taste in his time; for Milton has also too much a disposition to make the grotesque accessory to the terrible. Could Milton have written the lines on Ugolino? Perhaps he could. Those on Francesca? Not, I think, every line. Could Dante have planned such a poem as Paradise Lost? Not certainly, being Dante in 1300; but living when Milton did, perhaps he could. It is, however, useless to go on with questions that no one can fully answer. To compare the two poets, read two or three cantos of the Purgatory or Paradise, and then two or three hundred lines of Paradise Lost. Then take Homer, or even Virgil, the difference will be striking. Yet notwithstanding this analogy of their minds, I have not perceived that Milton imitates Dante very

Compared with Dante.

---

t The solemnity of Milton is striking in those passages where some other poets would indulge a little in voluptuousness, and the more so, because this is not wholly uncongenial to him. A few lines in Paradise Lost are rather too plain, and their gravity makes them worse.

often, probably from having committed less to memory while young (and Dante was not the favourite poet of Italy when Milton was there), than of Ariosto and Tasso.

30. Each of these great men chose the subject that suited his natural temper and genius. What, it is curious to conjecture, would have been Milton's success in his original design, a British story? Far less, surely, than in Paradise Lost; he wanted the rapidity of the common heroic poem, and would always have been sententious, perhaps arid and heavy. Yet even as religious poets, there are several remarkable distinctions between Milton and Dante. It has been justly observed that, in the Paradise of Dante, he makes use of but three leading ideas, light, music, and motion, and that Milton has drawn heaven in less pure and spiritual colours." The philosophical imagination of the former, in this third part of his poem, almost defecated from all sublunary things by long and solitary musing, spiritualises all that it touches. The genius of Milton, though itself subjective, was less so than that of Dante; and he has to recount, to describe, to bring deeds and passions before the eye. And two peculiar causes may be assigned for this difference in the treatment of celestial things between the Divine Comedy and the Paradise Lost; the dramatic form which Milton had originally designed to adopt, and his own theological bias towards anthropomorphism, which his posthumous treatise on religion has brought to light. This was no doubt in some measure inevitable in such a subject as that of Paradise Lost; yet much that is ascribed to God, sometimes with the sanction of Scripture, sometimes without it, is not wholly pleasing; such as " the oath that shook Heaven's whole circumference," and several other images of the same kind, which bring down the Deity in a manner not consonant to philosophical religion, however it may be borne out by the sensual analogies or mythic symbolism of Oriental writing.ˣ

ᵘ Quarterly Review, June, 1825. This article contains some good and some questionable remarks on Milton; among the latter I reckon the proposition that his contempt for women is shown in the delineation of Eve; an opinion not that of Addison or of many others, who have thought her exquisitely drawn.

ˣ Johnson thinks that Milton should have secured the consistency of this poem by keeping immateriality out of sight, and enticing his reader to drop it from

31. We rarely meet with feeble lines in Paradise Lost,' though with many that are hard, and in a 'common use of the word, might be called prosaic. Yet few are truly prosaic; few wherein the tone is not some way distinguished from prose. The very artificial style of Milton, sparing in English idiom, and his study of a rhythm, not always the most grateful to our ears, but preserving his blank verse from a trivial flow, is the cause of this elevation. It is at least more removed from a prosaic cadence than the slovenly rhymes of such contemporary poets as Chamberlayne. His versification is entirely his own, framed on a Latin and chiefly a Virgilian model, the pause less frequently resting on the close of the line than in Homer, and much less than in our own dramatic poets. But it is also possible that the Italian and Spanish blank verse may have had some effect upon his ear.

Elevation of his style.

32. In the numerous imitations, and still more numerous traces of older poetry which we perceive in Paradise Lost, it is always to be kept in mind that he had only his recollection to rely upon. His blindness seems to have been complete before 1654; and I scarcely think that he had begun his poem, before the anxiety and trouble into which the public strife of the Commonwealth and the Restoration had thrown him gave leisure for immortal occupations. Then the remembrance of early reading came over his dark and lonely path like the moon emerging from the clouds. Then it was that the muse was truly his; not only as she poured her creative inspiration into his mind, but as the daughter of Memory, coming with fragments of

His blindness.

his thoughts. But here the subject forbad him to preserve consistency, if indeed there be inconsistency in supposing a rapid assumption of form by spiritual beings. For though the instance that Johnson alleges of inconsistency in Satan's animating a toad was not necessary, yet his animation of the serpent was absolutely indispensable. And the same has been done by other poets, who do not scruple to suppose their gods, their fairies or devils, or their allegorical personages, inspiring thoughts, and even uniting themselves with the soul, as well as assuming all kinds of form, though their natural appearance is almost always anthropomorphic. And, 'after all, Satan does not animate a real toad, but takes the shape of one. "Squat like a toad close by the ear of Eve." But he does enter a real serpent, so that the instance of Johnson is ill chosen. If he had mentioned the serpent, every one would have seen that the identity of the animal serpent with Satan is part of the original account.

ʸ One of the few exceptions is in the sublime description of Death, where a wretched hemistich, "Fierce as ten furies," stands as an unsightly blemish.

ancient melodies, the voice of Euripides, and Homer, and Tasso; sounds that he had loved in youth, and treasured up for the solace of his age.   They who, though not enduring the calamity of Milton, have known what it is, when afar from books, in solitude or in travelling, or in the intervals of worldly care, to feed on poetical recollections, to murmur over the beautiful lines whose cadence has long delighted their ear, to recall the sentiments and images which retain by association the charm that early years once gave them — they will feel the inestimable value of committing to the memory, in the prime of its power, what it will easily receive and indelibly retain.   I know not indeed whether an education that deals much with poetry, such as is still usual in England, has any more solid argument among many in its favour, than that it lays the foundation of intellectual pleasures at the other extreme of life.

33. It is owing, in part, to his blindness, but more perhaps to his general residence in a city, that Milton, in the words of Coleridge, is "not a picturesque but a musical poet;" or as I would prefer to say, is the latter more of the two.   He describes visible things, and often with great powers of rendering them manifest, what the Greeks called ἐνάργεια, though seldom with so much circumstantial exactness of observation as Spenser or Dante, but he feels music.   The sense of vision delighted his imagination, but that of sound wrapped his whole soul in ecstasy.   One of his trifling faults may be connected with this, the excessive passion he displays for stringing together sonorous names, sometimes so obscure that the reader associates nothing with them, as the word Namancos in Lycidas, which long baffled the commentators.   Hence his catalogues, unlike those of Homer and Virgil, are sometimes merely ornamental and misplaced.   Thus the names of unbuilt cities come strangely forward in Adam's vision,[2] though he has afterwards gone over the same ground with better effect in Paradise Regained.   In this there was also a mixture of his pedantry.   But, though he was rather too ostentatious of learning, the nature of his subject demanded a good deal of episodical ornament.

His passion for music.

[2] Par. Lost, xi. 386.

And this, rather than the precedents he might have alleged from the Italians and others, is perhaps
the best apology for what some grave critics
have censured, his frequent allusions to fable and
mythology.   These give much relief to the severity of
the poem, and few readers would dispense with them.
Less excuse can be made for some affectation of science
which has produced hard and unpleasing lines; but he
had been born in an age when more credit was gained
by reading much than by writing well.   The faults,
however, of Paradise Lost are in general less to be called
faults than necessary adjuncts of the qualities we most
admire, and idiosyncrasies of a mighty genius.   The
verse of Milton is sometimes wanting in grace, and
almost always in ease; but what better can be said of
his prose?   His foreign idioms are too frequent in the
one; but they predominate in the other.

34. The slowness of Milton's advance to glory is now
generally owned to have been much exaggerated; we might say that the reverse was nearer
the truth.   "The sale of 1300 copies in two years," says
Johnson, "in opposition to so much recent enmity, and
to a style of versification new to all and disgusting to
many, was an uncommon example of the prevalence of
genius.   The demand did not immediately increase; for
many more readers than were supplied at first the nation
did not afford.   Only 3000 were sold in eleven years."
It would hardly however be said, even in this age, of a
poem 3000 copies of which had been sold in eleven
years, that its success had been small; and some, perhaps, might doubt whether Paradise Lost, published
eleven years since, would have met with a greater demand.   There is sometimes a want of congeniality in
public taste which no power of genius will overcome.
For Milton it must be said by every one conversant with
the literature of the age that preceded Addison's famous
criticism, from which some have dated the reputation of
Paradise Lost, that he took his place among great poets
from the beginning.   The fancy of Johnson that few
dared to praise it, and that "the revolution put an end
to the secrecy of love," is without foundation; the Government of Charles II. was not so absurdly tyrannical,
nor did Dryden, the court's own poet, hesitate, in his

preface to the State of Innocence, published soon after Milton's death, to speak of its original, Paradise Lost, as "undoubtedly one of the greatest, most noble, and most sublime poems which either this age or nation has produced."

35. The neglect which Paradise Lost never experienced seems to have been long the lot of Pa- Paradise
radise Regained. It was not popular with the. Regained.
world ; it was long believed to manifest a decay of the poet's genius, and in spite of all that the critics have written, it is still but the favourite of some whose pre-
dilections for the Miltonic style are very strong. The subject is so much less capable of calling forth the vast powers of his mind, that we should be unfair in comparing it throughout with the greater poem ; it has been called a model of the shorter epic, an action compre-
hending few characters and a brief space of time.[a] The love of Milton for dramatic dialogue, imbibed from Greece, is still more apparent than in Paradise Lost ; the whole poem, in fact, may almost be accounted a drama of primal simplicity, the narrative and descriptive part serving rather to diversify and relieve the speeches of the actors, than their speeches, as in the legitimate epic, to enliven the narration. Paradise Regained abounds with passages equal to any of the same nature in Paradise Lost ; but the argumentative tone is kept up till it produces some tediousness, and perhaps on the whole less pains have been exerted to adorn and elevate that which appeals to the imagination.

36. Samson Agonistes is the latest of Milton's poems ; we see in it, perhaps more distinctly than in Samson
Paradise Regained, the ebb of a mighty tide. Agonistes.
An air of uncommon grandeur prevails throughout, but the language is less poetical than in Paradise Lost ; the vigour of thought remains, but it wants much of its ancient eloquence. Nor is the lyric tone well kept up by the chorus ; they are too sententious, too slow in movement, and, except by the metre, are not easily dis-
tinguishable from the other personages. But this metre is itself infelicitous, the lines being frequently of a number of syllables not recognised in the usage of Eng-

[a] Todd's Milton, vol. v. p. 308.

lish poetry, and, destitute of rhythmical measure, fall into prose. Milton seems to have forgotten that the ancient chorus had a musical accompaniment.

37. The style of Samson, being essentially that of Paradise Lost, may show us how much more the latter poem is founded on the Greek tragedians than on Homer. In Samson we have sometimes the pompous tone of Æschylus, more frequently the sustained majesty of Sophocles; but the religious solemnity of Milton's own temperament, as well as the nature of the subject, have given a sort of breadth, an unbroken severity, to the whole drama. It is perhaps not very popular even with the lovers of poetry; yet upon close comparison we should find that it deserves a higher place than many of its prototypes. We might search the Greek tragedies long for a character so powerfully conceived and maintained as that of Samson himself; and it is but conformable to the sculptural simplicity of that form of drama which Milton adopted, that all the rest should be kept in subordination to it. "It is only," Johnson says, "by a blind confidence in the reputation of Milton, that a drama can be praised in which the intermediate parts have neither cause nor consequence, neither hasten nor retard the catastrophe." Such a drama is certainly not to be ranked with Othello and Macbeth, or even with the Œdipus or the Hippolytus; but a similar criticism is applicable to several famous tragedies in the less artificial school of antiquity, to the Prometheus and the Persæ of Æschylus, and, if we look strictly, to not a few of the two other masters.

38. The poetical genius of Dryden came slowly to perfection. Born in 1631, his first short poems, or, as we might rather say, copies of verses, were not written till he approached thirty; and though some of his dramas, not indeed of the best, belong to the next period of his life, he had reached the age of fifty before his high rank as a poet had been confirmed by indubitable proof. Yet he had manifested a superiority to his immediate contemporaries; his Astræa Redux, on the Restoration, is well versified; the lines are seldom weak; the couplets have that pointed manner which Cowley and Denham had taught the world to require; they are harmonious, but not so varied as the

Dryden. His earlier poems.

style he afterwards adopted. The Annus Mirabilis, in 1667, is of a higher cast; it is not so animated as the later poetry of Dryden, because the alternate quatrain, in which he followed Davenant's Gondibert, is hostile to animation; but it is not unfavourable to another excellence, condensed and vigorous thought. Davenant indeed and Denham may be reckoned the models of Dryden, so far as this can be said of a man of original genius, and one far superior to theirs. The distinguishing characteristic of Dryden, it has been said by Scott, was the power of reasoning and expressing the result in appropriate language. This indeed was the characteristic of the two whom we have named, and so far as Dryden has displayed it, which he eminently has done, he bears a resemblance to them. But it is insufficient praise for this great poet. His rapidity of conception and readiness of expression are higher qualities. He never loiters about a single thought or image, never labours about the turn of a phrase. The impression upon our minds that he wrote with exceeding ease is irresistible; and I do not know that we have any evidence to repel it. The admiration of Dryden gains upon us, if I may speak from my own experience, with advancing years, as we become more sensible of the difficulty of his style, and of the comparative facility of that which is merely imaginative.

39. Dryden may be considered as a satirical, a reasoning, a descriptive and narrative, a lyric poet, and as a translator. As a dramatist we must return to him again. The greatest of his satires is Absalom and Achitophel, that work in which his powers became fully known to the world, and which, as many think, he never surpassed. The admirable fitness of the English couplet for satire had never been shown before; in less skilful hands it had been ineffective. He does not frequently, in this poem, carry the sense beyond the second line, which, except when skilfully contrived, as it often is by himself, is apt to enfeeble the emphasis; his triplets are less numerous than usual, but energetic. The spontaneous ease of expression, the rapid transitions, the general elasticity and movement, have never been excelled. It is superfluous to praise the discrimination and vivacity of the chief characters, espe-

cially Shaftesbury and Buckingham. Satire, however, is so much easier than panegyric, that with Ormond, Ossory, and Mulgrave he has not been quite so successful. In the second part of Absalom and Achitophel, written by Tate, one long passage alone is inserted by Dryden. It is excellent in its line of satire, but the line is less elevated; the persons delineated are less important, and he has indulged more his natural proneness to virulent ribaldry. This fault of Dryden's writings, it is just to observe, belonged less to the man than to the age. No libellous invective, no coarseness of allusion, had ever been spared towards a private or political enemy. We read with nothing but disgust the satirical poetry of Cleveland, Butler, Oldham, and Marvell, or even of men whose high rank did not soften their style, Rochester, Dorset, Mulgrave. In Dryden there was, for the first time, a poignancy of wit which atones for his severity, and a discretion even in his taunts which made them more cutting.

40. The Medal, which is in some measure a continuation of Absalom and Achitophel, since it bears wholly on Shaftesbury, is of unequal merit, and on the whole falls much below the former. In Mac Flecknoe, his satire on his rival Shadwell, we must allow for the inferiority of the subject, which could not bring out so much of Dryden's higher powers of mind; but scarcely one of his poems is more perfect. Johnson, who admired Dryden almost as much as he could any one, has yet, from his proneness to critical censure, very much exaggerated the poet's defects. "His faults of negligence are beyond recital. Such is the unevenness of his compositions, that ten lines are seldom found together without something of which the reader is ashamed." This might be true, or more nearly true, of other poets of the seventeenth century. Ten good consecutive lines will, perhaps, rarely be found, except in Denham, Davenant, and Waller. But it seems a great exaggeration as to Dryden. I would particularly instance Mac Flecknoe as a poem of about four hundred lines, in which no one will be condemned as weak or negligent, though three or four are rather too ribaldrous for our taste. There are also passages, much exceeding ten lines, in Absalom and Achitophel, as well as in the

Mac Flecknoe.

later works, the Fables, which excite in the reader none
of the shame for the poet's carelessness with which Johnson has furnished him.

41. The argumentative talents of Dryden appear, more
or less, in the greater part of his poetry ; reason The Hind
in rhyme was his peculiar delight, to which he and
seems to escape from the mere excursions of Panther.
fancy.   And it is remarkable that he reasons better and
more closely in poetry than in prose.   His productions
more exclusively reasoning are the Religio Laici and
the Hind and Panther.   The latter is every way an
extraordinary poem.   It was written in the hey-day of
exultation, by a recent proselyte to a winning side, as
he dreamed it to be, by one who never spared a weaker
foe, nor repressed his triumph with a dignified moderation.   A year was hardly to elapse before he exchanged
this fulness of pride for an old age of disappointment and
poverty.   Yet then too his genius was unquenched, and
even his satire was not less severe.

42. The first lines in the Hind and Panther are justly
reputed among the most musical in our lan- Its singular
guage ; and perhaps we observe their rhythm fable.
the better because it does not gain much by the sense ;
for the allegory and the fable are seen, even in this commencement, to be awkwardly blended.   Yet, notwithstanding their evident incoherence, which sometimes
leads to the verge of absurdity, and the facility they give
to ridicule, I am not sure that Dryden was wrong in
choosing this singular fiction.   It was his aim to bring
forward an old argument in as novel a style as he could ;
a dialogue between a priest and a parson would have
made but a dull poem, even if it had contained some of
the excellent paragraphs we read in the Hind and
Panther.   It is the grotesqueness and originality of the
fable that give this poem its peculiar zest, of which no
reader, I conceive, is insensible ; and it is also by this
means that Dryden has contrived to relieve his reasoning by short but beautiful touches of description, such
as the sudden stream of light from heaven which announces the victory of Sedgmoor near the end of the
second book.[b]

b [I am indebted to a distinguished friend for the explanation of this line,
which I had misunderstood.—1853.]

43. The wit in the Hind and Panther is sharp, ready,
Its reason- and pleasant, the reasoning is sometimes admi-
ing.   rably close and strong; it is the energy of
Bossuet in verse.   I do not know, that the main argument of the Roman church could be better stated : all
that has been well said for tradition and authority, all
that serves to expose the inconsistencies of a vacillating
Protestantism, is in the Hind's mouth.   It is such an
answer as a candid man should admit to any doubts of
Dryden's sincerity.   He who could argue as powerfully
as the Hind may well be allowed to have thought himself in the right.   Yet he could not forget a few bold
thoughts of his more sceptical days; and such is his
bias to sarcasm that he cannot restrain himself from
reflections on kings and priests when he is most contending for them.°

44. The Fables of Dryden, or stories modernised from
The Fables. Boccaccio and Chaucer, are at this day pro-
        bably the most read and the most popular of
Dryden's poems.   They contain passages of so much
more impressive beauty, and are altogether so far more
adapted to general sympathy than those we have mentioned, that I should not hesitate to concur in this judgment.   Yet Johnson's accusation of negligence is better
supported by these than by the earlier poems.   Whether
it were that age and misfortune, though they had not
impaired the poet's vigour, had rendered its continual
exertion more wearisome, or, as is perhaps the better
supposition, he reckoned an easy style, sustained above
prose, in some places, rather by metre than expression,
more fitted to narration, we find much which might
appear slovenly to critics of Johnson's temper.   The
latter seems, in fact, to have conceived, like Milton, a
theory, that good writing, at least in verse, is never
either to follow the change of fashion, or to sink into
familiar phrase, and that any deviation from this rigour
should be branded as low and colloquial.   But Dryden
wrote on a different plan.   He thought, like Ariosto,
and like Chaucer himself, whom he had to improve, that

° By education most have been misled;
  So they believe because they so were
  bred.
  The priest continues what the nurse
  began,

And thus the child imposes on the
  man.—Part iii.
" Call you this backing of your
  friends ? " his new allies might have
  said.

a story, especially when not heroic, should be told in easy and flowing language, without too much difference from that of prose, relying on his harmony, his occasional inversions, and his concealed skill in the choice of words, for its effect on the reader. He found also a tone of popular idiom, not perhaps old English idiom, but such as had crept into society, current among his contemporaries ; and though this has in many cases now become insufferably vulgar, and in others looks like affectation, we should make some allowance for the times in condemning it. This last blemish, however, is not much imputable to the Fables. Their beauties are innumerable ; yet few are very well chosen ; some, as Guiscard and Sigismunda, he has injured through coarseness of mind, which neither years nor religion had purified ; and we want in all the power over emotion, the charm of sympathy, the skilful arrangement and selection of circumstance, which narrative poetry claims as its highest graces.

45. Dryden's fame as a lyric poet depends a very little on his Ode on Mrs. Killigrew's death, but almost entirely on that for St. Cecilia's Day, commonly called Alexander's Feast. The former, which is much praised by Johnson, has a few fine lines, mingled with a far greater number ill conceived and ill expressed ; the whole composition has that spirit which Dryden hardly ever wanted, but it is too faulty for high praise. The latter used to pass for the best work of Dryden, and the best ode in the language. Many would now agree with me that it is neither one nor the other, and that it was rather overrated during a period when criticism was not at a high point. Its beauties indeed are undeniable ; it has the raciness, the rapidity, the mastery of language which belong to Dryden; the transitions are animated, the contrasts effective. But few lines are highly poetical, and some sink to the level of a common drinking song. It has the defects as well as the merits of that poetry which is written for musical accompaniment.

His Odes—Alexander's Feast.

46. Of Dryden as a translator it is needless to say much. In some instances, as in an ode of Horace, he has done extremely well ; but his Virgil is, in my apprehension, the least successful of his chief works. Lines of consummate excellence are fre-

His translation of Virgil.

quently shot, like threads of gold, through the web, but the general texture is of an ordinary material. Dryden was little fitted for a translator of Virgil; his mind was more rapid and vehement than that of his original, but by far less elegant and judicious. This translation seems to have been made in haste; it is more negligent than any of his own poetry, and the style is often almost studiously, and as it were spitefully, vulgar.

47. The supremacy of Dryden from the death of Milton in 1674 to his own in 1700 was not only unapproached by any English poet, but he held almost a complete monopoly of English poetry. This latter period of the seventeenth century, setting aside these two great names, is one remarkably sterile in poetical genius. Under the first Stuarts, men of warm imagination and sensibility, though with deficient taste and little command of language, had done some honour to our literature; though once neglected, they have come forward again in public esteem, and if not very extensively read, have been valued by men of kindred minds full as much as they deserve. The versifiers of Charles II. and William's days have experienced the opposite fate; popular for a time, and long so far known, at least by name, as to have entered rather largely into collections of poetry, they are now held in no regard, nor do they claim much favour from just criticism. Their object in general was to write like men of the world—with ease, wit, sense, and spirit, but dreading any soaring of fancy, any ardour of moral emotion, as the probable source of ridicule in their readers. Nothing quenches the flame of poetry more than this fear of the prosaic multitude—unless it is the community of habits with this very multitude, a life such as these poets generally led, of taverns and brothels, or, what came much to the same, of the court. We cannot say of Dryden, that " he bears no traces of those sable streams; " they sully too much the plumage of that stately swan, but his indomitable genius carries him upwards to a purer empyrean. The rest are just distinguishable from one another, not by any high gifts of the muse, but by degrees of spirit, of ease, of poignancy, of skill and harmony in versification, of good sense and acuteness. They may easily be disposed of. Cleveland

Decline of poetry from the Restoration.

is sometimes humourous, but succeeds only in the lightest kinds of poetry. Marvell wrote some- Some minor poets enumerated. times with more taste and feeling than was usual, but his satires are gross and stupid. Oldham, far superior in this respect, ranks perhaps next to Dryden ; he is spirited and pointed, but his versification is too negligent, and his subjects temporary. Roscommon, one of the best for harmony and correctness of language, has little vigour, but he never offends, and Pope has justly praised his " unspotted bays." Mulgrave affects ease and spirit, but his Essay on Satire belies the supposition that Dryden had any share in it. Rochester, endowed by nature with more considerable and varied genius, might have raised himself to a higher place than he holds. Of Otway, Duke, and several more, it is not worth while to give any character. The Revolution did nothing for poetry ; William's reign, always excepting Dryden, is our *nadir* in works of imagination. Then came Blackmore with his epic poems of Prince Arthur and King Arthur, and Pomfret with his Choice, both popular in their own age, and both intolerable by their frigid and tame monotony in the next. The lighter poetry, meantime, of song and epigram did not sink along with the serious ; the state of society was much less adverse to it. Rochester, Dorset, and some more whose names are unknown, or not easily traced, do credit to the Caroline period.

48. In the year 1699, a poem was published, Garth's Dispensary, which deserves attention, not so much for its own merit, though it comes nearest to Dryden, at whatever interval, as from its indicating a transitional state in our versification. The general structure of the couplet through the seventeenth century may be called abnormous ; the sense is not only often carried beyond the second line, which the French avoid, but the second line of one couplet and the first of the next are not seldom united in a single sentence or a portion of one, so that the two, though not rhyming, must be read as a couplet. The former, when as dexterously managed as it was by Dryden, adds much to the beauty of the general versification ; but the latter, a sort of adultery of the lines already wedded to other companions at rhyme's altar, can scarcely ever be pleasing, unless it

be in narrative poetry, where it may bring the sound nearer to prose. A tendency, however, to the French rule of constantly terminating the sense with the couplet will be perceived to have increased from the Restoration. Roscommon seldom deviates from it, and in long passages of Dryden himself there will hardly be found an exception. But, perhaps, it had not been so uniform in any former production as in the Dispensary. The versification of this once famous mock-heroic poem is smooth and regular, but not forcible ; the language clear and neat ; the parodies and allusions happy. Many lines are excellent in the way of pointed application, and some are remembered and quoted, where few call to mind the author. It has been remarked that Garth enlarged and altered the Dispensary in almost every edition, and what is more uncommon, that every alteration was for the better. This poem may be called an imitation of the Lutrin, inasmuch as but for the Lutrin it might probably not have been written, and there are even particular resemblances. The subject, which is a quarrel between the physicians and apothecaries of London, may vie with that of Boileau in want of general interest ; yet it seems to afford more diversity to the satirical poet. Garth, as has been observed, is a link of transition between the style and turn of poetry under Charles and William, and that we find in Addison, Prior, Tickell, and Pope, during the reign of Anne.

Sect. IV.—On Latin Poetry.

49. The Jesuits were not unmindful of the credit their Latin verses had done them in periods more favourable to that exercise of taste than the present. Even in Italy, which had ceased to be a very genial soil, one of their number, Ceva, may deserve mention. His Jesus Puer is a long poem, not inelegantly written, but rather singular in some of its descriptions, where the poet has been more solicitous to adorn his subject than attentive to its proper character ; and the same objection might be made to some of its episodes. Ceva wrote also a phi-

Latin poets of Italy.

Ceva.

losophical poem, extolled by Corniani, but which has not fallen into my hands.[d] Averani, a Florentine of various erudition, Cappellari, Strozzi, author of a poem on chocolate, and several others, both within the order of Loyola and without it, cultivated Latin poetry with some success.[e] But, though some might be superior as poets, none were more remarkable or famous Sergardi. than Sergardi, best known by some biting satires under the name of Q. Sectanus, which he levelled at his personal enemy Gravina. The reputation, indeed, of Gravina with posterity has not been affected by such libels; but they are not wanting either in poignancy and spirit, or in a command of Latin phrase.[f]

50. The superiority of France in Latin verse was no longer contested by Holland or Germany. Of France Several poets of real merit belong to this —Quillet. period. The first in time was Claude Quillet, who, in his Callipædia, bears the Latinised name of Leti. This is written with much elegance of style and a very harmonious versification. No writer has a more Virgilian cadence. Though inferior to Sammarthanus, he may be reckoned high among the French poets. He has been reproached with too open an exposition of some parts of his subject; which applies only to the second book.

51. The Latin poems of Menage are not unpleasing; he has indeed no great fire or originality, but Menage. the harmonious couplets glide over the ear, and the mind is pleased to recognise the tesselated fragments of Ovid and Tibullus. His affected passion for Mademoiselle Lavergne and lamentations about her cruelty are ludicrous enough, when we consider the character of the man, as Vadius in the Femmes Savantes of Molière. They are perfect models of want of truth; but it is a want of truth to nature, not to the conventional forms of modern Latin verse.

52. A far superior performance is the poem on gardens by the Jesuit Réné Rapin. For skill in vary- Rapin on ing and adorning his subject, for a truly gardens. Virgilian spirit in expression, for the exclusion of feeble, prosaic, or awkward lines, he may perhaps be equal to

d Corniani, viii. 214; Salfi, xiv. 257.   238, et post.
e Bibl. Choisie, vol. xxii.; Salfi, xiv.   f Salfi, xiv. 299; Corniani, viii. 280.

'any poet, to Sammarthanus, or to Sannazarius himself. His cadences are generally very gratifying to the ear, and in this respect he is much above Vida.[g] But his subject, or his genius, has prevented him from rising very high; he is the poet of gardens, and what gardens are to nature, that is he to mightier poets. There is also too monotonous a repetition of nearly the same images, as in his long enumeration of flowers in the first book; the descriptions are separately good, and great artifice is shown in varying them; but the variety could not be sufficient to remove the general sameness that belongs to an horticultural catalogue. Rapin was a great admirer of box and all topiary works, or trees cut into artificial forms.

53. The first book of the Gardens of Rapin is on flowers, the second on trees, the third on waters, and the fourth on fruits. The poem is of about 3000 lines, sustained with equable dignity. All kinds of graceful associations are mingled with the description of his flowers, in the fanciful style of Ovid and Darwin; the violet is Ianthis, who lurked in valleys to shun the love of Apollo, and stained her face with purple to preserve her chastity; the rose is Rhodanthe, proud of her beauty, and worshipped by the people in the place of Diana, but changed by the indignant Apollo to a tree, while the populace, who had adored her, are converted into her thorns, and her chief lovers into snails and butterflies. A tendency to conceit is perceived in Rapin, as in the

two poets to whom we have just compared him.   Thus,
in some pretty lines, he supposes Nature to have "tried
her 'prentice hand" in making a convolvulus before she
ventured upon a lily.[h]

54. In Rapin there will generally be remarked a certain redundancy, which fastidious critics might call
tautology of expression.   But this is not uncommon in
Virgil.   The Georgics have rarely been more happily
imitated, especially in their didactic parts, than by
Rapin in the Gardens; but he has not the high flights
of his prototype; his digressions are short, and belong
closely to the subject; we have no plague, no civil war,
no Eurydice.   If he praises Louis XIV., it is more as
the founder of the garden of Versailles, than as the conqueror of Flanders, though his concluding lines emulate,
with no unworthy spirit, those of the last Georgic.[i]   It
may be added, that some French critics have thought the
famous poem of Delille on the same subject inferior to
that of Rapin.

55. Santeul (or Santolius) has been reckoned one of
the best Latin poets whom France ever pro- Santeul.
duced.   He began by celebrating the victories
of Louis and the virtues of contemporary heroes.   A
nobleness of thought and a splendour of language distinguish the poetry of Santeul, who furnished many
inscriptions for public monuments.   The hymns which
he afterwards wrote for the breviary of the church of
Paris have been still more admired, and at the request of
others he enlarged his collection of sacred verse.   But I
have not read the poetry of Santeul, and give only the
testimony of French critics.[k]

56. England might justly boast, in the earlier part of
the century, her Milton; nay, I do not know Latin
that, with the exception of a well-known and poetry in
very pleasing poem, though perhaps hardly of England.
classical simplicity, by Cowley on himself, Epitaphium

---

b Et tu rumpis humum, et multo te
    flore profundis,
Qui riguas inter serpis, convolvule, valles;
Dulce rudimentum meditantis lilia quon-
    dam
Naturæ, cum sese opera ad majora
    pararet.

i Hæc magni insistens vestigia sacra
    Maronis,
Re super hortensi, Claro de monte canebam.

Lutetia in magna; quo tempore Francica
    tellus
Rege beata suo, rebusque superba se-
    cundis,
Et sua per populos latè dare jura vo-
    lentes
Cœperat, et toti jam morem imponere
    mundo.

k Baillet; Biogr. Universelle.

Vivi Auctoris, we can produce anything equally good in
this period. The Latin verse of Barrow is forcible and
full of mind, but not sufficiently redolent of antiquity.[m]
Yet versification became, about the time of the Restoration, if not the distinctive study, at least the favourite
exercise, of the university of Oxford. The collection
entitled Musæ Anglicanæ, published near the end of the
century, contains little from any other quarter. Many
of these poems relate to the political themes of the day,
and eulogise the reigning king, Charles, James, or
William; others are on philosophical subjects, which
they endeavour to decorate with classical phrase. Their
character does not, on the whole, pass mediocrity; they
are often incorrect and somewhat turgid, but occasionally display a certain felicity in adapting ancient lines
to their subject, and some liveliness of invention. The
golden age of Latin verse in England was yet to come.

[m] The following stanzas on an erring conscience will sufficiently prove this:—

Tyranne vitæ, fax temeraria,
Infide dux, ignobile vinculum,
　Sidus dolosum, ænigma præsens,
　Ingenui labyrinthe voti,

Assensus errans, invalidæ potens
Mentis propago, quam vetuit Deus
　Nasci, sed ortæ principatum
　Attribuit, regimenque sanctum, &c.

CHAPTER VI.

HISTORY OF DRAMATIC LITERATURE, FROM 1650 TO 1700.

Section I.

Racine — Minor French Tragedians — Molière — Regnard, and other Comic Writers.

1. Few tragedies or dramatic works of any kind are now recorded by historians of Italian literature; those of Delfino, afterwards patriarch of Aquileia, which are esteemed among the best, were possibly written before the middle of the century, and were not published till after its termination. The Corradino of Caraccio, in 1694, was also valued at the time.[a] Nor can Spain arrest us longer; the school of Calderon in national comedy extended no doubt beyond the death of Philip IV. in 1665, and many of his own religious pieces are of as late a date; nor were names wholly wanting, which are said to merit remembrance, in the feeble reign of Charles II., but they must be left for such as make a particular study of Spanish literature.[b] We are called to a nobler stage. *Italian and Spanish drama.*

2. Corneille belongs in his glory to the earlier period of this century, though his inferior tragedies, more numerous than the better, would fall within the later. Fontenelle, indeed, as a devoted admirer, attributes considerable merit to those which the general voice both of critics and of the public had condemned.[c] Meantime, another luminary arose on *Racine's first tragedies.*

---

[a] Walker's Memoir on Italian Tragedy, p. 201; Salfi, xii. 57.
[b] Bouterwek.
[c] Hist. du Théâtre François, in Œuvres de Fontenelle, iii. 111. St. Evremond also despised the French public for not admiring the Sophonisbe of Corneille, which he had made too Roman for their taste.

the opposite side of the horizon.   The first tragedy of
Jean Racine, Les Frères Ennemis, was represented in
1664, when he was twenty-five years of age.   It is so far
below his great works as to be scarcely mentioned, yet
does not want indications of the genius they were to
display.   Alexandre, in 1665, raised the young poet to
more distinction.   It is said that he showed this tragedy
to Corneille, who praised his versification, but advised
him to avoid a path which he was not fitted to tread.
It is acknowledged by the advocates of Racine that the
characters are feebly drawn, and that the conqueror
of Asia sinks to the level of a hero in one of those
romances of gallantry which had vitiated the taste of
France.

3. The glory of Racine commenced with the repre-
Andro-
maque. sentation of his Andromaque in 1667, which was
not printed till the end of the following year.
He was now at once compared with Corneille, and the
scales long continued to oscillate.   Criticism, satire,
epigrams, were unsparingly launched against the rising
poet.   But his rival pursued the worst policy by obsti-
nately writing bad tragedies.   The public naturally
compare the present with the present, and forget the
past.   When he gave them Pertharite, they were dispensed from looking back to Cinna.   It is acknowledged
even by Fontenelle that, during the height of Racine's
fame, the world placed him at least on an equality with
his predecessor; a decision from which that critic, the
relation and friend of Corneille, appeals to what he takes
to be the verdict of a later age.

4. The Andromaque was sufficient to show that Racine
had more skill in the management of a plot, in the display of emotion, in power over the sympathy of the spectator, at least where the gentler feelings are concerned.
in beauty and grace of style, in all except nobleness of
character. strength of thought, and impetuosity of language.   He took his fable from Euripides, but changed
it according to the requisitions of the French theatre
and of French manners.   Some of these changes are for
the better, as the substitution of Astyanax for an unknown
Molossus of the Greek tragedian, the supposed son of
Andromache by Pyrrhus.   " Most of those," says Racine

himself very justly, " who have heard of Andromache, know her only as the widow of Hector and the mother of Astyanax. They cannot reconcile themselves to her loving another husband and another son." And he has finely improved this happy idea of preserving Astyanax, by making the Greeks, jealous of his name, send an embassy by Orestes to demand his life; at once deepening the interest and developing the plot.

5. The female characters, Andromache and Hermione, are drawn with all Racine's delicate perception of ideal beauty; the one, indeed, prepared for his hand by those great masters in whose school he had disciplined his own gifts of nature, Homer, Euripides, Virgil; the other more original and more full of dramatic effect. It was, as we are told, the fine acting of Mademoiselle de Champmelé in this part, generally reckoned one of the most difficult on the French stage, which secured the success of the play. Racine, after the first representation, threw himself at her feet in a transport of gratitude, which was soon changed to love. It is more easy to censure some of the other characters. Pyrrhus is bold, haughty, passionate, the true son of Achilles, except where he appears as the lover of Andromache. It is inconceivable and truly ridiculous that a Greek of the heroic age, and such a Greek as Pyrrhus is represented by those whose imagination has given him existence, should feel the respectful passion towards his captive which we might reasonably expect in the romances of chivalry, or should express it in the tone of conventional gallantry that suited the court of Versailles. But Orestes is far worse; love-mad, and yet talking in gallant conceits, cold and polite, he discredits the poet, the tragedy, and the son of Agamemnon himself. It is better to kill one's mother than to utter such trash. In hinting that the previous madness of Orestes was for the love of Hermione, Racine has presumed too much on the ignorance, and too much on the bad taste, of his audience. But far more injudicious is his fantastic remorse and the supposed vision of the Furies in the last scene. It is astonishing that Racine should have challenged comparison with one of the most celebrated scenes of Euripides in circumstances that deprived him of the possibility of rendering his own effec-

tive. For the style of the Andromaque, it abounds with grace and beauty; but there are, to my apprehension, more insipid and feeble lines, and a more effeminate tone, than in his later tragedies.

6. Britannicus appeared in 1669; and in this admirable
Britannicus. play Racine first showed that he did not depend on the tone of gallantry usual among his courtly hearers, nor on the languid sympathies that it excites. Terror and pity, the twin spirits of tragedy, to whom Aristotle has assigned the great moral office of purifying the passions, are called forth in their shadowy forms to sustain the consummate beauties of his diction. His subject was original and happy; with that historic truth which usage required, and that poetical probability which fills up the outline of historic truth without disguising it. What can be more entirely dramatic, what more terrible in the sense that Aristotle means (that is, the spectator's sympathy with the dangers of the innocent), than the absolute master of the world, like the veiled prophet of Khorasan, throwing off the appearances of virtue, and standing out at once in the maturity of enormous guilt? A presaging gloom, like that which other poets have sought by the hacknied artifices of superstition, hangs over the scenes of this tragedy, and deepens at its close. We sympathise by turns with the guilty alarms of Agrippina, the virtuous consternation of Burrhus, the virgin modesty of Junia, the unsuspecting ingenuousness of Britannicus. Few tragedies on the French stage, or indeed on any stage, save those of Shakspeare, display so great a variety of contrasted characters. None, indeed, are ineffective, except the confidante of Agrippina; for Narcissus is very far from being the mere confidant of Nero; he is, as in history, his preceptor in crime; and his cold villany is well contrasted with the fierce passion of the despot. The criticisms of Fontenelle and others on small incidents in the plot, such as the concealment of Nero behind a curtain that he may hear the dialogue between Junia and Britannicus, which is certainly more fit for comedy,[d] ought not to weigh against such excellence as we find in all the more essential requisites of a tragic drama. Racine

---

d It is, however, taken from Tacitus.

had much improved his language since Andromaque; the conventional phraseology about flames and fine eyes, though not wholly relinquished, is less frequent; and if he has not here reached, as he never did, the peculiar impetuosity of Corneille, nor given to his Romans the grandeur of his predecessor's conception, he is full of lines wherein, as every word is effective, there can hardly be any deficiency of vigour. It is the vigour indeed of Virgil, not of Lucan.

7. In one passage, Racine has, I think, excelled Shakspeare. They have both taken the same idea from Plutarch. The 'lines of Shakspeare are in Antony and Cleopatra:—

> Thy demon, that 's the spirit that keeps thee, is
> Noble, courageous, high, unmatchable,
> Where Cæsar's is not; but near him, thy angel
> Becomes a fear, as being o'erpowered.

These are, to my apprehension, not very forcible, and obscure even to those who know, what many do not, that by " a fear " he meant a common goblin, a supernatural being of a more plebeian rank than a demon or angel. The single verse of Racine is magnificent:—

> Mon génie étonné tremble devant le sien.

8. Berenice, the next tragedy of Racine, is a surprising proof of what can be done by a great master; Berenice. but it must be admitted that it wants many of the essential qualities that are required in the drama. It might almost be compared with Timon of Athens, by the absence of fable and movement. For nobleness and delicacy of sentiment, for grace of style, it deserves every praise; but is rather tedious in the closet, and must be far more so on the stage. This is the only tragedy of Racine, unless perhaps we except Athalie, in which the story presents an evident moral; but no poet is more uniformly moral in his sentiments. Corneille, to whom the want of dramatic fable was never any great objection, attempted the subject of Berenice about the same time with far inferior success. It required what he could not give, the picture of two hearts struggling against a noble and a blameless love.

9. It was unfortunate for Racine that he did not more

frequently break through the prejudices of the French
Bajazet. theatre in favour of classical subjects.   A field
was open of almost boundless extent, the mediæval history of Europe, and especially of France herself. His predecessor had been too successful in the Cid
to leave it doubtful whether an audience would approve
such an innovation at the hands of a favoured tragedian.
Racine however did not venture on a step which in the
next century Voltaire turned so much to account, and
which made the fortune of some inferior tragedies.   But
considering the distance of place equivalent, for the ends
of the drama, to that of time, he founded on an event in
the Turkish history not more than thirty years old, his
next tragedy, that of Bajazet.   The greater part indeed
of the fable is due to his own invention.   Bajazet is
reckoned to fall below most of his other tragedies in
beauty of style; but the fable is well connected; there
is a great deal of movement, and an unintermitting interest is sustained by Bajazet and Atalide, two of the
noblest characters that Racine has drawn.   Atalide has
not the ingenuous simplicity of Junie, but displays a
more dramatic flow of sentiment and not less dignity or
tenderness of soul.   The character of Roxane is conceived
with truth and spirit; nor is the resemblance some have
found in it to that of Hermione greater than belongs to
forms of the same type.   Acomat, the vizir, is more a
favourite with the French critics; but in such parts
Racine does not rise to the level of Corneille.   No poet
is less exposed to the imputation of bombastic exaggeration; yet in the two lines with which Acomat concludes
the fourth act, there is at least an approach to burlesque;
and one can hardly say that they would have been out of
place in Tom Thumb :—

> Mourons, moi, cher Osmin, comme un vizir, et toi,
> Comme le favori d'un homme tel que moi.

10. The next tragedy was Mithridate; and in this
Mithridate. Racine has been thought to have wrestled
against Corneille on his own ground, the display of the unconquerable mind of a hero.   We find in
the part of Mithridate a great depth of thought in compressed and energetic language.   But, unlike the masculine characters of Corneille, he is not merely senten-

tious. Racine introduces no one for the sake of the speeches he has to utter. In Mithridates he took what history has delivered to us, blending with it no improbable fiction according to the manners of the East. His love for Monime has nothing in it extraordinary, or unlike what we might expect from the king of Pontus; it is a fierce, a jealous, a vindictive love; the necessities of the French language alone, and the usages of the French theatre, could make it appear feeble. His two sons are naturally less effective; but the loveliness of Monime yields to no female character of Racine. There is something not quite satisfactory in the stratagems which Mithridates employs to draw from her a confession of her love for his son. They are not uncongenial to the historic character, but, according to our chivalrous standard of heroism, seem derogatory to the poetical.

11. Iphigénie followed in 1674. In this Racine had again to contend with Euripides in one of his most celebrated tragedies. He had even, in the character of Achilles, to contend, not with Homer himself, yet with the Homeric associations familiar to every classical scholar. The love, in fact, of Achilles, and his politeness towards Clytemnestra, are not exempt from a tone of gallantry a little repugnant to our conception of his manners. Yet the Achilles of Homer is neither incapable of love nor of courtesy, so that there is no essential repugnance to his character. That of Iphigenia in Euripides has been censured by Aristotle as inconsistent; her extreme distress at the first prospect of death being followed by an unusual display of courage. Hurd has taken upon him the defence of the Greek tragedian, and observes, after Brumoy, that the Iphigenia of Racine being modelled rather according to the comment of Aristotle than the example of Euripides, is so much the worse.* But his apology is too subtle, and requires too long reflection, for the ordinary spectator; and though Shakspeare might have managed the transition of feeling with some of his wonderful knowledge of human nature, it is certainly presented too crudely by Euripides, and much in the style which I have elsewhere observed to be too

_____
* Hurd's Commentary on Horace, vol. i. p. 115.

usual with our old dramatists.   The Iphigenia of Racine
is not a character, like those of Shakspeare, and of him,
perhaps, alone, which nothing less than intense meditation can develop to the reader, but one which a good
actress might compass, and a common spectator understand.   Racine, like most other tragedians, wrote for the
stage ; Shakspeare aimed at a point beyond it, and sometimes too much lost sight of what it required.

12.   Several critics have censured the part of Eriphile.
Yet Fontenelle, prejudiced as he was against Racine,
admits that it is necessary for the catastrophe, though he
cavils, I think, against her appearance in the earlier part
of the play, laying down a rule, by which our own tragedians would not have chosen to be tried, and which seems
far too rigid, that the necessity of the secondary characters should be perceived from their first appearance.ᶠ   The
question for Racine was in what manner he should manage
the catastrophe.   The *fabulous truth*, the actual sacrifice
of Iphigenia, was so revolting to the mind, that even
Euripides thought himself obliged to depart from it.   But
this he effected by a contrivance impossible on the French
stage, and which would have changed Racine's tragedy
to a common melodrame.   It appears to me that he very
happily substituted the character of Eriphile, who, as
Fontenelle well says, is the hind of the fable ; and whose
impetuous and somewhat disorderly passions both furnish a contrast to the ideal nobleness of Iphigenia throughout the tragedy, and reconcile us to her own fate at the
close.

13.   Once more, in Phédre, did the great disciple of
Phédre.   Euripides attempt to surpass his master.   In
          both tragedies the character of Phædra her-
self throws into shade all the others, but with this important difference, that in Euripides her death occurs
about the middle of the piece, while she continues in
Racine till the conclusion.   The French poet has borrowed much from the Greek, more, perhaps, than in any
former drama, but has surely heightened the interest,
and produced a more splendid work of genius.   I have
never read the particular criticism in which Schlegel
has endeavoured to elevate the Hippolytus above the

ᶠ Réflexions sur la Poëtique ; Œuvres de Fontenelle, vol. iii. p. 149.

Phédre. Many, even among French critics, have objected to the love of Hippolytus for Aricia, by which
Racine has deviated from the older mythological tradition, though not without the authority of Virgil. But
we are hardly tied to all the circumstance of fable ; and
the cold young huntsman loses nothing in the eyes of a
modern reader by a virtuous attachment. This tragedy
is said to be more open to verbal criticism than the Iphigénie ; but in poetical beauty I do not know that Racine
has ever surpassed it. The description of the death of
Hippolytus is, perhaps, his masterpiece. It is true
that, according to the practice of our own stage, long
descriptions, especially in elaborate language, are out of
use ; but it is not, at least, for the advocates of Euripides
to blame them.

14. The Phédre was represented in 1677 ; and after
this its illustrious author seemed to renounce   Esther.
the stage. His increasing attachment to the
Jansenists made it almost impossible, with any consistency, to promote an amusement which they anathema-
tised. But he was induced, after many years, in 1689,
by Madame de Maintenon, to write Esther for the purpose of representation by the young ladies whose education she protected at St. Cyr. Esther, though very much
praised for beauty of language, is admitted to possess
little merit as a drama. Much, indeed, could not be
expected in the circumstances. It was acted at St. Cyr ;
Louis applauded, and it is said that the Prince de Condé
wept. The greatest praise of Esther is that it encouraged
its author to write Athalie. Once more restored   Athalie.
to dramatic conceptions, his genius revived from
sleep with no loss of the vigour of yesterday. He was
even more in Athalie than in Iphigénie and Britannicus.
This great work, published in 1691, with a royal prohi-
bition to represent it on any theatre, stands by general
consent at the head of all the tragedies of Racine, for
the grandeur, simplicity, and interest of the fable, for
dramatic terror, for theatrical effect, for clear and judicious management, for bold and forcible, rather than
subtle delineation of character, for sublime sentiment and
imagery. It equals, if it does not, as I should incline to
think, surpass, all the rest in the perfection of style, and
is far more free from every defect, especially from feeble

politeness and gallantry, which of course the subject
could not admit. It has been said that he himself gave
the preference to Phédre; but it is more extraordinary
that not only his enemies, of whom there were many,
but the public itself, was for some years incapable of
discovering the merit of Athalie. Boileau declared it to
be a masterpiece, and one can only be astonished that
any could have thought differently from Boileau.   It
doubtless gained much in general esteem when it came
to be represented by good actors; for no tragedy in the
French language is more peculiarly fitted for the stage.

15. The chorus, which he had previously introduced in
Esther, was a very bold innovation (for the revival of
what is forgotten must always be classed as innovation),
and it required all the skill of Racine to prevent its
appearing in our eyes an impertinent excrescence.   But
though we do not, perhaps, wholly reconcile ourselves
to some of the songs, which too much suggest, by association, the Italian opera, the chorus of Athalie enhances
the interest as well as the splendour of the tragedy.   It
was, indeed, more full of action and scenic pomp than
any he had written, and probably than any other which
up to that time had been represented in France.   The
part of Athalie predominates, but not so as to eclipse the
rest.   The high-priest Joad is drawn with a stern zeal,
admirably dramatic, and without which the idolatrous
queen would have trampled down all before her during
the conduct of the fable, whatever justice might have
ensued at the last.   We feel this want of an adequate
resistance to triumphant crime in the Rodogune of Corneille. No character appears superfluous or feeble; while
the plot has all the simplicity of the Greek stage, it has
all the movement and continual excitation of the modern.

16. The female characters of Racine are of the greatest
beauty; they have the ideal grace and harmony
Racine's female characters. of ancient sculpture, and bear somewhat of the
same analogy to those of Shakspeare which that
art does to painting. Andromache, Monimia, Iphigenia,
we may add Junia, have a dignity and faultlessness
neither unnatural nor insipid, because they are only the
ennobling and purifying of human passions. They are
the forms of possible excellence, not from individual

models, nor likely, perhaps, to delight every reader, for
the same reason that more eyes are pleased by Titian
than by Raffaelle.   But it is a very narrow criticism
which excludes either school from our admiration, which
disparages Racine out of idolatry of Shakspeare.   The
latter, it is unnecessary for me to say, stands out of reach
of all competition.   But it is not on this account that we
are to give up an author so admirable as Racine.

17. The chief faults of Racine may partly be ascribed
to the influence of national taste, though we
must confess that Corneille has better avoided Racine
compared
with
Corneille.
them.   Though love, with the former, is always
tragic and connected with the heroic passions,
never appearing singly, as in several of our own dramatists, yet it is sometimes unsuitable to the character, and
still more frequently feeble and courtier-like in the expression.   In this he complied too much with the times;
but we must believe that he did not entirely feel that he
was wrong.   Corneille had, even while Racine was in
his glory, a strenuous band of supporters.   Fontenelle,
writing in the next century, declares that time has established a decision in which most seem to concur, that
the first place is due to the elder poet, the second to the
younger; every one making the interval between them
a little greater or less according to his taste.   But Voltaire, La Harpe, and in general, I apprehend, the later
French critics, have given the preference to Racine.   I
presume to join my suffrage to theirs.   Racine appears
to me the superior tragedian; and I must add that I
think him next to Shakspeare among all the moderns.
The comparison with Euripides is so natural that it can
hardly be avoided.   Certainly no tragedy of the Greek
poet is so skilful or so perfect as Athalie or Britannicus.
The tedious scenes during which the action is stagnant,
the impertinences of useless, often perverse morality, the
extinction, by bad management, of the sympathy that
had been raised in the earlier part of a play, the foolish
alternation of repartees in a series of single lines, will
never be found in Racine.   But, when we look only at
the highest excellences of Euripides, there is, perhaps,
a depth of pathos and an intensity of dramatic effect
which Racine himself has not attained.   The difference

between the energy and sweetness of the two languages
is so important in the comparison, that I shall give even
this preference with some hesitation.

18. The style of Racine is exquisite. Perhaps he is
Beauty of second only to Virgil among all poets. But I
his style. will give the praise of this in the words of a
native critic. " His expression is always so happy and
so natural, that it seems as if no other could have been
found ; and every word is placed in such a manner that
we cannot fancy any other place to have suited it as well.
The structure of his style is such that nothing could be
displaced, nothing added, nothing retrenched; it is one
unalterable whole. Even his incorrectnesses are often
but sacrifices required by good taste, nor would anything
be more difficult than to write over again a line of Racine.
No one has enriched the language with a greater number
of turns of phrase ; no one is bold with more felicity and
discretion, or figurative with more grace and propriety ;
no one has handled with more command an idiom often
rebellious, or with more skill an instrument always difficult ; no one has better understood that delicacy of style
which must not be mistaken for feebleness, and is, in fact,
but that air of ease which conceals from the reader the
labour of the work and the artifices of the composition ;
or better managed the variety of cadences, the resources
of rhythm, the association and deduction of ideas. In
short, if we consider that his perfection in these respects
may be opposed to that of Virgil, and that he spoke a
language less flexible, less poetical, and less harmonious,
we shall readily believe that Racine is, of all mankind,
the one to whom nature has given the greatest talent for
versification." [e]

19. Thomas, the younger and far inferior brother of
Thomas Pierre Corneille, was yet by the fertility of his
Corneille— pen, by the success of some of his tragedies, and
his Ariane. by a certain reputation which two of them have
acquired, the next name, but at a vast interval, to Racine.
Voltaire says he would have enjoyed a great reputation
but for that of his brother—one of those pointed sayings
which seem to convey something, but are really devoid
of meaning. Thomas Corneille is never compared with

---

[e] La Harpe, Éloge de Racine, as quoted by himself in Cours de Littérature, vol. vi.

his brother; and probably his brother has been rather serviceable to his name with posterity than otherwise. He wrote with more purity, according to the French critics, and it must be owned that, in his Ariane, he has given to love a tone more passionate and natural than the manly scenes of the older tragedian ever present. This is esteemed his best work, but it depends wholly on the principal character, whose tenderness and injuries excite our sympathy, and from whose lips many lines of great beauty flow. It may be compared with the Berenice of Racine, represented but a short time before; there is enough of resemblance in the fables to provoke comparison. That of Thomas Corneille is more tragic, less destitute of theatrical movement, and consequently better chosen; but such relative praise is of little value, where none can be given, in this respect, to the object of comparison. We feel that the prose romance is the proper sphere for the display of an affection, neither untrue to nature, nor unworthy to move the heart, but wanting the majesty of the tragic muse. An effeminacy uncongenial to tragedy belongs to this play; and the termination, where the heroine faints away instead of dying, is somewhat insipid. The only other tragedy of the younger Corneille that can be mentioned is the Earl of Essex. In this he has taken greater liberties with history than his critics approve; and though love does not so much predominate as in Ariane, it seems to engross, in a style rather too romantic, both the hero and his sovereign.

20. Neither of these tragedies, perhaps, deserves to be put on a level with the Manlius of La Fosse, to Manlius of which La Harpe accords the preference above La Fosse. all of the seventeenth century after those of Corneille and Racine. It is just to observe, what is not denied, that the author has borrowed the greater part of his story from the Venice Preserved of Otway. The French critics maintain that he has far excelled his original. It is possible that we might hesitate to own this general superiority; but several blemishes have been removed, and the conduct is perhaps more noble, or at least more fitted to the French stage. But when we take from La Fosse what belongs to another—characters strongly marked, sympathies powerfully contrasted, a develop-

ment of the plot probable and interesting, what will
remain that is purely his own? There will remain a
vigorous tone of language, a considerable power of description, and a skill in adapting, we may add with justice, in sometimes improving, what he found in a foreign
language.   We must pass over some other tragedies
which have obtained less honour in their native land,
those of Duché, Quinault, and Campistron.

21. Molière is perhaps, of all French writers, the one
Molière. whom his country has most uniformly admired,
and in whom her critics are most unwilling to
acknowledge faults ; though the observations of Schlegel
on the defects of Molière, and especially on his large
debts to older comedy, are not altogether without foundation.   Molière began with L'Etourdi in 1653, and his
pieces followed rapidly till his death in 1673.   About
one half are in verse ; I shall select a few without
regard to order of time, and first one written in prose,
L'Avare.

22. Plautus first exposed upon the stage the wretched-
L'Avare. ness of avarice, the punishment of a selfish love
of gold, not only in the life of pain it has cost
to acquire it, but in the terrors that it brings, in the
disordered state of mind, which is haunted, as by some
mysterious guilt, by the consciousness of secret wealth.
The character of Euclio in the Aulularia is dramatic,
and, as far as we know, original ; the moral effect requires perhaps some touches beyond absolute probability,
but it must be confessed that a few passages are over-
charged.   Molière borrowed L'Avare from this comedy ;
and I am not at present aware that the subject, though
so well adapted for the stage, had been chosen by any
intermediate dramatist.   He is indebted not merely for
the scheme of his play, but for many strokes of humour,
to Plautus.   But this takes off little from the merit of
this excellent comedy.   The plot is expanded without
incongruous or improbable circumstances ; new characters are well combined with that of Harpagon, and his
own is at once more diverting and less extravagant than
that of Euclio.   The penuriousness of the latter, though
by no means without example, leaves no room for any
other object than the concealed treasure, in which his
thoughts are concentred.   But Molière had conceived a

more complicated action.   Harpagon does not absolutely
starve the rats ; he possesses horses, though he feeds
them ill ; he has servants, though he grudges them
clothes ; he even contemplates a marriage supper at his
own expense, though he intends to have a bad one.   He
has evidently been compelled to make some sacrifices to
the usages of mankind, and is at once a more common
and a more theatrical character than Euclio.   In other
respects they are much alike : their avarice has reached
that point where it is without pride ; the dread of losing
their wealth has overpowered the desire of being thought
to possess it ; and though this is a more natural incident
in the manners of Greece than in those of France, yet
the concealment of treasure, even in the time of Molière,
was sufficiently frequent for dramatic probability.   A
general tone of selfishness, the usual source and necessary
consequence of avarice, conspires with the latter quality
to render Harpagon odious ; and there wants but a little
more poetical justice in the conclusion, which leaves the
casket in his possession.

23. Hurd has censured Molière without much justice.
" For the picture of the avaricious man, Plautus and
Molière have presented us with a fantastic, unpleasing
draught of the passion of avarice."   It may be answered
to this, that Harpagon's character is, as has been said
above, not so mere a delineation of the passion as that
of Euclio.   But as a more general vindication of Molière, it should be kept in mind, that every exhibition of
a predominant passion within the compass of the five
acts of a play must be coloured beyond the truth of
nature, or it will not have time to produce its effect.
This is one great advantage that romance possesses over
the drama.

24. L'Ecole des Femmes is among the most diverting
comedies of Molière.   Yet it has in a remark-   L'Ecole
able degree what seems inartificial to our own   des Femmes.
taste, and contravenes a good general precept of Horace ;
the action passes almost wholly in recital.   But this is
so well connected with the development of the plot and
characters, and produces such amusing scenes, that no
spectator, at least on the French theatre, would be sensible of any languor.   Arnolphe is an excellent modification of the type which Molière loved to reproduce ; the

selfish and morose cynic whose pretended hatred of the vices of the world springs from an absorbing regard to his own gratification. He has made him as malignant as censorious; he delights in tales of scandal; he is pleased that Horace should be successful in gallantry, because it degrades others. The half-witted and ill-bred child, of whom he becomes the dupe, as well as the two idiot servants, are delineated with equal vivacity. In this comedy we find the spirited versification, full of grace and humour, in which no one has rivalled Molière, and which has never been attempted on the English stage. It was probably its merit which raised a host of petty detractors, on whom the author revenged himself in his admirable piece of satire, La Critique de l'Ecole des Femmes. The affected pedantry of the Hôtel Rambouillet seems to be ridiculed in this retaliation; nothing in fact could be more unlike than the style of Molière to their own.

25. He gave another proof of contempt for the false taste of some Parisian circles in the Misanthrope; though the criticism of Alceste on the wretched sonnet forms but a subordinate portion of that famous comedy. It is generally placed next to Tartuffe among the works of Molière. Alceste is again the cynic, but more honourable and less openly selfish, and with more of a real disdain of vice in his misanthropy. Rousseau, upon this account, and many others after him, have treated the play as a vindication of insincerity against truth, and as making virtue itself ridiculous on the stage. This charge however seems uncandid; neither the rudeness of Alceste, nor the misanthropy from which it springs, are to be called virtues; and we may observe that he displays no positively good quality beyond sincerity, unless his ungrounded and improbable love for a coquette is to pass for such. It is true that the politeness of Philinthe, with whom the Misanthrope is contrasted, borders a little too closely upon flattery; but no oblique end is in his view; he flatters to give pleasure; and if we do not much esteem his character, we are not solicitous for his punishment. The dialogue of the Misanthrope is uniformly of the highest style; the female, and indeed all the characters, are excellently conceived and sustained: if this comedy fails of anything at pre-

sent, it is through the difference of manners, and, perhaps, in representation, through the want of animated action on the stage.

26. In Les Femmes Savantes, there is a more evident personality in the characters, and a more mali- Les Femmes cious exposure of absurdity, than in the Misan- Savantes. thrope; but the ridicule, falling on a less numerous class, is not so well calculated to be appreciated by posterity. It is, however, both in reading and representation, a more amusing comedy: in no one instance has Molière delineated such variety of manners, or displayed so much of his inimitable gaiety and power of fascinating the audience with very little plot, by the mere exhibition of human follies. The satire falls deservedly on pretenders to taste and literature, for whom Molière always testifies a bitterness of scorn in which we perceive some resentment of their criticisms. The shorter piece, entitled Les Précieuses Ridicules, is another shaft directed at the literary ladies of Paris. They had provoked a dangerous enemy; but the good taste of the next age might be ascribed in great measure to his unmerciful exposure of affectation and pedantry.

27. It was not easy, so late as the age of Molière, for the dramatist to find any untrodden field in the Tartuffe. follies and vices of mankind. But one had been reserved for him in Tartuffe—religious hypocrisy. We should have expected the original draft of such a character on the English stage; nor had our old writers been forgetful of their inveterate enemies, the Puritans, who gave such full scope for their satire. But choosing rather the easy path of ridicule, they fell upon the starch dresses and quaint language of the fanatical party; and where they exhibited these in conjunction with hypocrisy, made the latter more ludicrous than hateful. The Luke of Massinger is deeply and villanously dissembling, but does not wear so conspicuous a garb of religious sanctity as Tartuffe. The comedy of Molière is not only original in this character, but is a new creation in dramatic poetry. It has been doubted by some critics, whether the depth of guilt that it exhibits, the serious hatred that it inspires, are not beyond the strict province of comedy. But this seems rather a technical cavil. If subjects such as the Tartuffe are not fit for

comedy, they are at least fit for dramatic representation, and some new phrase must be invented to describe their class.

28. A different kind of objection is still sometimes made to this play, that it brings religion itself into suspicion. And this would no doubt have been the case, if the contemporaries of Molière in England had dealt with the subject. But the boundaries between the reality and its false appearances are so well guarded in this comedy, that no reasonable ground of exception can be thought to remain. No better advice can be given to those who take umbrage at the Tartuffe than to read it again. For there may be good reason to suspect that they are themselves among those for whose benefit it was intended; the Tartuffes, happily, may be comparatively few, but while the Orgons and Pernelles are numerous, they will not want their harvest. Molière did not invent the prototypes of his hypocrite; they were abundant at Paris in his time.

29. The interest of this play continually increases, and the fifth act is almost crowded by a rapidity of events, not so usual on the French stage as our own. Tartuffe himself is a masterpiece of skill. Perhaps in the cavils of La Bruyère there may be some justice; but the essayist has forgotten that no character can be rendered entirely effective to an audience without a little exaggeration of its attributes. Nothing can be more happily conceived than the credulity of the honest Orgon, and his more doting mother; it is that which we sometimes witness, incurable except by the evidence of the senses, and fighting every inch of ground against that. In such a subject there was not much opportunity for the comic talent of Molière; yet in some well-known passages, he has enlivened it as far as was possible. The Tartuffe will generally be esteemed the greatest effort of this author's genius; the Misanthrope, the Femmes Savantes, and the Ecole des Femmes will follow in various order, according to our tastes. These are by far the best of his comedies in verse. Among those in prose we may give the first place to L'Avare, and the next either to Le Bourgeois Gentilhomme, or to George Dandin.

30. These two plays have the same objects of moral

satire; on one hand the absurd vanity of plebeians in seeking the alliance or acquaintance of the no- *Bourgeois* bility; on the other, the pride and meanness *Gentil-* of the nobility themselves. They are both *George* abundantly diverting; but the sallies of hu- *Dandin.* mour are, I think, more frequent in the first three acts of the former. The last two acts are improbable and less amusing. The shorter pieces of Molière border very much upon farce; he permits himself more vulgarity of character, more grossness in language and incident, but his farces are seldom absurd, and never dull.

31. The French have claimed for Molière, and few perhaps have disputed the pretension, a supe- *Character of* riority over all earlier and later writers of *Molière.* comedy. He certainly leaves Plautus, the original model of the school to which he belonged, at a vast distance. The grace and gentlemanly elegance of Terence he has not equalled; but in the more appropriate merits of comedy, just and forcible delineation of character, skilful contrivance of circumstances, and humorous dialogue, we must award him the prize. The Italian and Spanish dramatists are quite unworthy to be named in comparison; and if the French theatre has, in later times, as is certainly the case, produced some excellent comedies, we have, I believe, no reason to contradict the suffrage of the nation itself, that they owe almost as much to what they have caught from this great model, as to the natural genius of their authors. But it is not for us to abandon the rights of Shakspeare. In all things most essential to comedy, we cannot acknowledge his inferiority to Molière. He had far more invention of characters, with an equal vivacity and force in their delineation. His humour was at least as abundant and natural, his wit incomparably more brilliant; in fact, Molière hardly exhibits this quality at all.[b] The Merry Wives of Windsor, almost the only pure comedy of Shakspeare, is surely not disadvantageously compared with George Dandin or Le Bourgeois Gentilhomme, or even with L'Ecole des Femmes. For the Tartuffe or the Misanthrope it is vain to seek a proper counterpart in

[b] [A French critic upon the first edition of this work has supposed *wit* to be the same as *esprit*, and is justly astonished that I should deny the latter quality to Molière, especially after the eulogies I have been passing on him.—1842.]

Shakspeare; they belong to a different state of manners. But the powers of Molière are directed with greater skill to their object; none of his energy is wasted; the spectator is not interrupted by the serious scenes of tragi-comedy, nor his attention drawn aside by poetical episodes. Of Shakspeare we may justly say that he had the greater genius, but perhaps of Molière, that he has written the best comedies. We cannot at least put any third dramatist in competition with him. Fletcher and Jonson, Wycherley and Congreve, Farquhar and Sheridan, with great excellences of their own, fall short of his merit as well as of his fame. Yet in humorous conception, our admirable play, the Provoked Husband, the best parts of which are due to Vanbrugh, seems to be equal to anything he has left. His spirited and easy versification stands of course untouched by any English rivalry; we may have been wise in rejecting verse from our stage, but we have certainly given the French a right to claim all the honour that belongs to it.

32. Racine once only attempted comedy. His wit was *Les Plaideurs of Racine.* quick and sarcastic, and in epigram he did not spare his enemies. In his Plaideurs there is more of humour and stage-effect than of wit. The ridicule falls happily on the pedantry of lawyers and the folly of suitors; but the technical language is lost in great measure upon the audience. This comedy, if it be not rather a farce, is taken from The Wasps of Aristophanes; and that Rabelais of antiquity supplied an extravagance very improbably introduced into the third act of Les Plaideurs, the trial of the dog. Far from improving the humour, which had been amusingly kept up during the first two acts, this degenerates into absurdity.

33. Regnard is always placed next to Molière among *Regnard— Le Joueur.* the comic writers of France in this, and perhaps in any age. The plays, indeed, which entitle him to such a rank are but few. Of these the best is acknowledged to be Le Joueur. Regnard, taught by his own experience, has here admirably delineated the character of an inveterate gamester; without parade of morality, few comedies are more usefully moral. We have not the struggling virtues of a Charles Surface, which the dramatist may feign that he may reward at the fifth

act; Regnard has better painted the selfish ungrateful being, who, though not incapable of love, pawns his mistress's picture, the instant after she has given it to him, that he may return to the dice-box. Her just abandonment, and his own disgrace, terminate the comedy with a moral dignity which the stage does not always maintain, and which in the first acts the spectator does not expect. The other characters seem to me various, spirited, and humorous; the valet of Valère the gamester is one of the best of that numerous class, to whom comedy has owed so much; but the pretended marquis, though diverting, talks too much like a genuine coxcomb of the world. Molière did this better in Les Précieuses Ridicules. Regnard is in this play full of those gay sallies which cannot be read without laughter; the incidents follow rapidly; there is more movement than in some of the best of Molière's comedies, and the speeches are not so prolix.

34. Next to Le Joueur among Regnard's comedies it has been usual to place Le Légataire, not by His other plays. any means inferior to the first in humour and vivacity, but with less force of character, and more of the common tricks of the stage. The moral, instead of being excellent, is of the worst kind, being the success and dramatic reward of a gross fraud, the forgery of a will by the hero of the piece and his servant. This servant is however a very comical rogue, and we should not perhaps wish to see him sent to the galleys. A similar censure might be passed on the comedy of Regnard which stands third in reputation, Les Menechmes. The subject, as explained by the title, is old—twinbrothers, whose undistinguishable features are the source of endless confusion; but what neither Plautus nor Shakspeare have thought of, one avails himself of the likeness to receive a large sum of money due to the other, and is thought very generous at the close of the play when he restores a moiety. Of the plays founded on this diverting exaggeration, Regnard's is perhaps the best; he has more variety of incident than Plautus; and by leaving out the second pair of twins, the Dromio servants, who render the Comedy of Errors almost too inextricably confused for the spectator or reader, as well as by making one of the brothers aware of the mistake, and a party in

the deception, he has given an unity of plot instead of a
series of incoherent blunders.

35. The Mère Coquette of Quinault appears a comedy
Quinault. of great merit. Without the fine traits of nature
Boursault. which we find in those of Molière, without the
sallies of humour which enliven those of Regnard, with
a versification perhaps not very forcible, it pleases us by
a fable at once novel, as far as I know, and natural, by
the interesting characters of the lovers, by the decency
and tone of good company, which are never lost in the
manners, the incidents, or the language. Boursault,
whose tragedies are little esteemed, displayed some originality in Le Mercure Galant. The idea is one which
has not unfrequently been imitated on the English as
well as French stage, but it is rather adapted to the
shorter drama than to a regular comedy of five acts.
The Mercure Galant was a famous magazine of light
periodical amusement, such as was then new in France,
which had a great sale, and is described in a few lines
by one of the characters in this piece.[i] Boursault places
his hero, by the editor's consent, as a temporary substitute in the office of this publication, and brings, in a
series of detached scenes, a variety of applicants for his
notice. A comedy of this kind is like a compound
animal ; a few chief characters must give unity to the
whole, but the effect is produced by the successive personages who pass over the stage, display their humour
in a single scene, and disappear. Boursault has been in
some instances successful ; but such pieces generally owe
too much to temporary sources of amusement.

36. Dancourt, as Voltaire has said, holds the same rank
Dancourt. relatively to Molière in farce, that Regnard does
in the higher comedy. He came a little after
the former, and when the prejudice that had been created
against comedies in prose by the great success of the
other kind had begun to subside. The Chevalier à la

---

i   Le Mercure est une bonne chose ;
On y trouve de tout, fable, histoire, vers,
    prose,
Sièges, combats, procès, mort, mariage,
    amour,
Nouvelles de province, et nouvelles de
    cour—
Jamais livre à mon gré ne fut plus
    nécessaire.   Act I. scene 2.

The Mercure Galant was established
in 1672 by one Visé : it was intended to
fill the same place as a critical record
of polite literature, which the Journal des Sçavans did in learning and science.

Mode is the only play of Dancourt that I know; it is much above farce, and if length be a distinctive criterion, it exceeds most comedies. This would be very slight praise, if we could not add that the reader does not find it one page too long, that the ridicule is poignant and happy, the incidents well contrived, the comic situations amusing, the characters clearly marked. La Harpe, who treats Dancourt with a sort of contempt, does not so much as mention this play. It is a satire on the pretensions of a class then rising, the rich financiers, which long supplied materials, through dramatic caricature, to public malignity, and the envy of a less opulent aristocracy.

37. The life of Brueys is rather singular. Born of a noble, Huguenot family, he was early devoted *Brueys.* to Protestant theology, and even presumed to enter the lists against Bossuet. But that champion of the faith was like one of those knights in romance, who first unhorse their rash antagonists, and then make them work as slaves. Brueys was soon converted, and betook himself to write against his former errors. He afterwards became an ecclesiastic. Thus far there is nothing much out of the common course in his history. But grown weary of living alone, and having some natural turn to comedy, he began, rather late, to write for the stage, with the assistance, or perhaps only under the name, of a certain Palaprat. The plays of Brueys had some success; but he was not in a position to delineate recent manners, and in the only comedy with which I am acquainted, Le Muet, he has borrowed the leading part of his story from Terence. The language seems deficient in vivacity, which, when there is no great naturalness or originality of character, cannot be dispensed with.

38. The French opera, after some ineffectual attempts by Mazarin to naturalise an Italian company, *Operas of* was successfully established by Lulli in 1672. *Quinault.* It is the prerogative of music in the melo-drame to render poetry its dependent ally; but the airs of Lulli have been forgotten and the verses of his coadjutor Quinault remain. He is not only the earliest, but by general consent the unrivalled poet of French music. Boileau indeed treated him with undeserved scorn, but probably

through dislike of the tone he was obliged to preserve, which in the eyes of so stern a judge, and one so insensible to love, appeared languid and effeminate. Quinault nevertheless was not incapable of vigorous and impressive poetry; a lyric grandeur distinguishes some of his songs; he seems to possess great felicity of adorning every subject with appropriate imagery and sentiment; his versification has a smoothness and charm of melody which has made some say that the lines were already music before they came to the composer's hands; his fables, whether taken from mythology or modern romance, display invention and skill. Voltaire, La Harpe, Schlegel, and the author of the life of Quinault in the Biographie Universelle, but most of all, the testimony of the public, have compensated for the severity of Boileau. The Armide is Quinault's latest and also his finest opera.

SECT. II.—ON THE ENGLISH DRAMA.

State of the Stage after the Restoration — Tragedies of Dryden, Otway, Southern — Comedies of Congreve and others.

39. THE troubles of twenty years, and, much more, the fanatical antipathy to stage-plays which the predominant party affected, silenced the muse of the buskin, and broke the continuity of those works of the elder dramatists, which had given a tone to public sentiment as to the drama from the middle of Elizabeth's reign. Davenant had, by a sort of connivance, opened a small house for the representation of plays, though not avowedly so called, near the Charter House in 1656. He obtained a patent after the Restoration. By this time another generation had arisen, and the scale of taste was to be adjusted anew. The fondness for the theatre revived with increased avidity; more splendid decoration, actors probably, especially Betterton, of greater powers, and above all, the attraction of female performers, who had never been admitted on the older stage, conspired with the keen appetite that long restraint produced, and with the general gaiety, or rather dissoluteness, of manners. Yet the multitude of places for

such amusement was not as great as under the first
Stuarts.   Two houses only were opened under royal
patents, granting them an exclusive privilege, one by
what was called the King's Company, in Drury Lane,
another by the Duke of York's Company, in Lincoln's
Inn Fields.   Betterton, who was called the English
Roscius, till Garrick claimed that title, was sent to Paris
by Charles II., that, taking a view of the French stage,
he might better judge of what would contribute to the
improvement of our own.   It has been said, and probably with truth, that he introduced moveable scenes,
instead of the fixed tapestry that had been hung across
the stage; but this improvement he could not have borrowed from France.   The king not only countenanced
the theatre by his patronage, but by so much personal
notice of the chief actors, and so much interest in all the
affairs of the theatre, as elevated their condition.

40. An actor of great talents is the best friend of the
great dramatists; his own genius demands theirs Change of
for its support and display; and a fine performer public
would as soon waste the powers of his hand on taste.
feeble music, as a man like Betterton or Garrick represent what is insipid or in bad taste.   We know that the
former, and some of his contemporaries, were celebrated in the great parts of our early stage, in those of
Shakspeare and Fletcher.   But the change of public
taste is sometimes irresistible by those who, as, in
Johnson's antithesis, they " live to please, must please
to live."   Neither tragedy nor comedy was maintained
at its proper level; and as the world is apt to demand
novelty on the stage, the general tone of dramatic representation in this period, whatever credit it may have
done to the performers, reflects little, in comparison with
our golden age, upon those who wrote for them.

41. It is observed by Scott, that the French theatre,
which was now thought to be in perfection, Its causes.
guided the criticism of Charles's court, and
afforded the pattern of those tragedies which continued
in fashion for twenty years after the Restoration, and
which were called rhyming or heroic plays.   Though
there is a general justice in this remark, I am not aware
that the inflated tone of these plays is imitated from any
French tragedy; certainly there was a nobler model in

the best works of Corneille. But Scott is more right in deriving the unnatural and pedantic dialogue which prevailed through these performances from the romances of Scudery and Calprenède. These were, about the era of the Restoration, almost as popular among our indolent gentry as in France; and it was to be expected that a style would gain ground in tragedy, which is not so widely removed from what tragedy requires, but that an ordinary audience would fail to perceive the difference. There is but a narrow line between the sublime and the tumid; the man of business or of pleasure who frequents the theatre must have accustomed himself to make such large allowances, to put himself into a state of mind so totally different from his every-day habits, that a little extraordinary deviation from nature, far from shocking him, will rather show like a further advance towards excellence. Hotspur and Almanzor, Richard and Aurungzebe, seem to him cast in the same mould; beings who can never occur in the common walks of life, but whom the tragedian has, by a tacit convention with the audience, acquired a right of feigning like his ghosts and witches.

42. The first tragedies of Dryden were what was called

Heroic tragedies of Dryden. heroic, and written in rhyme; an innovation which, of course, must be ascribed to the influence of the French theatre. They have occasionally much vigour of sentiment and much beautiful poetry, with a versification sweet even to lusciousness. The Conquest of Grenada is, on account of its extravagance, the most celebrated of these plays; but it is inferior to the Indian Emperor, from which it would be easy to select passages of perfect elegance. It is singular that although the rhythm of dramatic verse is commonly permitted to be the most lax of any, Dryden has in this play availed himself of none of his wonted privileges. He regularly closes the sense with the couplet, and falls into a smoothness of cadence which, though exquisitely mellifluous, is perhaps too uniform. In the Conquest of Grenada the versification is rather more broken.

43. Dryden may probably have been fond of this

His later tragedies. species of tragedy, on account of his own facility in rhyming, and his habit of condensing his sense. Rhyme, indeed, can only be rejected in our language from the tragic scene, because blank verse affords wider scope for the emotions it ought to excite; but for the tumid rhapsodies which the personages of his heroic plays utter, there can be no excuse. He adhered to this tone, however, till the change, in public taste, and especially the ridicule thrown on his own plays by the Rehearsal, drove him to adopt a very different, though not altogether faultless, style of tragedy. His principal works of this latter class are All for Love, in 1678, the Spanish Friar, commonly referred to 1682, and Don Sebastian, in 1690. Upon these the dramatic fame of Dryden is built; while the rants of Almanzor and Maximin are never mentioned but in ridicule. The chief excellence of the first tragedy appears to consist in the beauty of the language, that of the second in the interest of the story, and that of the third in the highly finished character of Dorax. Dorax is the best of Dryden's tragic characters, and perhaps the only one in which he has applied his great knowledge of the human mind to actual delineation. It is highly dramatic, because formed of those complex passions which may readily lead either to virtue or to vice, and which the poet can manage so as to surprise the spectator without transgressing consistency. The Zanga of Young, a part of some theatrical effect, has been compounded of this character, and of that of Iago. But Don Sebastian Don Sebastian. is as imperfect as all plays must be in which a single personage is thrown forward in too strong relief for the rest. The language is full of that rant which characterised Dryden's earlier tragedies, and to which a natural predilection seems, after some interval, to have brought him back. Sebastian himself may seem to have been intended as a contrast to Muley Moloch; but if the author had any rule to distinguish the blustering of the hero from that of the tyrant, he has not left the use of it in his reader's hands. The plot of this tragedy is ill conducted, especially in the fifth act. Perhaps the delicacy of the present age may have been too fastidious in excluding altogether from the drama this class of fables; because they may often excite great interest, give scope to impassioned poetry, and are admirably calculated for the ἀναγνώρισις, or discovery, which is so much dwelt upon by the critics; nor can the story of Œdipus, which has furnished one of the finest and most artful tragedies ever written, be well thought an improper subject even for representation. But they require, of all others, to be dexterously managed; they may make the main distress of a tragedy, but not an episode in it. Our feelings revolt at seeing, as in Don Sebastian, an incestuous passion brought forward as the make-weight of a plot, to eke out a fifth act, and to dispose of those characters whose fortune the main story has not quite wound up.

44. The Spanish Friar has been praised for what Johnson calls the " happy coincidence and coalition of the two plots." It is difficult to understand what can be meant by a compliment which seems either ironical or ignorant. Nothing can be more remote from the truth. The artifice of combining two distinct stories on the stage is, we may suppose, either to interweave the incidents of one into those of the other, or at least so to connect some characters with each intrigue, as to make the spectator fancy them less distinct than they are. Thus in the Merchant of Venice, the courtship of Bassanio and Portia is happily connected with the main plot of Antonio and Shylock by two circumstances: it is to set Bassanio forward in his suit that the fatal bond is first given; and it is by Portia's address that its forfeiture is explained away. The same play affords an instance of another kind of underplot, that of Lorenzo and Jessica, which is more episodical, and might perhaps be removed without any material loss to the fable; though even this serves to account for, we do not say to palliate, the vindictive exasperation of the Jew. But to which of these do the comic scenes in the Spanish Friar bear most resemblance? Certainly to the latter. They consist entirely of an intrigue which Lorenzo, a young officer, carries on with a rich usurer's wife; but there is not, even by accident, any relation between his adventures and the love and murder which go forward in the palace. The Spanish Friar, so far as it is a comedy, is reckoned the best performance of Dryden in that line. Father Dominic is very amusing, and has been copied very freely by succeeding dramatists, especially in the Duenna. But Dryden has no great abundance of wit in

this or any of his comedies. His jests are practical, and he seems to have written more for the eye than the ear. It may be noted as a proof of this, that his stage directions are unusually full. In point of diction, the Spanish Friar in its tragic scenes, and All for Love, are certainly the best plays of Dryden. They are the least infected with his great fault, bombast, and should perhaps be read over and over by those who would learn the true tone of English tragedy. In dignity, in animation, in striking images and figures, there are few or none that excel them; the power indeed of impressing sympathy, or commanding tears, was seldom placed by nature within the reach of Dryden.

45. The Orphan of Otway, and his Venice Preserved, will generally be reckoned the best tragedies of this period. They have both a deep pathos, *Otway.* springing from the intense and unmerited distress of women; both, especially the latter, have a dramatic eloquence, rapid and flowing, with less of turgid extravagance than we find in Otway's contemporaries, and sometimes with very graceful poetry. The story of the Orphan is domestic, and borrowed, as I believe, from some French novel, though I do not at present remember where I have read it; it was once popular on the stage, and gave scope for good acting, but is unpleasing to the delicacy of our own age. Venice Preserved is more frequently represented than any tragedy after those of Shakspeare; the plot is highly dramatic in conception and conduct; even what seems, when we read it, a defect, the shifting of our wishes, or perhaps rather of our ill wishes, between two parties, the senate and the conspirators, who are redeemed by no virtue, does not, as is shown by experience, interfere with the spectator's interest. Pierre indeed is one of those villains for whom it is easy to excite the sympathy of the half-principled and the inconsiderate. But the great attraction is in the character of Belvidera; and when that part is represented by such as we remember to have seen, no tragedy is honoured by such a tribute, not of tears alone, but of more agony than many would seek to endure. The versification of Otway, like that of most in this period, runs almost to an excess into the

line of eleven syllables, sometimes also into the *sdrucciolo* form, or twelve syllables with a dactylic close. These give a considerable animation to tragic verse.

46. Southern's Fatal Discovery, latterly represented
Southern. under the name of Isabella, is almost as familiar to the lovers of our theatre as Venice Preserved itself; and for the same reason, that whenever an actress of great tragic powers arises, the part of Isabella is as fitted to exhibit them as that of Belvidera. The choice and conduct of the story are, however, Southern's chief merits; for there is little vigour in the language, though it is natural, and free from the usual faults of his age. A similar character may be given to his other tragedy, Oroonoko; in which Southern deserves the praise of having, first of any English writer, denounced the traffic in slaves, and the cruelties of their West Indian bondage. The moral feeling is high in this tragedy, and it has sometimes been acted with a certain success; but the execution is not that of a
Lee. superior dramatist. Of Lee nothing need be said, but that he is, in spite of his proverbial extravagance, a man of poetical mind and some dramatic skill. But he has violated historic truth in Theodosius without gaining much by invention. The Mourning
Congreve. Bride of Congreve is written in prolix declamation, with no power over the passions. Johnson is well known to have praised a few lines in this tragedy as among the finest descriptions in the language; while others, by a sort of contrariety, have spoken of them as worth nothing. Truth is in its usual middle path; many better passages may be found, but they are well written and impressive.[k]

47. In the early English comedy, we find a large in-
Comedies of Chas. II.'s reign. termixture of obscenity in the lower characters, nor always confined to them, with no infrequent scenes of licentious incident and language. But these are invariably so brought forward as to manifest the dramatist's scorn of vice, and to excite no other sentiment in a spectator of even an ordinary degree of moral purity. In the plays that appeared after the Restoration, and that from the beginning, a

---

[k] Mourning Bride, act ii. scene 3; Johnson's Life of Congreve.

different tone was assumed. Vice was in her full career on the stage, unchecked by reproof, unshamed by contrast, and for the most part unpunished by mortification at the close. Nor are these less coarse in expression, or less impudent in their delineation of low debauchery, than those of the preceding period. It may be observed, on the contrary, that they rarely exhibit the manners of truly polished life, according to any notions we can frame of them, and are, in this respect, much below those of Fletcher, Massinger, and Shirley. It might not be easy perhaps to find a scene in any comedy of Charles II.'s reign where one character has the behaviour of a gentleman, in the sense which we attach to the word. Yet the authors of these were themselves in the world, and sometimes men of family and considerable station. The cause must be found in the state of society itself, debased as well as corrupted, partly by the example of the court, partly by the practice of living in taverns, which became much more inveterate after the Restoration than before. The contrast with the manners of Paris, as far as the stage is their mirror, does not tell to our advantage. These plays, as it may be expected, do not aim at the higher glories of comic writing; they display no knowledge of nature, nor often rise to any other conception of character than is gained by a caricature of some known class, or perhaps of some remarkable individual. Nor do they in general deserve much credit as comedies of intrigue; the plot is seldom invented with much care for its development; and if scenes follow one another in a series of diverting incidents, if the entanglements are such as produce laughter, above all, if the personages keep up a well-sustained battle of repartee, the purpose is sufficiently answered. It is in this that they often excel; some of them have considerable humour in the representation of character, though this may not be very original, and a good deal of wit in their dialogue.

48. Wycherley is remembered for two comedies, the Plain Dealer, and the Country Wife, the latter *Wycherley.* represented with some change, in modern times, under the name of the Country Girl. The former has been frequently said to be taken from the Misanthrope of Molière; but this, like many current asser-

tions, seems to have little if any foundation. Manly, the Plain Dealer, is, like Alceste, a speaker of truth; but the idea is at least one which it was easy to conceive without plagiarism, and there is not the slightest resemblance in any circumstance or scene of the two comedies. We cannot say the same of the Country Wife; it was evidently suggested by L'Ecole des Femmes; the character of Arnolphe has been copied; but even here the whole conduct of the piece of Wycherley is his own. It is more artificial than that of Molière, wherein too much passes in description; the part of Agnes is rendered still more poignant; and among the comedies of Charles's reign, I am not sure that it is surpassed by any.

49. Shadwell and Etherege, and the famous Afra Behn, have endeavoured to make the stage as grossly immoral as their talents permitted; but the two former, especially Shadwell, are not destitute of humour. At the death of Charles it had reached the lowest point; after the Revolution, it became not much more a school of virtue, but rather a better one of polished manners than before; and certainly drew to its service some men of comic genius whose names are now not only very familiar to our ears, as the boasts of our theatre, but whose works have not all ceased to enliven its walls.

Improvement after the Revolution.

50. Congreve, by the Old Bachelor, written, as some have said, at twenty-one years of age, but in fact not quite so soon, and represented in 1693, placed himself at once in a rank which he has always retained. Though not, I think, the first, he is undeniably among the first names. The Old Bachelor was quickly followed by the Double Dealer, and that by Love for Love, in which he reached the summit of his reputation. The last of his four comedies, the Way of the World, is said to have been coldly received; for which it is hard to assign any substantial cause, unless it be some want of sequence in the plot. The peculiar excellence of Congreve is his wit, incessantly sparkling from the lips of almost every character, but on this account it is accompanied by want of nature and simplicity. Nature indeed and simplicity do not belong as proper attributes to that comedy which, itself the crea-

Congreve.

ture of an artificial society, has for its proper business
to exaggerate the affectation and hollowness of the
world. A critical code which should require the comedy
of polite life to be natural would make it intolerable.
But there are limits of deviation from likeness which
even caricature must not transgress; and the type of
truth should always regulate the playful aberrations of
an inventive pencil. The manners of Congreve's comedies are not, to us at least, like those of reality; I am
not sure that we have any cause to suppose that they
much better represent the times in which they appeared.
His characters, with an exception or two, are heartless
and vicious; which, on being attacked by Collier, he
justified, probably by an afterthought, on the authority
of Aristotle's definition of comedy; that it is $\mu\iota\mu\eta\sigma\iota\varsigma$
$\phi\alpha\upsilon\lambda\sigma\tau\acute{\epsilon}\rho\omega\nu$, an imitation of what is the worse in human
nature.[m] But it must be acknowledged that, more than
any preceding writer among us, he kept up the tone of
a gentleman; his men of the world are profligate, but
not coarse; he rarely, like Shadwell, or even Dryden,
caters for the populace of the theatre by such indecencies as they must understand; he gave, in fact, a
tone of refinement to the public taste, which it never
lost, and which, in its progression, has almost banished
his own comedies from the stage.

51. Love for Love is generally reputed the best of
these. Congreve has never any great success *Love for*
in the conception or management of his plot; *Love.*
but in this comedy there is least to censure; several of
the characters are exceedingly humorous; the incidents
are numerous and not complex; the wit is often admirable. Angelica and Miss Prue, Ben and Tattle, have
been repeatedly imitated; but they have, I think, a
considerable degree of dramatic originality in themselves. Johnson has observed that " Ben the sailor is
not reckoned over natural, but he is very diverting."
Possibly he may be quite as natural a portrait of a mere
sailor, as that to which we have become used in modern
comedy.

52. The Way of the World I should perhaps incline
to place next to this; the coquetry of Milla- *His other*
mant, not without some touches of delicacy and *comedies.*

[m] Congreve's Amendments of Mr. Collier's false citations.

affection, the impertinent coxcombry of Petulant and Witwood, the mixture of wit and ridiculous vanity in Lady Wishfort, are amusing to the reader. Congreve has here made more use than, as far as I remember, had been common in England, of the all-important soubrette, on whom so much depends in French comedy. The manners of France happily enabled her dramatists to improve what they had borrowed with signal success from the ancient stage, the witty and artful servant, faithful to his master while he deceives every one besides, by adding this female attendant, not less versed in every artifice, nor less quick in repartee. Mincing and Foible, in this play of Congreve, are good specimens of the class; but speaking with some hesitation, I do not think they will be found, at least not so naturally drawn, in the comedies of Charles's time. Many would, perhaps not without cause, prefer the Old Bachelor, which abounds with wit, but seems rather deficient in originality of character and circumstance. The Double Dealer is entitled to the same praise of wit, and some of the characters, though rather exaggerated, are amusing; but the plot is so entangled towards the conclusion, that I have found it difficult,. even in reading, to comprehend it.

53. Congreve is not superior to Farquhar and Van-
Farquhar. brugh, if we might compare the whole of their
Vanbrugh. works. Never has he equalled in vivacity, in originality of contrivance, or in clear and rapid development of intrigue, the Beaux' Stratagem of the one, and much less the admirable delineation of the Wronghead family in the Provoked Husband of the other. But these were of the eighteenth century. Farquhar's Trip to the Jubilee, though once a popular comedy, is not distinguished by more than an easy flow of wit, and perhaps a little novelty in some of the characters; it is indeed written in much superior language to the plays anterior to the Revolution. But the Relapse and the Provoked Wife of Vanbrugh have attained a considerable reputation. In the former, the character of Amanda is interesting, especially in the momentary wavering and quick recovery of her virtue. This is the first homage that the theatre had paid, since the Restoration, to female chastity; and notwithstanding the vicious

tone of the other characters, in which Vanbrugh has gone as great lengths as any of his contemporaries, we perceive the beginnings of a re-action in public spirit, which gradually reformed and elevated the moral standard of the stage." The Provoked Wife, though it cannot be said to give any proofs of this sort of improvement, has some merit as a comedy; it is witty and animated, as Vanbrugh usually was; the character of Sir John Brute may not have been too great a caricature of real manners, such as survived from the debased reign of Charles; and the endeavour to expose the grossness of the older generation was itself an evidence that a better polish had been given to social life.

" This purification of English comedy has sometimes been attributed to the effects of a famous essay by Collier on the immorality of the English stage. But if public opinion had not been prepared to go along, in a considerable degree, with Collier, his animadversions could have produced little change. In point of fact, the subsequent improvement was but slow, and, for some years, rather shown in avoiding coarse indecencies than in much elevation of sentiment. Steele's Conscious Lovers is the first comedy which can be called moral ; Cibber, in those Parts of the Provoked Husband [that he wrote, carried this farther, and the stage afterwards grew more and more refined, till it became languid and sentimental.

CHAPTER VII.

HISTORY OF POLITE LITERATURE IN PROSE FROM 1650 TO 1700.

~~~~~~~~~~~~~~~~

SECTION I.

Italy — High Refinement of French Language — Fontenelle — St. Evremond — Sévigné — Bouhours and Rapin — Miscellaneous writers — English Style — and Criticism — Dryden.

1. IF Italy could furnish no long list of conspicuous
Low state of literature in Italy. names in this department of literature to our last period, she is far more deficient in the present. The Prose Fiorentine of Dati, a collection of what seemed the best specimens of Italian eloquence in this century, served chiefly to prove its mediocrity, nor has that editor, by his own panegyric on Louis XIV. or any other of his writings, been able to redeem its name.[a] The sermons of Segneri have already been mentioned; the eulogies bestowed on them seem to be founded, in some measure, on the surrounding barrenness. The letters of Magalotti, and still more of Redi, themselves philosophers, and generally writing on philosophy, seem to do more credit than anything else to this period.[b]

2. Crescimbeni, the founder of the Arcadian Society,
Crescimbeni. has made an honourable name by his exertions to purify the national taste, as well as by his diligence in preserving the memory of better ages than his own. His History of National Poetry is a laborious and useful work, to which I have sometimes been indebted. His treatise on the beauty of that poetry is only known to me through Salfi. It is written in dialogue, the speakers being Arcadians. Anxious to extir-

---

[a] Salfi, xiv. 25; Tiraboschi, xi. 412.   [b] Salfi, xiv. 17; Corniani, viii. 71.

pate the school of the Marinists, without falling back altogether into that of Petrarch, he set up Costanzo as a model of poetry. Most of his precepts, Salfi observes, are very trivial at present; but at the epoch of its appearance his work was of great service towards the reform of Italian literature.[c]

3. This period, the second part of the seventeenth century, comprehends the most considerable, and in every sense the most important and distinguished portion of what was once called the great age in France, the reign of Louis XIV. In this period the literature of France was adorned by its most brilliant writers; since, notwithstanding the genius and popularity of some who followed, we generally find a still higher place awarded by men of fine taste to Bossuet and Pascal than to Voltaire and Montesquieu. The language was written with a care that might have fettered the powers of ordinary men, but rendered those of such as we have mentioned more resplendent. The laws of taste and grammar, like those of nature, were held immutable; it was the province of human genius to deal with them, as it does with nature, by a skilful employment, not by a preposterous and ineffectual rebellion against their control. Purity and perspicuity, simplicity and ease, were conditions of good writing; it was never thought that an author, especially in prose, might transgress the recognised idiom of his mother-tongue, or invent words unknown to it, for the sake of effect or novelty; or, if in some rare occurrence so bold a course might be forgiven, these exceptions were but as miracles in religion, which would cease to strike us, or be no miracles at all, but for the regularity of the laws to which they bear witness even while they infringe them. We have not thought it necessary to defer the praise which some great French writers have deserved on the score of their language for this chapter. Bossuet, Malebranche, Arnauld, and Pascal, have already been commemorated; and it is sufficient to point out two causes in perpetual operation during this period which ennobled and preserved in purity the literature of France; one, the salutary influence of the Academy, the other, that

Age of Louis XIV. in France.

---

[c] Salfi, xiii. 450.

emulation between the Jesuits and Jansenists for public esteem, which was better displayed in their politer writings than in the abstruse and endless controversy of the five propositions. A few remain to be mentioned; and as the subject of this chapter, in order to avoid frequent subdivisions, is miscellaneous, the reader must expect to find that we do not, in every instance, confine ourselves to what he may consider as polite letters.

4. Fontenelle, by the variety of his talents, by their
Fontenelle application to the pursuits most congenial to
—his cha- the intellectual character of his contemporaries,
racter. and by that extraordinary longevity which made those contemporaries not less than three generations of mankind, may be reckoned the best representative of French literature. Born in 1657, and dying within a few days of a complete century, in 1757, he enjoyed the most protracted life of any among the modern learned; and that a life in the full sunshine of Parisian literature, without care and without disease. In nothing was Fontenelle a great writer; his mental and moral disposition resembled each other; equable, without the capacity of performing, and hardly of conceiving, anything truly elevated, but not less exempt from the fruits of passion, from paradox, unreasonableness, and prejudice. His best productions are, perhaps, the eulogies on the deceased members of the Academy of Sciences, which he pronounced during almost forty years, but these nearly all belong to the eighteenth century; they are just and candid, with sufficient, though not very profound, knowledge of the exact sciences, and a style pure and flowing, which his good sense had freed from some early affectation, and his cold temper as well as sound understanding restrained from extravagance. In his first works we have symptoms of an infirmity belonging more frequently to age than to youth; but Fontenelle was never young in passion. He there affects the tone of somewhat pedantic and frigid gallantry which seems to have survived the society of the Hôtel Rambouillet who had countenanced it, and which borders too nearly on the language which Molière and his disciples had well exposed in their coxcombs on the stage.

5. The Dialogues of the Dead, published in 1683, are

condemned by some critics for their false taste and perpetual strain at something unexpected and pa-   His Dia-
radoxical. The leading idea is, of course, bor-   logues of
rowed from Lucian ; but Fontenelle has aimed   the Dead.
at greater poignancy by contrast ; the ghosts in his dialogues are exactly those who had least in common with
each other in life, and the general object is to bring,
by some happy analogy which had not occurred to the
reader, or by some ingenious defence of what he had
been accustomed to despise, the prominences and de-
pressions of historic characters to a level. This is what
is always well received in the kind of society for which
Fontenelle wrote ; but if much is mere sophistry in his
dialogues, if the general tone is little above that of the
world, there is also, what we often find in the world,
some acuteness and novelty, and some things put in a
light which it may be worth while not to neglect.

6. Fenelon, not many years afterwards, copied the
scheme, though not the style, of Fontenelle in   Those of
his own Dialogues of the Dead, written for the   Fenelon.
use of his pupil the Duke of Burgundy. Some of these
dialogues are not truly of the dead ; the characters speak
as if on earth, and with earthly designs. They have
certainly more solid sense and a more elevated morality
than those of Fontenelle, to which La Harpe has preferred them. The noble zeal of Fenelon not to spare
the vices of kings, in writing for the heir of one so imperious and so open to the censure of reflecting minds,
shines throughout these dialogues ; but designed as they
were for a boy, they naturally appear in some places
rather superficial.

7. Fontenelle succeeded better in his famous dialogues
on the Plurality of Worlds, Les Mondes ; in   Fonte-
which, if the conception is not wholly original,   nelle's
he has at least developed it with so much spirit   Plurality of
and vivacity, that it would show as bad taste   Worlds.
to censure his work, as to reckon it a model for imitation. It is one of those happy ideas which have been
privileged monopolies of the first inventor ; and it will be
found accordingly that all attempts to copy this whim-
sical union of gallantry with science have been insipid
almost to a ridiculous degree. Fontenelle throws so
much gaiety and wit into his compliments to the lady

whom he initiates into his theory, that we do not confound them with the nonsense of coxcombs; and she is herself so spirited, unaffected, and clever, that no philosopher could be ashamed of gallantry towards so deserving an object. The fascinating paradox, as then it seemed, though our children are now taught to lisp it, that the moon, the planets, the fixed stars, are full of inhabitants, is presented with no more show of science than was indispensable, but with a varying liveliness that, if we may judge by the consequences, has served to convince as well as amuse. The plurality of worlds had been suggested by Wilkins, and probably by some Cartesians in France; but it was first rendered a popular tenet by this agreeable little book of Fontenelle, which had a great circulation in Europe. The ingenuity with which he obviates the difficulties that he is compelled to acknowledge, is worthy of praise; and a good deal of the popular truths of physical astronomy is found in these dialogues.

8. The History of Oracles, which Fontenelle published His History in 1687, is worthy of observation as a sign of of Oracles. the change that was working in literature. In the provinces of erudition and of polite letters, long so independent, perhaps even so hostile, some tendency towards a coalition began to appear. The men of the world especially, after they had acquired a free temper of thinking in religion, and become accustomed to talk about philosophy, desired to know something of the questions which the learned disputed; but they demanded this knowledge by a short and easy road, with no great sacrifice of their leisure or attention. Fontenelle, in the History of Oracles, as in the dialogues on the Plurality of Worlds, prepared a repast for their taste. A learned Dutch physician, Van Dale, in a dull work, had taken up the subject of the ancient oracles, and explained them by human imposture instead of that of the devil, which had been the more orthodox hypothesis. A certain degree of paradox, or want of orthodoxy, already gave a zest to a book in France; and Fontenelle's lively manner, with more learning than good society at Paris possessed, and about as much as it could endure, united to a clear and acute line of argument, created a popu-

larity for his History of Oracles, which we cannot reckon altogether unmerited.[d]

9. The works of St. Evremond were collected after his death in 1705; but many had been printed before, and he evidently belongs to the latter half of the seventeenth century. The fame of St. Evremond as a brilliant star, during a long life, in the polished aristocracy of France and England, gave for a time a considerable lustre to his writings, the greater part of which are such effusions as the daily intercourse of good company called forth. In verse or in prose, he is the gallant friend, rather than lover, of ladies who, secure probably of love in some other quarter, were proud of the friendship of a wit. He never, to do him justice, mistakes his character, which, as his age was not a little advanced, might have incurred ridicule. Hortense Mancini, Duchess of Mazarin, is his heroine; but we take little interest in compliments to a woman neither respected in her life, nor remembered since. Nothing can be more trifling than the general character of the writings of St. Evremond; but sometimes he rises to literary criticism, or even civil history; and on such topics he is clear, unaffected, cold, without imagination or sensibility; a type of the frigid being whom an aristocratic and highly polished society is apt to produce. The chief merit of St. Evremond is in his style and manner. He has less wit than Voiture, who contributed to form him, or than Voltaire, whom he contributed to form; but he shows neither the effort of the former, nor the restlessness of the latter. Voltaire, however, when he is most quiet, as in the earliest and best of his historical works, seems to bear a considerable resemblance to St. Evremond, and there can be no doubt that he was familiar with the latter's writings.

St. Evre-
mond.

10. A woman has the glory of being full as conspicuous in the graces of style as any writer of this famous age. It is evident that this was Madame de Sévigné. Her letters indeed were not published till the eighteenth century, but they were written in the mid-day of Louis's reign. Their ease and free-

Madame
de Sévigné.

---

d I have not compared, or indeed read, some of the reasoning, not the learning, Dale's work; but I rather suspect that of Fontenelle is original.

dom from affectation are more striking by contrast with
the two epistolary styles which had been most admired
in France, that of Balzac, which is laboriously tumid,
and that of Voiture, which becomes insipid by dint of
affectation.   Every one perceîves that in the Letters of
a mother to her daughter the public, in a strict sense, is
not thought of; and yet the habit of speaking and writing what men of wit and taste would desire to hear and
read, gives a certain mannerism, I will not say air of
effort, even to the letters of Madame de Sévigné.   The
abandonment of the heart to its casual impulses is not
so genuine as in some that have since been published.
It is at least clear that it is possible to become affected
in copying her unaffected style; and some of Walpole's
letters bear witness to this.   Her wit and talent of
painting by single touches are very eminent; scarcely
any collection of letters, which contain so little that can
interest a distant age, are read with such pleasure; if
they have any general fault, it is a little monotony and
excess of affection towards her daughter, which is repo-
ported to have wearied its object, and, in contrast with
this, a little want of sensibility towards all beyond her
immediate friends, and a readiness to find something
ludicrous in the dangers and sufferings of others.*

11. The French Academy had been so judicious both
The French in the choice of its members, and in the general
Academy.   tenor of its proceedings, that it stood very high
in public esteem, and a voluntary deference was commonly shown to its authority.   The favour of Louis
XIV., when he grew to manhood, was accorded as amply
as that of Richelieu.   The Academy was received by

---

* The proofs of this are numerous
enough in her letters.   In one of them
she mentions, that a lady of her acquaintance, having been bitten by a mad
dog, had gone to be dipped in the sea,
and amuses herself by taking off the
provincial accent with which she will
express herself on the first plunge.   She
makes a jest of La Voisin's execution;
and though that person was as little
entitled to sympathy as any one, yet,
when a woman is burned alive, it is not
usual for another woman to turn it into
drollery.

Madame de Sévigné's taste has been
arraigned for slighting Racine; and she
has been charged with the unfortunate
prediction: Il passera comme le café.
But it is denied that these words can be
found, though few like to give up so
diverting a miscalculation of futurity.
In her time, Corneille's party was so
well supported, and he deserved so much
gratitude and reverence, that we cannot
much wonder at her being carried a little
too far against his rival.   Who has ever
seen a woman just towards the rivals
of her friends, though many are just
towards their own?

the king, when they approached him publicly, with the same ceremonies as the superior courts of justice. This body had, almost from its commencement, undertaken a national dictionary, which should carry the language to its utmost perfection, and trace a road to the highest eloquence that depended on purity and choice of words; more than this could not be given by man. The work proceeded very slowly; and dictionaries were published in the mean time, one by Richelet in 1680, another by Furetière. The former seems to be little more than a glossary of technical or otherwise doubtful words; [f] but the latter, though pretending to contain only terms of art and science, was found, by its definitions and by the authorities it quoted, to interfere so much with the project of the academicians, who had armed themselves with an exclusive privilege, that they not only expelled Furetière from their body, on the allegation that he had availed himself of materials entrusted to him by the Academy for its own dictionary, but instituted a long process at law to hinder its publication. This was in 1685, and the dictionary of Furetière only appeared after his death at Amsterdam in 1690.[g] Whatever may have been the delinquency, moral or legal, of this compiler, his dictionary is praised by Goujet as a rich treasure, in which almost everything is found that we can desire for a sound knowledge of the language. It has been frequently reprinted, and continued long in esteem. But the dictionary of the Academy, which was published in 1694, claimed an authority to which that of a private man could not pretend. Yet the first edition seems to have rather disappointed the public expectation. Many objected to the want of quotations, and to the observance of an orthography that had become obsolete. The Academy undertook a revision of its work in 1700; and finally, profiting by the public opinion on which it endeavoured to act, rendered this dictionary the most received standard of the French language.[h]

12. The Grammaire Générale et Raisonnée of Lancelot, in which Arnauld took a considerable share, French Grammars. is rather a treatise on the philosophy of all

[f] Goujet, Baillet, n. 762.
[g] Pelisson, Hist. de l'Académie (continuation par Olivet), p. 47. Goujet.
Bibliothèque Française, i. 232, et post. Biogr. Univers., art. Furetière.
[h] Pelisson, p. 69; Goujet, p. 261.

language than one peculiar to the French. "The best critics," says Baillet, "acknowledge that there is nothing written by either the ancient or the modern grammarians with so much justness and solidity."[i] Vigneul-Marville bestows upon it an almost equal eulogy.[k] Lancelot was copied in a great degree by Lami, in his Rhetoric or Art of Speaking, with little of value that is original.[m] Vaugelas retained his place as the founder of sound grammatical criticism, though his judgments have not been uniformly confirmed by the next generation. His remarks were edited with notes by Thomas Corneille, who had the reputation of an excellent grammarian.[n] The observations of Ménage on the French language, in 1675 and 1676, are said to have the fault of reposing too much on obsolete authorities, even those of the sixteenth century, which had long been proscribed by a politer age.[o] Notwithstanding the zeal of the Academy, no critical laws could arrest the revolutions of speech. Changes came in with the lapse of time, and were sanctioned by the imperious rule of custom. In a book on grammar, published as early as 1688, Balzac and Voiture, even Patru and the Port-Royal writers, are called semi-moderns;[p] so many new phrases had since made their way into composition, so many of theirs had acquired a certain air of antiquity.

13. The genius of the French language, as it was esti-

Bouhours' Entretiens d'Ariste et d'Eugène.

mated in this age by those who aspired to the character of good critics, may be learned from one of the dialogues in a work of Bouhours, Les Entretiens d'Ariste et d'Eugène. Bouhours was a Jesuit, who affected a polite and lively tone, according to the fashion of his time, so as to warrant some degree of ridicule; but a man of taste and judgment, whom, though La Harpe speaks of him with disdain, his contemporaries quoted with respect. The first, and the most interesting at present, of these conversations, which are feigned to take place between two gentlemen of literary taste, turns on the French language.[q] This he

i Jugemens des Sçavans, n. 606. Goujet copies Baillet's words.
k Mélanges de Littérature, i. 124.
m Goujet, i. 56 ; Gibert, p. 351.
n Goujet, 146 ; Biogr. Univ.

o Id. 153.
p Bibliothèque Universelle, xv. 351. Perrault makes a similar remark on Patru.
q Bouhours points out several inno-

presumes to be the best of all modern—deriding the
Spanish for its pomp, the Italian for its finical effeminacy.' The French has the secret of uniting brevity
with clearness and purity with politeness. The Greek
and Latin are obscure where they are concise. The
Spanish is always diffuse. The Spanish is a turbid torrent, often overspreading the country with great noise ;
the Italian a gentle rivulet, occasionally given to inun-
date its meadows ; the French a noble river, enriching
the adjacent lands, but with an equal majestic course of
waters that never quits its level.' Spanish again he com-
pares to an insolent beauty, that holds her head high,
and takes pleasure in splendid dress ; Italian to a painted
coquette, always attired to please ; French to a modest
and agreeable lady, who, if you may call her a prude,
has nothing uncivil or repulsive in her prudery. Latin
is the common mother ; but while Italian has the sort
of likeness to Latin which an ape bears to a man, in
French we have the dignity, politeness, purity, and
good sense of the Augustan age. The French have rejected almost all the diminutives once in use, and do not,
like the Italians, admit the right of framing others. This
language does not tolerate rhyming sounds in prose, nor
even any kind of assonance, as *amertume* and *fortune*, near
together. It rejects very bold metaphors, as the zenith
of virtue, the *apogée* of glory ; and it is remarkable that
its poetry is almost as hostile to metaphor as its prose.'
" We have very few words merely poetical, and the language of our poets is not very different from that of the
world. Whatever be the cause, it is certain that a figurative style is neither good among us in verse nor in
prose." This is evidently much exaggerated, and in
contradiction to the known examples, at least, of dramatic poetry. All affectation and labour, he proceeds to

vations which had lately come into use.
He dislikes *avoir des ménagemens*, or
avoir de la considération, and thinks
these phrases would not last ; in which
he was mistaken. *Tour de visage* and
tour d'esprit were new : the words *fonds*,
mesures, *amitiés*, *compte*, and many more,
were used in new senses. Thus also
assez and *trop* ; as the phrase *je ne suis
pas trop de votre avis*. It seems on reflection, that some of the expressions he

animadverts upon must have been affected while they were new, being in opposition to the correct meaning of words ;
and it is always curious, in other languages as well as our own, to observe
the comparatively recent *nobility* of
many things quite established by present
usage. Entretiens d'Ariste et d'Eugène,
p. 95.

r P. 52 (edit. 1671).
s P. 77.   t P. 60.

say, are equally repugnant to a good French style. "If we would speak the language well, we should not try to speak it too well. It detests excess of ornament; it would almost desire that words should be as it were naked; their dress must be no more than necessity and decency require. Its simplicity is averse to compound words; those adjectives which are formed by such a juncture of two have long been exiled both from prose and verse." "Our own pronunciation," he affirms, " is the most natural and pleasing of any. The Chinese and other Asiatics sing; the Germans rattle (rallent); the Spaniards spout; the Italians sigh; the English whistle; the French alone can properly be said to speak; which arises, in fact, from our not accenting any syllable before the penultimate. The French language is best adapted to express the tenderest sentiments of the heart; for which reason our songs are so impassioned and pathetic, while those of Italy and Spain are full of nonsense. Other languages may address the imagination, but ours alone speaks to the heart, which never understands what is said in them."[u] This is literally amusing; and with equal patriotism Bouhours, in another place, has proposed the question, whether a German can, by the nature of things, possess any wit.

14. Bouhours, not deficient, as we may perceive, in self-confidence and proneness to censure, pre-

Attacked by Barbier d'Aucour. sumed to turn into ridicule the writers of Port-Royal, at that time of such distinguished reputation as threatened to eclipse the credit which the Jesuits had always preserved in polite letters. He alludes to their long periods, and the exaggerated phrases of invective which they poured forth in controversy.[x] But the Jansenist party was well able to defend itself. Barbier d'Aucour retaliated on the vain Jesuit by his Sentimens de Cleanthe sur les Entretiens

---

[u] P. 68.

[x] P. 150. Vigneul-Marville observes that the Port-Royal writers formed their style originally on that of Balzac (vol. 1. p. 107); and that M. d'Andilly, brother of Antony Arnauld, affected at one time a grand and copious manner like the Spaniards, as being more serious and imposing, especially in devotional writings; but afterwards finding the French were impatient of this style, that party abandoned it for one more concise, which it is by no means less difficult to write well, p. 139. Baillet seems to refer their love of long periods to the famous advocate Le Maistre, who had employed them in his pleadings, not only as giving more dignity, but also because the public taste at that time favoured them. Jugemens des Sçavans, n. 953.

d'Ariste et d'Eugène.   It seems to be the general opinion
of French critics, that he has well exposed the weak
parts of his adversary, his affected air of the world, the
occasional frivolity and feebleness of his observations;
yet there seems something morose in the censures of
the supposed Cleanthe, which renders this book less
agreeable than that on which it animadverts.

15. Another work of criticism by Bouhours, La Manière de Bien Penser, which is also in dialogue, *La Manière*
contains much that shows acuteness and deli- *de Bien*
cacy of discrimination, though his taste was *Penser.*
deficient in warmth and sensibility, which renders him
somewhat too strict and fastidious in his judgments.
He is an unsparing enemy of obscurity, exaggeration,
and nonsense, and laughs at the hyperbolical language
of Balzac, while he has rather overpraised Voiture.[y] The
affected, inflated thoughts, of which the Italian and Spanish writers afford him many examples, Bouhours justly
condemns, and by the correctness of his judgment may
deserve, on the whole, a respectable place in the second
order of critics.

16. The Réflexions sur l'Eloquence et sur la Poësie of
Rapin, another Jesuit, whose Latin poem on *Rapin's Re-*
Gardens has already been praised, are judi- *flections on*
cious, though perhaps rather too diffuse; his *Eloquence*
criticism is what would appear severe in our *and Poetry.*
times; but it was that of a man formed by the ancients,
and who lived also in the best and most critical age of
France.   The reflections on poetry are avowedly founded

[y] Voiture, he says, always takes a tone
of raillery when he exaggerates.   Le
faux devient vrai à la faveur de l'ironie,
p. 29.   But we can hardly think that
Balzac was not gravely ironical in some
of the strange hyperboles which Bouhours quotes from him.

In the fourth dialogue, Bouhours has
many just observations on the necessity
of clearness.   An obscurity arising from
allusion to things now unknown, such as
we find in the ancients, is rather a misfortune than a fault; but this is no excuse
for one which may be avoided, and arises
from the writer's indistinctness of conception or language.   Cela n'est pas intelligible, dit Philinthe (after hearing a
foolish rhapsody extracted from a funeral

sermon on Louis XIII.).   Non, répon-
dit Eudoxe, ce n'est pas tout-à-fait de
galimatias, ce n'est que du phébus.
Vous mettez donc, dit Philinthe, de la
différence entre le galimatias et le phébus?   Oui, repartit Eudoxe, le galimatias
renferme une obscurité profonde, et n'a
de soi-même nul sens raisonnable.   Le
phébus n'est pas si obscur, et a un bril-
lant qui signifie, ou semble signifier,
quelque chose; le soleil y entre d'or-
dinaire, et c'est peut-être ce qui a donné
lieu en notre langue au nom de phébus.
Ce n'est pas que quelquefois le phébus
ne devienne obscur, jusqu'à n'être pas
entendu; mais alors le galimatias s'en
joint; ce ne sont que brillans et que
ténèbres de tous côtés.   p. 342.

on Aristotle, but with much that is new, and with examples from modern poets to confirm and illustrate it. The practice at this time in France was to depreciate the Italians; and Tasso is often the subject of Rapin's censure; for want, among other things, of that grave and majestic character which epic poetry demands. Yet Rapin is not so rigorous, but that he can blame the coldness of modern precepts in regard to French poetry. After condemning the pompous tone of Brebœuf in his translation of the Pharsalia, he remarks that "we have gone since to an opposite extreme by too scrupulous a care for the purity of the language; for we have begun to take from poetry its force and dignity by too much reserve and a false modesty, which we have established as characteristics of our language, so as to deprive it of that judicious boldness which true poetry requires; we have cut off the metaphors and all those figures of speech which give force and spirit to words, and reduced all the artifices of words to a pure, regular style, which exposes itself to no risk by bold expression. The taste of the age, the influence of women who are naturally timid, that of the court which had hardly anything in common with the ancients, on account of its usual antipathy for learning, accredited this manner of writing."[x] In this Rapin seems to glance at the polite but cold criticism of his brother Jesuit, Bouhours.

17. Rapin, in another work of criticism, the Parallels His Paral- of Great Men of Antiquity, has weighed in the leis of scales of his own judgment Demosthenes and Great Men. Cicero, Homer and Virgil, Thucydides and Livy, Plato and Aristotle. Thus eloquence, poetry, history, and philosophy pass under review. The taste of Rapin is for the Latins; Cicero he prefers to Demosthenes, Livy on the whole to Thucydides, though this he leaves more to the reader; but is confident that none except mere grammarians have ranked Homer above Virgil.[a] The loquacity of the older poet, the frequency of his moral reflections, which Rapin thinks misplaced in an epic poem, his similes, the sameness of his transitions, are treated very freely; yet he gives him the preference over Virgil for grandeur and nobleness of nar-

[x] P. 147. [a] P. 158.

ration, for his epithets, and the splendour of his language. But he is of opinion that Æneas is a much finer character than Achilles. These two epic poets he holds, however, to be the greatest in the world ; as for all the rest, ancient and modern, he enumerates them one after another, and can find little but faults in them all.[b] Nor does he esteem dramatic and lyric poets, at least modern, much better.

18. The treatise on Epic Poetry by Bossu was once of some reputation. An English poet has thought fit to say that we should have stared, like Indians, at Homer, if Bossu had not taught us to understand him.[c] The book is, however, long since forgotten ; and we fancy that we understand Homer not the worse. It is in six books, which treat of the fable, the action, the narration, the manners, the machinery, the sentiments and expressions of an epic poem. Homer is the favourite poet of Bossu, and Virgil next to him ; this preference of the superior model does him some honour in a generation which was becoming insensible to its excellence. Bossu is judicious and correct in taste, but without much depth, and he seems to want the acuteness of Bouhours.

19. Fontenelle is a critic of whom it may be said, that he did more injury to fine taste and sensibility in works of imagination and sentiment than any man without his good sense and natural acuteness could have done. He is systematically cold ; if he seems to tolerate any flight of the poet, it is rather by caprice than by a genuine discernment of beauty ; but he clings, with the unyielding claw of a cold-blooded animal, to the faults of great writers, which he exposes with reason and sarcasm. His Reflections on Poetry relate mostly to dramatic composition, and to that of the French stage. Theocritus is his victim in the Dissertation on Pastoral Poetry ; but Fontenelle gave the Sicilian his revenge ; he wrote pastorals himself ; and we have altogether forgotten, or, when we again look at, can very partially approve, the idylls of the Boulevards, while those Doric

Bossu on epic poetry.

Fontenelle's critical writings.

b P. 175.

c Had Bossu never writ, the world had still,

Like Indians, view'd this mighty piece of wit.
MULGRAVE's *Essay on Poetry.*

dactyls of Theocritus linger still, like what Schiller has called soft music of yesterday, from our schoolboy reminiscences on our aged ears.

20. The reign of mere scholars was now at an end ;
no worse name than that of pedant could be

Preference of French language to Latin. imposed on those who sought for glory ; the admiration of all that was national in arts, in arms, in manners, as well as in speech, carried away like a torrent those prescriptive titles to reverence which only lingered in colleges. The superiority of the Latin language to French had long been contested ; even Henry Stephens has a dissertation in favour of the latter ; and in this period, though a few resolute scholars did not retire from the field, it was generally held either that French was every way the better means of expressing our thoughts, or at least so much more convenient as to put nearly an end to the use of the other. Latin had been the privileged language of stone ; but Louis XIV., in consequence of an essay by Charpentier, in 1676, replaced the inscriptions on his triumphal arches by others in French.[d] This of course does not much affect the general question between the two languages.

21. But it was not in language alone that the ancients were to endure the aggression of a disobedient

General superiority of ancients disputed. posterity. It had long been a problem in Europe whether they had not been surpassed —one perhaps which began before the younger generations could make good their claim. But time, the nominal ally of the old possessors, gave his more powerful aid to their opponents ; every age saw the proportions change, and new men rise up to strengthen the ranks of the assailants. In mathematical science, in natural knowledge, the ancients had none but a few mere pedants, or half-read lovers of paradox, to maintain their superiority ; but in the beauties of language, in eloquence and poetry, the suffrage of criticism had long been theirs. It seemed time to dispute even this. Charles

Charles Perrault. Perrault, a man of some learning, some variety of acquirement, and a good deal of ingenuity and quickness, published, in 1687, his famous " Parallel of the Ancients and Moderns in all that regards Arts

d Goujet, i. 13.

and Sciences." This is a series of dialogues, the parties being, first, a president, deeply learned and prejudiced in all respects for antiquity; secondly, an abbé, not ignorant, but having reflected more than read, cool and impartial, always made to appear in the right, or, in other words, the author's representative; thirdly, a man of the world, seizing the gay side of every subject, and apparently brought in to prevent the book from becoming dull. They begin with architecture and painting, and soon make it clear that Athens was a mere heap of pigsties in comparison with Versailles; the ancient painters fare equally ill. They next advance to eloquence and poetry, and here, where the strife of war is sharpest, the defeat of antiquity is chanted with triumph. Homer, Virgil, Horace, are successively brought forward for severe and often unjust censure : but of course it is not to be imagined that Perrault is always in the wrong; he had to fight against a pedantic admiration which surrenders all judgment; and having found the bow bent too much in one way, he forced it himself too violently into another direction. It is the fault of such books to be one-sided; they are not unfrequently right in censuring blemishes, but very uncandid in suppressing beauties. Homer has been worst used by Perrault, who had not the least power of feeling his excellence; but the advocate of the newer age in his dialogue admits that the Æneid is superior to any modern epic. In his comparison of eloquence Perrault has given some specimens of both sides in contrast; comparing, by means however of his own versions, the funeral orations of Pericles and Plato with those of Bourdaloue, Bossuet, and Fléchier, the description by Pliny of his country seat with one by Balzac, an epistle of Cicero with another of Balzac. These comparisons were fitted to produce a great effect among those who could neither read the original text, nor place themselves in the midst of ancient feelings and habits. It is easy to perceive that a vast majority of the French in that age would agree with Perrault; the book was written for the times.

22. Fontenelle, in a very short digression on the ancients and moderns, subjoined to his Discourse on Pastoral Poetry, followed the steps of Perrault. "The whole question as to pre-eminence be-

Fontenelle.

x 2

tween the ancients and moderns," he begins, "reduces itself into another, whether the trees that used to grow in our woods were larger than those which grow now. If they were, Homer, Plato, Demosthenes, cannot be equalled in these ages; but if our trees are as large as trees were of old, then there is no reason why we may not equal Homer, Plato, and Demosthenes." The sophistry of this is glaring enough; but it was logic for Paris. In the rest of this short essay there are the usual characteristics of Fontenelle, cool good sense, and an incapacity, by natural privation, of feeling the highest excellence in works of taste.

23. Boileau, in observations annexed to his translation
Boileau's defence of antiquity. of Longinus, as well as in a few sallies of his poetry, defended the great poets, especially Homer and Pindar, with dignity and moderation; freely abandoning the cause of antiquity where he felt it to be untenable. Perrault replied with courage, a quality meriting some praise where the adversary was so powerful in sarcasm and so little accustomed to spare it; but the controversy ceased in tolerable friendship.

24. The knowledge of new accessions to literature
First Reviews— Journal des Sçavans. which its lovers demanded had hitherto been communicated only through the annual catalogues published at Frankfort or other places. But these lists of title-pages were unsatisfactory to the distant scholar, who sought to become acquainted with the real progress of learning, and to know what he might find it worth while to purchase. Denis de Sallo, a member of the parliament of Paris, and not wholly undistinguished in literature, though his other works are not much remembered, by carrying into effect a happy project of his own, gave birth, as it were, to a mighty spirit which has grown up in strength and enterprise, till it has become the ruling power of the literary world. Monday, the 5th of January, 1665, is the date of the first number of the first review, the Journal des Sçavans, published by Sallo under the name of the Sieur de Hedouville, which some have said to be that of his servant.*

---

* Camusat, in his Histoire Critique des Journaux, in two volumes, 1734, which, notwithstanding its general title, is chiefly confined to the history of the Journal des Sçavans, and wholly to such as appeared in France, has not been able to clear up this interesting point; for there are not wanting those who assert

It was printed weekly, in a duodecimo or sexto-decimo form, each number containing from twelve to sixteen pages. The first book ever reviewed (let us observe the difference of subject between that and the last, whatever the last may be) was an edition of the works of Victor Vitensis and Vigilius Tapsensis, African bishops of the fifth century, by Father Chiflet, a Jesuit.[f] The second is Spelman's Glossary. According to the prospectus prefixed to the Journal des Sçavans, it was not designed for a mere review, but a literary miscellany; composed, in the first place, of an exact catalogue of the chief books which should be printed in Europe; not content with the mere titles, as the majority of bibliographers had hitherto been, but giving an account of their contents, and their value to the public; it was also to contain a necrology of distinguished authors, an account of experiments in physics and chemistry, and of new discoveries in arts and sciences, with the principal decisions of civil and ecclesiastical tribunals, the decrees of the Sorbonne and other French or foreign universities; in short, whatever might be interesting to men of letters. We find therefore some piece of news, more or less of a literary or scientific nature, subjoined to each number. Thus in the first number we have a double-headed child born near Salisbury; in the second, a question of legitimacy decided in the parliament of Paris; in the third, an experiment on a new ship or boat constructed by Sir William Petty; in the fourth, an account of a discussion in the college of Jesuits on the nature of comets. The scientific articles, which bear a large proportion to the rest, are illustrated by engravings. It was complained that the Journal des Sçavans did not pay much regard to polite or amusing literature; and this led to the publication of the Mercure Galant, by Visè, which gave reviews of poetry and of the drama.

25. Though the notices in the Journal des Sçavans are

that Hedouville was the name of an estate belonging to Sallo; and he is called in some public description, without reference to the Journal, Dominus de Sallo d'Hedouville in Parisiensi curia senator. Camusat, i. 13. Notwithstanding this, there is evidence that leads us to the valet; so that " amplius deliberandum censeo; Res magna est."

[f] Victoria Vitensis et Vigilii Tapsensis, Provinciæ Bisacenæ Episcoporum Opera, edente R. P. Chifletio, Soc. Jesu. Presb., in 4to. Divione. The critique, if such it be, occupies but two pages in small duodecimo. That on Spelman's Glossary, which follows, is but in half a page.

very short, and when they give any character, for the most part of a laudatory tone, Sallo did not fail to raise up enemies by the mere assumption of power which a reviewer is prone to affect. Menage, on a work of whose he had made some criticism, and by no means, as it appears, without justice, replied in wrath; Patin and others rose up as injured authors against the self-erected censor; but he made more formidable enemies by some rather blunt declarations of a Gallican feeling, as became a counsellor of the parliament of Paris, against the court of Rome; and the privilege of publication was soon withdrawn from Sallo.[g] It is said that he had the spirit to refuse the offer of continuing the journal under a previous censorship; and it passed into other hands, those of Gallois, who continued it with great success.[h] It is remarkable that the first review, within a few months of its origin, was silenced for assuming too imperious an authority over literature, and for speaking evil of dignities. " In cunis jam Jove dignus erat." The Journal des Sçavans, incomparably the most ancient of living reviews, is still conspicuous for its learning, its candour, and its freedom from those stains of personal and party malice which deform more popular works.

26. The path thus opened to all that could tempt a man who made writing his profession—profit, celebrity, a perpetual appearance in the public eye, the facility of pouring forth every scattered thought of his own, the power of revenge upon every enemy—could not fail to tempt more conspicuous men than Sallo or his successor Gallois. Two of very high reputation, at least of reputation that hence became very high, entered it, Bayle and Le Clerc. The former, in 1684, commenced a new review, Nouvelles de la République des Lettres. He saw, and was well able to improve, the opportunities which periodical criticism furnished to a mind eminently qualified for it; extensively, and, in some points, deeply learned; full of wit, acuteness, and a happy talent of writing in a lively tone

Reviews established by Bayle.

---

[g] Camusat, p. 23. Sallo had also attacked the Jesuits.

[h] 'Eloge de Gallois, par Fontenelle, in the latter's works, vol. v. p. 168. Biographie Universelle, arts. Sallo and Gallois. Gallois is said to have been a coadjutor of Sallo from the beginning, and some others are named by Camusat as its contributors, among whom were Gomberville and Chapelain.

without the insipidity of affected politeness. The scholar and philosopher of Rotterdam had a rival, in some respects, and ultimately an adversary, in a neighbouring city. Le Clerc, settled at Amsterdam as professor of belles lettres and of Hebrew in the Arminian seminary, undertook in 1686, at the age of twenty-nine, the first of those three celebrated series of reviews, to which he owes so much of his fame. This was the Bibliothèque Universelle, in all the early volumes of which La Croze, a much inferior person, was his coadjutor, published monthly in a very small form. Le Clerc had afterwards a disagreement with La Croze, and the latter part of the Bibliothèque Universelle (that after the tenth volume) is chiefly his own. It ceased to be published in 1693; and the Bibliothèque Choisie, which is, perhaps, even a more known work of Le Clerc, did not commence till 1703. But the fulness, the variety, the judicious analysis and selection, as well as the value of the original remarks, which we find in the Bibliothèque Universelle, render it of signal utility to those who would embrace the literature of that short but not unimportant period which it illustrates.

27. Meantime a less brilliant, but by no means less erudite, review, the Leipsic Acts, had commenced in Germany. The first volume of this series was published in 1682. But being written in Latin, with more regard to the past than to the growing state of opinions, and consequently almost excluding the most attractive, and, indeed, the most important subjects, with a Lutheran spirit of unchangeable orthodoxy in religion, and with an absence of anything like philosophy or even connected system in erudition, it is one of the most unreadable books, relatively to its utility in learning, which has ever fallen into my hands. Italy had entered earlier on this critical career; the Giornale de' Litterati was begun at Rome in 1668; the Giornale Veneto de' Litterati at Venice in 1671. They continued for some time, but with less conspicuous reputation than those above mentioned. The Mercure Savant, published at Amsterdam in 1684, was an indifferent production, which induced Bayle to set up his own Nouvelles de la République des Lettres in opposition to it. Two reviews were commenced in the German language within

the seventeenth century, and three in English. The first
of these latter was the Weekly Memorials for the Ingenious, London, 1682.   This, I believe, lasted but a short
time.   It was followed by one entitled The Works of the
Learned, in 1691 ; and by another, called History of the
Works of the Learned, in 1699.[i]

28. Bayle had first become known in 1682 by the

Bayle's
Thoughts
on the
Comet.

Pensées Diverses sur la Comète de 1680 ; a
work which I am not sure that he ever decidedly
surpassed.   Its purpose is one hardly worthy,
we should imagine, to employ him ; since those
who could read and reason were not likely to be afraid
of comets, and those who could do neither would be little
the better for his book.   But with this ostensible aim
Bayle had others in view ; it gave scope to his keen
observation of mankind, if we may use the word observation for that which he chiefly derived from modern books,
and to the calm philosophy which he professed.   There
is less of the love of paradox, less of a cavilling pyrrhonism, and though much diffuseness, less of pedantry and
irrelevant instances in the Pensées Diverses than in his
greater work.   It exposed him, however, to controversy ;
Jurieu, a French minister in Holland, the champion of
Calvinistic orthodoxy, waged a war that was only terminated with their lives ; and Bayle's defence of the
Thoughts on the Comet is full as long as the original performance, but far less entertaining.

29. He now projected an immortal undertaking, the

His Dic-
tionary.

Historical and Critical Dictionary.   Moreri, a
laborious scribe, had published, in 1673, a kind

---

i Jugler, Hist. Litteraria, cap. 9.
Bibliothèque Universelle, xiii. 41.—
[The first number of Weekly Memorials
for the Ingenious is dated Jan. 16, 1681-
2, and the first book reviewed is, Chris-
tiani Liberti Βιβλιοφιλια, Utrecht, 1681.
The editor proposes to transcribe from
the Journal des Sçavans whatever is
most valuable, and by far the greater
part of the articles relate to foreign
books.   This review seems to have lasted
but a year ; at least there is only one
volume in the British Museum.   The
Universal Historical Bibliothèque, which
began in January, 1686, and expired in
March, is scarcely worth notice : it is
professedly a compilation from the foreign reviews.   The History of the
Works of the Learned, published monthly
from 1699 to 1711, is much more respectable ; though in this also a very
large proportion is given to foreign
works, and probably on the credit of con-
tinental journals.   The books reviewed
are numerous and commonly of a learned
class.   The accounts given of them are
chiefly analytical, the reviewer seldom
interposing his judgment : if any bias is
perceptible, it is towards what was then
called the liberal side ; but for the most
part the rule adopted is to speak favour-
ably of every one.—1842.]

of encyclopedic dictionary, biographical, historical, and geographical ; Bayle professed to fill up the numerous deficiencies, and to rectify the errors of this compiler.   It is hard to place his dictionary, which appeared in 1694, under any distinct head in a literary classification which does not make a separate chapter for lexicography.   It is almost equally difficult to give a general character of this many-coloured web, which great erudition and still greater acuteness and strength of mind wove for the last years of the seventeenth century.   The learning of Bayle was copious, especially in what was most peculiarly required, the controversies, the anecdotes, the miscellaneous facts and sentences, scattered over the vast surface of literature for two preceding centuries.   In that of antiquity he was less profoundly versed, yet so quick in application of his classical stores that he passes for a better scholar than he was.   His original design may have been only to fill up the deficiencies of Moreri ; but a mind so fertile and excursive could not be restrained in such limits.   We may find, however, in this an apology for the numerous omissions of Bayle, which would, in a writer absolutely original, seem both capricious and unaccountable.   We never can anticipate with confidence that we shall find any name in his dictionary.   The notes are most frequently unconnected with the life to which they are appended ; so that, under a name uninteresting to us, or inapposite to our purpose, we may be led into the richest vein of the author's fine reasoning or lively wit.   Bayle is admirable in exposing the fallacies of dogmatism, the perplexities of philosophy, the weaknesses of those who affect to guide the opinions of mankind. But, wanting the necessary condition of good reasoning, an earnest desire to reason well, a moral rectitude from which the love of truth must spring, he often avails himself of petty cavils, and becomes dogmatical in his very doubts.   A more sincere spirit of inquiry could not have suffered a man of his penetrating genius to acquiesce, even contingently, in so superficial a scheme as the Manichean.   The sophistry of Bayle, however, bears no proportion to his just and acute observations.   Still less excuse can be admitted for his indecency, which almost assumes the character of monomania, so invariably does it recur, even where there is least pretext for it.

30. The Jugemens des Sçavans by Baillet, published in 1685 and 1686, the Polyhistor of Morhof in 1689, are certainly works of criticism as well as of bibliography. Baillet. Morhof. But neither of these writers, especially the latter, are of much authority in matters of taste; their erudition was very extensive, their abilities respectable, since they were able to produce such useful and comprehensive works; but they do not greatly serve to enlighten or correct our judgments, nor is the original matter in any considerable proportion to that which they have derived from others. I have taken notice of both these in my preface.

31. France was very fruitful of that miscellaneous The Ana. literature which, desultory and amusing, has the advantage of remaining better in the memory than more systematic books, and in fact is generally found to supply the man of extensive knowledge with the materials of his conversation, as well as to fill the vacancies of his deeper studies. The memoirs, the letters, the travels, the dialogues, and essays which might be ranged in so large a class as that we now pass in review, are too numerous to be mentioned, and it must be understood that most of them are less in request even among the studious than they were in the last century. One group has acquired the distinctive name of Ana; the reported conversation, the table-talk of the learned. Several of these belong to the last part of the sixteenth century, or the first of the next; the Scaligerana, the Perroniana, the Pithæana, the Naudæana, the Casauboniana; the last of which are not conversational, but fragments collected from the common-place books and loose papers of Isaac Casaubon. Two collections of the present period are very well known; the Menagiana, and the Mélanges de Littérature par Vigneul-Marville; which differs, indeed, from the rest in not being reported by others, but published by the author himself, yet comes so near in spirit and manner that we may place it in the same class. The Menagiana has the common fault of these Ana, that it rather disappoints expectation, and does not give us as much new learning as the name of its author seems to promise; but it is amusing, full of light anecdote of a literary kind, and interesting to all who love the recollections of that generation. Vigneul-Mar-

ville is an imaginary person;' the author of the Mélanges de Littérature is D'Argonne, a Benedictine of Rouen. This book has been much esteemed; the mask gives courage to the author, who writes not unlike a Benedictine, but with a general tone of independent thinking, united to good judgment and a tolerably extensive knowledge of the state of literature. He had entered into the religious profession rather late in life. The Chevræana and Segraisiana, especially the latter, are of little value. The Parrhasiana of Le Clerc are less amusing and less miscellaneous than some of the Ana; but in all his writings there is a love of truth and a zeal against those who obstruct inquiry, which to congenial spirits is as pleasing as it is sure to render him obnoxious to opposite tempers.

32. The characteristics of English writers in the first division of the century were not maintained in the second, though the change, as was natural, did not come on by very rapid steps. The pedantry of unauthorised Latinisms, the affectation of singular and not generally intelligible words from other sources, the love of quaint phrases, strange analogies, and ambitious efforts at antithesis, gave way by degrees; a greater ease of writing was what the public demanded, and what the writers after the Restoration sought to attain; they were more strictly idiomatic and English than their predecessors. But this ease sometimes became negligence and feebleness, and often turned to coarseness and vulgarity. The language of Sévigné and Hamilton is eminently colloquial; scarce a turn occurs in their writings which they would not have used in familiar society; but theirs was the colloquy of the gods, ours of men: their idiom, though still simple and French, had been refined in the saloons of Paris, by that instinctive rejection of all that is low which the fine tact of accomplished women dictates; while in our own contemporary writers, with little exception, there is what defaces the dialogue of our comedy, a tone not so much of provincialism, or even of what is called the language of the common people, as of one much worse, the dregs of vulgar ribaldry, which a gentleman must clear from his conversation before he can assert that name. Nor was this confined to those who

led irregular lives; the general manners being unpolished, we find in the writings of the clergy, wherever they are polemic or satirical, the same tendency to what is called *slang*; a word which, as itself belongs to the vocabulary it denotes, I use with some unwillingness. The pattern of bad writing in this respect was Sir Roger L'Estrange; his Æsop's Fables will present everything that is hostile to good taste; yet by a certain wit and readiness in raillery L'Estrange was a popular writer, and may even now be read, perhaps, with some amusement. The translation of Don Quixote, published in 1682, may also be specified as incredibly vulgar, and without the least perception of the tone which the original author has preserved.

33. We can produce nevertheless several names of those who laid the foundations at least, and in-

Hobbes.

deed furnished examples, of good style; some of them among the greatest, for other merits, in our literature. Hobbes is perhaps the first of whom we can strictly say that he is a good English writer; for the excellent passages of Hooker, Sidney, Raleigh, Bacon, Taylor, Chillingworth, and others of the Elizabethan or the first Stuart period are not sufficient to establish their claim; a good writer being one whose composition is nearly uniform, and who never sinks to such inferiority or negligence as we must confess in most of these. To make such a writer, the absence of gross faults is full as necessary as actual beauties; we are not judging as of poets, by the highest flight of their genius, and for-giving all the rest, but as of a sum of positive and nega-tive quantities, where the latter counterbalance and efface an equal portion of the former. Hobbes is clear, precise, spirited, and, above all, free, in general, from the faults of his predecessors; his language is sensibly less obsolete; he is never vulgar, rarely, if ever, quaint or pedantic.

34. Cowley's prose, very unlike his verse, as Johnson

Cowley.

has observed, is perspicuous and unaffected. His few essays may even be reckoned among the earliest models of good writing. In that, especially, on the death of Cromwell, till, losing his composure, he falls a little into the vulgar style towards the close, we find an absence of pedantry, an ease and graceful choice of idiom, an unstudied harmony of periods, which had been perceived in very few writers of the two preceding reigns. " His thoughts," says Johnson, " are natural, and his style has a smooth and placid equability which has never yet attained its due commendation. Nothing is far-sought or hard-laboured; but all is easy without feebleness, and familiar without grossness."

35. Evelyn wrote in 1651 a little piece, purporting to be an account of England by a Frenchman. It is very severe on our manners, especially in London; his abhorrence of the late revolutions in church and state conspiring with his natural politeness, which he had lately improved by foreign travel. It is worth reading as illustrative of social history; but I chiefly mention it here on account of the polish and gentlemanly elegance of the style, which very few had hitherto regarded in such light compositions. An answer by some indignant patriot has been reprinted together with this pamphlet of Evelyn, and is a good specimen of the bestial ribaldry which our ancestors seem to have taken for wit.[k] The later writings of Evelyn are such as his character and habits would lead us to expect, but I am not aware that they often rise above that respectable level, nor are their subjects such as to require an elevated style. *Evelyn.*

36. Every poem and play of Dryden, as they successively appeared, was ushered into the world by one of those prefaces and dedications which have made him celebrated as a critic of poetry and a master of the English language. The Essay on Dramatic Poesy, and its subsequent Defence, the Origin and Progress of Satire, the Parallel of Poetry and Painting, the Life of Plutarch, and other things of minor importance, all prefixed to some more extensive work, complete the catalogue of his prose. The style of Dryden was very superior to any that England had seen. Not conversant with our old writers, so little, in fact, as to find the common phrases of the Elizabethan age unintelligible,[m] he followed the taste of Charles's reign in emu- *Dryden.*

---

k Both these will be found in the late edition of Evelyn's Miscellaneous Works.
m Malone has given several proofs of this. Dryden's Prose Works, vol. i. part 2, p. 136, et alibi. Dryden thought expressions wrong and incorrect in Shakspeare and Jonson, which were the current language of their age.

lating the politest and most popular writers in the
French language.   He seems to have formed himself on
Montaigne, Balzac, and Voiture; but so ready was his
invention, so vigorous his judgment, so complete his
mastery over his native tongue, that, in point of style, he
must be reckoned above all the three.   He had the ease
of Montaigne without his negligence and embarrassed
structure of periods; he had the dignity of Balzac, with
more varied cadences, and without his hyperbolical
tumour; the unexpected turns of Voiture without his
affectation and air of effort.   In the dedications, especially, we find paragraphs of extraordinary gracefulness,
such as possibly have never been surpassed in our language.   The prefaces are evidently written in a more
negligent style; he seems, like Montaigne, to converse
with the reader from his arm-chair, and passes onward
with little connexion from one subject to another.[a]   In
addressing a patron, a different line is observable; he
comes with the respectful air which the occasion seems
to demand; but, though I do not think that Dryden
ever, in language, forgets his own position, we must
confess that the flattery is sometimes palpably untrue,
and always offensively indelicate.   The dedication of
the Mock Astrologer to the Duke of Newcastle is a masterpiece of fine writing; and the subject better deserved
these lavish commendations than most who received
them.   That of the State of Innocence to the Duchess of
York is also very well written; but the adulation is
excessive.   It appears to me that, after the Revolution,
Dryden took less pains with his style; the colloquial
vulgarisms, and these are not wanting even in his
earlier prefaces, become more frequent; his periods are
often of more slovenly construction; he forgets even in
his dedications that he is standing before a lord.   Thus,
remarking on the account Andromache gives to Hector
of her own history, he observes, in a style rather unworthy of him, " The devil was in Hector if he knew
not all this matter as well as she who told it him, for she
had been his bed-fellow for many years together; and if
he knew it then, it must be confessed that Homer in

---

[a] This is his own account.   " The
nature of a preface is rambling, never
wholly out of the way, nor in it. . .
This I have learned from the practice of
honest Montaigne."   Vol. iii. p. 605.

this long digression has rather given us his own character than that of the fair lady whom he paints." [o]

37. His Essay on Dramatic Poesy, published in 1668, was reprinted sixteen years afterwards, and it is curious to observe the changes which Dryden made in the expression. Malone has carefully noted all these; they show both the care the author took with his own style, and the change which was gradually working in the English language.[p] The Anglicism of terminating the sentence with a preposition is rejected.[q] Thus " I cannot think so contemptibly of the age I live in," is exchanged for " the age in which I live." " A deeper expression of belief than all the actor can persuade us to," is altered, " can insinuate into us." And, though the old form continued in use long after the time of Dryden, it has of late years been reckoned inelegant, and proscribed in all cases, perhaps with an unnecessary fastidiousness, to which I have not uniformly deferred; since our language is of a Teutonic structure, and the rules of Latin or French grammar are not always to bind us.

His Essay on Dramatic Poesy.

38. This Essay on Dramatic Poesy is written in dialogue; Dryden himself, under the name of Neander, being probably one of the speakers. It turns on the use of rhyme in tragedy, on the observation of the unities, and on some other theatrical questions. Dryden, at this time, was favourable to rhymed tragedies, which his practice supported. Sir Robert Howard having written some observations on that essay, and taken a different view as to rhyme, Dryden published a defence of his essay in a masterly style of cutting scorn, but one hardly justified by the tone of the criticism, which had been very civil towards him; and as he was apparently in the wrong, the air of superiority seems the more misplaced.

Improvements in his style.

o Vol. iii. p. 286. This is in the dedication of his third Miscellany to Lord Ratcliffe.

P Vol. i. pp. 136-142.

q " The preposition in the end of the sentence, a common fault with him (Ben Jonson), and which I have but lately observed in my own writings," p. 237. The form is, in my opinion, sometimes emphatic and spirited, though its frequent use appears slovenly. I remember my late friend, Mr. Richard Sharp, whose good taste is well known, used to quote an interrogatory of Hooker: " Shall there be a God to swear by, and none to pray to?" as an instance of the force which this arrangement, so eminently idiomatic, sometimes gives. In the passive voice, I think it better than in the active; nor can it always be dispensed with, unless we choose rather the feeble encumbering pronoun *which*.

39. Dryden, as a critic, is not to be numbered with
those who have sounded the depths of the human
mind, hardly with those who analyse the language and sentiments of poets, and teach others to judge
by showing why they have judged themselves.   He
scatters remarks sometimes too indefinite, sometimes too
arbitrary; yet his predominating good sense colours the
whole; we find in them no perplexing subtilty, no
cloudy nonsense, no paradoxes and heresies in taste to
revolt us.   Those he has made on translation in the
preface to that of Ovid's Epistles are valuable.   "No
man," he says, "is capable of translating poetry, who,
besides a genius *to* that art, is not a master both of his
author's language and of his own.   Nor must we understand the language only of the poet, but his particular
turn of thoughts and expression, which are the characters
that distinguish and as it were individuate him from all
other writers." [r]   We cannot pay Dryden the compliment
of saying that he gave the example as well as precept,
especially in his Virgil.   He did not scruple to copy
Segrais in his discourse on Epic Poetry.   "Him I follow,
and what I borrow from him am ready to acknowledge
to him; for, impartially speaking, the French are as
much better critics than the English as they are worse
poets." [s]

40. The greater part of his critical writings relates to
the drama, a subject with which he was very conversant;
but he had some considerable prejudices: he seems never
to have felt the transcendent excellence of Shakspeare;
and sometimes perhaps his own opinions, if not feigned,
are biassed by that sort of self-defence to which he
thought himself driven in the prefaces to his several
plays.   He had many enemies on the watch: the Duke
of Buckingham's Rehearsal, a satire of great wit, had
exposed to ridicule the heroic tragedies, [t] and many were
afterwards ready to forget the merits of the poet in the
delinquencies of the politician.   "What Virgil wrote,"

[r] Vol. iii. p. 19.
[s] P. 460.
[t] This comedy was published in 1672;
the parodies are amusing; and though
parody is the most unfair weapon that
ridicule can use, they are in most instances warranted by the original. Bayes,
whether he resembles Dryden or not, is
a very comic personage: the character is
said by Johnson to have been sketched
for Davenant, but I much doubt this
report. Davenant had been dead some
years before the Rehearsal was published, and could have been in no way
obnoxious to its satire.

he says, " in the vigour of his age, in plenty and in ease, I have undertaken to translate in my declining years; struggling with wants, oppressed by sickness, curbed in my genius, liable to be misconstrued in all I write; and my judges, if they are not very equitable, already prejudiced against me by the lying character which has been given them of my morals." [u]

41. Dryden will hardly be charged with abandoning too hastily our national credit, when he said the French were better critics than the English. We had scarcely anything worthy of notice to allege beyond his own writings. The Theatrum Poetarum by Philips, nephew of Milton, is superficial in every respect. Thomas Rymer, best known to mankind as the editor of the Fœdera, but a strenuous advocate for the Aristotelian principles in the drama, published in 1678, " The Tragedies of the last Age considered and examined by the Practice of the Ancients, and by the Common Sense of all Ages." This contains a censure of some plays of Beaumont and Fletcher, Shakspeare and Jonson. " I have chiefly considered the fable or plot, which all conclude to be the soul of a tragedy, which with the ancients is always found to be a reasonable soul, but with us for the most part a brutish, and often worse than brutish." [x] I have read only his criticisms on the Maid's Tragedy, King and No King, and Rollo; and as the conduct and characters of all three are far enough from being invulnerable, it is not surprising that Rymer has often well exposed them.

Rymer on Tragedy.

42. Next to Dryden, the second place among the polite writers of the period from the Restoration to the end of the century has commonly been given to Sir William Temple. His Miscellanies, to which principally this praise belongs, are not recommended by more erudition than a retired statesman might acquire with no great expense of time, nor by much originality of reflection. But if Temple has not profound knowledge, he turns all he possesses well to account; if his thoughts are not very striking, they are commonly just. He has less eloquence than Bolingbroke, but is also free from his restlessness and osten-

Sir William Temple's Essays.

[u] Vol. iii. p. 557.   [x] P. 4.

tation.   Much also, which now appears superficial in Temple's historical surveys, was far less familiar in his age; he has the merit of a comprehensive and a candid mind.   His style, to which we should particularly refer, will be found in comparison with his contemporaries highly polished, and sustained with more equability than they preserve, remote from anything either pedantic or humble.   The periods are studiously rhythmical; yet they want the variety and peculiar charm that we admire in those of Dryden.

43. Locke is certainly a good writer, relatively to the greater part of his contemporaries; his plain and manly sentences often give us pleasure by the wording alone.   But he has some defects; in his Essay on the Human Understanding he is often too figurative for the subject.   In all his writings, and especially in the Treatise on Education, he is occasionally negligent, and though not vulgar, at least according to the idiom of his age, slovenly in the structure of his sentences as well as the choice of his words; he is not, in mere style, very forcible, and certainly not very elegant.

Style of Locke.

44. The Essays of Sir George Mackenzie are empty and diffuse; the style is full of pedantic words to a degree of barbarism; and though they were chiefly written after the Revolution, he seems to have wholly formed himself on the older writers, such as Sir Thomas Browne, or even Feltham.   He affects the obsolete and unpleasing termination of the third person of the verb in *eth*, which was going out of use even in the pulpit, besides other rust of archaism.[y]   Nothing can be more unlike the manner of Dryden, Locke, or Temple.   In his matter he seems a mere declaimer, as if the world would any longer endure the trivial morality which the sixteenth century had borrowed from Seneca, or the dull ethics of sermons.   It is probable that. as Mackenzie was a man who had seen and read much, he must have some better passages than I have found in glancing shortly at his works.   His

Sir George Mackenzie's Essays.

[y] [It must be confessed that instances of this termination, though not frequent, may be found in the first years of George III., or even later. In the auxiliary *hath*, it is scarcely yet disused, at least in very grave writings.   But the unpleasing sound of *th* is a sufficient objection.—1842.]

countryman, Andrew Fletcher, is a better master of English style; he writes with purity, clearness, and spirit; but the substance is so much before his eyes that he is little solicitous about language. And a similar character may be given to many of the political tracts in the reign of William. They are well expressed for their purpose; their English is perspicuous, unaffected, often forcible, and upon the whole much superior to that of similar writings in the reign of Charles; but they do not challenge a place of which their authors never dreamed; they are not to be counted in the polite literature of England.

45. I may have overlooked, or even never known, some books of sufficient value to deserve mention; and I regret that the list of miscellaneous literature should be so short. But it must be confessed that our golden age did not begin before the eighteenth century, and then with him who has never since been rivalled in grace, humour, and invention. Walton's Complete Angler, published in 1653, seems by the title a strange choice out of all the books of half a century; yet its simplicity, its sweetness, its natural grace, and happy intermixture of graver strains with the precepts of angling, have rendered this book deservedly popular, and a model which one of the most famous among our late philosophers, and a successful disciple of Isaac Walton in his favourite art, has condescended to imitate.

46. A book, not indeed remarkable for its style, but one which I could hardly mention in any less miscellaneous chapter than the present, though, since it was published in 1638, it ought to have been mentioned before, is Wilkins's " Discovery of a New World, or a Discourse tending to prove that it is probable there may be another habitable World in the Moon, with a Discourse concerning the Possibility of a Passage thither." This is one of the births of that inquiring spirit, that disdain of ancient prejudice, which the seventeenth century produced. Bacon was undoubtedly the father of it in England; but Kepler, and above all Galileo, by the new truths they demonstrated, made men fearless in investigation and conjecture. The geographical discoveries indeed of Columbus and Ma-

Andrew Fletcher.

Walton's Complete Angler.

Wilkins's New World.

Y 2

gellan had prepared the way for conjectures, hardly more astonishing in the eyes of the vulgar than those had been. Wilkins accordingly begins by bringing a host of sage writers who had denied the existence of antipodes. He expressly maintains the Copernican theory, but admits that it was generally reputed a novel paradox. The arguments on the other side he meets at some length, and knew how to answer, by the principles of compound motion, the plausible objection that stones falling from a tower were not left behind by the motion of the earth. The spots in the moon he took for sea, and the brighter parts for land. A lunar atmosphere he was forced to hold, and gives reasons for thinking it probable. As to inhabitants he does not dwell long on the subject. Campanella, and long before him Cardinal Cusanus, had believed the sun and moon to be inhabited,[*] and Wilkins ends by saying: " Being content for my own part to have spoken so much of it as may conduce to show the opinion of others concerning the inhabitants of the moon, I dare not myself affirm anything of these Selenites, because I know not any ground whereon to build any probable opinion. But I think that future ages will discover more, and our posterity perhaps may invent some means for our better acquaintance with those inhabitants." To this he comes as his final proposition, that it may be possible for some of our posterity to find out a conveyance to this other world; and if there be inhabitants there, to have communication with them. But this chapter is the worst in the book, and shows that Wilkins, notwithstanding his ingenuity, had but crude notions on the principles of physics. He followed this up by what I have not seen, a " Discourse concerning a new Planet; tending to prove that it is possible our Earth is one of the Planets." This appears to be a regular vindication of the Copernican theory, and was published in 1640.

47. The cause of antiquity, so rudely assailed abroad by Perrault and Fontenelle, found support in Sir William Temple, who has defended it in one of his essays with more zeal than prudence

Antiquity defended by Temple.

---

[*] Suspicamur in regione solis magis esse solares, claros et illuminatos intellectuales habitatores, spiritualiores etiam quam in luna, ubi magis lunatici, et in terra magis materiales et crassi, ut illi intellectualis naturæ solares sint multum in actu et parum in potentiâ, terreni vero magis in potentiâ et parum in actu, lunares in medio fluctuantes, &c. Cusanus apud Wilkins, p. 103 (edit. 1802).

or knowledge of the various subjects on which he contends for the rights of the past.   It was in fact such a credulous and superficial view as might have been taken by a pedant of the sixteenth century.   For it is in science, taking the word largely, full as much as in works of genius, that he denies the ancients to have been surpassed.   Temple's Essay, however, was translated into French, and he was supposed by many to have made a brilliant vindication of injured antiquity.   But it was soon refuted in the most solid book that was written in any country, upon this famous dispute.   William Wotton published in 1694 his Reflections on Ancient and Modern Learning.[a]   He draws very well in this the line between Temple and Perrault, avoiding the tasteless judgment of the latter in poetry and eloquence, but pointing out the superiority of the moderns in the whole range of physical science. *(margin: Wotton's Reflections.)*

SECT. II.—ON FICTION.

French Romances — La Fayette and others — Pilgrim's Progress — Turkish Spy.

48.   SPAIN had about the middle of this century a writer of various literature, who is only known in Europe by his fictions, Quevedo.   His visions and his life of the great Tacaño were early translated, and became very popular.[b]   They may be reckoned superior to anything in comic romance, except Don Quixote, that the seventeenth century produced; and yet this commendation is not a high one.   In the picaresque style, the life of Tacaño is tolerably amusing; but Quevedo, like others, has long since been surpassed. The Sueños, or Visions, are better; they show spirit and *(margin: Quevedo's Visions.)*

[a] Wotton had been a boy of astonishing precocity; at six years old he could readily translate Latin, Greek, and Hebrew; at seven he added some knowledge of Arabic and Syriac.   He entered Catherine Hall, Cambridge, in his tenth year; at thirteen, when he took the degree of bachelor of arts, he was acquainted with twelve languages.   There being no precedent of granting a degree to one so young, a special record of his extraordinary proficiency was made in the registers of the university.   Monk's Life of Bentley, p. 7.

[b] The translation of this, " made English by a person of honour," takes great liberties with the original, and endeavours to excel it in wit by means of frequent interpolation.

sharpness with some originality of invention. But Las
Zahurdas de Pluton, which, like the other Visions, bears
a general resemblance to the Pilgrim's Progress, being
an allegorical dream, is less powerfully and graphically
written; the satire is also rather too obvious. "Lucian,"
says Bouterwek, "furnished him with the original idea
of satirical visions; but Quevedo's were the first of their
kind in modern literature. Owing to frequent imitations, their faults are no longer disguised by the charm
of novelty, and even their merits have ceased to interest." [c]

49. No species of composition seems less adapted to
French heroic romances.
the genius of the French nation in the reign of
Louis XIV. than the heroic romances so much
admired in its first years. It must be confessed
that this was but the continuance, and in some respect,
possibly, an improvement of a long-established style of
fiction. But it was not fitted to endure reason or ridicule, and the societies of Paris knew the use of both
weapons. Molière sometimes tried his wit upon the
romances; and Boileau, rather later in the day, when
the victory had been won, attacked Mademoiselle Scuderi
with his sarcastic irony in a dialogue on the heroes of
her invention.

50. The first step in descending from the heroic ro-
Novels of Madame La Fayette.
mance was to ground not altogether dissimilar.
The feats of chivalry were replaced by less
wonderful adventures; the love became less
hyperbolical in expression, though not less intensely
engrossing the personages; the general tone of manners
was lowered down better to that of nature, or at least
of an ideality which the imagination did not reject; a
style already tried in the minor fictions of Spain. The
earliest novels that demand attention in this line are
those of the Countess de la Fayette, celebrated, while
Mademoiselle de la Vergne, under the name of Laverna
in the Latin poetry of Menage.[d] Zayde, the first of

---

[c] Hist. of Spanish Literature, p. 471.

[d] The name Laverna, though well-
sounding, was in one respect unlucky,
being that given by antiquity to the god-
dess of thieves. An epigram on Menage,
almost, perhaps, too trite to be quoted, is
piquant enough:—

Lesbia nulla tibi, nulla est tibi dicta Co-
rinna;
Carmine laudatur Cynthia nulla tuo.
Sed cum doctorum compilas scrinia va-
tum,
Nil mirum, si sit culta Laverna tibi.

these, is entirely in the Spanish style ; the adventures are improbable, but various and rather interesting to those who carry no scepticism into fiction ; the language is polished and agreeable, though not very animated ; and it is easy to perceive that while that kind of novel was popular, Zayde would obtain a high place.   It has, however, the usual faults ; the story is broken by inter-vening narratives, which occupy too large a space ; the sorrows of the principal characters excite, at least as I should judge, little sympathy ; and their sentiments and emotions are sometimes too much refined in the alembic of the Hôtel Rambouillet.   In a later novel, the Princess of Cleves, Madame La Fayette threw off the affectation of that circle to which she had once belonged, and though perhaps Zayde is, or was in its own age, the more celebrated novel, it seems to me that in this she has excelled herself.   The story, being nothing else than the insuperable and insidious, but not guilty, attachment of a married lady to a lover, required a delicacy and correctness of taste which the authoress has well dis-played in it.   The probability of the incidents, the natural course they take, the absence of all complication and perplexity, give such an inartificial air to this novel, that we can scarcely help believing it to shadow forth some real event.   A modern novelist would probably have made more of the story ; the style is always calm, sometimes almost languid ; a tone of decorous politeness, like that of the French stage, is never relaxed ; but it is precisely by this means that the writer has kept up a moral dignity, of which it would have been so easy to lose sight.   The Princess of Cleves is perhaps the first work of mere invention (for though the characters are historical, there is no known foundation for the story) which brought forward the manners of the aristo-cracy ; it may be said, the contemporary manners ; for Madame La Fayette must have copied her own times. As this has become a popular style of fiction, it is just to commemorate the novel which introduced it.

51. The French have few novels of this class in the seventeenth century which they praise ; those of Madame Villedieu, or Des Jardins, may deserve to be excepted ; but I have not seen them.   Scarron, a man deformed and diseased, but en- *Scarron's Roman Comique.*

dowed with vast gaiety, which generally exuberated in buffoon jests, has the credit of having struck out into a new path by his Roman Comique. The Spaniards however had so much like this that we cannot perceive any great originality in Scarron. The Roman Comique is still well known, and if we come to it in vacant moments, will serve its end in amusing us; the story and characters have no great interest, but they are natural; yet, without the least disparagement to the vivacity of Scarron, it is still true that he has been left at an immense distance in observation of mankind, in humorous character, and in ludicrous effect, by the novelists of the eighteenth and nineteenth centuries. It is said that Scarron's romance is written in a pure style; and some have even pretended that he has not been without effect in refining the language. The Roman Bourgeois of Furetière appears to be a novel of middle life; it had some reputation, but I cannot speak of it with any knowledge.

52. Cyrano de Bergerac had some share in directing Cyrano de Bergerac. the public taste towards those extravagances of fancy which were afterwards highly popular. He has been imitated, as some have observed, by Swift and Voltaire, and I should add, to a certain degree, by Hamilton; but all the three have gone far beyond him. He is not himself a very original writer. His Voyage to the Moon, and History of the Empire of the Sun, are manifestly suggested by the True History of Lucian; and he had modern fictions, especially the Voyage to the Moon by Godwin, mentioned in our last volume, which he had evidently read, to imp the wings of an invention not perhaps eminently fertile. Yet Bergerac has the merit of being never wearisome; his fictions are well conceived, and show little effort, which seems also the character of his language in this short piece; though his letters had been written in the worst style of affectation. so as to make us suspect that he was turning the manner of some contemporaries into ridicule. The Segrais. novels of Segrais, such at least as I have seen, are mere pieces of light satire, designed to amuse by transient allusions the lady by whom he was patronised, Mademoiselle de Montpensier. If they deserve any regard at all, it is as links in the history of fiction between the mock-heroic romance, of which

Voiture had given an instance, and the style of fantastic invention, which was perfected by Hamilton.

53. Charles Perrault may, so far as I know, be said to have invented a kind of fiction which became extremely popular, and has had, even after it ceased to find direct imitators, a perceptible influence over the lighter literature of Europe. The idea was original, and happily executed. Perhaps he sometimes took the tales of children, such as the tradition of many generations had delivered them; but much of his fairy machinery seems to have been his own, and I should give him credit for several of the stories, though it is hard to form a guess. He gave to them all a real interest, as far as could be, with a naturalness of expression, an arch naïveté, a morality neither too obvious nor too refined, and a slight poignancy of satire on the world, which render the Tales of Mother Goose almost a counterpart in prose to the Fables of La Fontaine.

Perrault.

54. These amusing fictions caught the fancy of an indolent but not stupid nobility. The court of Versailles and all Paris resounded with fairy tales; it became the popular style for more than half a century. But few of these fall within our limits. Perrault's immediate followers, Madame Murat and the Countess D'Aunoy, especially the latter, have some merit; but they come very short of the happy simplicity and brevity we find in Mother Goose's Tales. It is possible that Count Antony Hamilton may have written those tales which have made him famous before the end of the century, though they were published later. But these, with many admirable strokes of wit and invention, have too forced a tone in both these qualities; the labour is too evident, and, thrown away on such trifling, excites something like contempt; they are written for an exclusive coterie, not for the world; and the world in all such cases will sooner or later take its revenge. Yet Hamilton's tales are incomparably superior to what followed; inventions alternately dull and extravagant; a style negligent or mannered, an immorality passing onward from the licentiousness of the Regency to the debased philosophy of the ensuing age, became the general characteristics of these fictions, which finally expired in the neglect and scorn of the world.

Hamilton.

55. The Télémaque of Fenelon, after being suppressed
Télémaque in France, appeared in Holland clandestinely
of Fenelon. without the author's consent in 1699. It is
needless to say that it soon obtained the admiration of
Europe, and perhaps there is no book in the French
language that has been more read. Fenelon seems to
have conceived that, metre not being essential, as he
assumed, to poetry, he had, by imitating the Odyssey in
Télémaque, produced an epic of as legitimate a character
as his model. But the boundaries between epic poetry,
especially such epics as the Odyssey, and romance were
only perceptible by the employment of verse in the
former; no elevation of character, no ideality of conception, no charm of imagery or emotion had been denied
to romance. The language of poetry had for two centuries been seized for its use. Télémaque must therefore
take its place among romances; but still it is true that
no romance had breathed so classical a spirit, none had
abounded so much with the richness of poetical language
(much, in fact, of Homer, Virgil, and Sophocles having
been woven in with no other change than verbal translation), nor had any preserved such dignity in its circumstances, such beauty, harmony, and nobleness in its
diction. It would be as idle to say that Fenelon was
indebted to D'Urfè and Calprenède, as to deny that some
degree of resemblance may be found in their poetical
prose. The one belonged to the morals of chivalry,
generous but exaggerated; the other to those of wisdom
and religion. The one has been forgotten because its
tone is false; the other is ever admired, and is only less
regarded because it is true in excess, because it contains
too much of what we know. Télémaque, like some other
of Fenelon's writings, is to be considered in reference to
its object; an object of all the noblest, being to form the
character of one to whom many must look up for their
welfare, but still very different from the inculcation of
profound truth. The beauties of Télémaque are very
numerous, the descriptions, and indeed the whole tone
of the book, have a charm of grace something like the
pictures of Guido; but there is also a certain languor
which steals over us in reading, and though there is no
real want of variety in the narration, it reminds us so
continually of its source, the Homeric legends, as to

become rather monotonous. The abandonment of verse has produced too much diffuseness; it will be observed, if we look attentively, that where Homer is circumstantial, Fenelon is more so; in this he sometimes approaches the minuteness of the romancers. But these defects are more than compensated by the moral, and even æsthetic excellence of this romance.

56. If this most fertile province of all literature, as we have now discovered it to be, had yielded so little even in France, a nation that might appear eminently fitted to explore it, down to the close of the seventeenth century, we may be less surprised at the deficiency of our own country. Yet the scarcity of original fiction in England was so great as to be inexplicable by any reasoning. The public taste was not incapable of being pleased; for all the novels and romances of the Continent were readily translated. The manners of all classes were as open to humorous description, the imagination was as vigorous, the heart as susceptible, as in other countries. But not only we find nothing good; it can hardly be said that we find anything at all that has ever attracted notice in English romance. The Parthenissa of Lord Orrery, in the heroic style, and the short novels of Afra Behn, are nearly as many, perhaps, as could be detected in old libraries. We must leave the beaten track before we can place a single work in this class. *Deficiency of English romances.*

57. The Pilgrim's Progress essentially belongs to it, and John Bunyan may pass for the father of our novelists. His success in a line of composition like the spiritual romance or allegory, which seems to have been frigid and unreadable in the few instances where it had been attempted, is doubtless enhanced by his want of all learning and his low station in life. He was therefore rarely, if ever, an imitator; he was never enchained by rules. Bunyan possessed in a remarkable degree the power of representation; his inventive faculty was considerable, but the other is his distinguishing excellence. He saw, and makes us see, what he describes; he is circumstantial without prolixity, and in the variety and frequent change of his incidents never loses sight of the unity of his allegorical fable. His invention was enriched, and rather his choice determined, by one rule *Pilgrim's Progress.*

he had laid down to himself, the adaptation of all the incidental language of Scripture to his own use. There is scarce a circumstance or metaphor in the Old Testament which does not find a place, bodily and literally, in the story of the Pilgrim's Progress ; and this peculiar artifice has made his own imagination appear more creative than it really is. In the conduct of the romance no rigorous attention to the propriety of the allegory seems to have been uniformly preserved. Vanity Fair, or the cave of the two giants, might, for anything we see, have been placed elsewhere ; but it is by this neglect of exact parallelism that he better keeps up the reality of the pilgrimage, and takes off the coldness of mere allegory. It is also to be remembered that we read this book at an age when the spiritual meaning is either little perceived or little regarded. In his language, nevertheless, Bunyan sometimes mingles the signification too much with the fable ; we might be perplexed between the imaginary and the real Christian ; but the liveliness of narration soon brings us back, or did at least when we were young, to the fields of fancy. Yet the Pilgrim's Progress, like some other books, has of late been a little overrated ; its excellence is great, but it is not of the highest rank, and we should be careful not to break down the landmarks of fame, by placing the John Bunyans and the Daniel De Foes among the Dii Majores of our worship.

58. I am inclined to claim for England not the invention, but, for the most part, the composition of another book, which, being grounded on fiction, may be classed here, The Turkish Spy. A secret emissary of the Porte is supposed to remain at Paris in disguise for above forty years, from 1635 to 1682. His correspondence with a number of persons, various in situation, and with whom, therefore, his letters assume various characters, is protracted through eight volumes. Much, indeed most, relates to the history of those times and to the anecdotes connected with it ; but in these we do not find a large proportion of novelty. The more remarkable letters are those which run into metaphysical and theological speculation. These are written with an earnest seriousness, yet with an extraordinary freedom, such as the feigned garb of a Mohammedan could hardly

have exempted from censure in Catholic countries.   Mahmud, the mysterious writer, stands on a sort of eminence above all human prejudice ; he was privileged to judge as a stranger of the religion and philosophy of Europe ; but his bold spirit ranges over the field of Oriental speculation.   The Turkish Spy is no ordinary production, but contains as many proofs of a thoughtful, if not very profound mind, as any we can find.   It suggested the Persian Letters to Montesquieu, and the Jewish to Argens ; the former deviating from his model with the originality of talent, the latter following it with a more servile closeness.   Probability, that is, a resemblance to the personated character of an Oriental, was not to be attained, nor was it desirable, in any of these fictions ; but Mahmud has something not European, something of a solitary insulated wanderer, gazing on a world that knows him not, which throws, to my feelings, a striking charm over the Turkish Spy ; while the Usbek of Montesquieu has become more than half Parisian ; his ideas are neither those of his birthplace, nor such as have sprung up unbidden from his soul, but those of a polite, witty, and acute society ; and the correspondence with his harem in Persia which Montesquieu has thought attractive to the reader, is not much more interesting than it is probable, and ends in the style of a common romance. As to the Jewish Letters of Argens, it is far inferior to the Turkish Spy, and, in fact, rather an insipid book.

59. It may be asked why I dispute the claim made by all the foreign biographers in favour of John Paul Marana, a native of Genoa, who is asserted to have published the first volume of the Turkish Spy at Paris in 1684, and the rest in subsequent years.[*]   Chiefly of English origin.

---

[*] The first portion was published at Paris, and also at Amsterdam. Bayle gives the following account:—Cet ouvrage a été contrefait à Amsterdam du consentement du libraire de Paris, qui l'a le premier imprimé. Il sera composé de plusieurs petits volumes qui contiendront les événemens les plus considérables de la chrétienté en général, et de la France en particulier, depuis l'année 1637 jusqu'en 1682.   Un Italien, natif de Gênes, Marana, donne ces relations pour des lettres écrites aux ministres de la Porte par un espion Turc qui se tenoit caché à Paris. Il prétend les avoir traduites de l'Arabe en Italien : et il raconte fort en long comment il les a trouvées. On soupçonne avec beaucoup d'apparence, que c'est un tour d'esprit Italien, et une fiction ingénieuse semblable à celle dont Virgile s'est servi pour louer Auguste, &c.   Nouvelles de la République des Lettres; Mars, 1684 ; in Œuvres diverses de Bayle, vol. i. p. 20.   The Espion Turc is not to be traced in the index to the Journal des Sçavans; nor is it noticed in the Bibliothèque Universelle.

But I am not disputing that Marana is the author of the thirty letters, published in 1684, and of twenty more in 1686, which have been literally translated into English, and form about half the first volume in English of our Turkish Spy.[f] Nor do I doubt in the least that the remainder of that volume had a French original, though I have never seen it. But the later volumes of the Espion Turc, in the edition of 1696, with the date of Cologne, which, according to Barbier, is put for Rouen,[g] are avowedly translated from the English. And to the second volume of our Turkish Spy, published in 1691, is prefixed an account, not very credible, of the manner in

---

[f] Salfi, xiv. 61 ; Biograph. Univers.

[g] Dictionnaire des Anonymes, vol. i. p. 406. Barbier's notice of L'Espion, dans les cours des princes Chrétiens, ascribes four volumes out of six, which appear to contain as much as our eight volumes, to Marana, and conjectures that the last two are by another hand; but does not intimate the least suspicion of an English original. And as his authority is considerable, I must fortify my own opinion by what evidence I can find.

The preface to the second volume (English) of the Turkish Spy begins thus: " Three years are now elapsed since the first volume of letters written by a Spy at Paris was published in English. And it was expected that a second should have come out long before this. The favourable reception which that found amongst all sorts of readers would have encouraged a speedy translation of the rest, had there been extant any French edition of more than the first part. *But after the strictest inquiry none could be heard of*; and, as for the Italian, our booksellers have not that correspondence in those parts as they have in the more neighbouring countries of France and Holland. So that it was a work despaired of to recover any more of this Arabian's memoirs. We little dreamed that the Florentines had been so busy in printing and so successful in selling the continued translation of these Arabian epistles, till it was the fortune of an English gentleman to travel in those parts last summer, and discover the happy news. I will not forestall his letter, which is annexed to this preface." A pretended

letter with the signature of Daniel Saltmarsh follows, in which the imaginary author tells a strange tale of the manner in which a certain learned physician of Ferrara, Julio de Medici, descended from the Medicean family, put these volumes, in the Italian language, into his hands. This letter is dated Amsterdam, Sept. 9, 1690, and as the preface refers it to the last summer, I hence conclude that the first edition of the second volume of the Turkish Spy was in 1691; for I have not seen that, nor any other edition earlier than the fifth, printed in 1702.

Marana is said by Salfi and others to have left France in 1689, having fallen into a depression of spirits. Now the first thirty letters, about one thirty-second part of the entire work, were published in 1684, and about an equal length in 1686. I admit that he had time to double these portions, and thus to publish one-eighth of the whole; but is it likely that between 1686 and 1689 he could have given the rest to the world? If we are not struck by this, is it likely that the English translator should have fabricated the story above mentioned, when the public might know that there was actually a French original which he had rendered? The invention seems without motive. Again, how came the French edition of 1696 to be an avowed translation from the English, when, according to the hypothesis of M. Barbier, the volumes of Marana had all been published in France? Surely, till these appear, we have reason to suspect their existence; and the *onus probandi* lies *now* on the advocates of Marana's claim.

which the volumes subsequent to the first had been pro-
cured by a traveller, in the original Italian ; no French
edition, it is declared, being known to the booksellers.
That no Italian edition ever existed is, I apprehend, now
generally admitted : and it is to be shown by those who
contend for the claims of Marana to seven out of the
eight volumes, that they were published in France
before 1691 and the subsequent years, when they appeared in English. The Cologne or Rouen edition of 1696
follows the English so closely, that it has not given the
original letters of the first volume, published with the
name of Marana, but rendered them back from the translation.

60. In these early letters, I am ready to admit, the
scheme of the Turkish Spy may be entirely traced.
Marana appears not only to have planned the historical
part of the letters, but to have struck out the more original
and striking idea of a Mohammedan wavering with religious scruples, which the English continuator has followed up with more philosophy and erudition.   The internal evidence for their English origin, in all the latter
volumes, is to my apprehension exceedingly strong ; but
I know the difficulty of arguing from this to convince a
reader.   The proof we demand is the production of these
volumes in French, that is, the specification of some
public or private library where they may be seen, in any
edition anterior to 1691, and nothing short of this can be
satisfactory evidence.[b]

---

[b] I shall now produce some direct evidence for the English authorship of seven
out of eight parts of the Turkish Spy.
. " In the life of Mrs. Manley, published
under the title of ' The Adventures of
Rivella,' printed in 1714, in pages 14
and 15 it is said, That her father, Sir
Roger Manley, was the genuine author
of the first volume of the Turkish Spy.
Dr. Midgley, an ingenious physician, related to the family by marriage, had the
charge of looking over his papers, among
which he found that manuscript, which
he easily reserved to his proper use ; and
both by his own pen and the assistance
of some others continued the work until
the eighth volume, without ever having
the justice to name the author of the first."
MS. note in the copy of the Turkish Spy
(edit. 1732) in the British Museum.
Another MS. note in the same volume
gives the following extract from Dunton's
Life and Errors :—" Mr. Bradshaw is the
best accomplished hackney writer I have
met with ; his genius was quite above
the common size, and his style was incomparably fine. . . . So soon as I saw
the first volume of the Turkish Spy, the
very style and manner of writing convinced me that Bradshaw was the author.
. . . Bradshaw's wife owned that Dr.
Midgley had engaged him in a work
which would take him some years to
finish, for which the Doctor was to pay
him 40s. per sheet . . . so that 'tis very
probable (for I cannot swear I saw him
write it) that Mr. William Bradshaw was
the author of the Turkish Spy ; were it

61. It would not, perhaps, be unfair to bring within
Swift's Tale the pale of the seventeenth century an effusion
of a Tub.   of genius sufficient to redeem our name in its
annals of fiction.   The Tale of a Tub, though not published till 1704, was chiefly written, as the author declares, eight years before ; and the Battle of the Books
subjoined to it has every appearance of recent animosity
against the opponents of Temple and Boyle, in the question of Phalaris.   The Tale of a Tub is, in my apprehension, the masterpiece of Swift ; certainly Rabelais
has nothing superior, even in invention, nor anything so
condensed, so pointed, so full of real meaning, of biting
satire, of felicitous analogy.   The Battle of the Books is
such an improvement of the similar combat in the Lutrin
that we can hardly own it is an imitation.

not for this discovery. Dr. Midgley had
gone off with the honour of that performance." It thus appears that in England
it was looked upon as an original work ;
though the authority of Dunton is not
very good for the facts he tells, and that
of Mrs. Manley much worse. But I do
not quote them as evidence of such facts,
but of common report. Mrs. Manley, who
claims for her father the first volume,
certainly written by Marana, must be set
aside ; as to Dr. Midgley and Mr. Bradshaw, I know nothing to confirm or refute
what is here said.

[The hypothesis of these notes, that all
the Turkish Spy, after the first of our eight
volumes, is of English origin, has been
controverted in the Gentleman's Magazine by persons of learning and acuteness.

I would surrender my own opinion, if I
could see sufficient grounds for doing so ;
but as yet Marana's pretensions are not
substantiated by the evidence which I
demanded, the proof of any edition in
French anterior to that of our Turkish
Spy, the second volume of which (there
is no dispute about Marana's authorship
of the first) appeared in 1691, with a preface denying the existence of a French
original. Those who have had recourse
to the arbitrary supposition that Marana
communicated his manuscript to some
English translator, who published it as
his own, should be aware that a mere possibility, without a shadow of evidence,
even if it served to explain the facts,
cannot be received in historical criticism
as truth.—1842.]

CHAPTER VIII.

HISTORY OF PHYSICAL AND OTHER LITERATURE, FROM 1650 TO 1700.

SECT. I.—ON EXPERIMENTAL PHILOSOPHY.

Institutions for Science at Florence —'London — Paris — Chemistry — Boyle and others.

1. WE have now arrived, according to the method pursued in corresponding periods, at the history of mathematical and physical science in the latter part of the seventeenth century. But I must here entreat my readers to excuse the omission of that which ought to occupy a prominent situation in any work that pretends to trace the general progress of human knowledge. The length to which I have found myself already compelled to extend these volumes might be an adequate apology; but I have one more insuperable in the slightness of my own acquaintance with subjects so momentous and difficult, and upon which I could not write without presumptuousness and much peril of betraying ignorance. The names, therefore, of Wallis and Huygens, Newton and Leibnitz, must be passed with distant reverence.

Reasons for omitting mathematics.

2. This was the age when the experimental philosophy to which Bacon had held the torch, and which had already made considerable progress, especially in Italy, was finally established on the ruins of arbitrary figments and partial inductions. This philosophy was signally indebted to three associations, the eldest of which did not endure long; but the others have remained to this day the perennial fountains of science; the Academy del Cimento at Florence, the

Academy del Cimento.

Royal Society of London, the Academy of Sciences at Paris. The first of these was established in 1657, with the patronage of the Grand „Duke Ferdinand II., but under the peculiar care of his brother Leopold. Both were, in a manner at that time remarkable, attached to natural philosophy ; and Leopold, less engaged in public affairs, had long carried on a correspondence with the learned of Europe. It is said that the advice of Viviani, one of the greatest geometers that Europe has produced, led to this institution. The name which this Academy assumed gave promise of their fundamental rule, the investigation of truth by experiment alone. The number of Academicians was unlimited ; and all that was required as an article of faith was the abjuration of all faith, a resolution to inquire into truth without regard to any previous sect of philosophy. This Academy lasted unfortunately but ten years in vigour : it is a great misfortune for any literary institution to depend on one man, and especially on a prince, who, shedding a factitious, as well as sometimes a genuine lustre round it, is not easily replaced without a diminution of the world's regard. Leopold, in 1667, became a cardinal, and was thus withdrawn from Florence ; others of the Academy del Cimento died or went away, and it rapidly sunk into insignificance. But a volume containing reports of the yearly experiments it made, among others the celebrated one proving, as was then supposed, the incompressibility of water, is generally esteemed.[a]

3. The germ of our Royal Society may be traced to
Royal
Society.
the year 1645, when Wallis, Wilkins, Glisson, and others less known, agreed to meet weekly at a private house in London, in order to converse on subjects connected with natural, and especially experimental, philosophy. Some of these soon afterwards settled in Oxford ; and thus arose two little societies in connexion with each other, those at Oxford being recruited by Ward, Petty, Willis, and Bathurst. They met at Petty's lodgings till he removed to Ireland in 1652 ; afterwards at those of Wilkins, in Wadham College, till he became Master of Trinity College, Cambridge, in 1659 ; about which time most of the Oxford philosophers

[a] Galluzzi, Storia del Gran Ducato, vol. vii. p. 240 ; Tiraboschi, xi. 204 ; Corniani, viii. 29.

came to London, and held their meetings in Gresham College.   They became more numerous after the Restoration, which gave better hope of a tranquillity indispensable for science; and on the 28th of November, 1660, agreed to form a regular society, which should meet weekly for the promotion of natural philosophy: their registers are kept from this time.[b]   The king, rather fond himself of these subjects, from the beginning afforded them his patronage; their first charter is dated 15th July, 1662, incorporating them by the style of the Royal Society, and appointing Lord Brouncker the first president, assisted by a council of twenty, the conspicuous names among which are Boyle, Kenelm Digby, Wilkins, Wren, Evelyn, and Oldenburg.[c]   The last of these was secretary, and editor of the Philosophical Transactions, the first number of which appeared March 1, 1665, containing sixteen pages in quarto.   These were continued monthly, or less frequently, according to the materials he possessed.   Oldenburg ceased to be the editor in 1667, and was succeeded by Grew, as he was by Hooke.   These early transactions are chiefly notes of conversations and remarks made at the meetings, as well as of experiments either then made or reported to the Society.[d]

4. The Academy of Sciences at Paris was established in 1666, under the auspices of Colbert.   The king assigned to them a room in the royal library for their meetings.   Those first selected were all mathematicians; but other departments of science, especially chemistry and anatomy, afterwards furnished associates of considerable name.   It seems, nevertheless, that this Academy did not cultivate experimental philosophy with such unremitting zeal as the Royal Society, and that abstract mathematics have always borne a larger proportion to the rest of their inquiries.   They published in this century ten volumes, known as Anciens Mémoires de l'Académie.   But near its close, in 1697, they received a regular institution from the king, organising them in a manner analogous

Academy of Sciences at Paris.

---

b Birch's Hist. of Royal Society, vol. i. p. 1.
c Id. p. 88.
d Id. vol. ii. p. 18 ; Thomson's Hist. of Royal Society, p. 7.

to the two other great literary foundations, the French Academy, and that of Inscriptions and Belles Lettres.[e]

5. In several branches of physics, the experimental philosopher is both guided and corrected by the eternal laws of geometry. In others he wants this aid, and, in the words of his master, "knows and understands no more concerning the order of nature than, as her servant and interpreter, he has been taught by observation and tentative processes." All that concerns the peculiar actions of bodies on each other was of this description; though in our own times even this has been in some degree brought under the omnipotent control of the modern analysis. Chemistry, or the science of the molecular constituents of bodies, manifested in such peculiar and reciprocal operations, had never been rescued from empirical hands till this period. The transmutation of metals, the universal medicine, and other inquiries utterly unphilosophical in themselves, because they assumed the existence of that which they sought to discover, had occupied the chemists so much that none of them had made any further progress than occasionally, by some happy combination or analysis, to contribute an useful preparation to pharmacy, or to detect an unknown substance. Glauber and Van Helmont were the most active and ingenious of these elder chemists; but the former has only been remembered by having long given his name to sulphate of soda, while the latter wasted his time on experiments from which he knew not how to draw right inferences, and his powers on hypotheses which a sounder spirit of the inductive philosophy would have taught him to reject.[f]

6. Chemistry, as a science of principles, hypothetical, no doubt, and in a great measure unfounded, but cohering in a plausible system, and better than the reveries of the Paracelsists and Behmenists, was founded by Becker in Germany, by Boyle and his contemporaries of the Royal Society in England. Becker, a native of Spire, who, after wandering from one city of Germany to another, died in London in 1685, by his Physica Subterranea, published in 1669, laid the foun-

State of Chemistry.

Becker.

[e] Fontenelle, vol. v. p. 23. Montucla, Hist. des Mathématiques, vol. ii. p. 557.
[f] Thomson's Hist. of Chemistry, i. 183.

dation of a theory which, having in the next century been perfected by Stahl, became the creed of philosophy till nearly the end of the last century. "Becker's theory," says an English writer, "stripped of everything but the naked statement, may be expressed in the following sentence : besides water and air there are three other substances, called earths, which enter into the composition of bodies, namely, the fusible or vitrifiable earth, the inflammable or sulphureous, and the mercurial. By the intimate combination of earths with water is formed an universal acid, from which proceed all other acid bodies ; stones are produced by the combination of certain earths, metals by the combination of all the three earths in proportions which vary according to the metal." [s]

7. No one Englishman of the seventeenth century after Lord Bacon raised to himself so high a reputation in experimental philosophy as Robert Boyle ; it has even been remarked that he was born in the year of Bacon's death, as the person destined by nature to succeed him. An eulogy which would be extravagant, if it implied any parallel between the genius of the two ; but hardly so if we look on Boyle as the most faithful, the most patient, the most successful disciple who carried forward the experimental philosophy of Bacon. His works occupy six large volumes in quarto. They may be divided into theological or metaphysical and physical or experimental. Of the former, we may mention as the most philosophical his Disquisition into the Final Causes of Natural Things, his Free Inquiry into the received Notion of Nature, his Discourse of Things above Reason, his Considerations about the Reconcileableness of Reason and Religion, his Excellency of Theology, and his Considerations on the Style of the Scriptures ; but the latter, his chemical and experimental writings, form more than two-thirds of his prolix works.

Boyle.

8. The metaphysical treatises, to use that word in a large sense, of Boyle, or rather those concerning Natural Theology, are very perspicuous, very free from system, and such as bespeak an

His metaphysical works.

§ Thomson's Hist. of Royal Society, p. 468.

independent lover of truth.   His Disquisition on Final
Causes was a well-timed vindication of that palmary
argument against the paradox of the Cartesians, who
had denied the validity of an inference from the manifest
adaptation of means to ends in the universe to an intelligent Providence.   Boyle takes a more philosophical
view of the principle of final causes than had been found
in many theologians, who weakened the argument itself
by the presumptuous hypothesis, that man was the sole
object of Providence in the creation.[h] His greater knowledge of physiology led him to perceive that there are
both animal, and what he calls cosmical, ends, in which
man has no concern.

9. The following passage is so favourable a specimen
Extract from one of them. of the philosophical spirit of Boyle, and so good
an illustration of the theory of *idols* in the No-
vum Organum, that, although it might better,
perhaps, have deserved a place in a former chapter, I
will not refrain from inserting it:—" I know not," he
says, in his Free Inquiry into the received Notion of
Nature, "whether it be a prerogative in the human
mind, that as it is itself a true and positive being, so is
it apt to conceive all other things as true and positive
beings also ; but whether or no this propensity to frame
such kind of ideas supposes an excellency, I fear it occasions mistakes, and makes us think and speak after the
manner of true and positive beings, of such things as are
but chimerical, and some of them negations or privations
themselves : as death, ignorance, blindness, and the like.
It concerns us therefore to stand very carefully upon our
guard, that we be not insensibly misled by such an innate
and unheeded temptation to error, as we bring into the
world with us."[i]

10. Boyle improved the air-pump and the thermometer,
His merits in physics and che-mistry. though the latter was first made an accurate
instrument of investigation by Newton.   He
also discovered the law of the air's elasticity,
namely, that its bulk is inversely as the pres-
sure upon it.   For some of the principles of hydrostatics
we are indebted to him, though he did not possess much
mathematical knowledge.   The Philosophical Transac-

---

h Boyle's Works, vol. v. p. 394.   i Vol. v. p. 161.

tions contain several valuable papers by him on this science.[k]　By his "Sceptical Chemist," published in 1661, he did much to overturn the theories of Van Helmont's school, that commonly called of the iatro-chemists, which was in its highest reputation; raising doubts as to the existence not only of the four elements of the peripatetics, but of those which these chemists had substituted. Boyle holds the elements of bodies to be atoms of different shapes and sizes, the union of which gives origin to what are vulgarly called elements.[m]　It is unnecessary to remark that this is the prevailing theory of the present age.

11. I shall borrow the general character of Boyle and of his contemporaries in English chemistry from a modern author of credit. "Perhaps Mr. Boyle may be considered as the first person neither connected with pharmacy nor mining, who devoted a considerable degree of attention to chemical pursuits. Mr. Boyle, though in common with the literary men of his age he may be accused of credulity, was both very laborious and intelligent; and his chemical pursuits, which were various and extensive, and intended solely to develope the truth without any regard to previously conceived opinions, contributed essentially to set chemistry free from the trammels of absurdity and superstition in which it had been hitherto enveloped, and to recommend it to philosophers as a science deserving to be studied on account of the important information which it was qualified to convey. His refutation of the alchemistical opinions respecting the constituents of bodies, his observations on cold, on the air, on phosphorus, and on ether, deserve particularly to be mentioned as doing him much honour. We have no regular account of any one substance or of any class of bodies in Mr. Boyle, similar to those which at present are considered as belonging exclusively to the science of chemistry. Neither did he attempt to systematise the phenomena, nor to subject them to any hypothetical explanation.

General character of Boyle.

12. "But his contemporary Dr. Hooke, who had a particular predilection for hypothesis, sketched in his Micrographia a very beautiful theoretical

Of Hooke and others.

k Thomson's Hist. of Royal Society, pp. 400, 411.　　m Thomson's Hist. of Chemistry, 1. 206.

explanation of combustion, and promised to develope his
doctrine more fully in a subsequent book; a promise
which he never fulfilled: though in his Lampas, published about twenty years afterwards, he has given a
very beautiful explanation of the way in which a candle
burns.   Mayow, in his Essays, published at Oxford
about ten years after the Micrographia, embraced the
hypothesis of Dr. Hooke without acknowledgment; but
clogged it with so many absurd additions of his own as
greatly to obscure its lustre and diminish its beauty.
Mayow's first and principal Essay contains some happy
experiments on respiration and air, and some fortunate
conjectures respecting the combustion of the metals;
but the most valuable part of the whole is the chapter
on affinities, in which he appears to have gone much
farther than any other chemist of his day, and to have
anticipated some of the best established doctrines of his
successors.   Sir Isaac Newton, to whom all the sciences
lie under such great obligations, made two most important contributions to chemistry, which constitute as
it were the foundation-stones of its two great divisions.
The first was pointing out a method of graduating ther-
mometers, so as to be comparable with each other in
whatever part of the world observations with them are
made.   The second was by pointing out the nature of
chemical affinity, and showing that it consisted in an
attraction by which the constituents of bodies were
drawn towards each other and united; thus destroying the
previous hypothesis of the hooks, and points, and rings,
and wedges, by means of which the different constituents of bodies were conceived to be kept together." [a]

13. Lemery, a druggist at Paris, by his Cours de
Chymie in 1675, is said to have changed the face
Lemery.   of the science; the change nevertheless seems
to have gone no deeper.   "Lemery," says Fontenelle,
"was the first who dispersed the real or pretended
obscurities of chemistry, who brought it to clearer and
more simple notions, who abolished the gross barbarisms
of its language, who promised nothing but what he knew
the art could perform; and to this he owed the success
of his book.   It shows not only a sound understanding,

but some greatness of soul, to strip one's own science of a false pomp." °   But we do not find that Lemery had any novel views in chemistry, or that he claims with any irresistible pretension the title of a philosopher. In fact, his chemistry seems to have been little more than pharmacy.

SECT. II.—-ON NATURAL HISTORY.

Zoology — Ray — Botanical Classifications — Grew — Geological Theories.

14. THE accumulation of particular knowledge in Natural History must always be progressive, where any regard is paid to the subject; every traveller in remote countries, every mariner may contribute some observation, correct some error, or bring home some new species.   Thus zoology had made a regular advance from the days of Conrad Gesner; yet with so tardy a step, that, reflecting on the extensive intercourse of Europe with the Eastern and Western world, we may be surprised to find how little Jonston, in the middle of the seventeenth century, had added, even in the most obvious class, that of quadrupeds, to the knowledge collected one hundred years before.   But hitherto zoology, confined to mere description, and that often careless or indefinite, unenlightened by anatomy, unregulated by method, had not merited the name of a science.   That name it owes to John Ray.

15. Ray first appeared in Natural History as the editor of the Ornithology of his highly accomplished friend Francis Willoughby, with whom he had travelled over the Continent.   This was published in 1676; and the History of Fishes followed in 1686.   The descriptions are ascribed to Willoughby, the arrangement to Ray, who might have considered the two works as in great part his own, though he has not interfered with the glory of his deceased friend.   Cuvier observes. that the History of Fishes is the more perfect work of the two, that many species are described which will

margin notes: Slow progress of zoology. | Before Ray.

ᴶ Eloge de Lemery, in Œuvres de Fontenelle, v. 361; Biogr. Universelle.

not be found in earlier ichthyologists, and that those of the Mediterranean especially are given with great precision.[p]

16. Among the original works of Ray we may select the Synopsis Methodica Animalium Quadrupedum et Serpentini Generis, published in 1693. This book makes an epoch in zoology, not for the additions of new species it contains, since there are few wholly such, but as the first classification of animals that can be reckoned both general and grounded in nature. He divides them into those with blood and without blood. The former are such as breathe through lungs, and such as breathe through gills. Of the former of these some have a heart with two ventricles, some have one only. And among the former class of these some are viviparous, some oviparous. We thus come to the proper distinction of Mammalia. But in compliance with vulgar prejudice, Ray did not include the cetacea in the same class with quadrupeds, though well aware that they properly belonged to it, and left them as an order of fishes.[q] Quadrupeds he was the first to divide into *ungulate* and *unguiculate*, hoofed and clawed, having himself invented the Latin words.[r] The former are *solidipeda, bisulca,* or *quadrisulca;* the latter are *bifida* or *multifida;* and these latter with undivided or with partially divided toes; which latter again may have broad claws, as monkeys, or narrow claws; and these with narrow claws he arranges according to their teeth, as either *carnivora* or *leporina,* now generally called *rodentia.* Besides all these quadrupeds which he calls *analoga,* he has a general division called *anomala,* for those without teeth or with such peculiar arrangements of teeth as we find in the insectivorous genera, the hedgehog and mole.[s]

17. Ray was the first zoologist who made use of comparative anatomy; he inserts at length every account of dissections that he could find; several had been made at Paris. He does not appear to be very

His Synopsis of Quadrupeds.

Merits of this work.

P Biographie Universelle, art. Ray.
q Nos ne a communi hominum opinione nimis recedamus, et ut affectatæ novitatis notam evitemus, cetaceum aquatilium genus, quamvis cum quadrupedibus vivi-

paris in omnibus fere præterquam in pilis et pedibus et elemento in quo degunt convenire videantur, piscibus annumerabimus. P. 55.
r P. 50.   s P. 56

anxious about describing every species; thus in the simian family he omits several well known.' I cannot exactly determine what quadrupeds he has inserted that do not appear in the earlier zoologists; according to Linnæus, in the twelfth edition of the Systema Naturæ, if I have counted rightly, they amount to thirty-two; but I have found him very careless in specifying the synonyms of his predecessors, and many, for which he only quotes Ray, are in Gesner or Jonston. Ray has however much the advantage over these in the brevity and closeness of his specific characters. "The particular distinction of his labours," says Cuvier, "consists in an arrangement more clear, more determinate than those of any of his predecessors, and applied with more consistency and precision. His distribution of the classes of quadrupeds and birds has been followed by the English naturalists almost to our own days; and we find manifest traces of that he has adopted as to the latter class in Linnæus, in Brisson, in Buffon, and in all other ornithologists." ᵘ

18. The bloodless animals, and even those of cold blood, with the exception of fishes, had occupied but little attention of any good zoologists till after the middle of the century. They were now studied with considerable success. Redi, established as a physician at Florence, had yet time for that various literature which has immortalised his name. He opposed, and in a great degree disproved by experiment, the prevailing doctrine of the equivocal generation of insects, or that from corruption; though where he was unable to show the means of reproduction, he had recourse to a paradoxical hypothesis of his own. Redi also enlarged our knowledge of intestinal animals, and made some good experiments on the poison of vipers.ˣ Malpighi, who combated, like Redi, the theory of the reproduction of organised bodies from mere corruption, has given one of the most complete treatises on the silkworm that we

Redi.

t Hoc genus animalium tum caudatorum tum cauda carentium species valde numerosæ sunt; non tamen multæ apud autores fide dignos descriptæ occurrunt. He only describes those species he has found in Clusius or Marcgrave, and what he calls Parisiensis, such, I presume, as

he had found in the Memoirs of the Académie des Sciences. But he does not mention the Simia Innus, or the S. Hamadryas, and several others of the most known species.

ᵘ Biogr. Univ.

ˣ Biogr. Univ.; Tiraboschi, xi. 252.

possess.[y] Swammerdam, a Dutch naturalist, abandoned
Swammer- his pursuits in human anatomy to follow up
dam.   that of insects, and by his skill and patience
in dissection made numerous discoveries in their structure.   His General History of Insects, 1669, contains
a distribution into four classes, founded on their bodily
forms and the metamorphoses they undergo.   A posthumous work, Biblia Naturæ, not published till 1738,
contains, says the Biographie Universelle, "a multitude of facts wholly unknown before Swammerdam; it
is impossible to carry farther the anatomy of these little
animals, or to be more exact in the description of their
organs."

19. Lister, an English physician, may be reckoned
Lister.   one of those who have done most to found the
science of conchology by his Historia sive Synopsis Conchyliorum, in 1685; a work very copious and
full of accurate delineations; and also by his three treatises on English animals, two of which relate to fluviatile
and marine shells.   The third, which is on spiders, is
not less esteemed in entomology.   Lister was also perhaps the first to distinguish the specific characters, such
at least as are now reckoned specific, though probably
not in his time, of the Asiatic and African elephant.
" His works in natural history and comparative anatomy
are justly esteemed, because he has shown himself an
exact and sagacious observer, and has pointed out with
correctness the natural relations of the animals that he
describes."[z]

20. The beautiful science which bears the improper
Comparative name of comparative anatomy, had but casually
anatomy.   occupied the attention of the medical profession.[a] It was to them, rather than to mere zoologists,
that it owed, and indeed strictly must always owe, its
discoveries, which had hitherto been very few.   It was
now more cultivated; and the relations of structure to

---

[y] Biogr. Univ.; Tiraboschi, xi. 252.
[z] Biogr. Univ.; Chalmers.
[a] It is most probable that this term
was originally designed to express a comparison between the human structure
and that of brutes, though it might also
mean one between different species of
the latter. In the first sense it is never
now used, and the second is but a part,
though an important one, of the science.
Zootomy has been suggested as a better
name, but it is not quite analogical to
anatomy; and on the whole it seems as
if we must remain with the old word,
protesting against its propriety.

the capacities of animal life became more striking as
their varieties were more fully understood ; the grand
theories of final causes found their most convincing
arguments.   In this period, I believe, comparative anatomy made an important progress, which in the earlier
part of the eighteenth century was by no means equally
rapid.   France took the lead in these researches.   " The
number of papers on comparative anatomy," says Dr.
Thomson, " is greater in the Memoirs of the French
Academy than in our national publication.   This was
owing to the pains taken during the reign of Louis XIV.
to furnish the Academy with proper animals, and the
number of anatomists who received a salary, and of
course devoted themselves to anatomical subjects."   There
are, however, about twenty papers in the Philósophical
Transactions before 1700 on this subject.[b]

21. Botany, notwithstanding the gleams of philosophical light which occasionally illustrate the   Botany.
writings of Cæsalpin and Columna, had seldom
gone farther than to name, to describe, and to delineate
plants with a greater or less accuracy and copiousness.
Yet it long had the advantage over zoology, and now,
when the latter made a considerable step in advance, it
still continued to keep ahead.   This is a period of great
importance in botanical science.   Jungius of   Jungius.
Hamburgh, whose posthumous Isagoge Phyto-
scopica was published in 1679, is said to have been the
first in the seventeenth century who led the way to a
better classification than that of Lobel ; and Sprengel
thinks that the English botanists were not unacquainted
with his writings ; Ray indeed owns his obligations to
them.[c]

22. But the founder of classification, in the eyes of the
world, was Robert Morison, of Aberdeen, pro-   Morison.
fessor of botany at Oxford ; who, by his Hortus
Blesensis, in 1669; by his Plantarum Umbelliferarum
Distributio Nova, in 1672 ; and chiefly by his great work,
Historia Plantarum Universalis, in 1678, laid the basis of
a systematic classification, which he partly founded, not on
trivial distinctions of appearance, as the older botanists,
but, as Cæsalpin had first done, on the fructifying organs.

b Thomson's Hist. of Royal Society,   c Sprengel, Hist. Rei Herbariæ, vol. ii.
p. 114.   p. 32.

He has been frequently charged with plagiarism from that great Italian, who seems to have suffered, as others have done, by failing to carry forward his own luminous conceptions into such details of proof as the world justly demands; another instance of which has been seen in his very striking passages on the circulation of the blood. Sprengel, however, who praises Morison highly, does not impute to him this injustice towards Cæsalpin, whose writings might possibly be unknown in Britain.[d]　And it might be observed also, that Morison did not, as has sometimes been alleged, establish the fruit as the sole basis of his arrangement. Out of fifteen classes, into which he distributes all herbaceous plants, but seven are characterised by this distinction.[e]　"The examination of Morison's works," says a late biographer, "will enable us to judge of the service he rendered in the reformation of botany. The great botanists, from Gesner to the Bauhins, had published works, more or less useful by their discoveries, their observations, their descriptions, or their figures. Gesner had made a great step in considering the fruit as the principal distinction of genera. Fabius Columna adopted this view; Cæsalpin applied it to a classification which should be regarded as better than any that preceded the epoch of which we speak. Morison had made a particular study of fruits, having collected 1500 different species of them, though he did not neglect the importance of the natural affinities of other parts. He dwells on this leading idea, insists on the necessity of establishing generic characters, and has founded his chief works on this basis. He has therefore done real service to the science; nor should the vanity which has made him conceal his obligations to Cæsalpin induce us to refuse him justice."[f]　Morison speaks of his own theory with excessive vanity, and depreciates all earlier botanists as full of confusion. Several English writers have been unfavourable to Morison, out of partiality to Ray, with whom he was on bad terms; but Tournefort declares that if he had not enlightened botany, it would still have been in darkness.

---

d Sprengel, p. 34.
e Pulteney, Historical Progress of Botany in England, vol. i. p. 307.
f Biogr. Universelle.

23. Ray, in his Methodus Plantarum Nova, 1682, and
in his Historia Plantarum Universalis, in three Ray.
volumes, the first published in 1686, the second
in 1688, and the third, which is supplemental, in 1704,
trod in the steps of Morison, but with more acknowledgment of what was due to others, and with some improvements of his own. He described 6900 plants, many of
which are now considered as varieties.[g] In the botanical
works of Ray we find the natural families of plants better
defined, the difference of complete and incomplete flowers
more precise, and the grand division of monocotyledons
and dicotyledons fully established. He gave much precision to the characteristics of many classes, and introduced several technical terms very useful for the perspicuity of botanical language; finally, he established
many general principles of arrangement which have
since been adopted.[h] Ray's method of classification was
principally by the fruit, though he admits its imperfec-
tions. "In fact, his method," says Pulteney, "though
he assumes the fruit as the foundation, is an elaborate
attempt, for that time, to fix natural classes."[i]

24. Rivinus, in his Introductio in Rem Herbariam,
Leipsic, 1690, a very short performance, struck Rivinus.
into a new path, which has modified to a great
degree the systems of later botanists. Cæsalpin and
Morison had looked mainly to the fruit as the basis of
classification; Rivinus added the flower, and laid down
as a fundamental rule that all plants which resemble
each other both in the flower and in the fruit, ought to
bear the same generic name.[k] In some pages of this
Introduction we certainly find the basis of the Critica
Botanica of Linnæus.[m] Rivinus thinks the arrangement
of Cæsalpin the best, and that Morison has only spoiled
what he took; of Ray he speaks in terms of eulogy, but
blames some part of his method. His own is primarily
founded on the flower, and thus he forms eighteen classes,
which, by considering the differences of the fruits, he
subdivides into ninety-one genera. The specific distinctions he founded on the general habit and appearance of
the plant. His method is more thoroughly artificial, as

g Pulteney. The account of Ray's life
and botanical writings in this work occupies nearly 100 pages.

h Biogr. Universelle.
i P. 259.
k Biogr. Universelle.   m Id.

opposed to natural ; that is, more established on a single principle, which often brings heterogeneous plants and families together, than that of any of his predecessors ; for even Ray had kept the distinction of trees from shrubs and herbs, conceiving it to be founded in their natural fructification.   Rivinus set aside wholly this leading division.   Yet he had not been able to reduce all plants to his method, and admitted several anomalous divisions.[n]

25. The merit of establishing an uniform and consist-

Tournefort.

ent system was reserved for Tournefort.   His Elémens de la Botanique appeared in 1694 ; the Latin translation, Institutiones Rei Herbariæ, in 1700.   Tournefort, like Rivinus, took the flower or corolla as the basis of his system ; and the varieties in the structure, rather than number, of the petals furnish him with his classes. • The genera—for, like other botanists before Linnæus, he has no intermediate division —are established by the flower and fruit conjointly, or now and then by less essential differences, for he held it better to constitute new genera than, as others had done, to have anomalous species.   The accessory parts of a plant are allowed to supply specific distinctions. But Tournefort divides vegetables, according to old prejudice—which it is surprising that, after the precedent of Rivinus to the contrary, he should have regarded— into herbs and trees ; and thus he has twenty-two classes. Simple flowers, monopetalous or polypetalous, form eleven of these ; composite flowers, three ; the apetalous, one ; the cryptogamous, or those without flower or fruit, make another class ; shrubs or *suffrutices* are placed in the seventeenth ; and trees, in five more, are similarly distributed, according to their floral characters.[o]   Sprengel extols much of the system of Tournefort, though he disapproves of the selection of a part so often wanting as the corolla for the sole basis ; nor can its various forms be comprised in Tournefort's classes.   His orders are well marked, according to the same author ; but he multiplied both his genera and species too much, and paid too little attention to the stamina.   His method was less repugnant to natural affinities and more convenient in

[n] Biogr. Univ. ; Sprengel, p. 56.
[o] Biogr. Univ. ; Thomson's Hist. of Royal Society, p. 34 ; Sprengel, p. 64.

practice than any which had come since Lobel.   Most of
Tournefort's generic distinctions were preserved by
Linnæus, and some which had been abrogated without
sufficient reason have since been restored.[p]   Ray opposed
the system of Tournefort, but some have thought that in
his later works he came nearer to it, so as to be called
magis corollista quam fructista.[q]   This, however, is not
acknowledged by Pulteney, who has paid great attention
to Ray's writings.

26. The classification and description of plants constitute what generally is called botany.   But Vegetable
these began now to be studied in connexion physiology.
with the anatomy and physiology of the vegetable world ;
terms not merely analogical, because as strictly applicable as to animals, but which had never been employed
before the middle of the seventeenth century.   This interesting science is almost wholly due to two men,
Grew and Malpighi.   Grew first directed his   Grew.
thoughts towards the anatomy of plants in
1664, in consequence of reading several books of animal
anatomy, which suggested to him that plants, being the
works of the same Author, would probably show similar
contrivances.   Some had introduced observations of this
nature, as Highmore, Sharrock, and Hooke, but only
collaterally ; so that the systematic treatment of the
subject, following the plant from the seed, was left quite
open for himself.   In 1670 he presented the first book
of his work to the Royal Society, who next year ordered
it to be printed.   It was laid before the society in print,
December, 1671 ; and on the same day a manuscript by
Malpighi on the same subject was read.   They went on
from this time with equal steps ; Malpighi, however,
having caused Grew's book to be translated for his own
use.   Grew speaks very honourably of Malpighi, and
without claiming more than the statement of facts permits him.[r]

27. The first book of his Anatomy of Plants, which is
the title given to three separate works, when   His Ana-
published collectively in 1682, contains the   tomy of
whole of his physiological theory, which is   Plants.
developed at length in those that follow.   The nature of

[p] Biogr. Universelle.   [q] Id.   Sprengel calls Grew's book opus abso-
[r] Pulteney; Chalmers; Biogr. Univ. lutum et immortale.

vegetation and its processes seem to have been unknown
when he began; save that common observation and the
more accurate experience of gardeners and others must
have collected the obvious truths of vegetable anatomy.
He does not quote Cæsalpin, and may have been unacquainted with his writings. No man perhaps who
created a science has carried it farther than Grew; he
is so close and diligent in his observations, making use
of the microscope, that comparatively few discoveries of
great importance have been made in the mere anatomy
of plants since his time;* though some of his opinions
are latterly disputed by Mirbel and others of a new
botanical school.

28. The great discovery ascribed to Grew is of the
sexual system in plants. He speaks thus of
what he calls the attire, though rather, I think,
in obscure terms:—" The primary and chief
use of the attire is such as hath respect to the
plant itself, and so appears to be very great and necessary. Because even those plants which have no flower
or foliature are yet some way or other attired, either
with the seminiform or the floral attire; so that it seems
to perform its service to the seeds as the foliature to the
fruit. In discourse hereof with our learned Savilian
professor Sir Thomas Millington, he told me he conceived that the attire doth serve, as the male, for the
generation of the seed. I immediately replied that I
was of the same opinion, and gave him some reasons for
it, and answered some objections which might oppose
them. But withal, in regard every plant is ἀρρενόθηλυς.
or male and female, that I was also of opinion that it
serveth for the separation of some parts as well as the
affusion of others."† He proceeds to explain his notion
of vegetable impregnation. It is singular that he should
suppose all plants to be hermaphrodite; and this shows
he could not have recollected what had long been known
as to the palm, or the passages in Cæsalpin relative to
the subject.

He discovers the sexual system.

29. Ray admitted Grew's opinion cautiously at first:
Nos ut verisimilem tantum admittimus. But in his
Sylloge Stirpium, 1694, he fully accedes to it. The real

---

* Biogr. Universelle.
† Book iv. ch. 1. He had hinted at some "primary and private use of the attire," in book i. ch. 5.

establishment of the sexual theory, however, is due
to Camerarius, professor of botany at Tübin- Camerarius
gen, whose letter on that subject, published confirms
1694, in the work of another, did much to this.
spread the theory over Europe. His experiments, indeed, were necessary to confirm what Grew had rather
hazarded as a conjecture than brought to a test; and he
showed that flowers deprived of their stamina do not
produce seeds capable of continuing the species." Woodward, in the Philosophical Transactions, illustrated the
nutrition of plants by putting sprigs of vegetables in
phials filled with water, and after some time determining the weight they had gained and the quantity they
had imbibed.ˣ These experiments had been made by
Van Helmont, who had inferred from them that water
is convertible into solid matter.ʸ

30. It is just to observe that some had preceded Grew
in vegetable physiology. Aromatari, in a letter Predeces-
of only four pages, published at Venice in sors of
1626, on the generation of plants from seeds, Grew.
which was reprinted in the Philosophical Transactions,
showed the analogy between grains and eggs, each containing a minute organised embryo, which employs the
substances enclosing it for its own development. Aromatari has also understood the use of the cotyledons.ᶻ
Brown, in his Inquiry into Vulgar Errors, has remarks
on the budding of plants, and on the quinary number
which they affect in their flower. Kenelm Digby, according to Sprengel, first explained the necessity in
vegetation for oxygen, or vital air, which had lately
been discovered by Bathurst.ᵃ Hooke carried the discoveries hitherto made in vegetable anatomy much further in his Micrographia. Sharrock and Lister contributed some knowledge; but they were rather later than
Grew. None of these deserve such a place as Malpighi.
Malpighi, who, says Sprengel, was not inferior
to Grew in acuteness, though, probably, through some
illusions of prejudice, he has not so well understood and

ᵘ Sprengel; Biogr. Univ.; Pulteney,
p. 338.
    ˣ Thomson's Hist. of Royal Society,
p. 58.
    ʸ Thomson's Hist. of Chemistry.
    ᶻ Sprengel; Biogr. Univ.

    ᵃ Sprengel, iii. 176. [It will be under-
stood that the name oxygen, though
Sprengel uses it, is modern; and also
that this gas is properly said to have been
discovered in 1774 by Priestley, who exhibited it in a separate state.—1842.]

explained many things. But the structure and growth of seeds he has explained better, and Grew seems to have followed him. His book is also better arranged and more concise.[b] The Dutch did much to enlarge botanical science. The Hortus Indicus Malabaricus of Rheede, who had been a governor in India, was published at his own expense in twelve volumes, the first appearing in 1686 ; it contains an immense number of new plants.[c] The Herbarium Amboinense of Rumphius was collected in the seventeenth century, though not published till 1741.[d] Several botanical gardens were formed in different countries; among others that of Chelsea was opened in 1686.[e]

31. It was impossible that men of inquiring tempers

Early notions of geology.

should not have been led to reflect on those remarkable phænomena of the earth's visible structure, which being in course of time accurately registered and arranged, have become the basis of that noble science, the boast of our age, geology. The first thing which must strike the eyes of the merest clown, and set the philosopher thinking, is the irregularity of the surface of our globe ; the more this is observed, the more signs of violent disruption appear. Some, indeed, of whom Ray seems to have been one,[f] were so much impressed by the theory of final causes that, perceiving the fitness of the present earth for its inhabitants, they thought it might have been created in such a state of physical ruin. But the contrary inference is almost irresistible. A still more forcible argument for great revolutions in the history of the earth is drawn from a second phænomenon of very general occurrence, the marine and other fossil relics of organised beings, which are dug up in strata far remote from the places where these bodies could now exist. It was common to account for them by the Mosaic deluge. But the depth at which they are found was incompatible with this hypothesis. Others fancied them to be not really organised, but sports of nature, as they were called, the casual resemblances of shells and fishes in stone. The

b Sprengel, p. 15.
c Biogr. Univ. The date of the first volume is given erroneously in the B. U.
d Id.

e Sprengel; Pulteney.
f See Ray's Three Physico-Theological Discourses on the Creation, Deluge, and final Conflagration. 1692.

Italians took the lead in speculating on these problems; but they could only arrive now and then at a happier conjecture than usual, and do not seem to have planned any scheme of explaining the general structure of the earth.[s] The Mundus Subterraneus of Athanasius Kircher, famous for the variety and originality of his erudition, contains probably the geology of his age, or at least his own. It was published in 1662. Ten out of twelve books relate to the surface or the interior of the earth, and to various terrene productions; the remaining two to alchemy and other arts connected with mineralogy. Kircher seems to have collected a great deal of geographical and geological knowledge. In England, the spirit of observation was so strong after the establishment of the Royal Society, that the Philosophical Transactions in this period contain a considerable number of geognostic papers, and the genius of theory was aroused, though not at first in his happiest mood.[h]

32. Thomas Burnet, master of the Charterhouse, a man fearless and somewhat rash, with more imagina-   Burnet's tion than philosophy, but ingenious and elo-   Theory of quent, published in 1694 his Theoria Telluris   Earth. Sacra, which he afterwards translated into English. The primary question for the early geologists had always been how to reconcile the phœnomena with which they were acquainted to the Mosaic narratives of the creation and deluge. Every one was satisfied that his own theory was the best; but in every case it has hitherto proved, whatever may take place in future, that the proposed scheme has neither kept to the letter of Scripture nor to the legitimate deductions of philosophy. Burnet gives the reins to his imagination more than any other writer on that which, if not argued upon by inductive reasoning, must be the dream of one man, little better in reality, though it may be more amusing, than the dream of another. He seems to be eminently ignorant of geological facts, and has hardly ever recourse to them as evidence. And, accordingly, though his book drew some attention as an ingenious romance, it does not appear that he made a single disciple. Whiston opposed Burnet's theory, but with one not less unfounded, nor

s Lyell's Principles of Geology, vol. i. p. 25.
h Thomson's Hist. of Royal Society.

with less ignorance of all that required to be known.

Other geologists. Hooke, Lister, Ray, and Woodward came to the subject with more philosophical minds, and with a better insight into the real phænomena. Hooke seems to have displayed his usual sagacity in conjecture; he saw that the common theory of explaining marine fossils by the Mosaic deluge would not suffice, and perceived that at some time or other a part of the earth's crust must have been elevated and another part depressed by some subterraneous power. Lister was aware of the continuity of certain strata over large districts, and proposed the construction of geological maps. Woodward had a still more extensive knowledge of stratified rocks; he was in a manner the founder of scientific mineralogy in England, but his geological theory was not less chimerical than those of his contemporaries.[i] It was first published in the Philosophical Transactions for 1695.[k]

33. The Protogæa of Leibnitz appears, in felicity of Protogæa of Leibnitz. conjecture and minute attention to facts, far above any of these. But this short tract was only published in 1749; and on reading it I have found an intimation that it was not written within the seventeenth century. Yet I cannot refrain from mentioning that his hypothesis supposes the gradual cooling of the earth from igneous fusion; the formation of a vast body of water to cover the surface, a part of his theory but ill established, and apparently the weakest of the whole; the subsidence of the lower parts of the earth, which he takes to have been once on the level of the highest mountains, by the breaking in of vaulted caverns within its bosom:[m] the deposition of sedimentary strata from inundations, their induration, and the subsequent covering of these by other strata through fresh inundations; with many other notions which have been gradually matured and rectified in the process of the science.[n] No

[i] Lyell, p. 31.

[k] Thomson, p. 207.

[m] Sect. 21. He admits also a partial elevation by intumescence, but says, ut vastissimæ Alpes ex solidâ jam terrâ eruptione surrexerint, minus consentaneum puto. Scimus tamen et in illis deprehendi reliquias maris. Cum ergo alterutrum factum oporteat, credibilius multo arbitror defluxisse aquas spontaneo nisu, quam ingentem terrarum partem incredibili violentiâ tam alte ascendisse. Sect. 22.

[n] Facies teneri adhuc orbis sæpius novata est; donec quiescentibus causis atque æquilibratis, consistentior emer-

one can read the Protogæa without perceiving that of all the early geologists, or indeed of all down to a time not very remote, Leibnitz came nearest to the theories which are most received in the English school at this day. It is evident that if the literal interpretation of Genesis, by a period of six natural days, had not restrained him, he would have gone much farther in his views of the progressive revolutions of the earth.[o] Leibnitz had made very minute inquiries for his age into fossil species, and was aware of the main facts which form the basis of modern geology.[p]

Sect. III.—On Anatomy and Medicine.

34. PORTAL begins the history of this period, which occupies more than 800 pages of his voluminous work, by announcing it as the epoch most favourable to anatomy : in less than fifty years the science put on a new countenance ; nature is interrogated, every part of the body is examined with an observing spirit : the mutual intercourse of nations diffuses the light on every side ; a number of great men appear, whose genius and industry excite our admiration.[q] But for this very reason I must in these concluding pages glide over a subject rather foreign to my own studies, and to those of the generality of my readers, with a very brief enumeration of names.

35. The Harveian theory gained ground, though obstinate prejudice gave way but slowly. It was confirmed by the experiment of transfusing blood, tried on dogs, at the instance of Sir

<small>Circulation of blood established.</small>

---

geret status rerum. Unde jam duplex origo intelligitur firmorum corporum ; una cum ignis fusione refrigescerent, altera cum reconcrescerent ex solutione aquarum. Neque igitur putandum est *lapides ex solâ esse fusione.* Id enim potissimum de primâ tantum massâ ex terræ basi accipio ; Nec dubito, postea materiam liquidam in superficie telluris procurrentem, quiete mox redditâ, ex ramentis subactis ingentem materiæ vim deposuisse, quorum alia varias terræ species formarunt, alia in saxa induruere, e quibus strata diversa sibi super imposita

diversas præcipitationum vices atque intervalla testantur. Sect. 4.

This he calls the incunabula of the world, and the basis of a new science, which might be denominated " naturalis geographia." But wisely adds, licet conspirent vestigia veteris mundi in præsenti facie rerum, tamen rectius omnia definient posteri, ubi curiositas eo processerit, ut per regiones procurrentia soli genera et strata describant. Sect. 5.

[o] See sect. 21, et alibi.

[p] Sect. 24, et usque ad finem libri.

[q] Hist. de l'Anatomie, vol. iii. p. 1.

Christopher Wren, in 1657, and repeated by Lower in 1661.[r] Malpighi in 1661, and Leeuwenhoek in 1690, by means of their microscopes, demonstrated the circulation of the blood in the smaller vessels, and rendered visible the anastomoses of the arteries and veins, upon which the theory depended.[s] From this time it seems to have been out of doubt. Pecquet's discovery of the thoracic duct (or rather of its uses, as a reservoir of the chyle from which the blood is elaborated, for the canal itself had been known to Eustachius) stands next to that of Harvey, which would have thrown less light on physiology without it, and like his was perseveringly opposed.[t]

36. Willis, a physician at Oxford, is called by Portal,

Willis.   who thinks all mankind inferior to anatomists,
Vieussens. one of the greatest geniuses that ever lived; his bold systems have given him a distinguished place among physiologers.[u] His Anatomy of the Brain, in which, however, as in his other works, he was much assisted by an intimate friend and anatomist of the first character, Lower, is, according to the same writer, a masterpiece of imagination and labour. He made many discoveries in the structure of the brain, and has traced the nerves from it far better than his predecessors, who had in general very obscure ideas of their course. Sprengel says that Willis is the first who has assigned a peculiar mental function to each of the different parts of the brain; forgetting, as it seems, that this hypothesis, the basis of modern phrenology, had been generally received, as I understand his own account, in the sixteenth century.[x] Vieussens of Montpellier carried on the discoveries in the anatomy of the nerves in his Neurographia Universalis, 1684; tracing those arising from the spinal marrow, which Willis had not done, and following the minute ramifications of those that are spread over the skin.[y]

37. Malpighi was the first who employed good micro-

Malpighi. scopes in anatomy, and thus revealed the secrets, we may say, of an invisible world, which Leeu-

[r] Sprengel, Hist. de la Médecine, vol. iv. p. 120.
[s] Ib., pp. 126, 142.
[t] Portal; Sprengel.
[u] P. 88. Biogr. Univ.

[x] Sprengel, vol. iv. p. 250. Compare vol. iii. p. 204.
[y] Portal, vol. iv. p. 5; Sprengel, p. 256; Biogr. Univ.

wenhoek afterwards, probably using still better instruments, explored with surprising success.   To Other anatomists. Malpighi anatomists owe their knowledge of the structure of the lungs.[z]   Graaf has overthrown many errors, and suggested many truths in the economy of generation.[a]   Malpighi prosecuted this inquiry with his microscope, and first traced the progress of the egg during incubation.   But the theory of evolution, as it is called, proposed by Harvey, and supported by Malpighi, received a shock by Leeuwenhoek's or Hartsoeker's discovery of spermatic animalcules, which apparently opened a new view of reproduction.   The hypothesis they suggested became very prevalent for the rest of the seventeenth century, though it is said to have been shaken early in the next.[b]   Borelli applied mathematical principles to muscular movements in his treatise De Motu Animalium.   Though he is a better mathematician than anatomist, he produces many interesting facts, the mechanical laws are rightly applied, and his method is clear and consequent.[c]   Duverney, in his Treatise on Hearing, in 1683, his only work, obtained a considerable reputation;   it threw light on many parts of a delicate organ, which by their minuteness had long baffled the anatomist.[d]   In Mayow's Treatise on Respiration, published in London, 1668, we find the necessity of what is now called oxygen to that function laid down;   but this portion of the atmosphere had been discovered by Bathurst and Henshaw in 1654, and Hooke had shown by experiment that animals die when the air is deprived of it.[e] Ruysch, a Dutch physician, perfected the art of injecting anatomical preparations, hardly known before, and thus conferred an inestimable benefit on the science.   He possessed a celebrated cabinet of natural history.[f]

38. The chemical theory of medicine which had descended from Paracelsus through Van Helmont, Medical theories. was propagated chiefly by Sylvius, a physician of Holland, who is reckoned the founder of what was called the chemiatric school.   His works were printed at Amsterdam in .1679, but he had promulgated his

[z] Portal, vol. iii. p. 120; Sprengel, p. 578.
[a] Portal, iii. 219; Sprengel, p. 303.
[b] Sprengel, p. 309.
[c] Portal, iii. 246; Biogr. Univ.
[d] Portal, p. 464. Sprengel, p. 288.
[e] Sprengel, iii. 176, 181.
[f] Id. p. 259; Biogr. Univ.

theory from the middle of the century. His leading principle was that a perpetual fermentation goes on in the human body, from the deranged action of which diseases proceed; most of them from excess of acidity, though a few are of alkaline origin. "He degraded the physician," says Sprengel, "to the level of a distiller or a brewer."[g] This writer is very severe on the chemiatric school, one of their offences in his eyes being their recommendation of tea; "the cupidity of Dutch merchants conspiring with their medical theories." It must be owned that when we find them prescribing also a copious use of tobacco, it looks as if the trade of the doctor went hand in hand with those of his patients. Willis, in England, was a partisan of the chemiatrics,[h] and they had a great influence in Germany; though in France the attachment of most physicians to the Hippocratic and Galenic methods, which brought upon them so many imputations of pedantry, was little abated. A second school of medicine, which superseded this, is called the iatro-mathematical. This seems to have arisen in Italy. Borelli's application of mechanical principles to the muscles has been mentioned above. These physicians sought to explain everything by statical and hydraulic laws; they were therefore led to study anatomy, since it was only by an accurate knowledge of all the parts that they could apply their mathematics. John Bernouilli even taught them to employ the differential calculus in explaining the bodily functions.[i] But this school seems to have had the same leading defect as the chemiatric; it forgot the peculiarity of the laws of organisation and life which often render those of inert matter inapplicable. Pitcairn and Boerhaave were leaders of the iatro-mathematicians; and Mead was reckoned the last of its distinguished patrons.[k] Meantime, a third school of medicine grew up, denominated the empirical; a name to be used in a good sense, as denoting their regard to observation and experience, or the Baconian principles of philosophy. Sydenham was the first of these in England; but they gradually prevailed, to the exclusion of all systematic theory. The

g Vol. v. p. 59; Biogr. Univ.
h Sprengel, p. 73.
i Id. p. 159.

k Id. p. 182. See Biographie Universelle, art. Boerhaave, for a general criticism of the iatro-mathematicians.

discovery of several medicines, especially the Peruvian bark, which was first used in Spain about 1640, and in England about 1654, contributed to the success of the empirical physicians, since the efficacy of some of these could not be explained on the hypotheses hitherto prevalent.[m]

SECT. IV.—ON ORIENTAL LITERATURE.

39. THE famous Polyglott of Brian Walton was published in 1657; but few copies appear to have been Polyglott of sold before the restoration of Charles II. in Walton. 1660, since those are very scarce which contain in the preface the praise of Cromwell for having facilitated and patronised the undertaking; praise replaced in the change of times by a loyal eulogy on the king. This Polyglott is in nine languages; though no one book of the Bible is printed in so many. Walton's Prolegomena are in sixteen chapters or dissertations. His learning perhaps was greater than his critical acuteness or good sense; such at least is the opinion of Simon and Le Long. The former, in a long examination of Walton's Prolegomena, treats him with all the superiority of a man who possessed both. Walton was assailed by some bigots at home for acknowledging various readings in the Scriptures, and for denying the authority of the vowel punctuation. His Polyglott is not reckoned so magnificent as the Parisian edition of Le Long; but it is fuller and more convenient.[n] Edmund Castell, the coadjutor of Walton in this work, published his Lexicon Heptaglotton in 1669, upon which he had consumed eighteen years and the whole of his substance. This is frequently sold together with the Polyglott.

40. Hottinger of Zurich, by a number of works on the Eastern languages, and especially by the Hottinger. Bibliotheca Orientalis, in 1658, established a reputation which these books no longer retain since the whole field of Oriental literature has been more Spencer. fully explored. Spencer, in a treatise of great

[m] Sprengel, p. 413.
[n] Simon, Hist. Critique du Vieux Tes- tament, p. 541; Chalmers; Biogr. Britan.; Biogr. Univ.; Brunet, Man. du Libraire.

erudition, De Legibus Hebræorum, 1685, gave some offence by the suggestion that several of the Mosaic institutions were borrowed from the Egyptian, though the general scope of the Jewish law was in opposition to the idolatrous practices of the neighbouring nations.

Bochart. The vast learning of Bochart expanded itself over Oriental antiquity, especially that of which the Hebrew nation and language is the central point; but his etymological conjectures have long since been set aside, and he has not in other respects escaped the fate of the older Orientalists.

41. The great services of Pococke to Arabic literature,

Pococke. which had commenced in the earlier part of the century, were extended to the present. His edition and translation of the Annals of Eutychius in 1658, that of the History of Abulfaragius in 1663, with many other works of a similar nature, bear witness to his industry; no Englishman probably has ever contributed so much to that province of learning.[o] A fine edition of the Koran, and still esteemed the best, was due to Marracci, professor of Arabic in the Sapienza or university of Rome, and published at the expense of Cardinal Barbadigo, in 1698.[p] But France had an

D'Herbelot. Orientalist of the most extensive learning in D'Herbelot, whose Bibliothèque Orientale must be considered as making an epoch in this literature. It was published in 1697, after his death, by Galland, who had also some share in arranging the materials. This work, it has been said, is for the seventeenth century what the History of the Huns by De Guignes is for the eighteenth; with this difference, that D'Herbelot opened the road, and has often been copied by his successor.[q]

42. Hyde, in his Religionis Persarum Historia, pub-

Hyde. lished in 1700, was the first who illustrated in a systematic manner the religion of Zoroaster, which he always represents in a favourable manner. The variety and novelty of its contents gave this book a credit which in some degree it preserves; but Hyde was ignorant of the ancient language of Persia, and is said to have been often misled by Mohammedan authorities.[r] The vast increase of Oriental information in

[o] Chalmers; Biogr. Univ.
[p] Tiraboschi, xi. 398.
[q] Biographie Universelle.
[r] Id.

modern times, as has been intimated above, renders it difficult for any work of the seventeenth century to keep its ground. In their own times, the writings of Kircher on China, and still more those of Ludolf on Abyssinia, which were founded on his own knowledge of the country, claimed a respectable place in Oriental learning. It is remarkable that very little was yet known of the Indian languages, though grammars existed of the Tamul, and perhaps some others, before the close of the seventeenth century.[a]

Sect. V.—On Geography and History.

43. The progress of geographical science long continued to be slow. If we compare the map of the world in 1651, by Nicolas Sanson, esteemed on all sides the best geographer of his age, with one by his son in 1692, the differences will not appear, perhaps, so considerable as we might have expected. Yet some improvement may be detected by the eye. Thus the Caspian sea has assumed its longer diameter from north to south, contrary to the old map. But the sea of Aral is still wanting. The coasts of New Holland, except to the east, are tolerably laid down, and Corea is a peninsula instead of an island. Cambalu, the imaginary capital of Tartary, has disappeared;[b] but a vast lake is placed in the centre of that region; the Altai range is carried far too much to the north, and the name of Siberia seems unknown. Africa and America have nearly the same outline as before; in the former, the empire of Monomotopa stretches to join that of Abyssinia in about the 12th degree of south latitude; and the Nile still issues, as in all the old maps, from a lake Zayre, in nearly the same parallel. The coasts of Europe, and especially of Scandinavia, are a little more accurate than before. The Sanson family, of whom several were publishers of maps, did not take pains enough to improve what their father had executed, though they might have

Maps of the Sansons.

---

[a] Eichborn, Gesch. der Cultur, v. 269.
[b] The Cambalu of Marco Polo is probably Pekin; but the geographers frequently placed this capital of Cathay north of the wall of China.

had material helps from the astronomical observations which were now continually made in different parts of the world.

44. Such was the state of geography when, in 1699, De Lisle, the real founder of the science, at the age of twenty-four, published his map of the world. He had been guided by the observations, and worked under the directions of Cassini, whose tables of the emersion of Jupiter's satellites, calculated for the meridian of Bologna, in 1668, and, with much improvement, for that of Paris, in 1693, had prepared the way for the perfection of geography. The latitudes of different regions had been tolerably ascertained by observation; but no good method of determining the longitude had been known before this application of Galileo's great discovery. It is evident that the appearance of one of those satellites at Paris being determined by the tables to a precise instant, the means were given, with the help of sufficient clocks, to find the longitudinal distance of other places by observing the difference of time; and thus a great number of observations having gradually been made, a basis was laid for an accurate delineation of the surface of the globe. The previous state of geography and the imperfect knowledge which the mere experience of navigators could furnish, may be judged by the fact that the Mediterranean sea was set down with an excess of 300 leagues in length, being more than one-third of the whole. De Lisle reduced it within its bounds, and cut off at the same time 500 leagues from the longitude of Eastern Asia. This was the commencement of the geographical labours of De Lisle, which reformed, in the first part of the eighteenth century, not only the general outline of the world, but the minuter relations of various countries. His maps amount to more than one hundred sheets.[u]

De Lisle's map of the world.

45. The books of travels, in the last fifty years of the seventeenth century, were far more numerous and more valuable than in any earlier period, but we have no space for more than a few names. Gemelli Carreri, a Neapolitan, is the first who

Voyages and Travels.

---

[u] Eloge de De Lisle, in Œuvres de Fontenelle. vol. vi. p. 253; Eloge de Cassini in vol. v. p. 328; Biogr. Univ.

claims to have written an account of his own travels round the world, describing Asia and America with much detail. His Giro del Mondo was published in 1699. Carreri has been strongly suspected of fabrication, and even of having never seen the countries which he describes; but his character, I know not with what justice, has been latterly vindicated.[x] The French justly boast the excellent travels of Chardin, Bernier, Thevenot, and Tavernier in the East; the account of the Indian archipelago and of China by Nieuhoff, employed in a Dutch embassy to the latter empire, is said to have been interpolated by the editors, though he was an accurate and faithful observer.[y] Several other relations of voyages were published in Holland, some of which can only be had in the native language. In English there were not many of high reputation: Dampier's Voyage Round the World, the first edition of which was in 1697, is better known than any which I can call to mind.

46. The general characteristics of historians of this period are neither a luminous philosophy, nor a rigorous examination of evidence. But, as before, we mention only a few names in this extensive province of literature. The History of the Conquest of Mexico by Antonio De Solis is " the last good work," says Sismondi, perhaps too severely as to others, " that Spain has produced; the last where purity of taste, simplicity, and truth are preserved; the imagination, of which the author had given so many proofs, does not appear."[z] Bouterwek is not less favourable; but Robertson, who holds De Solis rather cheap as an historian, does not fail to censure even his style. *Historians.* *De Solis.*

47. The French have some authors of history who, by their elegance and perspicuity, might deserve notice; such as St. Real, Father D'Orleans, and even Varillas, proverbially discredited as he is for want of veracity. The Memoirs of Cardinal De Retz rise above these; their animated style, their excellent portraitures of character, their acute and brilliant remarks distinguish their pages, as much as the similar *Memoirs of De Retz.*

[x] Tiraboschi, xi. 86; Salfi, xi. 442.   [y] Biogr. Univ.
[z] Littérature du Midi, iv. 101.

qualities did their author. "They are written," says
Voltaire, "with an air of greatness, an impetuosity and
an inequality which are the image of his life; his expression, sometimes incorrect, often negligent, but
almost always original, recalls continually to his readers
what has been so frequently said of Cæsar's Commentaries, that he wrote with the same spirit that he carried
on his wars."[a]   The Memoirs of Grammont, by Antony
Hamilton, scarcely challenge a place as historical, but
we are now looking more at the style than the intrinsic
importance of books.   Every one is aware of the peculiar felicity and fascinating gaiety which they display.

48. The Discourse of Bossuet on Universal History is
Bossuet on perhaps the greatest effort of his wonderful
universal genius.   Every preceding abridgment of so
history. immense a subject had been superficial and
dry.   He first irradiated the entire annals of antiquity
down to the age of Charlemagne with flashes of light that
reveal an unity and coherence which had been lost in
their magnitude and obscurity.   It is not perhaps an
unfair objection that, in a history calling itself that of
all mankind, the Jewish people have obtained a dispro-
portionate regard; and it might be almost as reasonable,
on religious grounds, to give Palestine an ampler space
in the map of the world, as, on a like pretext, to make
the scale of the Jewish history so much larger than that
of the rest of the human race.   The plan of Bossuet has
at least divided his book into two rather heterogeneous
portions.   But his conceptions of Greek, and still more
of Roman history, are generally magnificent; profound
in philosophy, with an outline firm and sufficiently
exact, never condescending to trivial remarks or petty
details; above all, written in that close and nervous
style which no one certainly in the French language
has ever surpassed.   It is evident that Montesquieu in
all his writings, but especially in the Grandeur et Dé-
cadence des Romains, had the Discourse of Bossuet
before his eyes; he is more acute, sometimes, and ingenious, and has reflected longer on particular topics of
inquiry, but he wants the simple majesty, the comprehensive eagle-like glance of the illustrious prelate.

---

[a] Biogr. Univ., whence I take the quotation.

49. Though we fell short in England of the historical reputation which the first part of the century might entitle us to claim, this period may be reckoned that in which a critical attention to truth, sometimes rather too minute, but always praiseworthy, began to be characteristic of our researches into fact. The only book that I shall mention is Burnet's History of the Reformation, written in a better style than those who know Burnet by his later and more negligent work are apt to conceive, and which has the signal merit of having been the first in English, as far as I remember, which is fortified by a large appendix of documents. This, though frequent in Latin, had not been so usual in the modern languages. It became gradually very frequent and almost indispensable in historical writings, where the materials had any peculiar originality.

English historical works.

Burnet.

*   *   *   *   *   *

50. The change in the spirit of literature and of the public mind in general, which had with gradual and never receding steps been coming forward in the seventeenth century, but especially in the latter part of it, has been so frequently pointed out to the readers of this and the last volume, that I shall only quote an observation of Bayle. " I believe," he says, " that the sixteenth century produced a greater number of learned men than the seventeenth ; and yet the former of these ages was far from being as enlightened as the latter. During the reign of criticism and philology, we saw in all Europe many prodigies of erudition. Since the study of the new philosophy and that of living languages has introduced a different taste, we have ceased to behold this vast and deep learning. But in return there is diffused through the republic of letters a more subtle understanding and a more exquisite discernment ; men are now less learned but more able."[b] The volumes which are now submitted to the public contain sufficient evidence of this intellectual progress both in philosophy and in polite literature.

General character of 17th century.

51. I here terminate a work, which, it is hardly ne-

[b] Dictionnaire de Bayle, art. Aconce, note D.

cessary to say, has furnished the occupation of not very few years, and which, for several reasons, it is not my intention to prosecute any farther. The length of these volumes is already greater than I had anticipated: yet I do not perceive much that could have been retrenched without loss to a part, at least, of the literary world. For the approbation which the first of them has received I am grateful: for the few corrections that have been communicated to me I am not less so; the errors and deficiencies of which I am not specially aware may be numerous; yet I cannot affect to doubt that I have contributed something to the general literature of my country, something to the honourable estimation of my own name, and to the inheritance of those, if it is for me still to cherish that hope, to whom I have to bequeath it.

Conclusion.

INDEX.

2 c 2

2 D 2

THE END.

LONDON : PRINTED BY WILLIAM CLOWES AND SONS, STAMFORD STREET, AND CHARING CROSS.

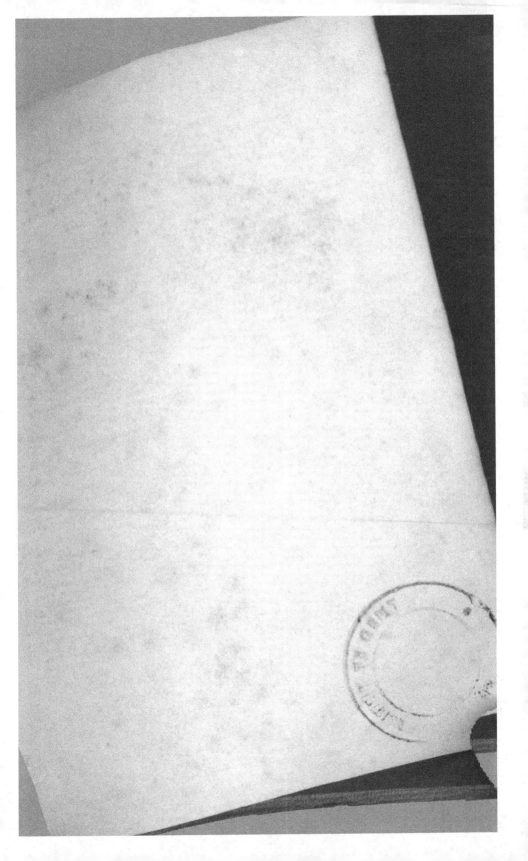

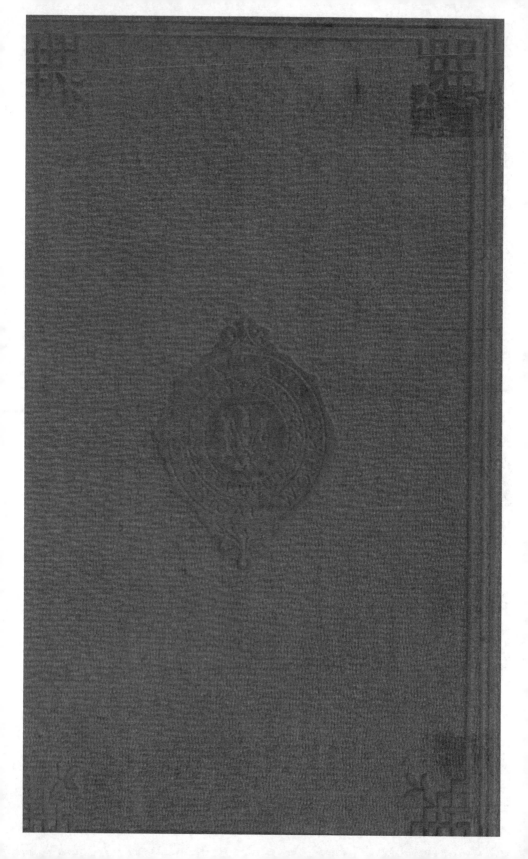